Justice, Crime and Ethics

Third Edition

MICHAEL C. BRASWELL – EAST TENNESSEE STATE UNIVERSITY

BELINDA R. McCARTHY – UNIVERSITY OF CENTRAL FLORIDA

BERNARD J. McCARTHY – UNIVERSITY OF CENTRAL FLORIDA

anderson publishing co.
2035 Reading Road
Cincinnati, OH 45202
800-582-7295

Justice, Crime and Ethics, Third Edition

Copyright © 1991, 1996, 1998
Anderson Publishing Co.
2035 Reading Rd.
Cincinnati, OH 45202

Phone 800.582.7295 or 513.421.4142
Web Site www.andersonpublishing.com

Library of Congress Cataloging-in-Publication Data

Justice, crime, and ethics / [edited by] Michael C. Braswell, Belinda R. McCarthy,
  Bernard J. McCarthy. -- 3rd ed.
      p.   cm.
  Includes bibliographical references and index.
  ISBN 0-87084-073-8 (pbk.)
  1. Criminal justice, Administration of--Moral and ethical aspects.
I. Braswell, Michael. II. McCarthy, Belinda Rodgers.
III. McCarthy, Bernard J., 1949-
HV7419.J87   1998
174'.9364--dc21   98-17914
                                                           CIP

Cover design by Tin Box Studio/Cincinnati, OH
Cover photo credit: Tony Stone Images/Gary Hush

EDITOR Ellen S. Boyne
ASSISTANT EDITOR Elizabeth A. Shipp
ACQUISITIONS EDITOR Michael C. Braswell

Dedication

*To our teachers: Jean Hendricks, Hans Toch and Vernon Fox
who taught us ethics through their actions.*

A Note About the Third Edition

The third edition of *Justice, Crime and Ethics* has been modified and expanded to meet the needs of students and instructors. Section I provides a broad philosophical foundation for exploring a wide range of criminal justice issues. Chapters in the remaining sections cover ethical issues on policing, courts, corrections, crime control policy and research, and an ethical framework for the future. While some classic articles have been retained intact, other articles have been updated and seven new chapters have been added to reflect today's criminal justice milieu.

To aid students in understanding and assessing ethical dilemmas, case studies and exercises have been included and the editors have added key concepts and discussion questions to both reprinted and original chapters. All persons and situations described in case studies and exercises are fictional and have been constructed to illustrate ethical dilemmas characteristic of the criminal justice field.

We would like to offer special thanks to Wayne Gillespie for his assistance on the text, Instructor's Guide and Student Study Guide and to Ellen Boyne for her efforts and contributions to this edition.

MB
BM
BM

Table of Contents

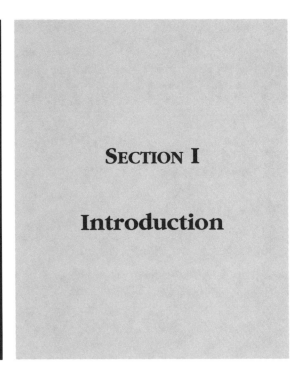

Vision brings a
new appreciation
of what there is.
It makes a
person see
things differently
rather than see
different things.

—Herbert Guenther

SECTION I

Introduction

Our personal and social values shape and color the way we perceive the world in which we live. While we are concerned with achieving personal goals and ambitions, we also come to realize at a rather early age that the needs and desires of others are also forces to be reckoned with. The question for us then becomes one of reconciling the pursuit of our individual dreams within the context of the larger community. Maintaining our individual integrity, our personal sense of right and wrong, and, at the same time, conforming to what is best for the majority of persons in our society can often become a perplexing challenge. Yet we are all connected to each other in one way or another, such as with parents and children, and inmates and correctional staff. We are even connected to our physical environment as evidenced in the quality of air we breathe and water we drink. As potential criminal justice practitioners, our professional choices and policies will emanate from our personal beliefs and values—from our personal philosophies. How much do we care about trying to honestly and effectively address the pressing justice issues of the day? Are we truly mindful of the ways we are connected to our problems? Do we have a long-term as well as short-term sense of what the costs of our proposed solutions will be?

Cultivating a greater understanding of our own philosophical perspectives can provide us with a foundation for making more informed decisions about the diverse social issues we face and the way our system of justice responds to such issues.

CHAPTER 1

Ethics, Crime and Justice:
An Introductory Note to Students

Michael C. Braswell

As you approach the study of ethics, crime and justice, it seems important that you view your study as a search, journey or exploration. This search in many ways will yield more questions than answers. It is a creative endeavor in which a number of your beliefs and assumptions will be challenged. Questions such as "Can moral or ethical behavior be illegal and legal actions be immoral?" and "Can we have a more equitable criminal justice system without addressing larger social problems like poverty and discrimination?" will test the limits of your personal values and beliefs (Braswell & LaFollette, 1988).[1] This study will also encompass a variety of disciplines that contribute to criminal justice, including law, economics, psychology, sociology, philosophy and theology. For the purposes of our exploration we will use the terms "ethical" and "moral" interchangeably.

> **KEY CONCEPTS:**
>
> ethics
>
> morals
>
> wholesight

What is "ethics"? In a general sense, ethics is the study of right and wrong, good and evil. Who decides what is right and wrong? What one person may believe is right, another person may feel is wrong. Our beliefs and values regarding right and wrong and good and evil are shaped by our parents and friends, by the communities we are a part of and by our own perceptions. Codes of conduct are also influenced by the law and our religious beliefs. Professional organizations involving such areas as law, medicine and criminal justice also offer professional codes of ethics as a benchmark for persons who fulfill those professional roles. This study involves all aspects of who we are— our minds, hearts, relationships with each other, and the intentions and motives for our actions regarding both our inner and outer environment. We are inclined to believe that ethical persons act in good or right ways, while unethical people commit evil acts and other forms of wrongdoing. Then again, it is not only a matter of a person acting "unethically"; also at issue are persons who could choose to do good, but instead do nothing, allowing others to do evil. So it is not simply a matter of my committing an evil or wrongful act, it is also a matter of my being an indirect accomplice to evil by silently standing by, letting evil occur when I could stand for what is right. As a result, unethical acts have to do both with the commission of wrongdoing and, by omission, allowing wrongdoing to occur. Thomas Merton, in examining a fundamental problem of omission, writes "moral paralysis . . . leaves us immobile, inert, passive, tongue-tied, ready and even willing to succumb."[2]

The study of justice and ethics, of the good and evil we do to each other, also involves a sense of community. We often hear that problems of crime and violence are the result of a breakdown in family and community values. What does our community consist of? Our community includes our family, neighbors, even the land we grow food on to eat and the air we breathe. Is it important that we act in ethical ways regarding our physical environment as well as with regard to the people we come in contact with? Within our community of interdependent parts exist three contexts, or perspectives, that can help us to approach a better understanding of justice, crime and ethics.

THREE CONTEXTS FOR UNDERSTANDING JUSTICE, CRIME AND ETHICS

The first context or perspective is the *personal* one. When we explore the study of right and wrong, good and evil, we find ourselves questioning and testing our own personal sense of values and ethics—our own ideas about what is good and evil and ethical and unethical. It is important that we do not approach the study of justice, crime and ethics with a cold, analytical eye. While our examination of the issues should be objective, it should also be personal. We need to take into account what we believe in and stand for personally. As we search for the truth and begin to understand various ethical concerns more fully, we may choose to revise and refine our value system. Still, the starting and ending point of the consequences of our journey will come back to the person we are and could possibly become. What do we personally believe about right and wrong, good and evil, justice and injustice? Do we even know what we believe? How will our personal values or lack of them affect the decisions we make and the direction our life takes?

Another broader context is the *social* one through which we relate to others in our community, both directly and indirectly. Persons do not commit crimes in isolation. Crimes require circumstances and victims. Crimes are related to social circumstances and conditions as well as being subject to the law and criminal justice system. Why did the abused wife kill her husband? In the broader social context, we might look at the abuse she suffered before making her husband a victim of homicide. What was her relationship to her parents and other family members? What about her neighbors? Did she have access to adequate social and support services? Could something have been done to prevent her own victimization and subsequent crime?

The social context of ethics suggests that we cannot be concerned only with criminals after they have committed crimes, but need to also better understand the conditions and environments that encourage people to become criminals, whether such offenders physically rape their victims or economically violate them through such means as stock market fraud.

The social context is not only concerned with how we judge others as being good or evil, but also how we judge ourselves in relationship to others. Frederick Buechner writes, "We are judged by the face that looks back at us from the bathroom mirror. We are judged by the faces of the people we love and by the faces and lives of our children and by our dreams. Each day finds us at the junction of many roads, and we are judged as much by the roads we have not taken as by the roads we have."[3]

The third context we can use in our efforts to better understand justice, crime and ethics is perhaps the most specific one and centers around the *criminal justice* process. Too often, the criminal justice process is the only context or perspective we consider. It is important that we include both the personal and social context of ethics when exploring the criminal justice process. Due process, police corruption, and punishment are examples of important issues that require us to consider personal beliefs, social factors and criminal justice consequences simultaneously. For example, I explore any new law being proposed regarding the punishment of offenders in terms of my personal beliefs. How does this proposed law square with my own value system? How do I feel about it? The proposed law also should be examined on the basis of how it will affect the social community. Is it just and fair to all parts and groups within the community? Will it contribute to the community's sense of safety and security, or is it perhaps more of a public relations or election-year gimmick? Can the criminal justice process and system effectively implement the law? Are there adequate resources to finance and manage the changes that will occur in the system as the result of the proposed law?

Figure 1.1: **Three Contexts for Understanding Justice, Crime and Ethics**

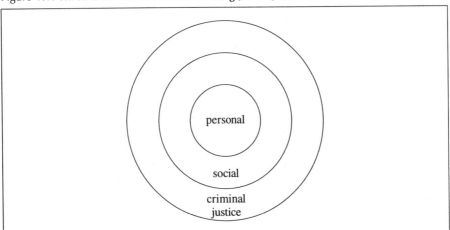

In addition to examining our study of ethics from a personal, social and criminal justice context, it is also useful to identify several specific goals as we begin to explore issues regarding justice, crime and ethics.

FIVE GOALS FOR EXPLORING ETHICS

The initial goal for exploring ethics is to *become more aware and open to moral and ethical issues.*

As we try to become more aware of ethical issues, we will discover a number of contradictions in our moral beliefs and values. We will find that there is often a difference between appearances and reality; that things are often not what they seem. What we are taught as children may be challenged by our adult experiences. As a result, some choices seem clearly to be right or wrong, while other events seem more ambiguous and less certain.

A part of our becoming more open includes our learning to be more aware of the full range and nature of moral and ethical issues, from telling a small lie to committing perjury; from cheating on one's income taxes to engaging in major bank fraud. This broad range of moral issues reminds us that where justice is concerned, personal values, social consequences, and criminal justice outcomes are often intertwined.

As we become more open to moral and ethical issues, it is important that we approach our second goal, which is to *begin developing critical thinking and analytical skills.*

As young children, we were often creative, as evidenced by our active imaginations. As we grew older, we learned to stand in line, follow instructions and be seen more than heard when it came to the process of learning. In a word, we learned to become obedient. And over time, we began to lose confidence in our point of view as being anything of value. In such a context, as students we are inclined to become more interested in asking how rather than why, in becoming more like technicians rather than philosophers. However, Albert Einstein, in discussing science and creativity, suggests that "To raise new questions, new possibilities, to regard old problems from a new angle, requires creative imagination and marks real advances in science."[4] In other words, if we do not first ask the right questions, our solutions, no matter how well intended and efficient, simply add to our difficulties. Asking why, then, is an important aspect of developing critical thinking and analytical skills.

Asking meaningful questions requires clarity in our thinking and a sense of mindfulness as we explore moral and ethical issues. Critical thinking and analytical skills help us to distinguish concepts such as justice and liberty from principles such as "the ends do not justify the means." For example, we might discuss capital punishment both as a concept and in principle. However, our critical thinking and analytical skills will allow us to go even further as we search for the truth regarding capital punishment. What are the short- and long-term costs of such a sanction? How does it affect our criminal justice system and our society in general? What will future generations think about our decisions, laws and policies regarding capital punishment? While we may never be able to arrive at an absolutely perfect position on capital punishment, critical thinking and analytical skills can aid us in exploring more openly and with more integrity the various issues surrounding capital punishment. These skills encourage openness and perseverance rather than blind acceptance and obedience based upon ignorance.

There will always be disagreement on such issues as capital punishment. As with any moral issue, there is a cost for the attitudes we hold and the choices we make; there is inevitably an upside and downside, a pro and con. As we explore such issues, critical thinking and analytical skills can help us see more clearly what the costs will be.

Becoming more open to moral and ethical issues and developing critical thinking and analytical skills will help us to more fully realize our third goal: **becoming more personally responsible.**

Before we can become more responsible, we must increase our ability to respond. The first two goals aid us in this endeavor. As we persevere in an open exploration and search for the truth regarding moral and ethical issues, we will feel more empowered and have more hope for the future.

A fourth goal of our ethics education is that we **understand how criminal justice is engaged in a process of coercion.**[5] Giving tickets to drivers who exceed the speed limit and sentencing offenders to prison are examples of this process. In exploring the morality of coercion, we come to realize that, in large part, criminal justice is about forcing people to do things they do not want to do. Having the authority to be coercive, and the discretionary nature of such authority, creates the potential for corruption and abuse. Can you think of any examples where the coercive role of police, courts or corrections could be corrupted? On a more personal level, how might parental or peer influences exercise coercion in an unethical way (Sherman, 1981)[6]?

The fifth goal of our exploration concerns what Parker Palmer refers to as **developing wholesight.**[7]

It is important that we become more open to moral and ethical issues, that we develop critical thinking and analytical skills, that we increase our sense of personal responsibility, and that we understand the morality of coercion. Yet all of these abilities and skills need to be tempered by our intuitive nature. We need to explore these issues not only with our minds, but also with our hearts. Our mind or intellect can often become more preoccupied with immediate problems and how to solve them. The heart asks why and looks not only to the immediate dilemma, but also to the deeper level of difficulty and asks what the costs might be in the long run. Wholesight creates a vision where our minds and hearts, our thinking and feeling, work together for the common good as we explore the ethical and moral issues we as individuals and as members of a community face.

Figure 1.2: **Five Goals for Exploring Ethics**

1. Greater awareness of moral/ethical issues

2. Develop critical thinking/analytical skills

3. Become personally responsible

4. Understanding coercion in criminal justice

5. Develop wholesight

The following sections of this book will introduce you to some of the philosophical theories that can provide a framework for you to study and analyze ethical and moral issues in crime and justice. The police, courts and corrections, which comprise the criminal justice system, will be explored in the light of ethical concerns. Criminal justice research and crime control policy will also be examined. Finally, a justice ethic for the future is offered for your consideration. What kind of future do you want to be a part of? What price are you willing to pay?

NOTES

1. Braswell, Michael and Hugh LaFollette (1988). "Seeking Justice: The Advantages and Disadvantages of Being Educated," *American Journal of Criminal Justice* (Spring): 135-147.

2. Ralph Woods (ed.), *The World Treasury of Religious Quotations* (New York: Garland Books, 1966), p. 647.

3. Frederick Buechner, *Wishful Thinking* (New York: Harper & Row, 1973), p. 48.

4. Tony Castle (ed.), *The New Book of Christian Quotations* (New York: Crossroad, 1988), p. 52.

5. Lawrence W. Sherman, *The Study of Ethics in Criminology and Criminal Justice* (Chicago: Joint Commission on Criminology and Criminal Justice Education and Standards, 1981).

6. Sherman.

7. Parker Palmer, *To Know As We Are Known* (San Francisco: Harper & Row, 1983).

DISCUSSION QUESTIONS

1. Define and discuss the term "ethics" from your own perspective.

2. Explain what "ethics" is using the three contexts presented in this chapter for understanding justice, crime and ethics.

3. Explain the five goals of exploring ethics and the impact that each has on the other.

CHAPTER 2

Utilitarian and Deontological Approaches to Criminal Justice Ethics

Jeffrey Gold

Over the past 10 to 15 years, interest in professional ethics has grown steadily. Business ethics, medical ethics and environmental ethics are all flourishing as components in most college and university curricula. Despite this fact, until recently, "higher education programs in criminology and criminal justice have largely neglected the systematic study of ethics."[1] This is unfortunate because the ethical issues that arise in the area of criminal justice are significant and complex. And, even though many of the ethical issues that arise in criminal justice are common to other professions, there are other issues that are specifically tailored to criminology and criminal justice. The most significant example, as mentioned in Chapter 1, involves the use of force and physical coercion. Sherman points out: "Force is the essence of criminal justice . . . The decisions of whether to use force, how much to use, and under what conditions are confronted by police officers, juries, judges, prison officials, probation and parole officers and others. All of them face the paradox . . . of using harm to prevent harm."[2] Because the use of force is central to criminal justice, this distinguishes criminal justice from other professions.

> **KEY CONCEPTS:**
>
> categorical imperative
>
> consequentialism
>
> deontology
>
> hypothetical imperative
>
> John Stuart Mill
>
> Immanuel Kant
>
> normative ethics
>
> universalizability
>
> utilitarianism
>
> utilitarian calculus

In addition to the issue concerning the use of force, there are other factors that seem to distinguish the moral decisions of criminal justice agents from other professionals. Sherman discusses two of them:

> First, criminal justice decisions are made on behalf of society as a whole, a collective moral judgement made in trust by a single person. That would entail a far greater responsibility than what other vocations are assigned. Second, the decisions criminal justice agents make are not just incidentally, but are primarily, moral decisions. An engineer designs a building that may or may not kill people, but the decision is primarily a physical one and only incidentally a moral one. When a police officer decides to arrest someone . . . when a judge decides to let that person out on a suspended sentence, the decisions are primarily moral ones.[3]

As we can see, the moral issues that arise in the field of criminal justice are both distinctive and significant.

It is sometimes helpful, when trying to solve certain specific ethical issues, to begin with more general, theoretical questions. When we get a handle on the more theoretical issue, we can apply that to a specific moral problem. So, with respect to criminal justice, we might begin by raising more general questions about the nature of justice. Theories of justice address broad social issues including human rights, equality and the distribution of wealth. We might even go up one more level of generality: justice is itself a branch of an even wider sphere, that of ethics. It seems important that we view issues in criminal justice from the larger framework of ethics and morality. It would be a mistake to assume that issues in criminal justice could emerge outside of the larger social and ethical context of our culture. Therefore, this essay will explore the field of ethics with the hope that such a study will provide us with a set of concepts that will shed some light on specific moral issues in the field of criminal justice. That shall be done by presenting a study of two of the major philosophical theories in the field of normative ethics.

NORMATIVE ETHICS

Normative ethics is the study of right and wrong. A normative ethical theorist tries to discover whether there are any basic, fundamental principles of right and wrong. If such principles are discovered, they are held to be the ground or foundation of all of our ethical judgments. For example, we ordinarily say lying, cheating, stealing, raping and killing are wrong. The ethical theorist asks: Do these very different activities of lying, stealing and killing all have something in common that makes them all wrong? If so, what is that common characteristic?

One of the most important figures in the history of Western philosophy, Socrates, was famous for seeking the universal in ethical matters.[4] In other words, when Socrates asked "What is Justice?" or "What is Virtue?", he was not asking for a list of actions that are just or a list of examples of virtue; rather, he was seeking the universal characteristic that all just or virtuous actions have in common.[5] Just as all squares, no matter how large they are or what color they are, have something in common (four equal sides and four right angles), the ethical theorist wants to know if all morally right actions (whether they are cases of honesty, charity or benevolence) also have something in common. If such a common characteristic is found, it is held to be the ground or foundation or fundamental principle of ethics. We shall now turn to our study of two standard ethical theories in an effort to locate such a foundation for ethics.

UTILITARIANISM

The most famous version of utilitarianism was developed in Great Britain in the eighteenth and nineteenth centuries by Jeremy Bentham and John Stuart Mill.[6] Utilitarianism is classified as a consequentialist ethical theory. In other words, the utilitarian holds that we judge the morality of an action in terms of the consequences or results of that action. Mill states: "All action is for the sake of some end, and rules of action, it seems natural to suppose, must take their whole character and color from the end to which they are subservient."[7] The insight that motivates consequentialism is this: a moral action produces something good; an immoral action produces a bad or harmful result. Put in the simplest possible way, cheating, stealing and murder are all wrong because they produce bad or harmful consequences, and charity and benevolence are good because they produce something beneficial. To summarize, the consequentialist holds that the morality of an action is determined by the consequences of that action—actions that are moral produce good consequences, actions that are immoral produce bad consequences.

At this point, two questions come up: (1) What do we mean by good consequences (and bad consequences)? (2) Consequences for whom? Actions have consequences for many different people. Which people should we consider when contemplating the consequences of our actions? By giving concrete answers to these two questions, the utilitarian carves out a unique and specific version or type of consequentialist moral theory.

In order to explain utilitarianism, we shall begin with the first question. How does the utilitarian define or characterize good and bad consequences? The most famous version of utilitarianism (the one advocated by Bentham and Mill) is called hedonistic utilitarianism. According to Mill, the fundamental good that all humans seek is happiness. Aristotle agrees with that point, even though he is not a utilitarian. In his discussion of the highest good, Aristotle says: "As far as its name is concerned, most people would agree: for both the common run of people and cultivated men call it happiness."[8] Mill holds that "there is in reality nothing desired except happiness."[9] Mill's view is that all people desire happiness and everything else they desire is either a part of happiness or a means to happiness. Thus, the basic and fundamental good, according to hedonistic utilitarianism (hereafter called utilitarianism), is happiness.

According to both Bentham and Mill, happiness is identified by pleasure. Mill claims: "By happiness is intended pleasure and the absence of pain; by unhappiness, pain and the privation of pleasure."[10] In his discussion of pleasure, Mill includes not only the pleasures of food, drink and sex, but also intellectual and aesthetic pleasures. In fact, Mill considers the "higher order" pleasures, that is the intellectual, emotional and aesthetic pleasures that nonhuman animals are not capable of experiencing, to be of a higher quality than the "lower order" pleasures that many species of animals experience. The pleasures of poetry and opera are, in Mill's view, qualitatively superior to the pleasures of drinking and playing pinball.

Consequentialism holds that the morality of an action is determined by the consequences produced by the action. For the utilitarian, the morally right action produces happiness (pleasure and the absence of pain) and the morally wrong action produces unhappiness (pain and suffering). Mill states: "The creed which accepts as the foundation of morals 'utility' or 'the greatest happiness principle' holds that actions are right in proportion as they tend to promote happiness; wrong as they tend to produce the reverse of happiness."[11] Bentham states, "By the principle of utility is meant that principle which approves or disapproves of every action whatsoever, according to the tendency which it appears to have to augment or diminish the happiness of the party whose interest is in question: or, what is the same thing in other words, to promote or to oppose the happiness."[12] Before we examine the theory in any more sophistication, we can already feel the intuitive appeal of the theory. Why do we think that murder, rape, cheating and lying are immoral? Because those actions cause pain to the victims and the families of the victims. Why do we think that charity and benevolence are righteous actions? Because they produce pleasure or happiness.

Let us now move to the second question. Since utilitarianism holds that we ought to produce happiness or pleasure, whose happiness or pleasure ought we to consider? After all, the thief gets a certain amount of pleasure from a successful burglary. The utilitarian answer to this is that we ought to consider all parties affected by the action, calculate the pain and pleasure of everyone who is influenced. After due consideration, the action that is morally correct is the one that produces the greatest good (amount of happiness) for the greatest number of people. If all the alternatives involve more pain than pleasure, the morally right action is the one that produces the least amount of pain.

For example, the thief wants money to accord himself a certain lifestyle. Stealing will bring him jewelry or other valuable items that he can trade for money that will make him feel good. However, such actions would also have another consequence: those persons who were stolen from would become victims with the accompanying feelings of sorrow, anger or, perhaps, even fear. As a result, their pain outweighs his pleasure. "The greatest good for the greatest number" creates the context for community. The proportionality of pain and pleasure must be judged in this context.

In calculating the amount of pleasure and pain produced by any action, many factors are relevant. Bentham creates a hedonistic calculus in which he lists those factors.[13] I shall briefly describe some of the major elements in Bentham's calculus. First, we must consider the *intensity* or strength of the pleasure or pain. A minor inconvenience is much less important than a major trauma. We must also consider the *duration* of the pleasure or pain. For example, in the case of a rape, psychological scars may last a lifetime. Additionally, we must consider the *long-term consequences* of an action. Certain actions may produce short-term pleasures, but in the long run, prove to be more harmful than good (for example alcohol and drugs). Finally, we must consider the *probability* or likelihood that our actions will produce the consequences we intend. For example, the prisons are full of thieves who in a personal (and not merely community) context did not make a good utilitarian choice. For instance, a certain offender commits an armed robbery to acquire money to spend on a lavish lifestyle that would make him or her feel good. Instead, because the offender did not consider the probability of being caught, he or she spends 15 years experiencing the pain of imprisonment.

Let me briefly summarize. The ethical theorist is interested in discovering the basic, fundamental principle of morality, a foundation upon which all moral judgments rest. The utilitarian claims to have found such a principle and identifies it as the greatest happiness principle. According to utilitarianism, an action ought to be done if and only if that action maximizes the total amount of pleasure (or minimizes the total amount of pain) of all parties affected by the action.

The entire criminal justice system can be justified on utilitarian grounds. Why do we need a police force? To serve and protect. That is to say, it is in the long-term interests of a society (produces the greatest amount of happiness for the greatest number of people) to pay police officers to protect the community from burglars, murderers, rapists and drunk drivers. The utilitarian would argue that what we call criminal activities tend to produce much more pain than pleasure. Therefore, a criminal justice system is instituted in order to lower the amount of crime, thereby lowering the amount of pain produced by crime.

Despite that fact that utilitarianism can be used to justify the criminal justice system, there are certain times when we say a police officer is justified in arresting (or ticketing) a citizen even though that arrest does not lead to the greatest good for the greatest number. For example, suppose a man is in a rush to pick up his daughter at school. He is driving on the freeway on a bright, sunny day and there is virtually no traffic. Suppose he exceeds the speed limit by 15 miles per hour (the speed limit is 55 mph and he is driving at 70 mph). The police officer stops him and gives him a ticket for $75. One might argue that, in this case, the painful consequences of giving a ticket outweigh the pleasurable consequences. First of all, the driver is caused pain by having to pay the ticket. Secondly, by getting the ticket, the driver is late to pick up his daughter, which causes the daughter anxiety. The delay also causes inconvenience for the principal at school. What are the pleasurable consequences for giving the ticket? Who is made happier? Had the officer just given the driver a warning, the driver, the principal and the child would all be happier. No one would be less happy. So, on on utilitarian grounds, the officer should not issue a ticket in the set of circumstances just described.

The previous example leads some people to say that the officer has a *duty* to issue the ticket regardless of the consequences. This leads us to our next moral theory, namely, deontological ethics.

DEONTOLOGICAL ETHICS

The word *deontology* comes from two Greek roots: *deos*, meaning duty, and *logos*, meaning study. Deontology is therefore the study of duty. Deontologists have argued that human beings sometimes have duties to perform certain actions regardless of the consequences. Police officers have a duty to issue traffic tickets even when doing so does not produce the greatest good for the greatest number. Teachers have the obligation or duty to fail students who do failing work even if failing that student produces more misery than happiness.

The most famous deontologist is Immanuel Kant, an eighteenth-century German philosopher. Kant believed that all consequentialist theories missed something crucial to ethics by neglecting the concept of duty. But that is not all. Kant also believed that by focusing solely on consequences, utilitarian-type theories missed something even more basic to morality, namely, a good will or the intention to do what is right. He begins his treatise on ethics as follows: "It is impossible to conceive anything at all in the world, or even out of it, which can be taken as good without qualification, except a *good will*."[14] In other words, the key to morality is human will or intention, not consequences.

Consider the following example: Suppose John is driving down the road and sees someone on the side of the road having difficulty with a flat tire. John notices that the car is a brand-new Cadillac and the driver of the car (an elderly woman) is wearing a mink coat. John thinks to himself, "If I help this woman, she will give me a large reward." So, John stops his car and helps the woman fix her flat tire. In the second case, Mary drives down the road and sees someone on the side of the road having difficulty with a flat tire. Mary says to herself, "That woman seems to be in trouble. I think I should help her." And she does help her. Kant would argue that there is a moral difference between case one and case two, despite the fact that the consequences in the two cases are identical. In both cases, John and Mary (on a utilitarian view) did the right thing by helping the woman, thereby producing the greatest good for the greatest number. However, Kant would argue that even though John and Mary both did the right thing (Kant would say they both acted in accordance with duty), there is still a moral difference. Mary did the act because it was her duty, whereas John was motivated by self-interest. Kant would not say that John was immoral. After all, he didn't do anything wrong. In fact, he did the right thing. But, because he didn't do it for the right reason, his action has no moral worth. He did the right thing for selfish reasons (which is still better than doing the wrong thing, that is to say performing an action inconsistent with duty). Kant draws a distinction between actions that are merely in accordance with duty and actions that are taken for the sake of duty.[15] And, he holds that only actions that are done for the sake of duty have moral worth.

Having established the importance of a good will (doing an act for the right reason), Kant moves to the question: What is our duty? In other words, just as the utilitarians have a fundamental principle of morality (act so as to produce the greatest good for the greatest number), Kant argues for a different fundamental principle of morality.

The Categorical Imperative

Kant calls the fundamental principle of morality the *categorical imperative*. An imperative is a command. It tells us what we ought to do or what we should do. The categorical imperative contrasts with what Kant calls hypothetical imperatives. A hypothetical imperative is a command that begins with "if," for example, *if* you want to get a good grade, you ought to study, or *if* you want to make a lot of money, you should work hard, or *if* you want to stay out of jail, you should not break the law. The categorical imperative is unhypothetical, no ifs whatsoever. Just do it! You ought to behave morally, period; not: *if* you want people to like you, you should behave morally; not: *if* you want to go to heaven, you should behave morally. It is just: you ought to behave morally. In other words, the categorical imperative commands absolutely and unconditionally.

What is the categorical imperative? Kant gives several formulations of it. We will focus on two formulations. The first formulation emphasizes a basic concept in ethics called "universalizability." The basic idea of universalizability is that for my action to be morally justifiable, I must be able to will that *anyone* in relevantly similar circumstances act in the same way. For example, I would like to cheat on my income tax, but could I will that *everyone* cheats on income taxes, thereby leaving the government insufficient funds to carry out programs I support? I would like to tell a lie to extricate myself from an uncomfortable situation, but could I will that someone else lie to me in order to get him or herself out of a difficult situation? Kant's formulation of the categorical imperative is as follows: "Act only on that maxim [a maxim is a principle of action] through which you can at the same time will that it should become a universal law."[16]

Kant's insight is that morality involves fairness or equality—that is, a willingness to treat everyone in the same way. I am acting immorally when I make myself an exception ("I wouldn't want others behaving this way, but it is fine for me to behave this way"). Put in that way, we see a similarity to the Golden Rule, which states, "Do unto others only as you would have them do unto you."[17] Kant's idea is that you should do only what you are willing to permit anyone else to do. The idea is that there is something inconsistent or irrational about saying that it is fine for me to lie to you, cheat you, steal from you, but it is not justified for you to do those things to me.

The next formulation of the categorical imperative focuses on the fact that human beings have intrinsic value (that is, value in and of themselves). Because human beings have intrinsic value, they ought always to be treated with reverence, and never to be treated as mere things. When I treat someone as a thing, an object, a tool or an instrument, I am treating that person as a means to my own ends. For example, if I marry someone to get her money, I am using her as a means to my own ends. I am not treating her with dignity, respect or reverence, but as a mere thing. It is the classic case of using someone. When I was about 10 years old, a friend and I wanted to go to a movie. My mother could drive one way but my friend's mother was busy and couldn't drive that day. So we decided to call a neighbor (Richard). I still remember the conversation. I said, "Hi, Richard. Would you like to go to a movie with me and Kenny?" Richard responded affirmatively, saying he would enjoy that very much. I then said, "Could your mother drive one way?" Well, Richard exploded. Richard immediately recognized that we were not inviting him because we especially wanted him to come, but rather we were using him to get a ride from his mother. Unfortunately, Richard was right. That was precisely why we called him.

Kant speaks of a human being as "something whose existence has in itself an absolute value."[18] He goes on to say that "man, and in general every rational being, exists as an end in himself, not merely as a means for arbitrary use by this or that will."[19] On the basis of this, he offers the following formulation of the categorical imperative: "Act in such a way that you always treat humanity, whether in your own person or in the person of any other, never simply as a means, but always at the same time as an end."[20]

Kant believed that these two seemingly different formulations of the categorical imperative really come to the same thing. Perhaps the reasoning goes as follows: What maxims or principles of action would I be willing to universalize? Only those that treated others as ends in themselves and not as things. Why? Because I want to be treated with reverence, respect and dignity. Since I want to be treated as a being with intrinsic value, I can only universalize maxims that treat other people as having intrinsic value.

COMPARING UTILITARIANISM AND DEONTOLOGY

Before concluding this essay, let us contrast deontological ethics with utilitarianism on a specific issue related to criminal justice. The issue is: What are the legitimate restraints a society should impose on police officers in the apprehension of suspected criminals? To limit this rather broad topic somewhat, let us focus on the use of techniques of deceit including entrapment, telephone bugging and undercover operations. In this example, I will not try to predict the answer that a utilitarian or a deontologist will give. Instead, I will simply contrast the approach or the strategy they will use in thinking about the issue.

Let's begin with utilitarianism. Utilitarianism is a consequentialist moral theory. We decide the legitimacy of deceptive tactics on the basis of the consequences of using those tactics. In particular, we must weigh the positive results against the negative results in deciding what to do. On the positive side are entrapment, bugging operations and undercover operations work. As a result of the use of such tactics, we are able to apprehend some criminals that might otherwise go free. And, as a result of apprehending those criminals, we may deter future crime in two ways: (1) We keep known criminals behind bars where they are unable to commit further crimes; and (2) We show, by example, what happens when someone breaks the law and, thereby, deter other citizens from risking incarceration.

On the negative side, we have certain individuals' right to privacy being violated by the use of deceptive tactics. The utilitarian will now weigh the positive benefits of apprehending criminals, and thereby protecting society, against the negative consequence of violating certain citizens' rights to privacy.

Kant would approach the issue from a very different reference point. As a deontologist, he would not approach this issue from the perspective of "What consequences are likely to occur?". Rather than focusing on the results or ends of the behavior, he or she would look at the behavior itself and see if it conforms to the categorical imperative. Concentrating on the universalizability formulation of the categorical imperative, a Kantian might ask: "Would I consent to having my telephone bugged if there were reason to suspect that I was guilty of a crime?"

Or, if we were to attend to the second formulation of the categorical imperative, a Kantian might ask: "Does the use of manipulative techniques in law enforcement constitute treating suspected criminals as mere means to our ends (by manipulating them, we are using them), or does it constitute treating them as ends in themselves (mature, responsible citizens who must answer to their behavior)?"

These are difficult questions to answer. But the point of the example is not to show how a utilitarian or deontologist would solve an ethical issue in criminal justice, but rather to illustrate how they would approach or think about such an issue.

JUSTICE AND DUTY

Both Kant's categorical imperative and Mill's principle of greatest happiness capture some of our moral intuitions. Treating people as ends and producing the greatest amount of happiness both seem to be credible guides to the moral life. Nonetheless, both theories seem to have trouble with a certain range of cases. Utilitarianism appears to have difficulty with certain cases of injustice, and Kant's deontology seems to have no way to handle cases of conflicting duties. In this final section, I will look at the weak points in both theories and propose an integrated Kantian-utilitarian ethic to handle the alleged weaknesses of both theories.[21]

According to utilitarianism, an action is moral when it produces the greatest amount of happiness for the greatest number of people. A problem arises, however, when the greatest happiness is achieved at the expense of a few. For example, if a large group were to enslave a very small group, the large group would gain certain comforts and luxuries (and the pleasure that accompanies those comforts) as a result of the servitude of the few. If we were to strictly follow the utilitarian calculus, the suffering of a few (even intense suffering) would be outweighed by the pleasure of a large enough majority. A thousand people's modest pleasure would outweigh the suffering of 10 others. Hence, utilitarianism would seem to endorse slavery when it produces the greatest total amount of happiness for the greatest number of people. This is obviously a problem for utilitarianism. Slavery and oppression are wrong regardless of the amount of pleasure accumulated by the oppressing class. In fact, when one person's pleasure results from the suffering of another, the pleasure seems all the more abhorrent.

The preceding case points to a weakness in utilitarianism, namely, the weakness in dealing with certain cases of injustice. Sometimes it is simply unjust to treat people in a certain way regardless of the pleasurable consequences for others. A gang rape is wrong even if 50 people enjoy it and only one suffers. It is wrong because it is unjust. To use Kant's formulation, it is always wrong to treat anyone as a mere means to one's own ends. When we enslave, rape and oppress, we are always treating the victim as a means to our own ends.

There are several cases related to criminal justice in which this issue comes up. However, when it comes up in these cases, it is not as simple as the slavery and gang-rape cases. It is complex, subtle and controversial. The cases I am considering involve the excessive use of force. Suppose, for example, that we want to keep order in our communities or in our prisons. Would we be justified in using excessive force on one offender as an example to the rest? If we were to beat a few citizens or prisoners severely for certain crimes, those public beatings might deter future crimes, thereby increasing the general happiness. But do we have the right to treat one offender with excessive violence in order to teach others a lesson? A case like this is apt to produce a lively debate, and the debate would involve utilitarian and Kantian sentiments. The utilitarian might point out that, although public canings are brutal, Singapore (which uses such punishments) is virtually crime-free. The Kantian would say that the beating of some citizens to protect others is too high a price. It is simply unjust to mistreat one citizen in order to benefit others. The ambivalent feelings we have in this case show how deeply we have internalized the voices of both Kant and Mill.

We see from the above cases (especially the slavery case) that utilitarianism has trouble dealing with situations involving the maximization of pleasure for the majority at the expense of the minority. We also see that Kant (with his emphasis on treating people as ends in themselves) can easily handle those cases. Kant's moral theory, however, has problems of its own. In particular, although Kant talks extensively of duty, he seems to have no way to deal with cases of conflicting duties. Suppose, for example, you borrow a gun from a friend for target practice, and promise to return the weapon. After you borrow the weapon, your friend becomes emotionally upset and vows to shoot someone. He then demands that you return the gun that you promised to return. He says he needs the gun back to commit a murder. On the one hand, you have a duty to keep your promises and return what you owe. On the other hand, you have a duty to try to prevent a murder. Kant gives us no guidance here. Treating people as ends and not means is a nice formula, but how does it apply in this case? If you do not return the gun, aren't you treating your friend as a means? If you do return the gun, aren't you treating the potential murder victim as a means? Kant provides no obvious solution. It is precisely at this point that a utilitarian calculus might help. The utilitarian would estimate the harm done by returning the gun against the harm done by keeping the gun. Presumably, much more harm would be caused by returning the weapon.

It appears, therefore, that Kant's theory is strong where Mill's is weak, and vice versa. Kant's emphasis on justice provides a moral reason to reject slavery even when it maximizes pleasure. And the utilitarian calculus gives us a method of determining what to do in cases of conflicting duties.

Perhaps we can combine the insights of both utilitarianism and deontology and formulate a "Utilitarian Kantian Principle." Cornman and Lehrer propose the following integrated principle:

> An action ought to be done in a situation if and only if 1. doing the action, (a) treats as mere means as few people as possible in the situation, and (b) treats as ends as many people as is consistent with (a), *and* 2. doing the action in the situation brings about as much overall happiness as is consistent with (1).[22]

This integrated Kantian utilitarian principle avoids the problem of the many enslaving the few because such an act would violate point 1. It also avoids the problem of conflicting duties because point 2 provides a way of deciding what to do when I am faced with a conflict of duties.

Deontology and utilitarianism are two of the most significant, influential ethical theories in Western thought. Much of the moral reasoning we daily engage in is guided by utilitarian and/or deontological reflection. This is true both generally and specifically in cases involving criminal justice. The criminal justice system itself is usually justified on either utilitarian grounds (it is in the best interest of most citizens to punish criminals) or Kantian grounds (it is our duty to punish wrongdoing). The hope is that this essay will provide some tools that we can use in trying to understand and solve some of the tough ethical decisions facing our criminal justice system.

NOTES

1. Lawrence W. Sherman, *The Study of Ethics in Criminology and Criminal Justice* (Chicago: Joint Commission on Criminology and Criminal Justice Education and Standards, 1981), p. 7.

2. Sherman, p. 30.

3. Sherman, p. 14.

4. In the *Metaphysics* (987b1), Aristotle states: "Now Socrates was engaged in the study of ethical matters, but not at all in the study of nature as a whole, yet in ethical matters he sought the universal and was the first to fix his thought on definitions."

5. See Plato, *Laches* 191c, *Euthyphro* 5c-d, *Meno* 72a.

6. See Jeremy Bentham, *The Principles of Morals and Legislation* (Darien, CT: Hafner Publishing Company, 1970); and John Stuart Mill, *Utilitarianism* (Indianapolis: Hackett Publishing Company, 1979).

7. Mill, p. 2.

8. Aristotle, *Nicomachean Ethics* 1095a15-20.

9. Mill, p. 37.

10. Mill, p. 7.

11. Mill, p. 7.

12. Bentham, p. 2.

13. Bentham, pp. 29-32.

14. Immanuel Kant, *Groundwork of the Metaphysic of Morals*, translated by H.J. Paton (New York: Harper & Row, 1964), p. 61.

15. Kant, pp. 65-67.

16. Kant, p. 88.

17. Matthew 7:12; Luke 6:31.

18. Kant, p. 95.

19. Kant, p. 95.

20. Kant, p. 96.

21. I first discovered the idea of integrating Kant and Mill in James Cornman and Keith Lehrer, *Philosophical Problems and Arguments: An Introduction*, 2d ed. (New York: Macmillan Publishing Co., 1974), pp. 504-508.

22. Cornman and Lehrer, p. 506.

DISCUSSION QUESTIONS

1. Compare and contrast utilitarianism and deontology. Which of the two do you feel explains human behavior most effectively? Why?

2. Explain and discuss Kant's categorical imperative. How appropriate are his views in today's criminal justice field?

3. Think of a difficult ethical decision that someone working in the criminal justice field might be facing. Using one of the theories discussed in this chapter, illustrate how it might be used to improve upon that situation, including the person's understanding of his or her dilemma.

CASE STUDY

Chapter 2:
Utilitarian and
Deontological
Approaches to
Criminal Justice
Ethics

POLICE OFFICER
OR
SOCIAL WORKER?

Jack and Ann Smith are a married couple with three children ranging in age from five months to six years. Jack is unemployed and is 60 percent disabled from a wound he received in Vietnam. Ann has to provide primary care for the children and also has a part-time job at a nearby grocery store. Jack and Ann live in a housing project where the rent is based on the government welfare checks they receive.

It is near the end of the month and the food stamps have almost been depleted. Jack spent what little money they had left on beer for himself and his friends. Over the years, Jack has continued to feel bitter about his disability and apparently tries to drown his problems with alcohol.

Jack and Ann had an argument earlier in the day over the amount of money Jack spends on beer and wine. Ann was also becoming increasingly upset over Jack frequenting bars and not trying to help with household responsibilities and chores. Ann even accused Jack of feeling sorry for himself and of being a failure in general. Jack responded by slapping Ann several times and leaving the house in a fit of temper.

While Jack was gone, the two eldest children began fighting with each other, which resulted in the youngest child crying. Although Ann had carefully cleaned the apartment the day before, the children had again made a mess of the house. Her patience wearing thin, Ann rocked the youngest child in a rocking chair in an effort to stop his crying. After substantial threats from their mother, the two oldest children started playing in the kitchen and eventually broke several dish-

From Larry S. Miller and Michael Braswell, *Human Relations and Police Work,* 4th ed. (Prospect Heights, IL: Waveland Press), 1997. Reprinted with permission.

es that were on the table. That was the last straw! Ann began whipping [beating] the oldest child for breaking the dishes. Full of anger and frustration, she whipped the child so hard that he fainted and was apparently unconscious.

Jack came back to the apartment a short time later, intoxicated and still upset over the argument in which he and Ann had engaged earlier. He found the younger children crying, the oldest child badly beaten, and Ann sitting in a kitchen chair sobbing. In a fit of rage, Jack began beating Ann.

The next-door neighbor, aware of what was happening, called the police and explained the situation.

You are a patrol officer assigned to the call. Your partner is a female officer with little police experience. Not knowing for sure what the situation is, you do not call for a backup car. In your opinion, at this point, it is a routine family disturbance call.

As you stand outside the Smiths' apartment door, you hear children sobbing. No one answers the door or speaks to you when you knock. You think to yourself, "These people need a social worker, not a police officer." Your partner looks at you, uncertain and waiting for instructions. You take a deep breath and try to decide what the best course of action will be.

Based on what you have read, answer the following questions:

> Examine this case from utilitarian and deontological perspectives. How would each approach differ from the other in resolving the crisis? How would they be similar? Which approach do you feel would be best?

CHAPTER 3

Peacemaking, Justice and Ethics

Michael C. Braswell & Jeffrey Gold

The evolution of legal and social justice in America often has found itself pulled between the retribution and punishment agendas of such ancient traditions as the law of Moses, the Koran, and the rehabilitation and redemption traditions of New Testament Christianity. The tension between these traditions of retribution and rehabilitation, and punishment and reform, has been substantial.

Peacemaking as a justice and criminology perspective has been heralded in some quarters as a contemporary, "new age" phenomenon. The New Age movement itself appears to be essentially a middle-class movement that focuses on such issues as metaphysical inquiry, mind control, emotional healing, and financial well-being. While peacemaking concerns may be compatible with some of these issues, it seems more grounded in age-old traditions such as Christianity, Judaism, Islamism, Buddhism and Hinduism. In particular, these ancient traditions emphasize the value and usefulness of suffering and service, which is often deemphasized or nonexistent in New Age movements.[1]

Peacemaking, as evolved from ancient spiritual and wisdom traditions, has included the possibility of mercy and compassion within the framework of justice. To put such thinking in a more personal perspective, we might consider our own experiences—times when we have been the victim and other occasions when we have been the offender. Perhaps we have never committed a crime and, hopefully, most of us have never been harmed by an offender. Yet, in our own way we have been both victim and offender. We have been betrayed by those we trusted, whether the heartbreak of a romance gone sour, or the cruel gossip of a broken confidence. How did we feel when we were betrayed? What did we want from the one who hurt us? Typically, we wanted to strike back; we wanted revenge, retribution, our pound of flesh. What about the occasions when we have been the offender; when we have committed the betrayal? When our best friend

> **KEY CONCEPTS:**
>
> caring
>
> connectedness
>
> mindfulness
>
> peacemaking

found out that we were the source of the criticism or cruel gossip, what did we want? As the one who offended, what did we hope for? Did we hope for mercy and forgiveness, perhaps another chance? Can we have it both ways? Can we be for revenge and violence when we are the victim and for mercy and peace when we are the offender? Can we expect to have it both ways?

What we will try to do in this chapter is explore three themes of peacemaking: (1) connectedness, (2) care, and (3) mindfulness. It is our hope that through this exploration we will be able to better understand the possibilities of peacemaking for us as criminal justice professionals as well as on a personal level.

CONNECTEDNESS

The first and perhaps most important theme is demonstrated in the dedication to the book *Inner Corrections: Finding Peace and Peace Making*, which says, "to the keeper and the kept, the offender and the victim, the parent and the child, the teacher and the student, and the incarcerator and the liberator that is within each of us."[2] This simple statement suggests what Eastern philosophers such as Lao-tzu and Western philosophers such as Plato advocated ages ago—that human beings are not simply isolated individuals, but that each one of us is integrally "connected" and bonded to other human beings and the environment. This environment includes not only the outer physical environment, but our inner psychological and spiritual environment as well. Chief Seattle of the Duwamish tribe, in a letter to the president of the United States, wrote the following in 1852:

> Every part of this earth is sacred to my people. Every shining pine needle, every sandy shore, every mist in the dark woods, every meadow, every humming insect . . . . We know the sap which courses through the trees as we know the blood that courses through our veins. We are part of the earth and it is part of us. The perfumed flowers are our sisters. The bear, the deer, the great eagle, these are our brothers. The rocky crests, the juices in the meadow, the body heat of the pony, and man, all belong to the same family . . . This we know: the earth does not belong to man, man belongs to the earth. All things are connected like the blood that unites us all. Man did not weave the web of life, he is merely a strand in it. Whatever he does to the web, he does to himself.[3]

In that letter, Chief Seattle emphasizes our connection to the natural world. One can find a similar position in several different Eastern philosophies. Bo Lozoff, articulating the position found in Yoga, states: "In Truth, we (everybody and everything in the Universe) are all connected; most of us just can't see the glue."[4]

The idea that we just can't see the glue (that is, we can't see the connection linking ourselves to others) is the Hindu concept that we misperceive ourselves as isolated and disconnected from one another and the world. As we become more aware of how we are connected to all that we are a part of, we are encouraged to take more personal responsibility to do the best we can. Wendell Berry, a noted conservationist, writes, "A man who is willing to undertake the discipline and the difficulty of mending his own ways is worth more to the conservation movement than a hundred who are insisting merely that the government and industries mend *their* ways."[5] Thomas Merton suggests that "instead of hating the people you think are war makers, hate the appetites and the disorder in your own soul, which are the causes of war."[6] Insofar as we see ourselves as apart from nature rather than a part of nature, we end up with pollution, acid rain, destruction of forests and the depletion of the ozone layer. As Berry and Merton indicate, an important aspect of connectedness is looking within, taking personal responsibility and acting in a more responsible way.

In this regard, it is interesting to contrast two metaphors concerning the earth. The older metaphor of "mother earth" contrasts dramatically with the contemporary metaphor of the earth as a collection of "natural resources." A mother is someone to whom we feel connected and bound. To perceive the earth as one's mother is to see oneself as coming out of the earth. The connection could not be any more intimate. To perceive the earth as an assortment of natural resources is another matter entirely. To conceive of the earth as merely a provider of goods for our own purposes is, to borrow Kant's expression, to see the earth as merely a means of our own ends. The danger in that attitude is now obvious. Insofar as we do not consider the earth to be sacred or precious (as Chief Seattle did), but instead see it as a commodity with no intrinsic worth, we find ourselves in a world with places like Prince William Sound, Three Mile Island, Love Canal and Chernobyl. To put such thinking in a Judeo-Christian context, does "dominion over the earth" refer to our being responsible stewards of the earth and its resources, or does it allow us to attempt to dominate the earth, exploiting its resources for profit and convenience with little or no regard for breaking environmental laws or for our children's future?

Once we accept the assumption that we are connected to everyone and everything around us, it becomes clear that our actions do not take place in a vacuum but within a complex web of interconnected people and things. Whatever I do has an impact upon those around me. My actions have consequences. This is the Hindu and Buddhist concept of karma. The law of karma is the law of cause and effect. All actions have effects or consequences. The law of karma is neither good or bad. It simply is what it is.

When we integrate the notion of karma (lawful consequences) with the notion of connectedness, it becomes clear that, since we are connected to everyone around us, our actions affect those who are connected to us even when we cannot see the connections. Insofar as we have an impact on someone we are connected with, we have an impact upon ourselves. In other words, our actions ultimately come back to us. What goes around comes around. What we do to others, in one way or another, we also do to ourselves. It is the biblical idea that we reap what we sow. It is Chief Seattle's idea that "Man did not weave the web of life, he is merely a strand in it. Whatever he does to the web, he does to himself. Plant seeds of violence and reap violent fruits. Plant seeds of compassion and reap compassionate fruits." Bo Lozoff states: "Every thought, word, and deed is a seed we plant in the world. All our lives, we harvest the fruits of those seeds. If we plant desire, greed, fear, anger and doubt, then that's what will fill our lives. Plant love, courage, understanding, good humor, and that's what we get back. This isn't negotiable; it's a law of energy, just like gravity."[7]

When we speak of karma, we are not talking about retribution, revenge or punishment. Rather, we are speaking of the consequences of actions. We do not say of someone who jumps from a third-story window that his broken leg is a punishment for jumping. It is simply a consequence. Rather than thinking of karma as retribution, it is better to think of it as the principle, "You've made your bed, now you must lie in it." We must inhabit the world we create. If we pollute the world, we must live in a polluted world. If we act violently or choose to ignore violence and injustice, we must live in a violent and unjust world.

According to proponents of the idea of karma (the idea that each one of us reaps what he or she sows), no one can ever get away with one's actions. Perhaps we won't get caught by the police, but the action still has an impact on our own life. For a philosopher like Plato the consequences are consequences for our own psyche. In Plato's *Gorgias,* Socrates compares physical health with psychological health.[8] To understand this comparison, consider the following example. I live a sedentary life, eat a diet of junk food and soda pop, smoke cigarettes and drink alcohol excessively. This life of no exercise, poor nutrition, cigarettes and alcohol will eventually catch up with me. After I become adjusted and acclimated to it, I may believe that I feel just fine. But from the fact that I believe that I feel fine, it does not follow that I am in an optimal state of physical health. The reason that I believe that I feel fine is precisely because I no longer even know what it is like to feel healthy. It is like a severely nearsighted child who has never worn glasses. He will not know that his sight is not optimal; he will think the world is supposed to look the way he sees it. He will not know that there is a better way to see. Similarly, the person who lives a sedentary life and eats exclusively at fast food restaurants may not know that there is a better way to feel. But the fact that he does not know it does not stop the junk food and cigarettes from continuing to affect his physical condition. One simply cannot avoid the consequences of an unhealthy diet and lifestyle.

This is also a useful analogy for understanding suffering and violence within families. There is often a sense of disconnectedness, inconsistency and neglect regarding relationships in unhealthy and abusive families. Over a period of years trust becomes nonexistent and feelings of anger and unhappiness begin to appear normal to such families. They forget how it felt to be happy and at peace (if they ever experienced such feelings). When children grow up full of pain and inconsistencies, they, along with their families, often reap a harvest of drug abuse, spousal battering and other forms of criminality—even suicide or homicide. They did not realize things had gotten so bad. In a sense, the connections, both hidden and obvious, that animate the consequences of our actions are like a dance (and there are no spectators in the dance of life). "The flailing arms of the abusive parent and the contortions of the victim-child are locked in a dance of pain and sorrow no less significant than the dance of joy experienced by the loving elderly couple."[9]

In *Gorgias*, Plato argues that the same is true with injustice and psychological health. One can never escape the consequences of injustice. One may escape detection by the police, one may never be brought to trial, one may never go to prison—but injustice continues to affect one's psyche, whether we know it or not. We must inhabit the unjust world that we have created. According to Plato, injustice brings strife, disharmony and conflict. There will be strife and conflict in an unjust city. Similarly, there will be strife and conflict in an unjust individual (a lack of psychic health and wholeness). Just as the physically unhealthy man may not know he is unhealthy and the nearsighted child may not know his eyesight is poor, the unjust man may not know that he is in a state of psychic disharmony and imbalance. That is because he has become adjusted and acclimated to an unjust and violent life. He simply doesn't know what it is like to feel balanced, harmonious and whole. Of course, consequences of poor physical or psychic health may also offer a person opportunity to learn and grow from his or her experience. For example, what does it mean when a person who ridicules and feels prejudice toward disabled persons finds him or herself the parent of a disabled child? Some persons might suggest that such a consequence is a form of punishment. Perhaps on a deeper level, the consequence is also an opportunity—another chance for the disconnected person to see and experience the connection, that his or her disabled child is lovable and an important part of the web of life. The same can be said of the harsh, uncaring critic of the drug addict, who comes to find that his own daughter or son suffers from such an affliction.

To summarize, according to what we are calling theories of connectedness, people are not isolated, disconnected beings. Rather, we are earthly beings and social beings; that is, we are creatures integrally connected to the earth and to other people on the earth. What we do has direct consequence on those to whom we are connected whether or not we see the connection. Our actions directly affect the world in which we live. We must live in the world created by our own actions. If we act violently, cruelly and unjustly, we will live in a world filled with violence, cruelty and injustice. If we act compassionately and benevolently, we will live in a world that is more compassionate and benevolent.

This metaphysical view naturally leads to an ethics of nonviolence. The Sanskrit word *ahimsa,* meaning nonviolence, is a fundamental concept in Hinduism and Buddhism. Mahatma Gandhi, who advocated an ethic of nonviolence, is a contemporary representative of that idea. A Christian representative is Martin Luther King, Jr. Both believed in changing the world and rectifying the injustices they saw, but both insisted on using nonviolent strategies. Martin Luther King, Jr., accepting the Nobel Peace Prize, said, "The nonviolent resisters can summarize their message in the following simple terms: We will not obey unjust laws or submit to unjust practices. We will do this peacefully, openly, cheerfully, because our aim is to persuade. We adopt the means of nonviolence because our end is a community at peace with itself."[10] The idea is that violence breeds violence. You don't fight fire with fire, rather you put out fire with water. You don't end violence by violently resisting it. Perhaps that is what Jesus meant by "resist not evil."[11] You don't end violence by creating more of it. If we must inhabit the world we create and we want to live in a world which is just and peaceful, we ought to act in just and peaceful ways. Richard Quinney writes, "Instead of a war on crime ("on criminals") we need to be waging peace on the economy, in the society, and within ourselves."[12] In other words, we need to wage peace, not war.

An example of the relevance of this to criminal justice can be found in our contemporary prisons. Contemporary prisons are typically violent institutions that tend to perpetuate rather than diminish violence. According to the theories presented in this section, we must begin to treat criminals in less violent and more compassionate ways. We must stop thinking in terms of revenge, retribution and recrimination, and begin to think in terms of reconciliation, compassion and forgiveness. In recent years, there have been innovations and increasing numbers of alternative programs on mediation, conflict resolution, restitution and community action. They are a part of an emerging criminology of peacemaking, a criminology that seeks to end suffering and reduce crime.[13] This approach to corrections is not a weak, "bleeding heart" approach. Sometimes love may have to be firm love. Still, if we choose to acknowledge our connectedness and desire to be peacemakers, we will insist on treating persons as a part of our humanity whether they deserve such treatment or not.

The following Zen story presents this philosophy in its most radical form:

> One evening as Shichiri Kojun was reciting sutras a thief with a sharp sword entered, demanding either his money or his life. Shichiri told him: "Do not disturb me. You can find the money in that drawer." Then he resumed his recitation. A little while afterwards he stopped and called: "Don't take it all. I need some to pay taxes with tomorrow." The intruder gathered up most of the money and started to leave. "Thank a person when you receive a gift," Shichiri added. The man thanked him and made off. A few days afterwards the fellow was caught and confessed, among others, the offence against Shichiri. When Shichiri was called as a witness he said: "This man is no thief, at least as far as I am concerned. I gave him the money and he thanked me for it." After he had finished his prison term, the man went to Shichiri and became his disciple.[14]

Along the same lines, Jesus teaches that if anyone sues you for your coat, let him also have your cloak.[15] He goes on to say: "Love your enemies, bless them that curse you, do good to them that hate you, and pray for them who despitefully use you, and persecute you."[16] The radical message of these philosophies is that we should cease to repay violence with violence, whether that repayment be called "retribution" or "just deserts." Instead, we must learn to, as Paul puts it, "overcome evil with good."[17] Jesus also reminds us that whatever we do to the "least of those" in our society, we do to Him. In terms of criminal justice, that would involve a complete reform of what we now call "corrections."

CARING

In the previous chapter, we presented reasons in support of the utilitarian version of the fundamental rule of morality, namely, that we ought to produce the greatest good for the greatest number. We advanced Kant's arguments for what he considers to be the basic moral principle, that we ought to treat others as ends in themselves and not as mere means. We have just explored how theories of connectedness defend the moral absolute of nonviolence. Though each of the three theories differ from one another, all share a similarity of approach. All attempt to prove, by means of argument, justification and reason, a specific moral rule or principle. According to Nel Noddings, proving, justifying and arguing for rules and principles is a masculine approach to ethics. In *Caring: A Feminine Approach to Ethics & Moral Education,* she outlines an alternative. Noddings claims:

> Ethics, the philosophical study of morality, has concentrated for the most part on moral reasoning . . . Even though careful philosophers have recognized the difference between "pure" or logical reason and "practical" or moral reason, ethical argumentation has frequently proceeded as if it were governed by the logical necessity characteristic of geometry. It has concentrated on the establishment of principles and that which can be logically derived from them. One might say that ethics has been discussed largely in the language of the father: in principles and propositions, in terms such as justification, fairness, justice. The mother's voice has been silent. Human caring and the memory of caring and being cared for, which I shall argue form the foundation of ethical response, have not received attention except as outcomes of ethical behavior. One is tempted to say that ethics has so far been guided by Logos, the masculine spirit, whereas the more natural and perhaps stronger approach would be through Eros, the feminine spirit.[18]

According to Noddings, the masculine approach (the approach of the father) is a detached perspective that focuses on law and principle, whereas the feminine approach (the approach of the mother) is rooted in receptivity, relatedness and responsiveness.[19] Noddings advocates the feminine perspective. She goes on to point out that "this does not imply that all women will accept it [the feminine perspective] or that men will reject it; indeed, there is no reason why men should not embrace it."[20]

The masculine perspective is an approach to ethics, an approach through justification and argument. The feminine perspective, on the other hand, "shall locate the very wellspring of ethical behavior in human affective response."[21] Noddings's point is that ethical caring is ultimately grounded in natural caring— for example, the natural caring a mother has for her child. Noddings's emphasis on natural caring leads her to the conclusion "that in truth, the moral viewpoint is prior to any notion of justification."[22] In other words, rather than viewing reason and justification as the process by which one comes to the moral perspective, Noddings indicates that the moral perspective is a natural perspective, as natural as a mother caring for her infant.

An ancient Chinese philosophy, Taoism, advocates a position that is similar to the one we find in Noddings. The two major Taoist philosophers, Lao-tzu and Chuang-tzu, suggest that not only is natural caring prior to reason, justification and principle, it is superior to those activities. In fact, the Taoists claim that principles of ethics actually interfere with caring. Just as Nel Noddings is responding to a particular masculine tradition in Western ethics, the Taoists are responding to a particular tradition in Chinese ethics, namely, Confucianism. The Confucianists were very rule- and principle-oriented—rules for filial piety, rules for those who govern, rules for those who are governed. The Taoists responded by claiming that those rules, because of their artificiality, destroyed true, natural caring and replaced it with forced or legislated "caring."

From the Taoist perspective, the danger of advocating ethical rules and principles is that they will replace something far superior to those principles, namely natural caring. Chuang-tzu says: "Because [the doctrine of] right and wrong appeared, the Way was injured."[23]

Lao-tzu makes a similar claim. Lao-tzu doesn't make the strong claim that the doctrine of right and wrong destroyed the Way (the Tao). However, he does claim that only in unnatural states does the doctrine of right and wrong arise. In the *Tao Te Ching*, Lao-tzu says:

> Therefore, when Tao [the natural Way] is lost, only then does the doctrine of virtue arise.
>
> When virtue is lost, only then does the doctrine of humanity arise.
>
> When humanity is lost, only then does the doctrine of righteousness arise.
>
> When righteousness is lost, only then does the doctrine of propriety arise.
>
> Now, propriety is a superficial expression of loyalty and faithfulness, and the beginning of disorder.[24]

Notice how Lao-tzu concludes by discussing the superficiality of notions of propriety and how such notions are the beginning of disorder. In another section of the *Tao Te Ching*, Lao-tzu summarizes the preceding by saying, "When the great Tao [Natural Way] declined, the doctrine of humanity and righteousness arose."[25] Lao-tzu is saying that artificial doctrines of virtue, humanity, and righteousness, doctrines that tell us how we ought to behave, arise only in unhealthy situations. Something is already terribly wrong when we tell a mother she ought to feed her child or that she has a duty to feed her child. Feeding one's child is a natural, caring response. Lao-tzu says: "When the six family relationships are not in harmony, there will be the advocacy of filial piety and deep love to children."[26]

Given that we live in and are inculcated into a patriarchal society, a society of rules, principles and laws, do the Taoists have any suggestions as to how to break free from patriarchal modes of thought, how to return to a more natural and caring way of living in the world? As you might expect, the answer to this is yes. The Taoist position can be put in the following way: Moral reasoning is the product of a mind that discriminates and draws distinctions (between right and wrong, good and bad, just and unjust). According to Taoism, these categories and distinctions are artificial and conventional, not natural. To put oneself into a more natural state, which according to the Taoist view on human nature would be a more caring state, one must undo, erase or transcend all the conventional, artificial dualisms that have been inculcated into us. We perceive the world the way we have been taught to perceive the world. So, we must begin to unlearn the categories that have been programmed into us.

In a more contemporary vein, Myers and Chiang[27] also compared the prevailing legalistic, masculine approach to law enforcement—which focuses on analysis, rationalization and punishment—with the feminine perspective of nurturing and care, and treatment.

Martin[28] examined the usefulness of incorporating transpersonal psychology into the justice and corrections process. This discipline integrates Western scientific and Eastern and Western spiritual traditions, which could open a fresh way to develop policy and treatment strategies that are more positive and growth-oriented.

An ancient story involving the teacher, Ryokan, and his delinquent nephew offers another interesting, if unorthodox, approach in utilizing the ethic of care:

> Once his brother asked Ryokan to visit his house and speak to his delinquent son. Ryokan came but did not say a word of admonition to the boy. He stayed overnight and prepared to leave the next morning. As the wayward nephew was lacing up Ryokan's sandals, he felt a drop of warm water. Glancing up, he saw Ryokan looking down at him, his eyes full of tears. Ryokan then returned home, and the nephew changed for the better.[29]

It goes without saying that caring is not the exclusive property of Taoism or Yoga. Mother Teresa, a recipient of the Nobel Peace Prize, encompasses this ethic of caring from a Christian perspective. She started her work as a one-woman mission in Calcutta, India, ministering to and caring for the dying. Generally speaking, in some ways we might consider the dying poor even more undesirable than incarcerated offenders. Yet Mother Teresa's Missionaries of Charity grew from a one-woman operation to a group of active missions found all over the world. When asked how she could emotionally handle constantly being around so many dying persons, she responded that when she looked into the eyes of the dying she saw "Christ in a distressing disguise."[30]

MINDFULNESS

Mother Teresa is perhaps the embodiment of the ethic of care. Internalizing such an approach requires that one develop a compassionate vision through mindfulness. The following example from one of her public addresses demonstrates such a vision in action:

> A gentleman came to our house and he told me, "There is a Hindu family with about eight children who have not eaten for a long time." So I took some rice quickly and went to their family and I could see real hunger on the small faces of these children and yet the mother had the courage to divide the rice into two and she went out. When she came back, I asked her, "Where did you go? What did you do?" And she said: "They are hungry also." "Who are they?" "The Muslim family next door with as many children." She knew that they were hungry. What struck me most was that she knew and because she knew she gave until it hurt. I did not bring more rice that night because I wanted them to enjoy the joy of giving, of sharing. You should have seen the faces of those little ones. They just understood what their mother did. Their faces were brightened with smiles. When I came in they looked hungry, they looked so miserable. But the act of their mother taught them what true love was.[31]

Mindfulness allows us to experience a more transcendent sense of awareness. It allows us to be fully present, aware of what is immediate, yet also at the same time to become more aware of the larger picture both in terms of needs and possibilities. Mindfulness allowed the Hindu mother not only to receive the rice from Mother Teresa with gratitude, but also allowed her to see how she was connected to the hungry Muslim family and how to have the courage to care enough to share her meager resources, thus teaching her own children one of life's greatest lessons.

Mindfulness can encourage us to move from the passion of single-minded self-interest to a growing sense of compassion that includes others and their needs. We often wring our hands about those who are victims of physical abuse and the homeless. Yet how often do we volunteer to help?[32] Mindfulness can help us, like the Hindu mother, to act on our concerns. As Wang Yang Ming states, "To know and not to do is in fact, not to know."[33] Developing wholesight can help us to become more mindful in turning our knowing into doing. As mentioned in Chapter 1, Parker Palmer suggests that wholesight includes both the heart and the head in one's decisionmaking.[34]

A strategy or process that can help us become more mindful is meditation. Meditation is a practice through which the meditator quiets or stills the contents of the mind: the thoughts, the emotions, the desires, the inner chatter. Successful meditation culminates in the cessation of mental activity, a profound inner stillness. (See Figure 3.1.)

Figure 3.1
A Guide for A Simple Meditation

1. Find a quiet, special *place* in which to meditate.
2. Find a *time* to practice meditation when the area is quiet and there are no distractions, preferably twice daily. Many persons practice meditation at the beginning of the day and at the end of the day.
3. Try to meditate for a designated period of time during each meditation experience, usually at least 10 minutes, and preferably 20 minutes.
4. Sit in a straight-backed chair, keeping the spine as straight as possible.
5. For the designated period of time, practice the following sequence:
   A) Sit silently for a few moments and become *aware* of how you are breathing;
   B) Gently and gradually begin to breathe more *smoothly;*
   C) Now begin to breathe a little more *deeply,* gradually increasing the depth of your breathing;
   D) Finally, begin to *slow* down the rate of your breathing;
   E) No matter what distractions or thoughts may occur, simply acknowledge them and let them pass, then return to breathing *smoothly, deeply* and *slowly* for the designated period of time.

Recall that Taoism teaches us to return to a more natural state, a state in which we are not controlled by the artificial modes of thought that have been inculcated into us by our society. The practice of meditation can teach us to control and still those modes of thought. By freeing ourselves from conventional ways of thinking, we return to a more natural state, a more connected and caring state. Some persons are concerned that emptying the mind meditatively could lead to some form of mind control. The truth of the matter is that meditation is more likely to lead to a greater sense of self-control, since most of us stay preoccupied with thoughts of things to do or things left undone. Busy, noisy minds often result in confused and unclear thoughts. We are less likely to be misled or do something we regret if our minds are quiet, strong and clear.

The relevance of this approach in ethics to criminal justice can be seen in the work of Bo Lozoff, director of the Prison Ashram Project. Lozoff works with prisoners, teaching them techniques of meditation. Lozoff is "helping prisoners to use their cells as ashrams [places of spiritual growth], and do their time as 'prison monks' rather than convicts."[35] In his book *We're All Doing Time,* Lozoff has a chapter on meditation in which he describes and teaches a number of meditation techniques. Much of his work in prisons involves teaching these techniques to convicts.

Lozoff describes meditation as "sitting perfectly still—silence of body, silence of speech and silence of mind. The Buddha called this 'The Noble Silence.' It's just a matter of STOPPING."[36] To connect this with Taoism, we might say that by achieving a state of inner silence in which we stop all the conventional modes of thinking and reasoning that have been inculcated into us, we return to a more natural state, a more caring state. And from this caring and compassionate state, we can become more mindful of how our inner and outer experiences are connected to those around us, even to our physical environment. This awareness can become a kind of awakening, encouraging us to make more informed and ethical decisions about the way we live our lives.

CONCLUSION

If we choose to develop a greater capacity for peacemaking through connectedness, care and mindfulness, it should follow that as persons and criminal justice professionals we will act more morally and ethically. In addition, we are more likely to teach offenders such values from the inside-out, since we will be living that way ourselves. For peacemaking to work, we have to take it personally first. We have to be grounded in the reality of where we are in terms of criminal justice problems, but at the same time, peacemaking encourages us to have a vision of what we can become. Peacemaking offers us a vision of hope grounded in the reality of which we are a part. John Gibbs suggests that "the best strategy for individual peacemakers is to adopt one which emphasizes personal transformation, has a spiritual base, and avoids ideology."[37] Mother Teresa writes, "There can be no peace in the world, including peace in the streets and peace in the home, without peace in our mind. What happens within us, happens outside us. The inner and outer are one."[38]

If we choose to try to become peacemakers, it does not necessarily follow that our lives will be less difficult. As Frederick Buechner suggests in discussing the teachings of Jesus "peace seems to have meant not the absence of struggle but the presence of love."[39] Bo Lozoff, who along with his wife, Sita, have dedicated their lives to teaching offenders peacemaking, writes in response to an inmate's letter:

> Life is funny that way. We tend to expect a nice, easy, smooth life as a result of prayer and meditation. But more often than not, our spiritual practice seems to create *more* problems instead of fewer. And then we often freak out and miss the point entirely.
>
> Pain, separation, misfortune are a part of human life . . . . Did the martyrs of every religion avoid being tortured for their beliefs? Divine beings, saints and sages have come into this world to show us how to *respond* to pain, separation, misfortune, and death—not how to escape them. By their example, they have shown us the humility, patience, forgiveness, courage, compassion, and ultimate freedom which are our own divine nature.[40]

Peacemaking acknowledges that while we do not control what life brings us, we do have a choice in how to respond to whatever life brings us. Through connectedness, care and mindfulness, we can begin to change ourselves first, then others by our example, and finally our system of justice—from the inside-out.

Figure 3.2
Thoughts on Peacemaking

I have decided to stick with love. Hate is too great a burden to bear.

—Martin Luther King Jr.

Love cures people—both the ones who give it and the ones who receive it.

—Karl Menninger

Love has no middle term; either it destroys or it saves.

—Victor Hugo

The love we give away is the only love we keep.

—Elbert Hubbard

In all conflict with evil, the method to be used is love and not force. When we use evil methods to defeat evil, it is evil that wins.

—Sri Rodhakrishnan

The inner ear of each man's soul hears the voice of life, (find your work, and do it!). Only by obedience to this command can he find peace.

—Frank Crane

If you do your work with complete faithfulness . . . you are making as genuine a contribution to the substance of the universal good as is the most brilliant worker whom the world contains.

—Phillips Brooks

The vocation of every man and woman is to serve other people.

—Leo Tolstoy

In real love you want the other person's good. In romantic love you want the other person.

—Margaret Anderson

Once we learn to touch this peace, we will be healed and transformed. It is not a matter of fact; it is a matter of practice.

—Thich Nhat Hanh

He who knows when enough is enough will always have enough.

—Lao-tzu

NOTES

1. Clemens Bartollas and Michael Braswell, "Correctional Treatment, Peacemaking, and the New Age Movement," *Journal of Crime & Justice* 16:43-59, 1993.

2. Bo Lozoff and Michael Braswell, *Inner Corrections: Finding Peace and Peace Making* (Cincinnati: Anderson Publishing Co., 1989).

3. The entire letter can be found in Joseph Campbell, *The Power of Myth* (New York: Doubleday, 1988), pp. 32-35.

4. Bo Lozoff, *We're All Doing Time* (Durham, NC: Human Kindness Foundation, 1987), p. 11.

5. Sy Safransky (ed.) *Sunbeams* (Berkley: North Atlantic Books, 1990), p. 51.

6. Safransky, p. 115.

7. Lozoff, p. 9.

8. Plato, *Republic*, 351d-352a.

9. Michael Braswell, *Journey Homeward* (Chicago: Franciscan Herald Press, 1990), p. 87.

10. Carl Cohen, *Civil Disobedience* (New York: Columbia University Press, 1971), p. 40.

11. Matthew 5:39.

12. Richard Quinney, "A Life of Crime: Criminology and Public Policy As Peacemaking," *Journal of Crime & Justice* 16:3-11, 1993.

13. Quinney, 3-11.

14. Paul Reps (ed.), *Zen Flesh, Zen Bones: A Collection of Zen and Pre-Zen Writings* (Garden City, NY: Doubleday, 1919), p. 41.

15. Matthew 5:40.

16. Matthew 5:44.

17. Romans 12:21.

18. Nel Noddings, *Caring: A Feminine Approach to Ethics and Moral Education* (Berkeley: University of California Press, 1986), p. 1.

19. Noddings, p. 2.

20. Noddings, p. 2.

21. Noddings, p. 3.

22. Noddings, p. 95.

23. Chuang-tzu, *Basic Writings* (New York: Columbia University Press, 1964), p. 37.

24. Lao-tzu, *The Way of Lao-tzu* (Tao Te Ching) (Indianapolis: Bobbs-Merrill, 1963), p. 167.

25. Lao-tzu, p. 131.

26. Id.

27. Laura Myers and Chau-Pu Chiang, "Law Enforcement Officer & Peace Officer: Reconciliation Using the Feminine Approach," *Journal of Crime & Justice* 16:31-43, 1993.

28. Randy Martin, "Transpersonal Psychology and Criminological Theory: Rethinking the Paradigm," *Journal of Crime & Justice* 16:43-59, 1993.

29. Safransky (ed.), p. 115-116.

30. From the documentary film, *Mother Teresa*, directed by Richard Attenborough.

31. Teresa de Bertodano (ed.), *Daily Readings with Mother Teresa* (London: Fount, 1993), p. 53.

32. Michael Braswell, "Peacemaking: A Missing Link in Criminology," *The Criminologist* 15:1, 3-5, 1990.

33. Lozoff & Braswell, p. 63.

34. Parker Palmer, *To Know As We Are Known* (San Francisco: Harper & Row, 1983).

35. Lozoff, p. xvii.

36. Lozoff, p. 29.

37. John Gibbs, "Spirituality, Ideology, and Personal Transformation: Some Considerations for Peacemaking." Unpublished paper, p. 2, 1993.

38. de Bertodano, p. 7.

39. Frederick Buechner, *Wishful Thinking* (New York: Harper & Row, 1973), p. 39.

40. Bo Lozoff, "Letters," *Human Kindness Foundation Newsletter*, p. 5, 1994.

DISCUSSION QUESTIONS

1. List and discuss the three themes of peacemaking and explain the impact they have on traditional police or corrections values.

2. In your opinion, can peacemaking, justice and ethics ever become fully realized? Why or why not?

3. Choose one theme of peacemaking and explain why you think it would have the greater impact on justice and ethics.

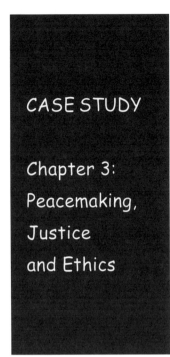

CASE STUDY

Chapter 3:
Peacemaking,
Justice
and Ethics

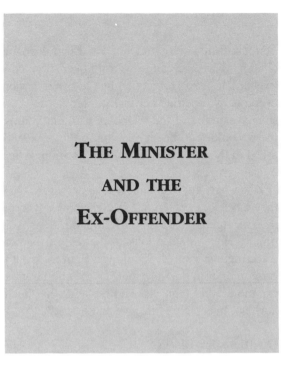

THE MINISTER
AND THE
EX-OFFENDER

As one of your community's leading ministers, you have always spoken out for progressive correctional reform. Your congregation has usually backed you, and on the few occasions when they did not, they still remained tolerant of your views. Now, however, things are different. Sally, a former member of your church, was once active in working with the church youth. She has since been convicted of embezzlement from the local bank where she worked and sentenced to a year in prison.

As her minister, you kept in contact with her from the beginning of her imprisonment. No one ever really believed she would have to serve time; since the money was returned, no one expected that her boss would even bring charges against her. Everyone has financial burdens at one time or another, and Sally had experienced a succession of problems over a long period of time. The clincher was her husband's permanent disability as a result of an accident. The bills began to pile up faster than she could get them paid. They had mortgaged their house and sold one of their two cars. Finally, in desperation, Sally "borrowed" several thousand dollars from the bank where she had worked as a teller for years. When her crime was discovered, her world crumbled around her.

She has now returned to the community after serving a prison term for embezzlement. When you talked to her the day after she returned, you realized that she was a broken woman. Her daughter had dropped out of school to care for the father, and his disability check was their primary source of income. You counseled her and encouraged her to try and regain her place in the community.

From Michael Braswell, Tyler Fletcher and Larry S. Miller, *Human Relations and Corrections,* 4th ed. (Prospect Heights, IL: Waveland Press), 1997. Reprinted with permission.

You also helped her find work and had even suggested that she return to your church where she had previously been very active. She was reluctant to rejoin the church, fearing rejection by the congregation. You tried to reassure her that everyone was behind her and wanted her to return to the church. In fact, a substantial number of the members had told you as much. When you learned that there would soon be an opening in the Sunday School for a youth director, you asked Sally to consider taking the position. After several days of thinking about it, she agreed.

You have now brought her name before the Sunday School Committee and they have, to a person, refused to allow her to be the youth leader. Their bitterness has taken you totally by surprise; their words remain all too clear in your mind: "How would it look to the rest of the community to have an ex-convict directing our youth?" Should you fight for what you believe is right and risk dissension or even possibly splitting the church, or should you tell her that her fears are more valid than you had thought; that her former fellow church members have not been able to forgive and forget?

Questions for Discussion:

> Evaluate this case from a peacemaking perspective. What course of action should the minister take?

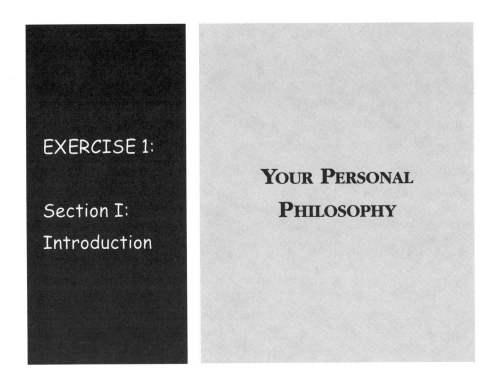

EXERCISE 1:

Section I: Introduction

YOUR PERSONAL PHILOSOPHY

What is your personal/professional philosophy? The most important aspect of our personal and professional growth involves the values and beliefs that we hold dear. Now that you have covered the first three chapters, with which theories and ideas do you agree or disagree? What are your personal values and what beliefs are they based upon? How do you plan to put these values and beliefs into practice in the work environment of your chosen profession?

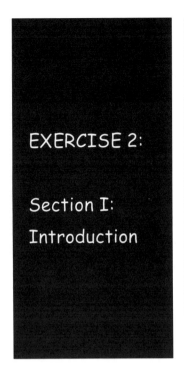

EXERCISE 2:

Section I:

Introduction

THE ETHICS OF DRUG CONTROL POLICY

The United States is currently confronting a drug crisis. While drug use in the general population seems to be declining, drug use and sales among criminals is continuing to increase. Some citizens are calling for stiffer penalties for illegal drug use, while others are calling for decriminalization and even legalization of certain drugs. Suppose you were a staff assistant to a congressperson whose committee was investigating the ethics of drug control policy.

What issues would be relevant to this assessment?

How could a morally correct approach to drug/crime policy be developed?

Whose rights would have to be protected?

What societal benefits and deficits would you consider?

How could this policy be developed in a way that promoted caring and concern for all in society?

> Man becomes
> great exactly
> in the degree
> in which he
> works for the
> welfare of
> his fellow-man.
>
> —Mahatma Gandhi

SECTION II

Ethical Issues in Policing

Police work has been called a "morally dangerous" endeavor, and with good reason. Not only are the temptations faced by the average patrol officer much greater than those confronted in other occupations, but the nature of the work itself requires activities that can easily cross over the line from acceptable to unethical conduct.

Police corruption is a broad area of concern. For some observers it includes everything from the simple acceptance of a free meal from a small business owner, to the receipt of kickbacks from attorneys and tow truck drivers, to police-organized theft.

Many of the problems of police corruption are linked to the tremendous amount of discretion possessed by the patrol officer. Most of us would agree that it is sometimes acceptable to use this discretion to avoid giving a ticket or making an arrest. When good judgment determines that no action is necessary or there are other means of addressing the problem, discretion is clearly being put to good use. But, when these discretions are influenced by offers of money, drugs or sexual favors, the use of discretion becomes tainted, and the actions corrupt.

Situations confronting police officers offer temptations of their own. The money found on a drunk, the cash and drugs found at the scene of a crime—these can tempt officers who are on their honor to report what they find. In the area of narcotics control, such temptations are always present.

There are still other dilemmas confronting the police officer who does not give in to the temptations of corruption. In many ways, crime control efforts foster an "ends justifies the means" mentality. To the extent that due process guarantees are seen as somehow interfering with crime control efforts, attempts to work

47

around these "technicalities" come to be viewed as justified. This is especially true in regard to the control of vice and narcotics activities, where proactive and deceptive methods, such as "sting" operations and undercover work, are routine.

In many ways, police officers must walk a fine line. Overzealousness and the use of unnecessary force is undesirable, but so is a reluctance to intervene or back up another officer when the situation requires it. When officers use patrol time to avoid their responsibilities rather than to execute them, the professional image of the entire department suffers.

To avoid corruption, police departments must attempt to recruit and hire honorable men and women. These persons must be educated and trained to deal with whatever problems they confront. There is also a need for the police organization to take steps to keep standards high. These efforts include the development of explicit policy covering the variety of potentially corrupting situations and the implementation of active internal affairs units. Perhaps more important, however, is the creation of an organizational climate that fosters candid and open public examination of police practices, and a responsiveness to line officers and the dilemmas they confront.

CHAPTER 4

Learning Police Ethics

Lawrence Sherman

There are two ways to learn police ethics. One way is to learn on the job, to make your moral decisions in haste under the time pressures of police work. This is by far the most common method of learning police ethics, the way virtually all of the half million police officers in the United States decide what ethical principles they will follow in their work. These decisions are strongly influenced by peer group pressures, by personal self-interest, by passions and emotions in the heat of difficult situations.

There is another way. It may even be a better way. You can learn police ethics in a setting removed from the heat of battle, from the opinions of co-workers, and from the pressures of supervisors. You can think things through with a more objective perspective on the issues. You should be able to make up your mind about many

KEY CONCEPTS:

apologia

contingencies

ethics

metamorphosis

moral career

moral experience

morals

occupational career

difficult choices before you actually have to make them. And you can take the time to weigh all sides of an issue carefully, rather than making a snap judgment.

The purpose of this article is to provide a basis for this other, less common way of learning police ethics, by making the alternative—the usual way of learning police ethics—as clear as possible. This portrait of the on-the-job method is not attractive, but it would be no more attractive if we were to paint the same picture for doctors, lawyers, judges, or college professors. The generalizations we make are not true of all police officers, but they do reflect a common pattern, just as similar patterns are found in all occupations.

Lawrence Sherman, "Learning Police Ethics," (as appeared in *Criminal Justice Ethics*, Volume 1, Number 1 [Winter/Spring 1982] pp. 10-19). Reprinted by permission of the Institute for Criminal Justice Ethics, 899 Tenth Avenue, New York, NY 10019-1029.

Learning New Jobs

Every occupation has a learning process (usually called "socialization") to which its new members are subjected. The socialization process functions to make most "rookies" in the occupation adopt the prevailing rules, values, and attitudes of their senior colleagues in the occupation. Very often, some of the existing informal rules and attitudes are at odds with the formal rules and attitudes society as a whole expects members of the occupation to follow. This puts rookies in a moral dilemma: Should the rookies follow the formal rules of society or the informal rules of their senior colleagues?

These dilemmas vary in their seriousness from one occupation and one organization to the next. Young college professors may find that older professors expect them to devote most of their time to research and writing, while the general public (and their students) expects them to devote most of their time to teaching. With some luck, and a lot of work, they can do both.

Police officers usually face much tougher dilemmas. Like waiters, longshoremen, and retail clerks, they may be taught very early how to steal—at the scene of a burglary, from the body of a dead person, or in other opportunities police confront. They may be taught how to commit perjury in court to insure that their arrests lead to conviction, or how to lie in disciplinary investigations to protect their colleagues. They may be taught how to shake people down, or how to beat people up. Or they may be fortunate enough to go to work in an agency, or with a group of older officers, in which none of these violations of official rules is ever suggested to them.

Whether or not rookie police officers decide to act in ways the wider society might view as unethical, they are all subjected to a similar process of being taught certain standards of behavior. Their reactions to that learning as the years pass by can be described as their *moral careers:* the changes in the morality and ethics of their behavior. But the moral career is closely connected to the *occupational career:* the stages of growth and development in becoming a police officer.

This article examines the process of learning a new job as the context for learning police ethics. It then describes the content of the ethical and moral values in many police department "cultures" that are conveyed to new police officers, as well as the rising conflict within police agencies over what those values should be. Finally, it describes the moral career of police officers, including many of the major ethical choices officers make.

Becoming a Police Officer

There are four major stages in the career of anyone joining a new occupation:[1]

- the *choice* of occupation
- the *introduction* to the occupation

- the first *encounter* with doing the occupation's work

- the *metamorphosis* into a full-fledged member of the occupation

Police officers go through these stages, just as doctors and bankers do. But the transformation of the police officer's identity and self-image may be more radical than in many other fields. The process can be overwhelming, changing even the strongest of personalities.

Choice

There are three aspects of the choice to become a police officer. One is the *kind of person* who makes that choice. Another is the *reason* the choice is made, the motivations for doing police work. The third is the *methods* people must use as police officers. None of these aspects of choice appears to predispose police officers to be more or less likely to perform their work ethically.

Many people toy with the ideal of doing police work, and in the past decade the applicants for policing have become increasingly diverse. Once a predominately white male occupation, policing has accepted many more minority group members and attracted many more women. More college-educated people have sought out police work, but this may just reflect the higher rate of college graduates in the total population.

What has not changed, apparently, is the socioeconomic background of people who become police. The limited evidence suggests police work attracts the sons and daughters of successful tradespeople, foremen, and civil servants— especially police. For many of them, the good salary (relative to the educational requirements), job security, and prestige of police work represent a good step up in the world, an improvement on their parents' position in life.

The motivation to become a police officer flows naturally from the social position of the people who choose policing. People do not seem to choose policing out of an irrational lust for power or because they have an "authoritarian personality"; The best study on this question showed that New York City police recruits even had a *lower* level of authoritarian attitudes than the general public (although their attitudes become more authoritarian as they become adapted to police work, rising to the general public's level of authoritarian attitudes).[2] Police applicants tend to see police work as an adventure, as a chance to do work out of doors without being cooped up in an office, as a chance to do work that is important for the good of society, and not as a chance to be the "toughest guy on the block." Nothing in the motivation to apply for a police position seems to predispose police officers towards unethical behavior.

Nor do the methods of selecting police officers seem to affect their long-term moral careers. There was a time when getting on the force was a matter of bribery or political favors for local politicians, or at least a matter of knowing the right people involved in grading the entrance examinations and sitting on the selection committees. But in the 1980s the selection process appears to be highly bureaucratic, wherein impersonal multiple-choice tests scored by computers play the most important role in the process.

To be sure, there are still subjective background investigations, personal interviews, and other methods that allow biases to intrude upon the selection process. But these biases, if anything, work in the direction of selecting people who have backgrounds of unquestioned integrity. Combined with the high failure rate among all applicants—sometimes less than one in twenty is hired, which makes some police departments more selective in quantitative terms than the Harvard Law School—the selection process probably makes successful applicants feel that they have been welcomed into an elite group of highly qualified people of very high integrity.

Introduction

But this sense of high ideals about police work may not last for long. The introduction to policing provided by most police academies begins to convey folklore that shows the impossibility of doing things "by the book" and the frequent necessity of "bending the rules."

Police recruit training has changed substantially over the past thirty years. Once highly militaristic, it has recently taken on more the atmosphere of the college classroom. The endurance test-stress environment approach, in which trainees may be punished for yawning or looking out the window, may still be found in some cities, but it seems to be dying out. Dull lectures on the technical aspects of police work (such as how to fill out arrest reports) and the rules and regulations of the department are now often supplemented by guest lectures on theories of crime and the cultures of various ethnic groups.

But the central method of *moral* instruction does not appear to have changed. The "war story" still remains the most effective device for communicating the history and values of the department. When the instructor tells a "war story," or an anecdote about police work, the class discipline is relaxed somewhat, the interest and attention of the class increase, and an atmosphere of camaraderie between the class and the instructor is established. The content of the war story makes a deep impression on the trainees.

The war stories not only introduce police work as it is experienced by police officers—rather than as an abstract ideal—they also introduce the ethics of police work as something different from what the public, or at least the law and the press, might expect. Van Maanen recounts one excerpt from a police academy criminal law lecture that, while not a "story," indicates the way in which the hidden values of police work are conveyed:

> I suppose you guys have heard of Lucky Baldwin? If not, you sure will when you hit the street. Baldwin happens to be the biggest burglar still operating in this town. Every guy in this department from patrolman to chief would love to get him and make it stick. We've

> busted him about ten times so far, but he's got an asshole lawyer and money so he always beats the rap. . . . If I ever get a chance to pinch the SOB, I'll do it my way with my thirty-eight and spare the city the cost of a trial.[3]

Whether the instructor would actually shoot the burglary suspect is open to question, although he could do so legally in most states if the suspect attempted to flee from being arrested. More important is the fact that the rookies spend many hours outside the classroom debating and analyzing the implications of the war stories. These discussions do help them decide how they would act in similar circumstances. But the decisions they reach in these informal bull sessions are probably more attributable to peer pressure and the desire to "fit in" to the culture of the department than to careful reflection on moral principle.

Encounter

After they leave the academy, the rookies are usually handed over to Field Training Officers (FTOs). In the classic version of the first day on patrol with the rookie, the FTO says, "Forget everything they taught you in the academy, kid; I'll show you how police work is really done." And show they do. The rookie becomes an observer of the FTO as he or she actually does police work. Suddenly the war stories come alive, and all the questions about how to handle tough situations get answered very quickly and clearly, as one police veteran recalls:

> On this job, your first partner is everything. He tells you how to survive on the job . . . how to walk, how to stand, and how to speak and how to think and what to say and see.[4]

The encounter with the FTO is only part of the rookie's "reality shock" about police work. Perhaps even more important are the rookie's encounters with the public. By putting on the uniform, the rookie becomes part of a visible minority group. The self-consciousness about the new appearance is heightened by the nasty taunts and comments the uniform attracts from teenagers and others.[5] The uniform and gun, as symbols of power, attract challenges to that power simply because they are there.[6] Other people seek out the uniform to manipulate the rookie to use the power on behalf of their personal interests. Caught frequently in the cross fire of equally unreasonable citizen demands, the rookie naturally reacts by blaming the public. The spontaneous reaction is reinforced by one of the central values of the police culture: the public as enemy.[7]

This is not different from the way many doctors view their patients, particularly patients with a penchant for malpractice suits. Nor is it different from the view many professors have of their students as unreasonable and thick-headed, particularly those who argue about grades. Like police officers, doctors and professors wield power that affects other people's lives, and that power is always subject to counterattack. Once again, Van Maanen captures the experience of the rookie:

> [My FTO] was always telling me to be forceful, to not back down and
> to never try to explain the law or what we are doing to a civilian. I real-
> ly didn't know what he was talking about until I tried to tell some kid
> why we have laws about speeding. Well, the more I tried to tell him
> about traffic safety, the angrier he got. I was lucky just to get his John
> Hancock on the citation. When I came back to the patrol car, [the
> FTO] explains to me just where I'd gone wrong. You really can't talk
> to those people out there; they just won't listen to reason.[8]

It is the public that transforms the rookie's self-conception, teaching him or her the pains of exercising power. The FTO then helps to interpret the encounters with the public in the light of the values of the police culture, perhaps leading the rookie even further away from the values of family or friends about how police should act.

The FTO often gives "tests" as he or she teaches. In many departments, the tests are as minor as seeing if the rookie will wait patiently outside while the FTO visits a friend. In other departments, the test may include getting the rookie involved in drinking or having sex on duty, a seriously brutal slugfest against an arrestee, or taking bribes for nonenforcement. The seriousness of the violations may vary, but the central purpose of the test does not: seeing if the rookie can keep his or her mouth shut and not report the violations to the supervisors. A rookie who is found to be untrustworthy can be, literally, hounded and harassed from the department.

Finally, in the encounter stage, the rookie gets the major reality shock in the entire process of becoming a police officer. The rookie discovers that police work is more social work than crime fighting, more arbitration of minor disputes than investigations of major crimes, more patching of holes in the social fabric than weaving of webs to catch the big-time crooks. The rookie's usual response is to define most of the assignments received as "garbage calls," not *real* police work. Not quite sure whom to blame for the fact that he or she was hired to do police work but was assigned everything else, the rookie blames the police executive, the mayor and city council, and even previous U.S. presidents (for raising public expectations). But most of all the rookie blames the public, especially the poor, for being so stupid as to have all these problems, or so smart as to take advantage of welfare and other social programs.

Metamorphosis

The result of those encounters is usually a complete change, a total adaptation of the new role and self-conception as a "cop." And with that transformation comes a stark awareness of the interdependence cops share with all other cops. For all the independence police have in making decisions about how to deal with citizens, they are totally and utterly dependent on other police to save their lives, to respond to a call of an officer in trouble or in need of assistance, and to lie on their behalf to supervisors to cover up minor infractions of the many rules the department has. This total change in perspective usually means that police accept several new assumptions about the nature of the world:

- loyalty to colleagues is essential for survival

- the public, or most of it, is the enemy

- police administrators are also the enemy.

- any discrepancy between these views and the views of family and friends is due simply to the ignorance of those who have not actually done police work themselves.

These are their new assumptions about the *facts* of life in police work, the realities which limit their options for many things, including the kinds of moral principles they can afford to have and still "survive," to keep the job, pay the mortgage, raise the kids, and vest the pension. This conception of the facts opens new police officers to learning and accepting what may be a new set of values and ethical principles. By the time the metamorphosis has been accomplished, in fact, most of these new values have been learned.

CONTENT OF POLICE VALUES TEACHING

Through the war stories of the academy instructor, the actions and stories of the FTO, the bull sessions with other rookies and veterans, and the new officer's encounters with the public, a fairly consistent set of values emerges. Whether the officer accepts these values is another question. Most students of police work seem to agree that these are the values (or some of them) that are taught:

1. Discretion A: *Decisions about whether to enforce the law, in any but the most serious cases, should be guided by both what the law says and who the suspect is.* Attitude, demeanor, cooperativeness, and even race, age, and social class are all important considerations in deciding how to treat people generally, and whether or not to arrest suspects in particular.

2. Discretion B: *Disrespect for police authority is a serious offense that should always be punished with an arrest or the use of force.* The "offense" known as "contempt of cop" or P.O.P.O. (pissing off a police officer) cannot be ignored. Even when the party has committed no violation of the law, a police officer should find a safe way to impose punishment, including an arrest on fake charges.

3. Force: *Police officers should never hesitate to use physical or deadly force against people who "deserve it," or where it can be an effective*

way of solving a crime. Only the potential punishments by superior officers, civil litigation, citizen complaints, and so forth should limit the use of force when the situation calls for it. When you can get away with it, use all the force that society should use on people like that—force and punishment which bleeding-heart judges are too soft to impose.

4. Due Process: *Due process is only a means of protecting criminals at the expense of the law-abiding and should be ignored whenever it is safe to do so.* Illegal searches and wiretaps, interrogation without advising suspects of their Miranda rights, and if need be (as in the much-admired movie, *Dirty Harry*), even physical pain to coerce a confession are all acceptable methods for accomplishing the goal the public wants the police to accomplish: fighting crime. The rules against doing those things merely handcuff the police, making it more difficult for them to do their job.

5. Truth: *Lying and deception are an essential part of the police job, and even perjury should be used if it is necessary to protect yourself or get a conviction on a "bad guy."* Violations of due process cannot be admitted to prosecutors or in court, so perjury (in the serious five percent of cases that ever go to trial) is necessary and therefore proper. Lying to drug pushers about wanting to buy drugs, to prostitutes about wanting to buy sex, or to congressmen about wanting to buy influence is the only way, and therefore a proper way, to investigate these crimes without victims. Deceiving muggers into thinking you are an easy mark and deceiving burglars into thinking you are a fence are proper because there are not many other ways of catching predatory criminals in the act.

6. Time: *You cannot go fast enough to chase a car thief or traffic violator nor slow enough to get to a "garbage" call; and when there are no calls for service, your time is your own.* Hot pursuits are necessary because anyone who tries to escape from the police is challenging police authority, no matter how trivial the initial offense. But calls to nonserious or social-work problems, like domestic disputes or kids making noise, are unimportant, so you can stop to get coffee on the way or even stop at the cleaner's if you like. And when there are no calls, you can sleep, visit friends, study, or do anything else you can get away with, especially on the midnight shift, when you can get away with a lot.

7. Rewards: *Police do very dangerous work for low wages, so it is proper to take any extra rewards the public wants to give them, like free meals, Christmas gifts, or even regular monthly payments (in some*

cities) for special treatment. The general rule is: take any reward that doesn't change what you would do anyway, such as eating a meal, but don't take money that would affect your job, like not giving traffic tickets. In many cities, however, especially in the recent past, the rule has been to take even those awards that do affect your decisions, as long as they are related only to minor offenses—traffic, gambling, prostitution, but not murder.

8. Loyalty: *The paramount duty is to protect your fellow officers at all costs, as they would protect you, even though you may have to risk your own career or your own life to do it.* If your colleagues make a mistake, take a bribe, seriously hurt somebody illegally, or get into other kinds of trouble, you should do everything you can to protect them in the ensuing investigation. If your colleagues are routinely breaking the rules, you should never tell supervisors, reporters, or outside investigators about it. If you don't like it, quit—or get transferred to the police academy. But never, ever, blow the whistle.

THE RISING VALUE CONFLICTS

None of these values is as strongly or widely held as in the past. Several factors may account for the breakdown in traditional police values that has paralleled the breakdown of traditional values in the wider society. One is the increasing diversity of the kinds of people who join police departments: more women, minorities, and college graduates. Another is the rising power of the police unions which defend individual officers who get into trouble—sometimes even those who challenge the traditional values. A third factor is the rise of investigative journalism and the romantic aura given to "bucking the system" by such movies as *Serpico.* Watergate and other recent exposés of corruption in high places—especially the attitude of being "above the law"—have probably made all public officials more conscious of the ethics of their behavior. Last but not least, police administrators have increasingly taken a very stern disciplinary posture towards some of these traditional police values and gone to extraordinary lengths to counteract them.

Consider the paramount value of loyalty. Police reformer August Vollmer described it in 1931 as the "blue curtain of secrecy" that descends whenever a police officer does something wrong, making it impossible to investigate misconduct. Yet in the past decade, police officers in Cincinnati, Indianapolis, New York, and elsewhere have given reporters and grand juries evidence about widespread police misconduct. In New York, police officers have even given evidence against their colleagues for homicide, leading to the first conviction there (that anyone can recall) of a police officer for murder in the line of duty. The code of silence may be far from breaking down, but it certainly has a few cracks in it.

The ethics of rewards have certainly changed in many departments over the past decade. In the wake of corruption scandals, some police executives have taken advantage of the breakdown in loyalty to assign spies, or "field associates," to corruption-prone units to detect bribe-taking. These officers are often recruited for this work at the police academy, where they are identified only to one or two contacts and are generally treated like any other police officer. These spies are universally hated by other officers, but they are very hard to identify. The result of this approach, along with other anti-corruption strategies, has been an apparent decline in organized corruption.[9]

The ethics of force are also changing. In the wake of well-publicized federal prosecutions of police beatings, community outrage over police shootings, and an explosion in civil litigation that has threatened to bankrupt some cities, the behavior and possibly the attitude of the police in their use of force have generally become more restrained. In Los Angeles, Kansas City, Atlanta, New York, Chicago, and elsewhere, the number of killings of citizens by police has declined sharply.[10] Some officers now claim that they risk their lives by hesitating to use force out of fear of being punished for using it. Even if excessive use of force has not been entirely eliminated, the days of unrestrained shooting or use of the "third degree" are clearly gone in many cities.

The increasing external pressures to conform to legal and societal values, rather than to traditional police values, have generated increasing conflict among police officers themselves. The divide-and-conquer effect may be seen in police officers' unwillingness to bear the risks of covering up for their colleagues now that risks are much greater than they have been. Racial conflicts among police officers often center on these values. At that national level, for example, the National Organization of Black Law Enforcement Executives (NOBLE) has been battling with the International Association of Chiefs of Police (IACP) since at least 1979 over the question of how restrictive police department firearms policies should be.

These conflicts should not be over-emphasized, however. The learning of police ethics still takes place in the context of very strong communication of traditional police values. The rising conflicts are still only a minor force. But they are at least one more contingency affecting the moral choices police officers face as they progress through their careers, deciding which values to adopt and which ethical standards to live by.

THE POLICE OFFICER'S MORAL CAREER

There are four major aspects of moral careers in general that are directly relevant to police officers.[11] One is the *contingencies* the officer confronts. Another is the *moral experiences* undergone in confronting these contingencies. A third is the *apologia,* the explanation officers develop for changing the ethical principles they live by. The fourth and most visible aspect of the moral careers of police officers is the *stages* of moral change they go through.

Contingencies

The contingencies shaping police moral careers include all the social pressures officers face to behave one way rather than another. Police departments vary, for example, in the frequency and seriousness of the rule-breaking that goes on. They also vary in the openness of such rule-breaking, and in the degree of teaching of the *skills* of such rule-breaking. It is no small art, for example, to coax a bribe offer out of a traffic violator without directly asking for it. Even in a department in which such bribes are regularly accepted, a new officer may be unlikely to adopt the practice if an older officer does not teach him or her how. In a department in which older officers explicitly teach the techniques, the same officer might be more likely to adopt the practice. The difference in the officer's career is thus shaped by the difference in the contingencies he or she confronts.

The list of all possible contingencies is obviously endless, but these are some of the more commonly reported ones:

- the values the FTO teaches
- the values the first sergeant teaches
- the kind of citizens confronted in the first patrol assignment
- the level of danger on patrol
- whether officers work in a one-officer or two-officer car (after the training period)
- whether officers are assigned to undercover or vice work
- whether there are conflicts among police officers over ethical issues in the department
- the ethical "messages" sent out by the police executive
- the power of the police union to protect officers from being punished
- the general climate of civic integrity (or lack of it)
- the level of public pressure to control police behavior

Contingencies alone, of course, do not shape our behavior. If we were entirely the products of our environment, with no freedom of moral choice, there would be little point in writing (or reading) books on ethics. What contingencies like these do is push us in one direction or another, much like the waves in the ocean. Whether we choose to swim against the tide or flow with the waves is up to us.

Moral Experiences

The moral experience is a major turning point in a moral career. It can be an agonizing decision about which principles to follow or it can be a shock of recognition as you finally understand the moral principles implicit in how other people are behaving. Like the person asleep on a raft drifting out to sea, the police officer who has a moral experience suddenly discovers where he or she is and what the choices are.

Some officers have had moral experiences when they found out the system they worked for was corrupt: when the judge dismissed the charges against the son of a powerful business executive, or when a sergeant ordered the officer not to make arrests at an illegal after-hours bar. One leading police executive apparently went through a moral experience when he was first assigned to the vice squad and saw all the money that his colleagues were taking from gamblers. Shocked and disgusted, he sought and obtained a transfer to a less corrupt unit within a few weeks.

Other officers have had moral experiences in reaction to particular incidents. One Houston police rookie was out of the academy for only several weeks when he witnessed a group of his senior colleagues beat up a Mexican-American, Joe Campos Torres, after he resisted arrest in a bar. Torres drowned after jumping or being pushed from a great height into a bayou, and no one knew how he had died when his body was found floating nearby. The officer discussed the incident with his father, also a Houston police officer, and the father marched the young man right into the Internal Affairs Division to give a statement. His testimony became the basis of a federal prosecution of the other officers.

Other officers may have a moral experience when they see their ethics presented in public, outside of the police culture. New York City police captain Max Schmittberger, for example, who had been a bagman collecting graft for his superiors in New York's Tenderloin district, was greatly moved by the testimony of prostitutes he heard at the hearings of the Lexow Committee investigating police corruption in 1893. He told muckraking reporter Lincoln Steffens that the parade of witnesses opened his eyes to the reality of the corruption, so he decided to get on the witness stand himself to reveal even more details of the corruption.

No matter what contingencies occur to prompt a moral experience, the police officer faces relatively few choices about how to react. One option is to drift with the tide, letting things go on as they have been. Another option is to seek an escape route, such as a transfer, that removes the moral dilemma that may prompt the moral experience. A third option is to leave police work altogether, although the financial resources of police officers are not usually great enough to allow the luxury of resigning on principle. The fourth and most difficult option is to fight back somehow, either by blowing the whistle to the public or initiating a behind-the-scenes counterattack.

Not all moral experiences are prompted by criminal acts or even by violations of rules and regulations. Racist jokes or language, ethnic favoritism by commanders, or other issues can also prompt moral experiences. With some officers, though, nothing may ever prompt a moral experience; they may drift out to sea, or back to shore, sound asleep and unaware of what is happening to them.

Apologia

For those officers with enough moral consciousness to suffer a moral experience, a failure to "do the right thing" could be quite painful to live with. "Even a bent policeman has a conscience," as a British police official who resigned on principle (inadequate police corruption investigations in London) once observed.[12] In order to resolve the conflict between what they think they should have done and what they actually did, officers often invent or adopt an acceptable explanation for their conduct. The explanation negates the principle they may have wished they actually had followed, or somehow makes their behavior consistent with that principle.

Perhaps the most famous apologia is the concept of "clean graft": bribes paid to avoid enforcement of laws against crimes that don't hurt people. Gambling and prostitution bribes were traditionally labeled as "clean graft," while bribes from narcotics pushers were labeled "dirty graft." (As narcotics traffic grew more lucrative, however, narcotics bribes were more often labeled "clean.")

The apologia for beating a handicapped prisoner in a moment of anger may draw on the police value system of maintaining respect for authority and meting out punishment because the courts will not. The apologia for stopping black suspects more often than white suspects may be the assumption that blacks are more likely to be guilty. No matter what a police officer does, he or she is apt to find *situationally justified* reasons for doing it. The reasons are things only the officer can understand, because only the officer knows the full story, all the facts of the *situation*. The claim of situational expertise, of course, conveniently avoids any attempt to apply a general moral principle to conduct. The avoidance is just as effective in the officer's own mind as it would be if the apologia were discussed with the officer's spouse, clergyman, or parents.

Perhaps the most important effect of the apologia is that it allows the officer to live with a certain moral standard of behavior, to become comfortable with it. This creates the potential for further apologias about further changes in moral standards. The process can clearly become habit-forming, and it does. The progression from one apologia to the next makes up the stages of moral change.

Stages

The stages of moral change are points on a moral continuum, the different levels of moral improvement or of the "slippery slope" of moral degeneration. Such descriptions sound trite and old-fashioned, but they are commonly used by officers who get into serious trouble—such as being convicted for burglary—to account for their behavior.

The officers caught in the Denver police burglary ring in 1961, for example, appear to have progressed through many stages in their moral careers before forming an organized burglary ring:

1. First they suffered moral experiences that showed them that the laws were not impartially enforced and that judges were corrupt.

2. Then they learned that other police officers were dishonest, including those who engaged in "shopping," i.e., stealing goods at the scene of a nighttime commercial burglary, with the goods stolen by the police thus indistinguishable from the goods stolen by others.

3. They joined in the shopping themselves and constructed an apologia for it ("the insurance pays for it all anyway").

4. The apologia provided a rationale for a planned burglary in which they were burglars ("the insurance pays for it anyway").

5. The final stage was to commit planned burglaries on a regular basis.

These stages are logically available to all police officers. Many, perhaps most, officers progress to Stage 3 and go no further, just as most professors steal paper clips and photocopying from their universities, but not books or furniture. Why some people move into the further stages and others do not is a problem for sociology of deviance, not ethics. The fact is that some officers do move into the more serious stages of unethical conduct after most officers have established the custom in the less serious, but still unethical, stages.

Each aspect of police ethics, from force to time to due process, has different sets of stages. Taken together, the officer's movement across all the stages on all the ethical issues makes up his or her moral career in police work. The process is not just one way; officers can move back closer to legal principles as well as away from them. But the process is probably quite connected across different issues. Your moral stage on stealing may parallel your moral stage on force.

Learning Ethics Differently

This article has treated morality as if it were black and white, i.e., as if it consisted of clear-cut principles to be obeyed or disobeyed. Many issues in police ethics are in fact clear-cut, and hold little room for serious philosophical analysis. One would have a hard time making a rational defense of police officers stealing, for example.

But what may be wrong with the way police ethics is now taught and learned is just that assumption: that all police ethical issues are as clear-cut as stealing. They are not. The issues of force, time, discretion, loyalty, and others are all very complex, with many shades of gray. To deny this complexity, as the formal approaches of police academies and police rule books often do, may simply encourage unethical behavior. A list of "dos" and "don'ts" that officers must follow because they are ordered to is a virtual challenge to their ingenuity: catch me if you can. And in the face of a police culture that has already established values quite contrary to many of the official rules, the black-and-white approach to ethics may be naive.

As indicated above, an alternative approach may be preferred. This would consider both clear-cut and complex ethical issues in the same fashion: examining police problems in the light of basic moral principles and from the moral point of view. While there may be weaknesses in this alternative approach, it may well be the sounder road to ethical sensitivity in the context of individual responsibility.

NOTES

1. See John Van Maanen, "On Becoming a Policeman," in *Policing: A View from the Street*, eds. Peter Manning and John Van Maanen (Santa Monica, CA: Goodyear, 1978).

2. See John McNamara, "Uncertainties in Police Work: The Relevance of Recruits' Backgrounds and Training," in *The Police: Six Sociological Studies*, ed. David J. Bordua (New York: Wiley, 1967).

3. Van Maanen, "On Becoming a Policeman," p. 298.

4. Ibid., p. 301.

5. See William Westley, *Violence and the Police* (Cambridge, MA: M.I.T. Press, 1970), pp. 159-60.

6. See William Ker Muir, Jr., *Police: Streetcorner Politicians* (Chicago: University of Chicago Press, 1977).

7. See Westley, *Violence*, pp. 48-108.

8. Van Maanen, "On Becoming a Policeman," p. 302.

9. See Lawrence Sherman, "Reducing Police Gun Use" (Paper presented at the International Conference on the Management and Control of Police Organizations, Breukelen, the Netherlands, 1980).

10. Ibid.

11. Cf. Erving Goffman, "The Moral Career of the Mental Patient," in *Asylum: Essays on the Social Situation of Mental Patients and Other Inmates* (Garden City, NY: Anchor Books, 1961), pp. 127-69.

12. See Sherman, "Reducing Police Gun Use."

DISCUSSION QUESTIONS

1. Why is it difficult for police officers to make moral judgments that are not in line with those of their peers? Do you think you would "buck the system"? Why or why not?

2. Why do you feel there are value conflicts between citizens and police? If you were a police chief, how would you resolve the conflicts between citizens and your department?

3. What type of instruction would be of the greatest value to new recruits in the police academy regarding professional ethics?

4. Can you demonstrate professional ethics without having personal ethics? Why or why not?

CASE STUDY

Chapter 4:
Learning
Police Ethics

LIBERTY AND JUSTICE
FOR ALL

You are a police officer in a large metropolitan city. For the past eight months you worked in a middle- and upper-class suburban patrol zone. Most of the people with whom you came in contact were respectable members of the community. You had good rapport with most of the community and they were generally quite cooperative with the police. Now you are being transferred to another patrol zone which is in a lower-class area near the inner city.

The first week you are in the new zone, you are assigned to work with Mike, a veteran officer who has been working this zone for almost four years. Mike drives you around, pointing out informants, drunks, thieves, and places where they hang out. You immediately notice that Mike has a somewhat harsh, even punitive attitude regarding the people with whom he comes in contact on his beat.

"You have to treat these people tough, intimidation is the only way to communicate with them," Mike explains.

After one week in your new zone, you become aware of a great difference in police work with different types of people. You rarely made arrests in your old zone. Most problems there could be worked out by talking rationally with the people with whom you came in contact. In this zone, however, you have made more arrests and have had to use more force with people. It becomes apparent to you that there are even more drunks and criminals living in the new zone than you had ever expected. People living in the slums seem to be more apathetic as well.

Mike has told you that if you need information on criminal activity, just pick somebody up and threaten to arrest them if they do not tell you what you need

From Larry S. Miller and Michael Braswell, *Human Relations and Police Work*, 4th ed. (Prospect Heights, IL: Waveland Press), 1997. Reprinted with permission.

to know. This method worked, as your new partner seemed to demonstrate frequently. Mike would "plant" drugs or a gun on somebody, then threaten to arrest them if they did not give him information or become an informant for him. Mike has occasionally beat confessions out of suspects, then threatened to "get them" if they did not plead guilty to offenses.

You become aware of more violent crimes in you new zone. There are more murders, assaults, and rapes here than would happen in the middle- and upper-class neighborhoods. Mike defines rape "victims" as those persons who did not get paid for their services. "Not even worth writing a report on," Mike tells you. Murder investigations are routinely handled by the investigators in this zone. The detectives seldom perform a comprehensive investigation on any offense here. In the middle- and upper-class zone, all offenses were investigated thoroughly and the victims were given excellent attention by investigating officers.

You find that more police officers are assaulted in the lower-class zone than in your old zone. The people living in the lower-class zone do not appear to respect the police. It seems they only respect force.

"Don't ever turn your back on these people. And if you have to put one of these thugs down, be sure there ain't no damned video camera around," Mike advises you. Mike also advises you to have your gun ready at all times.

"Shotgun's the best, they're really scared of 'em," says Mike. You also notice that more officers in this zone use deadly force than officers in other zones of the city. The police shot five people here last year.

"And probably a few more they didn't count," Mike chuckles.

After working in the new zone for two months and seeing what kind of people live in this area, you find yourself agreeing more and more with Mike's attitudes and methods. You and Mike receive a radio call to back up another unit a couple of blocks away. As you pull up beside the other cruiser, you see two police officers beating up a young man in the alley.

"C'mon Mike, you want a piece of this?" shouts one of the officers. Mike takes out his slapjack and moves in with the other two officers beating the youth.

"What did he do?" you ask.

"He made the mistake of calling us names," responds one of the officers. "We're going to let this one be an example."

The young man could not be over seventeen years old and appears to be badly hurt. You know the officers will leave him in the alley when they are finished beating him. Of course, there will be no arrest.

You begin to think about how you have changed. Mike always says, "Fight fire with fire." Right now you are wondering who the criminals are. What should you do?

Questions:

1. Explain the metamorphosis of the officer taken out of his middle-class environment. Why would there be increased conflict between citizens and police in the lower-class neighborhood? Could this increased conflict explain the behavior of the other veteran officers in this precinct?

2. From a deontological perspective, what must this new officer do to preserve his moral integrity?

3. How might an *apologia* be used to defend the actions of the veteran officers? Would utilitarianism allow for the battering of a minor in this case?

CHAPTER 5

Do Cops Really Need a Code of Ethics?

Michael Davis

My title may seem rhetorical. "Of course the cops need a code of ethics," it will be said. "You have only to look at today's newspaper to see that." Okay, let's look.

Today is March 12, 1991. My newspaper is the *Wall Street Journal*. The headline on the left side of its front page reads: "LA Law: A Video-taped Beating Highlights Problems of Los Angeles Police—Years of Brutality Alleged; Critics Cite Department's Authoritarian Approach—High Tech, Low Manpower." The story, building for a week in other papers, has finally reached the *Journal*:

KEY CONCEPTS:

code of ethics

ethics

moral ideals

moral principles

moral rules

morality

> On March 3, after a high speed chase, Los Angeles police stopped Rodney King, a 25-year-old unemployed construction worker. What happened then is uncertain. What an unseen citizen's video camera began recording a few minutes later is not: King lay on the ground, bound and motionless. Around him stood fifteen uniformed men. Most, including the sergeant in command, just looked on. But three kicked King again and again or struck him with nightsticks, their movements not wild, like sharks in a frenzy, but precise and deliberate. They seemed to be taking turns.[1]

That beating was not unique in the history of policing. It probably has kin in every state in the Union, in every country, and indeed in every significant police force as far back as we can trace the police function. Though some police

Michael Davis, "Do Cops Really Need a Code of Ethics?" (as appeared in *Criminal Justice Ethics*, Volume 10, Number 2 [Summer/Fall 1991] pp. 14-28). Reprinted by permission of the Institute for Criminal Justice Ethics, 899 Tenth Avenue, New York, NY 10019-1029.

departments are doubtless much less brutal than others, we in fact know little about such differences. About all that seems clear is that better education, better training, better pay, better equipment, and other technical improvements do not seem to have had much effect. The Los Angeles Police Department remains a leader in that kind of "professionalization."[2]

We have looked at today's newspaper. The conclusion may now seem obvious. Since using unnecessary force is morally wrong, police who engage in the use of such force definitely need better ethics. The first step to better ethics is a code of ethics that spells out right and wrong. So, whatever else the police need, they need a code of ethics.

That's the argument I want to examine. I shall try to show that it relies on several mistakes about what codes of ethics are and how they work, mistakes that can distort the whole process by which police (or, rather, those who manage police) write a code of ethics, justify its provisions, and seek to enforce them. Los Angeles police did not need a code of ethics to know that beating Rodney King was both illegal and immoral.[3] If they need a code of ethics at all, it is as part of a larger project, organizing police work as a profession (in a sense to be explained). Police may have legitimate reasons not to want to organize in that way.

My purpose here is not to argue that police should or should not organize as a profession but to clarify what that would mean, especially the place of a code of ethics in that difficult undertaking.

MORALITY AND ETHICS

The terms "morality" and "ethics" have been used in so many different ways lately that I must, I think, begin by explaining what I mean by them.

Morality, as used here, may be divided into three standards of conduct: rules, principles, and ideals. All guide the choice of action and provide a basis for justifying or evaluating what we do (just as nonmoral rules, principles, and ideals do). They differ from one another only in how they do that. Other aspects of morality may be defined in terms of these standards. For example, a certain moral virtue—say, justice—would be a settled disposition to deliberate in accordance with the principles of justice; good character, a complex or moral (and certain nonmoral) virtues; and so on.[4]

Moral rules are those standards of conduct each of us (rational persons) wants every other to follow even if everyone else's following them means we must do the same. Moral rules are requirements (or prohibitions) one is supposed to obey all the time (unless the conduct in question is justified under an exception). Among moral rules relevant to police work are: "Don't kill," "Don't deprive of liberty," "Don't cause pain," "Don't steal," and "Keep your promises." Moral rules can also be stated with "shall;" for example, "You shall not kill."

Moral rules have exceptions. The exceptions resemble the rules in at least two ways. First, exceptions are as rule-like as the rules themselves. For example, among the exceptions to "Don't kill" are "except in self-defense" and "except in defense of an innocent person." Second, exceptions are justified in much the way that rules are. A would-be exception is actually an exception only if everyone is willing to allow everyone else the same freedom from the rule as he wants for himself. Exceptions provide terms of justification for what would otherwise be the morally unjustified (a simple violation of a moral rule). So, for example, self-defense is an exception (in part at least) because each of us wants to be able to repel unjustified attacks even if our being able to do that means being repelled in turn should we unjustifiably attack another. Having "Don't kill" with the exception, we are safer than we would be without it. We can control whom we unjustifiably attack but not who unjustifiably attacks us.

If you don't do as a moral rule requires, and have no justification, your conduct is morally wrong; and if you don't have even a good excuse for what you did, you deserve blame and perhaps punishment.

Moral principles differ from moral rules in much the way that Ronald Dworkin has suggested legal principles differ from legal rules.[5] While rules require (or forbid) acts, principles do not. Principles merely state considerations that should have a certain weight in choice of action (what is good to do or bad to omit doing). While moral rules can be rewritten using "shall" without significant change of meaning, moral principles cannot. They naturally take "should" rather than "shall." The difference between rule and principle is, then, not like that between duties that are enforceable and those that are not, or like that between obligations that must be kept no matter what and those that can be overridden, or like that between responsibilities leaving me some discretion, or like that between standards concerned with action and those concerned with quality of life. The difference between rule and principle is where in deliberation the two standards fit.

Consider the moral principle, "Help the needy." Though grammatically similar to "Keep your promises," "Help the needy" requires no act. Though I am now at my desk writing, rather than helping the needy, I am not doing anything wrong (as I would be if I were sitting here when I had a promise to keep). Though I should always help the needy if I can, and I can help them even now (for example, by writing a check), my conduct satisfies the principle "Help the needy" if their needs weigh in my deliberations enough to outweigh otherwise decisive considerations (and I am acting accordingly).

Normally, giving due weight to the needs of the needy will mean that I help the needy now and then. Moral principles are morally important because, in morally decent people, they create tendencies to act which, being realized in action often enough, maintain (more or less) a state of affairs that all rational persons want. We prefer moral principles to moral rules when we do not want the relatively determinate conduct a rule imposes or cannot agree on what the rule should be. Moral principles allow us more flexibility in choice of acts than rules do but at the risk of making actions less predictable than when they are subject to rule. Moral principles work best for conduct where predictability is less important—for example, when what is involved is doing good, or the harm to be prevented is relatively minor.

Since moral principles do not (directly) require conduct, conduct cannot (as such) violate a principle; and since no conduct can violate a principle, we cannot blame people for conduct because it violates a principle. We can, however, still blame people for not giving a principle due weight in deliberations. For example, if someone's acts, words, or some combination of these show a tendency to discount the principle "Help the needy," we can say that she is stingy or uncharitable (that is, that she lacks the disposition to give due weight to the needs of the needy). To say that is to blame her for how she decides to act rather than for what she in fact did. The way she decided is crucial.

While moral principles provide grounds for moral blame, they do not do the same for moral praise. In this, they resemble moral rules. Like rules, principles help to define minimal decency. A minimally decent (or upright) person merely obeys the moral rules and gives moral principles the weight due them. Her conduct is merely satisfactory. To say of someone, for example, that she is "merely upright" is to "damn with faint praise." We expect more of people than that. Though we do not require more, we withhold praise until we get it. We do not, for example, describe a merely decent person as "virtuous," "just," or even "good."

That brings me to moral ideals. These take us beyond mere decency. They are ways of acting that everyone wants everyone else to support, including ourselves (so long as such support is consistent with obeying moral rules and giving due weight to moral principles). We support conduct by encouraging it with compliments or donations, by removing obstacles such as taxes or zoning laws, or by excusing from otherwise deserved punishment. Ideals are easy to recognize. Consider the golden rule.[6]

While we are willing to have others praise, reward, and otherwise encourage people to treat each other as they themselves would like to be treated (and, indeed, to give such moral support ourselves), we are not willing to require people to do what the golden rule says. We do not want that much regimentation. The golden rule cannot be rewritten with "shall" without changing its meaning. It is not a moral rule (in our sense).

For similar reasons, the golden rule cannot be a moral principle. The corresponding moral principle would require us, in all deliberations, to give the interests of others at least as much weight as our own. Few of us are willing to be so benevolent (except in such special circumstances as administering a public charity). Though the golden rule can be written with "should," the "should" has a different sense than it has in a moral principle. The golden rule is an ideal.

Ideals are to principles much as principles are to rules. Because they demand more, we allow more freedom in the way people respond to them. I can fall far short of an ideal without necessarily deserving blame. Indeed, I can fall far short and still deserve praise—if I come closer than people like me normally do. One can be praised even when being far from perfect.[7]

I do not think these distinctions necessarily reflect actual usage (except in cases of especially careful speakers). Instead, I offer them as a useful way to discipline ordinary language. So, for example, though we often speak of people as being "ethical" or "highly ethical" when we wish to praise them for coming closer to a moral ideal than people normally do, I believe we would be better off if, whenever possible, we described such conduct as "morally good," saving "ethical" for morally good conduct of a special sort.

Ethics, as I shall use the term, refer to moral standards applying to all members of a group simply because they are members of that group. "Standard" here refers to a rule, principle, or ideal. Ethics differs from group to group. Legal ethics applies to lawyers, not to police or politicians; Hopi ethics, to Hopis; Catholic ethics, to Catholics. Different groups can, of course, have equivalent standards, standards beyond those of ordinary morality, but they still will not have the same ethics. For example, suppose both Catholics and Hopis have a rule forbidding divorce. A divorced Catholic can remarry in violation of the Catholic rule, but she would not be in violation of the Hopi rule (unless she is also a Hopi). She must be a Hopi to come under the Hopi rule. A group is defined by a single practice in which all (and only) its members participate.

Ethics resembles law in applying to persons only insofar as they belong to a group (rather than insofar as they are rational persons as such). Ethics also resembles law in not being entirely deducible from ordinary morality (even in combination with situational factors). Like law, ethics is made, not merely found, and therefore capable of being made in more than one way. Morality constrains what can be ethics without totally determining it.

Ethics differs from law in being (by definition) part of morality (though distinct from ordinary morality). Ethics differs from ordinary morality only in adding rules, principles, or ideals—for example, by turning a moral ideal into an ethical principle or rule. Ethics is "morality plus. . . ." How ethics can be both part of morality and yet more than ordinary morality I shall explain later.

Because ethical standards are, by definition, moral standards (in at least the minimum sense of being morally permissible), "Nazi ethics," "criminal ethics," and the like can be ethics only in the degenerate sense in which counterfeit money is still money. Ethics has no more to do with ethic or ethos than morality does with morale or mores.

This use of "ethics" differs from two other common uses. "Ethics" is often a mere synonym for "morality." "Ethics," as used here, is not. Instead, it names a special domain of morality, one with its own rules, principles, or ideals (in addition to and consistent with those of ordinary morality).

"Ethics," as used here, also differs from what philosophers generally mean by that term. It does not name the study of morality, the theory of the good, the attempt to describe an ideal or rationally defensible morality, or even the successful outcome of such an attempt. Like "morality," "ethics" here names a practice that is not merely intellectual.

Given how this use of "ethics" differs from others, I should perhaps give my reasons for adopting it. There are two. First, I believe my use generally corresponds to what professionals mean when they talk about their profession's ethics. Second, I believe that thinking about ethics my way is more helpful in discussions of professional ethics than thinking about ethics in other ways. While I shall not explicitly defend either claim here, making sense of police ethics will provide evidence for both. In any case, I have already defended both claims elsewhere.[8]

CODES OF ETHICS AND THE POLICE

A code of ethics is a formal statement of a group's ethics, whether a description of a preexisting practice (like a dictionary's definition) or a formula creating the practice (like a definition in a contract). We may distinguish three distinct kinds of code: statements of ideal ("credos" or "aspirations"); statements of principle ("guidelines" or "ethical considerations"); and statements of requirement ("codes of conduct," "mandatory rules," or simply "duties"). While I would prefer to reserve "codes of ethics" for the last of these, I cannot do that here without risking confusion. Not only has "code of ethics" been used indiscriminately for codes of each kind, it has also been used for codes placing statements of one kind next to statements of another, without any suggestion that, for example, some are requirements while others are mere ideals. Codes of police ethics are at least as likely to do this as those of other professions. The consequences are not good.

Consider, for example, the code the International Association of Chiefs of Police (IACP) adopted in 1987 to govern its members' conduct.[9] Section 2 begins: "IACP members shall be dedicated to the highest ideals of honor and integrity to maintain the respect and confidence of their governmental officials, subordinates, the public and their fellow police executives." The initial "shall" suggests a requirement, but what is required is dedication to an ideal. To dedicate oneself is to set oneself apart for a sacred undertaking, to give oneself up wholly (for a time at least) to some purpose. How can police chiefs give themselves up wholly to pursuing honor and integrity? Such dedication is not a minimum below which no chief can fall without deserving blame or punishment. "Shall" seems out of place.

The rest of Section 2 confirms the impression that "shall" is out of place. The two subsections use "should," not "shall." For example, the first reads: "Members should conduct themselves so as to maintain public confidence in their profession, their department, and in their performance of the public trust." The "should" here seems to state a principle rather than an ideal. A police chief who did not give great weight to maintaining public confidence would deserve blame. He would not simply have fallen well short of an ideal. So, Section 2 seems to mix ideal and principle in a way likely to confuse.

If Section 2 suggests a code of principles or ideals, other sections of the code suggest something more rigorous. For example, Subsection 3a reads: "At all times, members shall completely and accurately represent their credentials, including prior employment, education, certification and personal history." Always representing one's credentials "completely and accurately" seems a manageable requirement (so long as the standard of completeness and accuracy is not too high). The subsection's content is consistent with its being read as a rule (though it does not require that reading). The use of "should" rather than "shall" in the next subsection provides more support for that reading. Subsection 3b begins, "Members seeking a police executive position should demonstrate professional respect for incumbents and those seeking the same position." Why "should" rather than "shall"? Since this standard does not seem intrinsically harder to satisfy than completeness and accuracy in representing credentials, the only explanation for the switch from "shall" to "should" (apart from careless drafting or elegant variation) seems to be that this subsection, unlike the one before, states a guideline, not a requirement.

This IACP code is, of course, not a "real police code." The IACP's members are police executives; their concerns are not primarily those of the officer on patrol. I have nonetheless started with this IACP code because it seems better thought through than the "real police" equivalent, the IACP's "Law Enforcement Code of Ethics" (1957).[10] The "Law Enforcement Code of Ethics" seems to be a statement of ideals (that is, standards few humans would want to be held to). Yet, the ideals are stated as if they were mandatory rules. Thus, the first paragraph begins: "As a Law Enforcement Officer, my fundamental duty is to serve . . . ."[11] The next two paragraphs, while dropping "duty," replace it with the equally mandatory language of oath or promise; for example, "I will keep my private life unsullied . . ." and "I will never act officiously or permit personal feelings, prejudices, animosities or friendships to influence my decisions." Any officer who takes this mandatory language seriously will quickly learn that he cannot do what the code seems to require. He will then either have to quit the force or consign its mandates to "code heaven."[12]

The United Nations' "Draft Code of Conduct for Law Enforcement Officials" is only somewhat better. The preamble indicates that the code is to serve "as a body of principles for observance by law enforcement officials of all nations." But Article 1 does not sound like a mere principle (in our sense): "Law enforcement officials must at all times fulfill the duty imposed upon them by law, by serving the community and by protecting all persons against illegal acts, consistent with the high degree of responsibility required by their profession." Both that initial "must" and subsequent "high degree of responsibility required" at least suggest that Article 1 is a rule, not a principle (in our sense). The language of Article 2 confirms that suggestion by switching to language appropriate to principles. Article 2 uses "should" rather than "must" (as do two other articles): "In the performance of their duty, law enforcement officials should respect and protect human dignity and maintain and uphold the human rights of all persons." Two other Articles use "may never" and "No law enforcement officer may" (rather than "must" or "should"). They sound like rules (that is, denials of permission). But understanding them that way makes the code's equally common use of "must" troublesome. Why not, for example, say that law enforcement officers "may not" fail in their duty rather than saying they "must" fulfill it? Is there some distinction between these constructions, or is the alternation between them merely pretty?[13]

Though the UN code (wisely) puts a "Commentary" after each article, the commentaries seldom help with such questions. For example, Article 3 says, "Law enforcement officials may never use more force than necessary in the performance of their duty." While that sounds like a flat prohibition of unnecessary force, the commentary softens the impression. Paragraph (a) informs us, "This provision emphasizes that the use of force by law enforcement officials should be exceptional." Why that "should" rather than "must"? We are not told. The next paragraph informs us that the use of more force than "reasonable under the circumstances" is "not tolerable." What is the difference between "reasonable" and "necessary"? All necessary force may be reasonable, but is all reasonable force necessary? The last paragraph—"[in] no case . . . should this provision be interpreted to authorize the use of force which is disproportionate to the legitimate objective to be achieved"—suggests that even some necessary force might be unreasonable (because disproportionate). The overall effect of this commentary is to suggest that Article 3 asks nothing more than a strong tendency to avoid the use of force. Could that have been the intention of its authors?

The confusions I have been at pains to point out are not merely academic. They affect the code's usefulness. For example, let us assume that the UN code applies to the LAPD and that Article 3 states a requirement. We can then cite the UN code to show that the three officers who beat Rodney King acted unethically (as well as illegally and immorally). If the police cannot justify their use of force under some exception, that ends the matter. Their conduct is blameworthy (whether or not they have an excuse for it, that is, whether or not they deserve the blame). If, however, Article 3 merely sates a principle, the question becomes whether the officers gave the principle due weight in the circumstances. Determining whether their conduct was unethical becomes more complicated (though, in these circumstances, not much more so). If, however, we interpreted Article 3 as a statement of ideal (as the IACP's "Law Enforcement of Ethics" seems to), we would have no basis in the code for blaming the officers. Falling short of an ideal is not, as such, blameworthy. The question becomes how well others have done in similar circumstances.

So, anyone drafting a code of ethics should decide early on what kind of code it will be: a statement of ideals, of principles, or of requirements—or a mixture. If the code is to be a mixture, great care should be taken to make clear which statements are ideals, which principles, and which rules. A code's drafters need not accept the conventions I have suggested, but they will risk serious confusion if they do not adopt something like them.[14]

Should mixed codes be avoided? The history of the American Bar Association's old "Model Code of Professional Responsibility" (1969) may suggest that the answer is yes. That code was a carefully drawn mixed code. The ideals ("Canons"), principles ("Ethical Considerations"), and requirements ("Mandatory Rules") were all clearly labeled. The Preamble explained the distinction. Yet, that mixture proved too much for the lawyers. In 1981, the ABA adopted "The Model Rules of Professional Conduct," which so far seems to be doing better. Like the UN's "Draft Code of Law Enforcement," it has the preamble, mandatory rules, and commentary characteristic of a model statute (though—after much debate—one mandatory rule is now written with "should" rather than "shall" to indicate that it cannot provide an occasion for formal discipline).

Still, I do not think we should conclude from the ABA's experience that mixed codes are necessarily too complicated to work. The National Society of

Professional Engineers (NSPE) has had a mixed code of ethics for a long time. Though the NSPE amends it from time to time and offers interpretations regularly, it seems happy with it overall.

A PRACTICAL CODE

A code of ethics sets standards for some domain of conduct. What that domain is is relevant to how the code should be written. The more important the conduct governed is to the lives of those affected, the more reason there is for the code to state requirements; the less important the conduct, the more reason for it to state considerations or ideals. Use of unnecessary force, for example, seems something police should be required to avoid. Avoiding unnecessary force should not be a mere ideal or consideration in police decisions. In contrast, avoiding dishonesty "in thought and deed" (as the IACP's 1957 code put it) seems too much to require of police. How many of us, police or not, are willing to accept as a requirement no dishonest thoughts, no white lies, and so on? Any code concerned to reduce dishonesty should therefore include honesty as principle or ideal (or demand certain sorts of honesty by rules much more narrowly drawn).

In general, a code of rules will be substantially longer than a code of principles or ideals. In part, that is because rules should be stated with their exceptions. But, in part too, codes of rules tend to be longer because a standard bearing directly on conduct, the way rules do, invites more specificity than standards that bear less directly, the way principles or ideals do. Because the violation of a rule is much easier to recognize than discounting a principle or ignoring an ideal, and so much easier to condemn or punish, we generally insist on much more detail in rules. We want the boundaries of conduct as clearly defined as possible, not open to challenge or to wildly different interpretations.

Let us suppose we are trying to draft a code of police ethics. For any proposed provision, the first question should be, "Does this state the minimum below which no officer should fall?" If the answer is yes, the provision is a candidate for becoming a mandatory rule. Otherwise, the provision can only be a principle or ideal (assuming it belongs in the code at all). To decide which it is, principle or ideal (or not code material at all), we must answer two more questions.

One is: "Can an officer make good police decisions without giving some weight to this consideration?" If the answer is no, the consideration is a possible principle. If, however, the answer is yes, we must ask one more question: "Would it still be good for an officer to do as this provision says?" If the answer is yes, the standard is a possible ideal. Otherwise, it is not. So, for example, "honesty in thought and deed" seems a possible principle. An officer who gave no weight to honesty would be a perpetual embarrassment to the force, dangerous to his partners, and useless to the courts. On the other hand, "honesty in thought and deed" probably cannot be an ideal for police. "Going undercover," though a practice about which many have grave doubts, is an established and practiced form of police work. If (as it seems) gathering intelligence by going undercover is part of the normal police function, police cannot commit themselves to complete honesty, even as an ideal. Lying, falsification, and dissembling may be part of good police work. Honesty thus differs from, for example, "being constantly mindful of the welfare of others," a state good for police to achieve, however hard in practice.

That honesty can be a principle but not an ideal of police ethics suggests the complex relationship between principles and ideals. Principles are not simply standards meant to bring out conduct inherently easier to achieve than that which ideals call for. Principles and ideals differ in the way they obtain conduct. Ideals identify a state of affairs to be aimed at—and, if possible, achieved. Nothing can be our ideal if we do not want to achieve it. In this respect, ideals are more like rules, which also identify a desired state of affairs (though one mandated rather than merely urged). Principles, in contrast, do not identify a state of affairs to aim at or achieve, only considerations to be taken into account. There need be no ideal corresponding to a principle (except an "ideal of deliberation"). We can want some matter always considered—for example, honesty—even if we never want our conduct determined solely by that consideration. In this respect, principles bear less directly on conduct than do ideals. That is why honesty can be a principle of police work even if it cannot be a rule or ideal.

I have so far spoken only of "possible" rules, principles, or ideals. What distinguishes possible from actual? Answering that question will take us to the most important part of understanding police ethics, the problem of putting ethics into practice.

A code of ethics must set standards beyond ordinary morality if it is to be a code of ethics at all. It must require something more than ordinary morality requires, lay down principles ordinary morality does not, or set an ideal ordinary morality does not. That follows from our definition of ethics. Yet, if a code is to be realized in practice, it cannot ask more than most of those subject to it are willing to give. A code must "buy" obedience. The more the code demands of those subject to it, the more it must "pay" them to obey. How can a code of ethics get those subject to it to obey? We may distinguish four possibilities: command, reward, oath, and convention.

By "command," I mean obtaining obedience by stating what is wanted and attaching bad consequences to failure to comply. The bad consequences might include boycott, undesirable assignment, fine, suspension, or imprisonment. Command (in this sense) does not presuppose good motives on the part of those subject to it. The command might be an alien imposition made potent by strict surveillance and swift response to each individual's disobedience. Command pays for obedience in goods external to morality. Command is the characteristic means by which law, especially criminal law, is enforced. Command works better with rules than with principles or ideals.

By "reward," I mean obtaining obedience by stating what is wanted and attaching good consequences to compliance. The good consequences may be money, honors, better assignments, or the like. Like command, reward does not presuppose good motives on the part of those rewarded. Like command, reward must rely on a capacity to detect obedience and disobedience, and to respond accordingly. Reward differs from command only in the consequences those imposing the standard attach (good consequences for obedience rather than bad consequences for disobedience). If command is characteristic of the way the law secures obedience, reward is characteristic of the way a market secures it.

By "oath," I mean any way of taking on a moral obligation more or less independent of the content. "Oath" includes swearing, pledging, promising, and other formal undertakings. Oath, unlike command or reward, does presuppose some good motives in those from whom it is to be exacted. Oath-takers must be relatively decent persons, that is, beings who respect an oath. While law or market can obtain even immoral conduct (for example, by threatening to punish one who does not do as told or by offering a large reward to those who do), oath cannot (except through misunderstanding). An oath ordinarily motivates only insofar as it seems morally obliging and can morally oblige only insofar as what it requires is morally permissible. Ethics by oath is therefore internal to morality in a way ethics by command and ethics by reward are not. Ethics by oath makes direct appeal to conscience. So, it can secure obedience in circumstances where difficulties of supervision mean that (mere) command and reward cannot. Ethics by oath fits principles and ideals better than ethics by command or reward does.

Oaths, though internal to morality, are still external to ethics (in our sense), that is, they have no necessary connection with groups. A particular oath can bind just one individual. Nothing in an oath as such requires oath-takers to work together, even if the oath binds more than one. The obligations of each oath-taker may endure in spite of whatever other oath-takers do (just as my mortgage obliges me even if all others default on theirs).

Oaths are external to ethics in another way. An oath is usually a condition of taking an office (or other responsible position). A police officer, for example, is supposed to be sworn in before he can exercise the police power. This use of oath at least suggests that the officer cannot be trusted with that power until he gives his word to use it as the oath proscribes. In such instances the obligations of office are treated as morally independent of occupying the office. Even if regularly re-administered, an oath treats the office as if it did not itself impose obligations on its occupant. Convention, my last means of gaining obedience to a code of ethics, is not like that.

By "convention," I mean a practice in which the participation of each is valuable only insofar as others participate as well. Many games are conventions in this sense. Stud poker, for example, requires at least two players (and is best with five to eight). Conventions are cooperative undertakings. Each participant benefits from what others do while helping to make possible similar benefits for the others by doing as they do. These benefits are essential to what makes participation worth the trouble.

Conventions can create moral obligations. When each voluntarily participates in a morally permissible practice to obtain the benefits that the practice creates, each has a moral obligation not to disobey the rules generating these benefits. Disobeying the rules of such a practice is cheating. Cheating is (ordinarily) morally wrong. So, for example, cheating at stud poker is morally wrong. Anyone who voluntarily sits down to play poker is morally obliged to play by the rules. That obligation continues until she gets up from the table, informs the other players that she no longer intends to play by the rules, or otherwise quits the game.[15]

Conventions can also create moral responsibilities (in the sense of that term in which one's responsibilities are something more than the sum of one's obligations). So, for example, while the rules of stud poker do not require a player to try to win, a player would be acting irresponsibly if he did not try to win. Not only would he probably disappoint those he played against, he would also not be playing as he should. He would be ignoring a principle of the game. While "obligation" (like "duty") seems to be a term corresponding to "rule," "responsibility" seems to correspond to "principle." Principles state our responsibilities, just as rules state our obligations or duties. We do not seem to have a similar term corresponding to "ideal."

Treating a code of ethics as a convention (in this sense) means treating ethics as a practice in which the reasons for obedience must be internal to the practice itself. Ethics by convention will differ sharply from ethics by command, reward, or oath. Police ethics can be treated as convention. People voluntarily join the force and can quit at will. If police ethics can be treated as convention, the question becomes, should it be?

A PROFESSIONAL CODE

Command or reward can put almost any standard into practice, including many that are morally permissible. Fear and greed are powerful incentives. Those employing such incentives need only concern themselves with how closely the conduct in question can be supervised and how much enforcement will cost.

What is true of standards in general is true of codes of ethics in particular (except that no morally impermissible standard can be part of a code of ethics). Those putting a code of ethics into practice by command or reward will not necessarily be able to trust those subject to it. Command and reward presuppose close supervision.

Unlike ethics by command or reward, ethics by oath does not presuppose close supervision. Conscience can serve instead. Ethics by oath nonetheless resembles ethics by command and reward in being largely independent of what the code actually says. Virtually any morally permissible oath is (morally) binding, however arduous or unsatisfying the conduct it commits one to. The oath need only be taken voluntarily. Those willing to pay morally decent people to take the oath (for example, by making the oath a condition of otherwise attractive employment) will have little trouble finding such oath-takers.

The same is not true of ethics by convention. While, like ethics by oath, ethics by convention depends on conscience, it differs from ethics by oath in the way conscience is brought in. Conscience will make no claim unless the convention in question itself generates enough in benefits to make voluntary participation attractive. The code is therefore subject to constraints on content that ethics by command, reward, or oath is not. We cannot set standards very high without making participation too burdensome. But we also cannot set standards very low. Standards must produce enough (morally permissible) benefits to make participants want the practice. A code of ethics cannot do that without setting a standard significantly higher (morally better) than would otherwise prevail.

What internal benefits can make obedience to a code of police ethics attractive? The answer depends in part on what police want out of their work and in part on what they are willing to pay to get it. The answer may vary from department to department. If, for example, police merely want to make money, caring little about what others think of them, probably no code of ethics can provide internal benefits sufficient to make participation attractive. If such police are to have a code of ethics, the legislature, city council, or police commission will probably have to rely on some combination of command, reward, and oath to motivate them to obey. The code will, in effect, be indistinguishable from other regulations governing only the police. Talk of "ethics" will be uninformative (though not inaccurate).

If, however, the police in a department consist largely of people who want to serve their fellow citizens by helping to maintain good order, who want their uniform to bring special respect, or who otherwise see police work as more than just another way to earn a living, the benefits they seek will depend (in part at least) on what other police do. For example, no police officer can maintain good order alone or assure respect for the uniform. Such achievements require the cooperation of other officers (as well as the appropriate public response). Such achievements require police to work together as voluntary participants in a common enterprise the primary purpose of which goes beyond what law, market, and ordinary morality exact. In other words, such achievements require police to think of themselves as sharing a common profession. Insofar as they think of themselves in that way, they will probably be able to write a code generating enough internal beliefs to make participation in the profession that the code defines attractive.[16]

I have just used the much-used word "profession" in a sense different from the merely technical sense I gave it when speaking of the Los Angeles Police Department earlier. That was no slip. The connection people commonly make between "profession" and "code of ethics" would be incomprehensible if "profession" were a mere synonym for "highly skilled occupation." Profession, as I understand it, is not a matter of mere skill or knowledge. Whatever else a profession is, it is at least a voluntary cooperative undertaking, the (primary) purpose of which is public service. Such an undertaking imposes obligations defined (in part at least) by the profession's code of ethics. Professionals differ from other people in having obligations that others do not. Being a professional means belonging to a profession.

This point needs stressing. Police sometimes justify having a code of ethics as a way to get privileges, status, or income comparable to that of lawyers, doctors, or other "true professionals." Police tend to think of professional status itself as something society grants, in the way the state grants a license to practice medicine or law. That is a mistake. Privilege, status, and high income are external to professions. Some professions have relatively low income, low status, and few privileges. Think, for example, of priests, teachers, or nurses. And many people with relatively high income, high status, and great privilege are not professionals. Think, for example, of movie stars, "professional athletes," or stockbrokers. Police need to remember that. If they do not, any infatuation with ethics is likely to be short-lived and disappointing. Police do not have high income, high status, or great privilege in any free society. They probably never will, code of ethics or no.

But they can be professionals in a free society, something not so easy in what we somewhat misleadingly call a "police state," that is, a country where the government maintains power by force rather than by consent. Under such a government, the police are often required to torture, execute without trial, and otherwise engage in morally impermissible conduct. They cannot be professionals in the morally worthy sense, however they long to be, however much technical skill they develop, and however many privileges an oppressive government accords them as a means of remaining in office.

In a free society, the police have little control over how society will treat them. What they have instead is the ability to conduct themselves in ways everyone should recognize as morally good. They can conduct themselves by a code setting standards beyond what is merely morally decent. They can work in the company of people who (generally) maintain those standards. They can develop a basis for justified self-respect and professional pride, whatever the larger society knows or thinks.

The police are not, of course, even potentially, a "free profession" in the way law and medicine are (or at least, were until recently). Like engineers and teachers, military officers and clergy, the police belong to a "captive profession," a profession the members of which must work within institutions over which they have only limited control. Those in charge, whether the police chief or the officers under him, will be chosen by those above, not by those below. Departmental regulations will also come from above. That makes achieving ethics by convention harder—but not impossible.

Police, like engineers and teachers, have in fact been able to maintain significant freedom of action despite departmental regulations and elaborate systems of inspection, investigation, and recording. They have that freedom for much the same reason engineers and teachers do. Their superiors require their judgment, judgment that cannot be reduced to rules or exercised from above. Few departments can afford the supervision necessary to assure that the ordinary officer obeys regulations. Probably no department would in fact want to pay the cost, either in efficiency or morale, of such supervision.[17] So, almost everyone in a police department, or served by it, is likely (in the long run at least) to benefit from a department in which ordinary officers generally consider their code of ethics as a standard each should follow in part because the others are doing the same. That, in turn, means everyone has an interest in having the police adopt a code that can work (in part at least) as a convention. That interest is, however, not the only interest involved. Other interests weigh against ethics by convention.

THE PROBLEM OF THE MISSING HIGHER STANDARD

If a code of ethics must set a standard of conduct higher than law, market, and ordinary morality do, most actual codes of police ethics do not seem to be codes of ethics at all. Consider again the UN's "Code of Conduct for Law Enforcement Officials" and the beating of Rodney King. Two of the code's ten short articles are directly relevant. Article 3 forbids police the "use of more force than necessary in the performance of their duty;" and Article 4 does the same thing for "inflicting, instigating, or tolerating any act of torture or other cruel, inhuman, or degrading treatment or punishment." These provisions (except perhaps for "tolerating") do not seem to go significantly beyond law and ordinary morality. Beating King was both illegal and immoral, UN code or no. The police did not need a code of ethics to tell them not to beat King. What need then for a code of police ethics?

The question is clearest for the unnecessary use of force, but it is a question that can be asked about most provisions of most codes of police ethics (except those that set unrealistically high standards). I will give only one more example. Among the standards of the IACP's 1957 "Law Enforcement Code of Ethics" was "honesty in thought and deed in both my personal and official life." We noted earlier that this seems to be a principle rather than an ideal or rule. Yet, if a principle, it is a principle all morally decent people share, not a higher standard. We should all be honest in thought and deed.

If codes of police ethics do not in fact state a standard of conduct higher than ordinary morality, they differ in an important way from those of most other professions. All professional codes include some provisions restating ordinary morality. Such provisions counteract the special temptations or pressures to ignore moral standards characteristic of the profession's work. But most codes of ethics include much that goes beyond ordinary morality. So, for example, the NSPE's Code of Ethics specifically requires an employed engineer to notify her employer before accepting a second job (III.1.c) and forbids engineers who employ others to accept payment from either an employee or an employment agency for given employment (III.6.a).

Why do police codes characteristically fail to set a standard higher than ordinary morality? There are probably many reasons, including the confusion caused by the very language in which police codes are written. But a large part of the answer, I think, is that police find it harder than most of us to maintain minimum standards of decency. That is not because they were "criminal types" before they joined the force. Police work itself seems to have a strong tendency to corrupt. Police see much more of the underside of life than the rest of us do, not only the worst people but even good people at their worst. Police are far more likely to be offered a substantial bribe than most of us, to be threatened with death or wounds, and to hear of other people's wrongdoing. Their sense of what is normal must suffer in consequence. They are also much more likely than most of us to feel like failures. My "clients" generally graduate, get jobs and do pretty well. Most of the people the police see regularly end up dead, in jail, on the run, or just down and out. "Bitterness" seems as much of an occupational disease of the police as brutality, suspicion, cynicism, and petty theft.[18]

For the police, then, the object of ethics must be somewhat different from that of most other professions. The police will do well to remain decent human beings. The problem of police ethics (and of police administration, too) is to help them do that. A code can help police to maintain ordinary moral decency in at least three ways. First, a code can simply serve to remind police of what is (and, therefore, of what is not) expected of them. Second, it can provide a common vocabulary for discussion of hard cases. Third, the emotional language so common in police codes might also help to inspire an officer to do more than she would otherwise do.

Whether police codes in fact significantly support minimally decent conduct in any of these ways is, of course, an empirical question, one about which social scientists should tell us more. We might guess, though, that while reading a stirring code may do as much good as listening to a Sunday sermon or making a New Year's resolution, it is unlikely to do more. If that were all police codes were good for, they would not be good for much.

More important here, if police codes only restate ordinary morality—moral ideals as police ideals, moral principles as police principles, and moral rules as police rules—they are not codes of ethics (in our sense). They do not set a higher standard. What then do "police ethics" have to do with ethics? Article 8 of the UN's Code suggests an answer, but one that will probably make most police uncomfortable. That article not only (redundantly) requires law enforcement officials to "refrain from" conduct violating the code, but it also requires them to "prevent and rigorously oppose all violations of this code." Once a violation has occurred (or can be expected), a law enforcement officer "should report the matter within the chain of command, or take such other actions as are lawfully open . . . including, when necessary, the reporting to any agency with reviewing or remedial power."

Article 8 is the only explicit "whistleblowing" provision I have seen in a code of police ethics.[19] Such a provision is, however, necessary to any police code that is to be more than a mere restatement of what law, market, and ordinary morality exact. Part of the specifically professional responsibility of police, probably the most important, is helping other police do the right thing. That may, on occasion, mean breaking "the code of silence," the rule that helps the police to protect themselves from outside interference and so to preserve enough autonomy to make professional judgment possible.

While I believe police need to think carefully about ways of preserving autonomy that are less likely than the code of silence to shield corruption, I need not argue that here. Much can be done to help police maintain minimum standards of moral decency without breaching that code. Putting a fellow officer "on report" is not the only way, or even the best way, to maintain professional standards. Consider, for example, what might have happened if, as the King beating began, one of the officers standing there had fired his revolver into the air and said something like this: "Did we join the police force to beat up on this helpless man? Isn't our job to protect everyone from the monsters of this world, not to become monsters ourselves?" Words like that might have cleared the air. The police certainly knew that they were doing something wrong (though they probably also thought that their superiors condoned what they did).[20] Had an officer (or supervisor) spoken up in time, there might have been no wrongdoing to report.[21]

CONCLUSIONS

We can, I think, now draw six conclusions. First, police do not need a code of ethics just because they use unnecessary force. They generally know that using unnecessary force is morally wrong, code or no code. Publishing a code forbidding such practices adds nothing to an officer's moral knowledge. Neither does it add to his moral duties. Even requiring officers to swear an oath to obey the code will not change the substance of those duties. Closer supervision, harsher discipline, less pressure from above for "results," or alternative methods for handling the problems that now lead police to use unnecessary force would seem more likely to reduce police brutality than any code that simply restates ordinary morality.

Second, a code of police ethics (that is, a code that goes beyond ordinary morality) can help prevent undesirable conduct only insofar as the police can be kept morally decent people (people over whom conscience exercises considerable authority). Because some police work seems to be inherently corrupting, police departments need to be more careful than they are about the work they do. For example, they probably need to take on less undercover work than they now do. They also need to be more careful about making officers work such long or irregular hours that they lose touch with the world beyond police work. Departments may even want to require "sabbatical leaves" every few years.

Third, a code of ethics can help prevent undesirable conduct only if police think of themselves as professionals in the morally interesting sense. Insofar as police think of themselves as mere individual employees, a "code of ethics," whatever its substance, will be no more than another departmental regulation. Its moral foundation will be the employment contract (whether or not supplemented by a special oath).

Fourth, because what distinguishes a code of ethics from other regulations governing police conduct is its connection with policing as a profession, giving police a living code of ethics means something more than issuing another regulation, making police swear an oath as a condition of employment, or even regularly informing them of their duties. Giving police a living code means choosing its term so that police benefit enough from having it in force that it becomes reasonable for them to help enforce it. That, in turn, probably means giving them a central part in writing, interpreting, and enforcing the code. Codes that seem to come from above generally do not touch the world below. So, police departments need to think about ways to combine their quasi-military organization with the decentralized controls characteristic not only of free professions like law and medicine but of captive professions like education and engineering. Decentralized control (autonomy) is part of what makes a profession possible.

Fifth, since the primary standards of a police code probably cannot in practice demand much more of police than ordinary morality does, the important part of a code of ethics for police will not be the primary standards (for example, those forbidding unnecessary brutality or urging honesty in thought and deed), but the secondary standards (for example, those making the conduct of each police officer the professional responsibility of every other). While few police codes include such secondary standards, all should. Otherwise, a police officer reading the code could properly conclude that he is responsible only for his own conduct. So long as he satisfies the primary standards, he has done all he should. He is a true professional.

Sixth, the teaching of police ethics probably needs to be changed accordingly. Right now the emphasis seems to be on the individual police officer doing his duty and "keeping his nose clean." Little, if anything, is said about an officer's responsibility for helping fellow police officers do the right thing.[22] Yet, in police work, as in other professions, moral support is an important part of maintaining standards. Police clearly have a support system in place, "the code of silence."[23] The problem is to turn that into a system of moral support. Doing that means, among other things, teaching police how to talk about the profession's ethics with each other.

Answering the Question with Which We Began

Most of us, sufficiently provoked, are capable of giving someone in Rodney King's position a kick or two. Luckily, few of us have the opportunity. Police often do. They will take that opportunity far more often than we would like unless those they work with help them keep in mind the reasons they have to show restraint. The Los Angeles police force, more than 8,000 officers, will not quickly live down what they did to Rodney King, even though only three officers actually struck King and only a dozen or so more stood by.

Do cops really need a code of ethics? That's one for the cops. My purpose here has been to clarify who should answer the question, why, and how—not to answer it for them.

NOTES

I should like to thank John Kleinig for encouraging me to think about the subject of this paper, for directing me to many of the works cited here, and (along with one anonymous reviewer) for helpful comments on one or another draft. I should also like to thank Sohair ElBaz for helping me to track down many of the works cited here.

1. Some may think that racism explains the way the police mistreated King. He is black; all fifteen of the officers, white. King thinks otherwise. The left side of an earlier *Journal* front page seems to support King's view. It described how Officer Gamble of the Dayton (Ohio) police repeatedly touched a hot clothes iron to the bare skin of a handcuffed suspect's chest and stomach. Gamble's partner, who had been holding the suspect in place, stopped the torture only when Gamble, having pulled down the suspect's pants, seemed about to place the iron on the suspect's genitals. Both Gamble and his victim were black. Kotlowitz, "Hidden Casualties: Drug War's Emphasis on Law Enforcement Takes a Toll on Police," *Wall Street Journal,* Jan. 11, 1991, p. 1.

2. Nazario and Jefferson, "LA Law: A Videotaped Beating Highlights Problems of Los Angeles Police," *Wall Street Journal,* Mar. 12, 1991, p. 1.

3. One piece of evidence for this claim, if any is needed, is that the LAPD has a code of ethics forbidding use of unnecessary force. All California police officers, including the LAPD, are required by law to subscribe to the International Association of Police Chiefs' 1957 Law Enforcement Code of Ethics discussed below. Muehlelsen, "A Matter of Ethics—The Old Code Switch," *National Reporter,* June 1991, p. 11.

4. While I do not wish to turn this paper into a debate between virtue-theorists and rule-theorists, I should at least suggest why I have largely ignored virtue here. It seems to me that when I deliberate, rules, principles, and ideals, not virtues, are the standards that guide my choice of action. Following those standards may in time develop the corresponding virtues (in accordance with Aristotle's well-known dictum), but then my deliberations will be shorter. The virtues, as such, will not appear in my deliberations. For a fuller discussion of this point, see my "Civic Virtue, Corruption, and the Structure of Moral Theories," 13 *Midwest Stud. Philosophy,* 352-66 (1988).

5. See especially Ronald Dworkin, "Taking Rights Seriously" 14-43 (1977). Dworkin's distinction between rules and principles does not seem to correspond to any of the distinctions traditionally lumped together under "perfect and imperfect duties [or obligations]." For a list of possibilities, see Campbell, "Perfect and Imperfect Obligations," 52 *Modern Schoolman* 285-94 (1975).

6. Since there is a notable tendency to revise the golden rule until it can indeed seem a plausible rule of conduct (in my sense), perhaps it is worth quoting it exactly: "Therefore all things whatsoever ye would that men should do to you, do ye even so to them: for this is the law and the prophet" (Matthew 7:12). Taken literally, that "all" seems to leave no time for looking after oneself.

7. For an explanation of the (minimal) moral theory lying behind this way of putting things, see my "The Moral Legislature: Morality Without an Archimedean Point," *Ethics,* forthcoming.

8. I have dealt with aspects of professional codes in the following works: "Thinking Like an Engineer: The Place of a Code of Ethics in the Practice of a Profession," 20 *Phil. & Pub. Aff.* 150-67 (1991); "The Ethics Boom: What and Why," 34 *Centennial Review I* 163-86 (1990); "The Discipline of Science: Law or Profession?" I *Accountablity in Research* 137-45 (1990); "The Special Roles of Professionals in Business Ethics," 7 *Business & Professional Ethics Journal* 51-62 (1988); *Codes of Ethics in Business* (Center for the Study of Ethics in Society: Kalamazoo, Michigan, 1988); "Professional Means Putting Your Profession First," 2 *Georgetown Journal of Legal Ethics* 341-57 (1988); "Vocational Teachers, Confidentiality, and Pro-

fessional Ethics," *International Journal of Applied Philosophy,* Spring 1988, pp. 11-20; "Ethics in the City of Chicago," 18 *Teaching Philosophy* 329-38 (1987); "The Use of Professions," 22 *Business Economics* 5-10 (1987); and "The Moral Authority of a Professional Code," 29 *Nomos* 302-37 (1987). The first two and the last of these are especially relevant here.

9. "Rule XXXIV: International Association of Chiefs of Police Code of Ethics," *Police Chief,* February 1987, pp. 11-12. There is also a confusing alternation between "will" and "shall" not relevant here. Note that unlike most codes of ethics, this one includes specific provisions for enforcement (including complaint, investigation, hearing, and punishment).

10. The IACP replaced this code of police ethics with another on October 17, 1989. See "Law Enforcement Code of Ethics," *Police Chief,* June 1990, p. 10, for text and accompanying explanation: Gruber, "President's Message: Changes and Innovations," p. 8. I ignore that new code here for two reasons. First, few police will know much about it. Indeed, its chances of replacing the old one in any major department looks slim. For an explanation, see Muehlelsen, supra note 3. The other reason I ignore that code here is that it does not seem much of an advance over the 1957 code.

11. Could "duty" here mean "imperfect" rather than "perfect" duty? That, of course, depends on what we mean by "perfect" and "imperfect" here. Following Campbell, we might distinguish five possibilities: (1) culpable/supererogatory, (2) important/trivial, (3) legal/moral, (4) specific/vague, and (5) correlative/non-correlative. Clearly, "serving mankind" could be an imperfect duty in two of these senses, the uninteresting ones. It could be a moral and vague duty rather than a legal specific one. But, in the remaining three senses, "serving mankind" seems to be a perfect duty, not an imperfect one. "Serving mankind" is neither a trivial duty nor one merely good for police to perform. It is, as the code says, a "fundamental duty." Police who do not serve mankind deserve blame and, indeed, punishment. Mankind, or at least the general public, has a right to that service. That is what the public pays police for. That is what they have contracted to provide.

12. Discussions of this code have a curiously automatic (and homiletic) quality explained, perhaps, by the confusion close reading generates. Compare, for example, G. T. Payton, *Patrol Procedures* 4-26 (3d ed. 1967); Bruining, "Law Enforcement Code of Ethics," *Police Chief,* October 1973 p. 68 ff; and Moore, "Law Enforcement Code of Ethics: A Guide to Police/Community Relations," *Police Chief,* March 1975, p. 56. While Bruining often seems to paraphrase Payton, he never mentions him.

13. Mueller, "The United Nations Draft Code of Conduct for Law Enforcement Officials," 1 *Police Studies* 17-21 (1978). For an explanation (and defense) of this draft (including information about its ratification), see Bossard, "Police Ethics and International Police Cooperation," in *The Social Basis of Criminal Justice: Ethical Issues for the 1980's* (F. Schmalleger & R. Gustafon eds. 1981), 23-37. For another code with similar problems, see the *American Acadamy for Professional Law Enforcement, Ethical Standards in Law Enforcement* (1974). I am, of course, assuming that the code's drafters chose their words carefully, for example, that they meant something more by "must" than by "should." How plausible is that assumption? In the case of the UN Code, the answer is clear. As adopted (December 17, 1979), the code no longer includes the language to which I have objected.

14. Compare, for example, the preamble of the *Association for Computing Machinery, Code of Professional Conduct* (1975): "The verbs 'shall' (imperative) and 'should' (encouragement) are used purposefully in the Code. The Canons and Ethical Considerations are not, however, binding rules . . . [etc]."

15. This implicit appeal to the principle of fairness ("Don't cheat") should raise no red flags, even though the principle itself has been under a cloud ever since the seemingly devastating criticism it received in R. Nozick, *Anarchy, State, and Utopia* (1974). I have, it should be noted, limited my use to obligations generated by voluntarily claiming benefits of a cooperative practice that would not exist but for the practice. Most attacks on the principle of fairness have

addressed the "involuntary benefits" version. And even those attacks are not decisive. See my "Nozick's Argument for the Legitimacy of the Welfare State," 97 *Ethics* 576-94 (1987), which shows that Nozick's original criticism, and most subsequent criticism, depend on examples that, upon careful examination, fail to support the criticism. For a positive defense of the "involuntary benefits" version (somewhat revised), see Arneson, "The Principle of Fairness and Free-Rider Problems," 92 *Ethics* 616-33 (1982).

16. Anyone writing a code of ethics would benefit from reading J. Kultgen, *Ethics and Professionalism* (1988), especially pp. 201-51. Yet I must point out an important difference between his analysis and mine. Kultgen seems to suppose that there is some objectively right way to write a code with which politics usually interferes. As I understand writing a code, politics is essential. So, on my view, the imposition of a code of ethics by outsiders (for example, a legislature) is much more problematic than Kultgen seems to think. This does not mean that outsiders should not participate, only that they probably cannot dominate if the code is to have the support of those it must govern.

17. Perhaps this is the place to note that the empirical evidence suggests that the more police feel they have to hide, the more they are likely to resist outside control. Shame or guilt tends to make police more clannish, more committed to the code of silence, and so harder to regulate. Ethics, then, is not necessarily opposed to outside control. See, e.g., Shernock, "The Effects of Patrol Officers' Defensiveness Toward the Outside World on Their Ethical Orientations," *Criminal Justice Ethics,* Summer/Fall 1990, pp. 24-42. On the other hand, outside control, or at least control by those above the officer on patrol, may actually discourage ethical conduct. See, e.g., "Attitudes of Police Officers Toward Their Professional Ethics," 12 *Journal of Criminal Justice* 211-20 (1984). What police now lack is the formal procedures of peer review that, for example, lawyers or accountants typically have. Can such procedures ever be built into the quasi-military structure characteristic of police organization? Do we need that quasi-military structure anymore?

18. See, e.g., G.T. Payton, supra note 12, p. 6 ("easy to become bitter") 11 ("dealing with moral degenerates"), 12 ("reproach or ridicule, he must expect . . . as part of his job"), 16 ("easy . . . to become discouraged"), 17 ("must vent your anger upon them"), 18 ("good police officers who have just lost their heads"), and 22 ("a known fact that a person's ethics normally decrease with the years"); or, fifteen years later, Johnson & Copus, "Law Enforcement Ethics: A Theoretical Analysis," in F. Schmalleger & R. Gustafson, supra note 13, pp. 39-83. For a theoretical framework in which this tendency makes sense, see my "Explaining Wrongdoing," *Journal of Social Philosophy,* Summer/Fall 1989, pp. 74-90.

19. Beside the codes cited above, I have examined the following: *Western Australia Police Force Code of Ethics* (1990); *New South Wales, Maxims for General Guidance for Members of the Police Force* (1870) and *NSW Police Force Circular* (1981), both in Hawkes, "Ethics," *NSW Police News,* Dec. 1982, pp. 13-18.

20. See, e.g., "L.A. Cops on Tape Detail 'Big Time' Beating," *Chicago Tribune,* Mar. 19, 1991, p. 1, col. 3.

21. Compare my "Avoiding the Tragedy of Whistleblowing," 8 *Business & Professional Ethics Journal* (1989) 3-19.

22. The question of police response to police wrongdoing is, however, not altogether ignored. See, e.g., Chicago Police Academy, Training Division, Course Lesson Plan, "Unit Title: Police Morality" (five classroom hours). Discussion case III.F, one of five cases assigned for a single hour session, takes up the use of force. Among the seventeen questions appended for discussion, about a third concern response to a partner's brutality. The last of these (like the other four) is a good example of what police should be discussing regularly and often throughout their careers, not just in their initial (all too brief) training:

In a situation like this, if you felt that your partner was a dedicated and professional officer who had just had an understandable human reaction in slapping the prisoner, would you lie under oath to protect him? Could you justify this in your own mind? Why or why not? Also assume that he is a close personal friend.

Calling the course "police morality" (as Chicago does) may be understood in two related ways: first, as showing confusion (also evident in the teaching materials) about whether the course is reinforcing ordinary moral standards or teaching something new (professional ethics); and, second, as recognizing how little beyond ordinary morality the IAPC's "Code of Ethics" (included in the course) goes. The course lacks a framework for dealing with the hard questions it eventually puts to its trainees. Perhaps that is why so little time is allowed for discussion.

23. Because the "code of silence" is so often treated as an unredeemable conspiracy against the good, I should perhaps briefly explain why I do not treat it that way here. The code of silence is an expression of loyalty among people who must, now and then at least, trust each other with their lives. Loyalty, while a virtue more likely than most to be put in the service of vice, is still a virtue the police would probably be considerably worse off without. The problem is to channel it, not to decry it. For an examination of loyalty useful in this context (though one arguing that loyalty is not a virtue), see Erwin, "Loyalty: The Police," *Criminal Justice Ethics,* Summer/Fall 1990, pp. 3-15.

Discussion Questions

1. Do police officers really need a code of ethics? Explain.

2. Should a code of ethics be a statement of ideals, principles, requirements, or a mixture? Support your position.

3. List and discuss the six conclusions stated by the author.

CHAPTER 6

Police Lies and Perjury: A Motivation-Based Taxonomy

Thomas Barker & David L. Carter

Lying and other deceptive practices are an integral part of the police officer's working environment. At first blush, one's reaction to this statement might be rather forthright. Police officers should not lie. *If you can't trust your local police, who can you trust?* However, as with most issues, the matter is not that simple.

We are all aware that police officers create false identities for undercover operations. We know that they make false promises to hostage takers and kidnappers. We also know officers will strain the truth in order to spare the feelings of a crime victim and his/her loved ones. Police officers are trained to lie and be deceptive in these law enforcement practices. They are also trained to use techniques of interrogation which require deception and even outright lying.

Police officers learn much of this in the police academy, where they are also warned about the impropriety of perjury and the need to record all incidents fully and accurately in all official reports. The recruit learns that all rules and regulations must be obeyed. He/she learns of the danger of lying to internal affairs or a supervisor. The recruit is told to be truthful in his dealings with the noncriminal element of the public in that mutual trust is an important element in police community relations. Once the recruit leaves the academy—and some departments where officers work in the field before attending rookie school—the officer

KEY CONCEPTS:

accepted lying

blue code

deviant lying

encouragement

entrapment

perjury

tolerated lying

undercover operations

From Thomas Barker and David L. Carter, *Police Deviance,* 3rd ed. (Cincinnati, OH: Anderson Publishing), 1994, Chapter 8.

soon learns from his/her peers that police lying is the norm under certain circumstances.

Our purpose is to discuss the patterns of lying which might occur in a police organization, the circumstances under which they occur and the possible consequences of police lying.

TAXONOMY OF POLICE LIES

Accepted Lying

Certain forms of police lying and/or deception are an accepted part of the police officer's working environment. The lies told in this category are accepted by the police organization because they fulfill a defined police purpose. Administrators and individual police officers believe that certain lies are necessary to control crime and to "arrest the guilty." In these instances, the organization will freely admit the intent to lie and define the acts as a legitimate policing strategy. On face value, most would agree with the police that lies in this category are acceptable and necessary. However, a troubling and difficult question is "to what extent, if at all, is it *proper* for law enforcement officials to employ trickery and deceit as part of their law enforcement practices?" (Skolnick, 1982, italics added). As we shall see, the answer to this question is not so easy. Acceptable lies may be very functional for the police but are they always proper, moral, ethical, and legal?

The most readily apparent patterns of "accepted" police lying are the deceptive practices that law enforcement officers believe are necessary to perform undercover operations or detect other forms of secret and consensual crimes. Police officers engaged in these activities must not only conceal their true identity but they must talk, act, and dress out of character, fabricating all kinds of stories in order to perform these duties. One could hardly imagine that FBI Special Agent Joseph Pistone could have operated for six years in the Mafia without the substantial number of lies that he had to tell (Pistone, 1987). However, the overwhelming majority of the undercover operations are neither as fascinating nor as dangerous as working six years with the Mafia or other organized crime groups. The most common police undercover operations occur in routine vice operations dealing with prostitution, bootlegging, gambling, narcotics, bribery of public officials (e.g., ABSCAM, MILAB, BRILAB) and sting operations.

These deceptive practices in undercover operations are not only acceptable to the law enforcement community but considered necessary for undercover operations to be effective. Nevertheless, such activities are not without problems. The "Dirty Harry" problem in police work raises the question as to what extent morally good police practices warrant or justify ethically, politically, or legally suspect means to achieve law enforcement objectives (Klockars, 1980). Marx also raises the issue that many of the tactics used by law enforcement officers in such recent undercover operations as ABSCAM, MILAB, BRILAB, police-run fencing or sting operations and anti-crime decoy squads may have lost sight of "the profound difference between carrying out an investigation to determine if a suspect is, in fact, breaking the law, and carrying it out to determine if an individual can be induced to break the law" (Marx, 1985:106). One congressman involved in the ABSCAM case refused the first offer of a cash bribe only later to accept the money after federal agents, concluding that he was an alcoholic, gave him liquor (Marx, 1985:104).

Encouraging the commission of a crime may be a legally accepted police practice when the officer acts as a willing victim or his/her actions facilitate the commission of a crime that was going to be committed in the first place. However, it is possible for "encouragement" to lead the suspect to raise the defense of entrapment. According to *Black's Law Dictionary* entrapment is "the act of officers or agents of the government in inducing a person to commit a crime not contemplated by him, for the purpose of instituting a criminal prosecution against him" (Black, 1983:277). For the defense of entrapment to prevail the defendant must show that the officer or his/her agent has gone beyond providing the encouragement and opportunity for the commission of a crime and through trickery, fraud, or other deception has induced the suspect to commit a crime. This defense is raised far more times than it is successful because the current legal criteria to determine entrapment is what is known as the "subjective test."

In the subjective test the predisposition of the offender, rather than the objective methods of the police, is the key factor in determining entrapment (Marx, 1985; Skolnick, 1982; Stitt and James, 1985). This makes it extremely difficult for a defendant with a criminal record to claim that he/she would not have committed the crime except for the actions of the officer. The "objective test" of entrapment raised by a minority of the Supreme Court has focused on the nature of the police conduct rather than the predisposition of the offender (Stitt and James, 1985). For example, the objective test probably would examine whether the production of crack by a police organization for use in undercover drug arrests is proper and legal. According to an Associated Press story, the Broward County Florida Sheriff's Department, not having enough crack to supply undercover officers, has started manufacturing their own crack. The sheriff's department chemist has made at least $20,000 worth of the illegal substance. Local defense attorneys have raised the issue of entrapment. In fact, one public defender stated:

> I think there's something sick about this whole system where the
> police make the product, sell the product and arrest people for buy-
> ing the product (*Birmingham Post-Herald*, April 19, 1989:B2).

The issue of deception aside, this practice raises a number of ethical and legal issues concerning police practices. At what point do we draw the line to make a police undercover operation convincing?

In addition to the accepted practices of lying and deception required for undercover operations, members of the police community often believe that it is proper to lie to the media or the public when it is necessary to protect the innocent, protect the image of the department, or calm the public in crisis situations. The department's official policy may be one of openness and candor when dealing with the media. However, as a practical matter, members of the department may deny the existence of an investigation or "plant" erroneous information to protect an ongoing investigation (i.e., disinformation). The untimely revelation of facts may alert the suspects and drive them underground or cause them to cease their illegal activities. Nevertheless, one could argue that public exposure of certain criminal activities or the possibility of them might decrease the risk of injury to persons or property. This issue was raised in the recent terrorist bombing of PanAm Flight 103 over Lockerbie, Scotland. What was the best course of action? Tell the public of all threats against airliners—most of which were unfounded—and create fear? Or keep all threats confidential and hope that airline and government officials effectively deal with the threats?

In some crimes, such as kidnapping, the publication of accurate information, or any information at all, might lead to the murder of the victim. Therefore, under these circumstances, police administrators might view lies told to protect the victim as perfectly acceptable and necessary.

Police administrators are well aware of the possibility that the entire organization may be labeled deviant because of the deviant acts of its members. The "rotten apple" theory of police corruption has often been used as an impression management technique by police administrators who are aware of this possibility (Barker, 1977). It is easier to explain police deviance as a result of individual aberrations than to admit the possibility of systemic problems and invite public scrutiny. However, candor and public scrutiny may be the best way to ensure that corruption and other forms of police deviance do not occur or continue in an organization (see Cooper and Belair, 1978).

Thus, accepted lies are those that the organization views as having a viable role in police operations. The criteria for the lie to be accepted are:

- It must be in furtherance of a legitimate organizational purpose.

- There must be a clear relationship between the need to deceive and the accomplishment of an organizational purpose.

- The nature of the deception must be one wherein officers and the management structure acknowledge that deception will better serve the public interest than the truth.

- The ethical standing of the deception and the issues of law appear to be collateral concerns.

Tolerated Lying

A second category of police lies are those that are recognized as "lies" by the police organization but are tolerated as "necessary evils." Police administrators will admit to deception or "not exactly telling the whole truth" when confronted with the facts. These types of situational or "white" lies are truly in the gray area of propriety and the police can provide logical rationales for their use. When viewed from an ethical standpoint they may be "wrong," but from the police perspective they are necessary (i.e., tolerated) to achieve organizational objectives or deal with what Goldstein has termed the basic problems of police work (Goldstein, 1977:9).

The basic problems of police work arise from the mythology surrounding police work; e.g., statutes usually require and the public expects the police to enforce all the laws all the time, the public holds the police responsible for preventing crime and apprehending all criminals, the public views the police as being capable of handling all emergencies, etc. (Goldstein, 1977). Most police administrators will not publicly admit that they do not have the resources, the training or the authority to do some of the duties that the public expects. In fact, many police administrators and police officers lacking the education and insight into police work would be hard pressed to explain police work, particularly discretionary decisionmaking, to outside groups. Therefore, they resort to lies and deception to support police practices.

Police administrators often deny that their departments practice anything less than full enforcement of all laws rather than attempt to explain the basis for police discretionary decisions and selective enforcement. We continually attempt to deal with social problems through the use of criminal sanctions and law enforcement personnel. Mandatory sentencing for all offenders committing certain felony and misdemeanor offenses is often seen as a panacea for these offenses. For example, in recent years many politically active groups such as Mothers Against Drunk Drivers (MADD) had pressured legislators for stronger laws with mandatory enforcement in drunk driving cases. However, their sentiment in cases not involving accidents may not be shared by the general public (Formby and Smykla, 1984) or the police. One can only speculate as to the number of discretionary decisions still being made by police officers in DUI offenses in departments where full enforcement is the official policy. One of the authors learned of an individual who had two DUI offenses reduced and asked a police supervisor about it.

> *Barker:* The chief has said that all DUI suspects are charged and those over the legal blood alcohol level never have the charge reduced. In fact, he said this at a MADD meeting. Yet, I heard that [   ] had two DUI offenses reduced.
>
> *Supervisor:* This is true Tom. However, [   ] is helping us with some drug cases. MADD may not understand but they do not have to make drug busts.

The point of note is that the police, in response to political pressure, make a policy on DUI cases and vow that the policy will be followed. However, in this case, that vow was not true. The police made a discretionary judgment that the assistance of the DUI offender in drug investigations was of greater importance than a DUI prosecution. Thus, this policy deviation was tantamount to a lie to the MADD membership—a lie tolerated by the police department.

The public also expects the police to handle any disorderly or emergency situations. The American public believes that one of the methods for handling any problem is "calling the cops" (Bittner, 1971). However, in many of these order-maintenance situations the police do not have the authority, resources or training to deal with the problem. They often face a situation "where something must be done now" yet an arrest is not legally possible or would be more disruptive. The officer is forced to reach into a bag of tricks for a method of dealing with the crisis. Lying to the suspects or the complainants is often that method. For example, police officers may tell noisy teenagers to move along or be arrested when the officers have neither the intention nor legal basis for an arrest. They often tell complainants that they will follow up on their complaint or turn it over to the proper agency when they have no intention of doing so. The police see these lies as a way of handling the "nuisance work" that keeps them from doing "real police work" or as a way of dealing with a problem beyond their means. In these cases, the lie is used as a tool of expediency—arguably an abuse of police discretion but one which is tolerated.

In domestic disturbances police officers face volatile situations where the necessary conditions for an arrest often are not present. Frequently there is a misdemeanor where the officer does not have a warrant, an offense has not been committed in his/her presence, and the incident occurred in a private residence. However, the officer may feel that something must be done. Consequently, the officer may lie and threaten to arrest one or both combatants, or take one of the parties out to the street or the patrol car to discuss the incident and arrest them for disorderly conduct or public intoxication when they reach public property. Another option is to make an arrest appear legal. Obviously, the latter strategy will not be a tolerated pattern of lying. It would fall into the pattern of deviant lying to be discussed later.

Officers soon learn that the interrogation stage of an arrest is an area where certain lies are tolerated and even taught to police officers. The now-famous *Miranda v. Arizona* case decided by the U.S. Supreme Court in 1966 quoted excerpts from Inbau and Reid's *Criminal Interrogation and Confessions* text to show that the police used deception and psychologically coercive methods in their interrogation of suspects (George, 1966:155-266). The latest edition of this same text gives examples of deceptive and lying practices for skilled interrogators to engage in (Inbau, Reid and Buckley, 1986).

As an illustration of these techniques, the reader is told that the interrogator should put forth a facade of sincerity so convincingly that "moisture may actually appear in his eyes" (p. 52). Another recommended effective practice of deception is that the interrogator have a *simulated* evidence case folder on hand during the course of the interrogation if an actual case file does not exist (p. 54). The interrogator may also make inferences such as a large number of investigators are working on the case and drew the same evidentiary conclusion about the suspect's guilt, even if, in reality, the interrogator is the only person working the case (p. 85). The inference is that the case against the suspect is strong because of the number of people involved in the investigation and the consequent weight of the evidence.

One particularly troublesome piece of advice for interviewing rape suspects is that:

> Where circumstances permit, the suggestion might be offered that the rape victim had acted like she might have been a prostitute and that the suspect had assumed she was a willing partner. In fact, the interrogator may even say that the police knew she had engaged in prostitution on other occasions . . . (p. 109).

As a final illustration, the book notes that an effective means to interrogate multiple suspects of a crime is "playing one offender against the other." In this regard it is suggested that the "interrogator may merely intimate to one offender that the other has confessed, or else the interrogator *may actually tell the offender so*" (emphasis added, p. 132).

It is difficult to say whether or not these tolerated forms of lying are "wrong"—many investigators would argue that they are not really "lies" but good interrogation techniques. One could also argue that the end justifies the means as long as the actions of the officers are not illegal. However, one can hypothesize that deception in one context increases the probability of deception in other contexts (cf., Skolnick, 1982; Stitt and James, 1985). As a veteran police officer told one of the authors while they were discussing ways to convince a suspect to agree to a consent search . . .

> *Barker:* That sure sounds like telling a lot of lies.
>
> *Officer:* It is not police lying; it is an art. After all, the criminal has constitutional protection. He can lie through his teeth. Why not us? What is fair is fair.

This attitude, which is borne in the frustrations of many officers, sets a dangerous precedent for attitudes related to civil liberties. When law enforcement officers begin to tolerate lies because it serves their ends—regardless of constitutional and ethical implications of those lies—then fundamental elements of civil rights are threatened.

Deviant Police Lying

The last example raises the possibility of the third category of policy lying—deviant lies. After all, "he (the suspect) can lie through his teeth. Why not us?" Deviant police lies are those that violate substantive or procedural law and/or police department rules and regulations. The deviant lies which violate substantive or procedural law are improper and should not be permitted. However, organization members (including supervisors) and other actors in the criminal justice system are often aware of their occurrence. Noted defense attorney Alan Dershowitz states that police lying is well known by actors in the criminal justice system. He clearly illustrates these as the "Rules of the Justice Game." In part, the rules include:

Rule IV: Almost all police lie about whether they violated the Constitution in order to convict guilty defendants.

Rule V: All prosecutors, judges, and defense attorneys are aware of Rule IV.

Rule VI: Many prosecutors implicitly encourage police to lie about whether they violated the Constitution in order to convict guilty defendants.

Rule VII: All judges are aware of Rule VI.

Rule VIII: Most trial judges pretend to believe police officers who they know are lying.

Rule IX: All appellate judges are aware of Rule VIII, yet many pretend to believe the trial judges who pretend to believe the lying police officers. (Dershowitz, 1983: xxi-xxii).

This may be an extreme position. However, other criminal defense attorneys believe that the police will lie in court. In fact, one study concluded that "the possibility of police perjury is a part of the working reality of criminal defense attorneys" (Kittel, 1986:20). Fifty-seven percent of the 277 attorneys surveyed in this study believed that police perjury takes place very often or often (Kittel, 1986:16). Police officers themselves have reported that they believe their fellow officers will lie in court (Barker, 1978). An English barrister believes that police officers have perjured themselves on an average of three out of ten trials (Wolchover, 1986).

As part of the research for this chapter, one of the authors asked an Internal Affairs (IA) investigator of a major U.S. police department about officer lying:

Carter: During the course of IA investigations, do you detect officers lying to you?

IA Investigator: Yes, all the time. They'll lie about anything, everything.

Carter: Why is that?

IA Investigator: To tell me what I want to hear. To help them get out of trouble. To make themselves feel better—rationalizing I guess. They're so used to lying on the job, I guess it becomes second nature.

An analysis of deviant lies reveals that the intent of the officer in telling deviant lies may be either in support of perceived legitimate goals or illegitimate goals.

Deviant Lies in Support of Perceived Legitimate Goals

The deviant lies told by the officer to achieve perceived legitimate goals usually occur to put criminals in jail, prevent crime, and perform various other policing responsibilities. The police officer believes that because of his/her unique experiences in dealing with criminals and the public he/she knows the guilt or innocence of those arrested (Manning, 1978). Frequently, officers feel this way independently of any legal standards. However, the final determination of guilt or innocence is in the judicial process. The officer(s), convinced that the suspect is factually guilty of the offense, may believe that necessary elements of legal guilt are lacking, e.g., no probable cause for a "stop," no *Miranda* warning, not enough narcotics for a felony offense, etc. Therefore, the officer feels that he/she must supply the missing elements. One police officer told one of the authors that it is often necessary to "fluff up the evidence" to get a search warrant or ensure conviction. The officer will attest to facts, statements or evidence which never occurred or occurred in a different fashion. Obviously when he/she does this under oath, perjury has then been committed. Once a matter of record, the perjury must continue for the officer to avoid facing disciplinary action and even criminal prosecution.

Charges were dropped in a case against an accused cop killer and three Boston police officers were suspended with pay pending a perjury investigation. The perjury involved a Boston detective who "invented" an informant. The detective maintained that the informant gave critical information which was cited in the affidavit for a search warrant (*New York Times*, 1989:K9). The "no knock" search warrant's execution led to the death of a Boston detective. The officer(s) who lies in these instances must employ creative writing skills in official reports to ensure that the written chronology of events is consistent with criminal procedures regardless of what actually occurred.

These lies are rationalized by the officer because they are necessary to ensure that criminals do not get off on technicalities. A central reason for these deviant lies is officer frustration. There is frustration with the criminal justice system because of the inability of courts and corrections to handle large caseloads. Frustration with routinized practices of plea negotiations and intricate criminal procedures that the officer may not fully understand. The officer sees the victims of crimes and has difficulty in reconciling the harm done to them with the wide array of due process protections afforded to defendants. Nevertheless, the officer has fallen into "the avenging angel syndrome" in which the end justifies the means. The officer can easily rationalize lying and perjury to accomplish what is perceived to be the right thing. The officer's views are shortsighted and provincial. There is no recognition that such behavior is a threat to civil liberties and that perjury is as fundamentally improper as the criminal behavior of the accused.

Deviant Lies In Support of Illegitimate Goals

Lies in this category are told to effect an act of corruption or to protect the officer from organizational discipline or civil and/or criminal liability. Deviant lies may be manifest in police perjury as the officer misrepresents material elements of an arrest or search in order to "fix" a criminal prosecution for a monetary reward. Lying and/or perjury in court is an absolute necessity in departments in which corrupt acts occur on a regular basis. Sooner or later every police officer who engages in corrupt acts or observes corrupt acts on the part of other officers will face the possibility of having to lie under oath to protect him/herself, or fellow officers. Skolnick has suggested that perjury and corruption are both systematic forms of police deviance which occur for the same sort of reason: "Police know that other police are on the take and police know that other police are perjuring themselves" (Skolnick, 1982:42).

It is also possible that other forms of police deviance will lead to deviant lying. For example, the officer who commits an act of police brutality may have to lie on the report to his/her supervisor and during testimony to avoid the possibility of criminal sanction, a civil lawsuit, or department charges. The officer who has sex, sleeps or drinks on duty may have to lie to a supervisor or internal affairs to avoid department discipline. The officer who causes an injury or death to a suspect in a way that is not strictly according to law or police policy may have to lie to protect himself or his fellow officers from criminal and/or civil liability.

As an illustration, one of the authors assisted a police department which was under a federal court injunction related to an extensive number of civil rights violations for excessive force and harassment. During one series of inquiries, the following conversation occurred:

> *Carter:* Did you ever talk to other accused officers before giving your deposition in these cases?
>
> *Officer:* Of course. [NOTE: The tone of the response was almost incredulous.]
>
> *Carter:* Would you discuss the facts of the allegation?
>
> *Officer:* Sure. We had to be sure our stories were straight.

The implications from these statements and the continued conversations were clear: Officers were willing to lie during the sworn deposition to protect themselves and others. They would swear to the truth of facts that were plainly manufactured for their protection. Moreover, their remorse was not that they lied, but that they got caught in misconduct. Similarly, a police chief in West Virginia recently told a federal judge he lied to investigators in order to cover up for four officers accused of beating handcuffed prisoners (*Law Enforcement News,* March 15, 1989, p. 2). Again, the illegitimate goal of "protection" surfaces as a motive for lying.

The typical police bureaucracy is a complex organization with a myriad of rules and regulations. The informal organization, including many supervisors, overlooks these rules until someone decides to "nail someone." Given the plethora of rules and regulations in most large urban police departments, it is virtually impossible to work a shift without violating one. It may be common practice to eat a free meal, leave one's beat for personal reasons, not wear one's hat when out of the car, to live outside the city limits, etc. All of these acts may be forbidden by a policy, rule, or regulation. When a supervisor decides to discipline an officer for violating one of these acts, the officer, and often fellow officers, may resort to lies to protect themselves and each other. After all, such "minor" lies are inherent in the "Blue Code." Manning observes that rule enforcement by police supervisors represents a mock bureaucracy where ritualistic and punitive enforcement is applied after the fact (Manning, 1978). The consequences of these seemingly understandable lies can be disastrous when discovered. The officer(s) may be suspended, reduced in rank, or dismissed. The same organization where members routinely engage in acceptable, tolerated, and deviant lying practices can take on a very moralistic attitude when it discovers that one of its own has told a lie to avoid internal discipline. Nevertheless, the lies told in these examples are told in support of the illegitimate goal of avoiding departmental discipline.

CONCLUSION

The effects of lying, even those which are acceptable or tolerated, are multifold. Lies can and do create distrust within the organization. When the public learns members of the police department lie or engage in deceptive practices, this can undermine citizen confidence in the police. As we have seen, some police lies violate citizens' civil rights and other lies are told to cover up civil rights violations. Police lying contributes to police misconduct and corruption, and undermines the organization's discipline system. Furthermore, deviant police lies undermine the effectiveness of the criminal justice system. What should the organization do to deal with the reality of police lies? An important first step is to establish a meaningful code of ethics and value statements for the organization. Importantly, this should go beyond the development of documents. The operational and managerial levels of the police department must know that the code of ethics and value statements are guides to police moral and ethical behavior. There should never become another set of rules and procedures to be used when necessary to "nail someone." Once ethics and values are embodied, it is essential to develop a support structure consisting of directives, training, and supervision. This will create a moral environment throughout the organization and establish parameters of acceptable behavior giving notice to employees about management.

References

Barker, T. (1978). "An Empirical Study of Police Deviance Other Than Corruption," *Journal of Police Science and Administration* 6, 3: 264-272.

Barker, T. (1977). "Peer Group Support for Police Occupational Deviance," *Criminology* 15, 3: 353-366.

Bittner, E. (1971). *The Functions of the Police in Modern Society*, Washington, DC: U.S. Government Printing Office.

Birmingham Post-Herald (1988). "Sheriff's Chemist Makes Crack," April 19:B2.

Black, H.C. (1983). *Black's Law Dictionary*, Abridged 5th Ed. St. Paul, MN: West Publishing Co.

Cooper, G.R. and R.R. Belair (1978). *Privacy and Security of Criminal History Information: Privacy and the Media*. U.S. Department of Justice. Washington, DC: U.S. Government Printing Office.

Dershowitz, A.M. (1983). *The Best Defense*, New York: Vintage Books.

Formby, W.A. and J.O. Smykla (1984). "Attitudes and Perception Toward Drinking and Driving: A Simulation of Citizen Awareness," *Journal of Police Science and Administration* 12, 4: 379-384.

George, J.B. (1966). *Constitutional Limitations on Evidence in Criminal Cases*. Ann Arbor, Michigan: Institute of Continuing Legal Education.

Goldstein, H. (1977). *Policing A Free Society*. Cambridge, MA: Ballinger Publishing Company.

Inbau, F.E., J.E. Reid and J.P. Buckley (1986). *Criminal Interrogation and Confessions*, 3rd Ed., Baltimore, MD: Williams and Wilkins.

Kittel, N.G. (1986). "Police Perjury: Criminal Defense Attorneys' Perspective," *American Journal of Criminal Justice* XI, 1 (Fall): 11-22.

Klockars, C.B. (1980). "The Dirty Harry Problem," *The Annals*, 452 (November): 33-47.

Law Enforcement News (1989). March 15: 2.

Manning, P.K. (1978). "Lying, Secrecy and Social Control." In P.K. Manning and J. Van Maanen (Eds.) *Policing: A View from the Street*, Santa Monica, CA: Goodyear Publishing Co. 238-255.

Marx, G.T. (1985). "Who Really Gets Stung? Some Issues Raised By The New Police Undercover Work." In F.A. Elliston and M. Feldberg (Eds.) *Moral Issues in Police Work*. Totowa, NJ: Rowan and Allanheld.

New York Times (1989). "Dead Officer, Dropped Charges: A Scandal in Boston." March 20: K9.

Pistone, J.D. (1987). *Donnie Brasco: My Undercover Life in the Mafia*. New York, NY: Nail Books.

Skolnick, J. (1982). "Deception By Police," *Criminal Justice Ethics*, 1, 2 (Summer/Fall): 40-54.

Stitt, B.G. and G.G. James (1985). "Entrapment: An Ethical Analysis." In F.A. Elliston and M. Feldberg (Eds.) *Moral Issues in Police Work*. Totowa, NJ: Rowan and Allanheld.

Wolchover, D. (1986). "Police Perjury in London." *New Law Journal* (Feb.): 180-184.

Discussion Questions

1. What are the different types of lying (deception) by police? How could one form contribute to another? What is the best course of action for a department to take concerning police lying? Explain.

2. Examine deviant police lying from both deontological and utilitarian perspectives. How does deviant police lying differ under each system? Which system might consider motive?

3. Should police be allowed to break the law in order to apprehend a violent criminal? How do we balance individual rights with police discretion and deception? What is the difference between encouragement and entrapment?

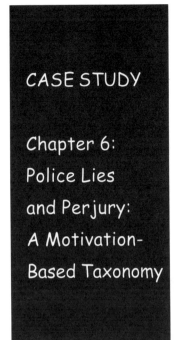

CASE STUDY

Chapter 6:
Police Lies
and Perjury:
A Motivation-
Based Taxonomy

SUPER COP

Bill Hammonds's name appears once again on the "Best Detective of the Month" roster.

It is the sixth time in a row that Hammonds has received the honor. Hammonds was promoted from patrol to investigations just nine months ago.

"How does he do it?" you ask yourself aloud.

"Hammonds is doing a damn good job, isn't he?" Pete Rowe comments as he steps up to the bulletin board.

"That's not the word for it. Look at the difference in all of our case loads and conviction rates and then look at Hammonds'. His conviction rate is almost 80 percent while the average is around 20 percent," you point out.

"Well, I've heard that he's got a whole army of snitches working for him," Pete says as he walks away from the bulletin board.

"Snitches" is a slang word for informants. Without good informants, an investigator can do very little with an investigation. But it takes time for an investigator to develop good informants.

Hammonds did not seem to have any trouble developing informants during his first weeks as an investigator. It took you almost two months to develop a couple of snitches, and Hammonds seemed to have an "army" of snitches working for him during the first several weeks of his detective assignment.

From Larry S. Miller and Michael Braswell, *Human Relations and Police Work*, 4th ed. (Prospect Heights, IL: Waveland Press), 1997. Reprinted with permission.

"How does he do it?" you ask yourself again.

That afternoon your captain calls you into his office. "Mike, how's that investigation coming on the country club burglary?" the captain asks.

"It's a pretty tight case, Captain. I've got a couple of leads and I'm waiting for a response from the crime lab," you explain.

"I've been getting some pressure up the ranks to get this thing resolved. You've been working on the case for about two weeks. I'm going to put both you and Hammonds on the case and see if we can't get this thing solved," the captain says.

Walking out of the captain's office, you feel as though you have been slapped in the face. It seems obvious that the captain feels you are not as competent as Hammonds would be in solving the case. It is an insult, but one you will have to live with.

The next day, Hammonds walks up to you, sporting a grin.

"Mike, I hear you're having trouble with a burglary at the country club?" Bill asks, somewhat snidely.

"Very funny, Hammonds. C'mon, let's contact some of your snitches and see if they know anything," you retort as you grab your overcoat.

Hammonds will not allow you to talk with any of his informants. Hammonds always insists that you stay in the car while he gets out to talk. You are not very concerned because several other detectives are "protective" of their sources and do not like others around while talking with them. After a while, you begin to wonder what kind of informants Hammonds has working for him. Almost all of Hammonds' snitches seem to be either drug users or pushers.

"Now all we have to do is sit back and wait for a phone call," Hammonds says as he begins to drive back to the station.

"Did any of your snitches know anything?" you ask.

"No, not yet. But one will turn up something real soon," Hammonds says as he begins to drive back to the station.

That afternoon, Hammonds comes into the detective office with a warrant in his hand. "This is it, Mike. I've got a warrant for Jake Lennan, the one that broke into the country club." Hammonds says as he waves the warrant in your face.

"Ok, Hammonds, now tell me how you did it," you say, looking over the warrant.

"It was easy, Mike. My snitches came through with the information. Besides, I think there is a real good chance that Mr. Jake Lennan will want to talk and confess to the break-in as well as return the stolen property," Hammonds comments.

You look at Hammonds in disbelief. Hammonds, noticing the expression on your face, continues to explain.

"Look, if this Jake guy doesn't talk and confess I'd sure hate to be in his shoes when my snitches get hold of him."

Hammonds' last statement puts a thought in your mind. Apparently Hammonds is using his informants to do the investigative work for him. Hammonds' informants may even be using force on suspects like Jake Lennan to confess and return stolen property. It seems Pete was right about Hammonds having an army of snitches. You begin to wonder what Hammonds is giving his informants in return for their services.

"What're you paying your snitches for doing your work for you?" you ask with increasing skepticism.

"Nothing much. I may let them slide on a few things they may be involved with," Hammonds responds as he turns and walks away.

It is becoming more apparent to you that Hammonds may be solving cases by using his informants to do the investigation work, as well as engaging in other inappropriate activities. Hammonds' use of drug addicts and pushers as informants led you to other possible conclusions. He could be ignoring violations of narcotics laws by his informants in return for information and services. You decide to confront Hammonds with your suspicions.

"Well, why not?" I'm solving more cases than anyone else here. Why not let snitches slide on some things in return for good convictions? I haven't put one thug in jail that didn't deserve to go. It's throwing back the little fish for the big ones," Hammonds argues.

Hammonds continues to explain to you how he has been using his informants to "catch" the crooks and make them confess to their crimes.

As you think about what Hammonds said, you wonder if that is the way an investigation should be handled. His argument seems to have some merit and does produce results. It does not seem right to you that a police officer should ignore the illegal activities of one group and arrest others. You decide to ask your captain.

"Look, Mike, in our business it's give and take. We have to look at our priorities. We have to look at the worst offenses and let the others slide. We can use that to our advantage the way Hammonds is doing. We've all done it as investigators—maybe not to the extent that Hammonds has, but if all of us would take that advantage, we would solve more cases," your captain explains.

The captain's statement still does not satisfy you. You still believe Hammonds' methods are unethical, even if "that's the way it is" in detective work.

You wonder what you will have to do to become "Detective of the Month."

Questions:

1. Justify the actions of Hammonds from a utilitarian perspective.

2. What types of problems may be generated by Hammonds's actions?

3. Do you agree with the Captain and Hammonds?

CHAPTER 7

The Ethics of Deceptive Interrogation

Jerome H. Skolnick & Richard A. Leo

INTRODUCTION

As David Rothman and Aryeh Neier have recently reported, "third degree" police practices—torture and severe beatings—remain commonplace in India, the world's largest democracy.[1] Police brutality during interrogation flourishes because it is widely accepted by the middle classes.[2] Although this may seem uncivilized to most Americans, it was not so long ago that American police routinely used physical violence to extract admissions from criminal suspects.[3] Since the 1960s, and especially since *Miranda* [*v. Arizona*], police brutality during interrogation has virtually disappeared in America. Although one occasionally reads about or hears reports of physical violence during custodial questioning,[4] police observers and critics agree that the use of physical coercion during interrogation is now exceptional.

> ## KEY CONCEPTS:
> fabricated evidence
>
> Fourteenth Amendment
>
> interrogation
>
> interview
>
> *Miranda v. Arizona*
>
> role playing
>
> slippery slope argument
>
> Wickersham Report

This transformation occurred partly in response to the influential Wickersham report,[5] which disclosed widespread police brutality in the United States during the 1920s; partly in response to a thoughtful and well-intentioned police professionalism, as exemplified by Fred Inbau and his associates; and partly in

Jerome H. Skolnick and Richard Leo, "The Ethics of Deceptive Interrogation," (as appeared in *Criminal Justice Ethics*, Volume II, Number 1 [Winter/Spring 1992] pp. 3-12). Reprinted by permission of the Institute for Criminal Justice Ethics, 899 Tenth Avenue, New York, NY 10019-1029.

response to changes in the law which forbade police to "coerce" confessions but allowed them to elicit admissions by deceiving suspects who have waived their right to remain silent. Thus, over the last fifty to sixty years, the methods, strategies, and consciousness of American police interrogators have been transformed: psychological persuasion and manipulation have replaced physical coercion as the most salient and defining features of contemporary police interrogation. Contemporary police interrogation is routinely deceptive.[6] As it is taught and practiced today, interrogation is shot through with deception. Police are instructed to, are authorized to—and do—trick, lie, and cajole to elicit so-called "voluntary" confessions.

Police deception, however, is more subtle, complex, and morally puzzling than physical coercion. Although we share a common moral sense in the West that police torture of criminal suspects is so offensive as to be impermissible—a sentiment recently reaffirmed by the violent images of the Rodney King beating—the propriety of deception by police is not nearly so clear. The law reflects this ambiguity by being inconsistent, even confusing. Police are permitted to pose as drug dealers, but not to use deceptive tactics to gain entry without a search warrant, nor are they permitted to falsify an affidavit to obtain a search warrant.

The acceptability of deception seems to vary inversely with the level of the criminal process. Cops are permitted to, and do, lie routinely during investigation of crime, especially when, working as "undercovers," they pretend to have a different identity.[7] Sometimes they may, and sometimes may not, lie when conducting custodial interrogations. Investigative and interrogatory lying are each justified on utilitarian crime control grounds. But police are never supposed to lie as witnesses in the courtroom, although they may lie for utilitarian reasons similar to those permitting deception at earlier stages.[8] In this article, we focus on the interrogatory stage of police investigation, considering (1) how and why the rather muddled legal theory authorizing deceptive interrogation developed; (2) what deceptive interrogation practices police, in fact, engage in; and—a far more difficult question—(3) whether police should ever employ trickery and deception during interrogation in a democratic society valuing fairness in its judicial processes.

THE JURISPRUDENCE OF POLICE INTERROGATION

The law of confessions is regulated by the Fifth, Sixth, and Fourteenth Amendments. Historically, the courts have been concerned almost exclusively with the use of *coercion* during interrogation. Although a coerced confession has been inadmissible in federal cases since the late nineteenth century, the Supreme Court did not proscribe physically coercive practices in state cases until 1936.[9] In *Brown v. Mississippi*, three black defendants were repeatedly whipped and pummeled until they confessed. This was the first in a series of state cases in which the Court held that confessions could not be "coerced," but had to be "voluntary" to be admitted into evidence.[10]

Whether a confession meets that elusive standard is to be judged by "the totality of the circumstances." Under that loose and subjective guideline, an admission is held up against "all the facts" to decide whether it was the product of a "free and rational will" or whether the suspect's will was "overborne" by police pressure. Over the years, however, certain police practices have been designated as presumptively coercive. These include physical force, threats of harm or punishment, lengthy or incommunicado interrogation, denial of food and/or sleep, and promises of leniency.[11] In 1940, the Supreme Court ruled—in a case in which a suspect was first threatened with mob violence, then continuously questioned by at least four officers for five consecutive days—that psychological pressure could also be coercive.[12]

One reason for excluding admissions obtained through coercion is their possible falsity. But, beginning with *Lisenba v. California*[13] in 1941, and followed by *Ashcraft v. Tennessee*[14] three years later, the Supreme Court introduced the criterion of *fairness* into the law. Whether in the context of searches or interrogations, evidence gathered by police methods that "shock the conscience" of the community or violate a fundamental standard of fairness are to be excluded, regardless of reliability.[15] This rationale is sometimes twinned with a third purpose: deterring offensive or unlawful police conduct.

In its watershed *Miranda* decision, the Supreme Court in 1966, prescribed specific limitations on custodial interrogation by police.[16] The five-to-four majority deplored a catalog of manipulative and potentially coercive psychological tactics employed by police to elicit confessions from unrepresented defendants. In essence, the court could not reconcile ideas such as "fairness" and "voluntariness" with the increasingly sophisticated and psychologically overbearing methods of interrogation. In response, it fashioned the now familiar prophylactic rules to safeguard a criminal defendant's Fifth Amendment right against testimonial compulsion. As part of its holding, *Miranda* requires that (1) police advise a suspect of her right to remain silent and her right to an attorney, and (2) the suspect "voluntarily, knowingly and intelligently" have waived these rights before custodial interrogation can legally commence. An interrogation is presumed to be coercive unless a waiver is obtained. Once obtained, however, the "due process-voluntariness" standard governs the admissibility of any confession evidence. In practice, once a waiver is obtained, most of the deceptive tactics deplored by the majority become available to the police.

In retrospect, *Miranda* seems to be an awkward compromise between those who argue that a waiver cannot be made "intelligently" without the advice of an attorney, who would usually advise her client to remain silent, and those who would have preferred to retain an unmodified voluntariness standard because police questioning is "a particularly trustworthy instrument for screening out the innocent and fastening on the guilty," and because the government's obligation is "not to counsel the accused but to question him."[17]

In sum, then, three sometimes competing principles underlie the law of confessions: first, the truth-finding rationale, which serves the goal of *reliability* (convicting an innocent person is worse than letting a guilty one go free); second, the substantive due process or *fairness* rationale, which promotes the goal of the system's integrity; and third, the related *deterrence* principle, which proscribes offensive or lawless police conduct.

The case law of criminal procedure has rarely, however, and often only indirectly, addressed the troubling issue of trickery and deceit during interrogation. We believe this is the key issue in discussing interrogation since, we have found, interrogation usually implies deceiving and cajoling the suspect.

Police deception that intrudes upon substantive constitutional rights is disallowed. For example, the Supreme Court has ruled that an officer cannot trick a suspect into waiving his *Miranda* rights. But apart from these constraints, the use of trickery and deception during interrogation is regulated solely by the due process clause of the Fourteenth Amendment, and is proscribed, on a case-by-case basis, only when it violates a fundamental conception of fairness or is the product of egregious police misconduct. The courts have offered police few substantive guidelines regarding the techniques of deception during interrogation. Nor have the courts successfully addressed the relation between fairness and the lying of police, or the impact of police lying on the broader purposes of the criminal justice system, such as convicting and punishing the guilty. As we shall see, the relations among lying, conceptions of fairness, and the goals of the criminal justice system raise intriguing problems.

A TYPOLOGY OF INTERROGATORY DECEPTION

Because police questioning remains shrouded in secrecy, we know little about what actually happens during interrogation. Police rarely record or transcribe interrogation sessions.[18] Moreover, only two observational studies of police interrogation have been reported, and both are more than two decades old.[19] Most articles infer from police training manuals what must transpire during custodial questioning. Our analysis is based on Richard Leo's dissertation research. It consists of a reading of the leading police training manuals from 1942 to the present; from attending local and national interrogation training seminars and courses; from listening to tape-recorded interrogations; from studying interrogation transcripts; and from ongoing interviews with police officials.

A. "Interview" versus "Interrogate"

The Court in *Miranda* ruled that warnings must be given to a suspect who is in custody, or whose freedom has otherwise been significantly deprived. However, police will question suspects in a "non-custodial" setting—which is defined more by the suspect's state of mind than by the location of the questioning—so as to circumvent the necessity of rendering warnings. This is the most fundamental, and perhaps the most overlooked, deceptive stratagem police employ. By telling the suspect that he is free to leave at any time, and by having him acknowledge that he is voluntarily answering their questions, police will transform what would otherwise be considered an interrogation into a non-custodial interview. Thus, somewhat paradoxically, courts have ruled that police questioning outside of the station may be custodial,[20] just as police questioning inside the station may be non-custodial.[21] The line between the two is the "objective" restriction on the suspect's freedom. Recasting the interrogation as an interview is the cleanest deceptive police tactic since it virtually removes police questioning from the realm of judicial control.

B. *Miranda* Warnings

When questioning qualifies as "custodial," however, police must recite the familiar warnings. The Court declared in *Miranda* that police cannot trick or deceive a suspect into waiving *Miranda* rights.[22] The California Supreme Court has additionally ruled that police cannot "soften up" a suspect prior to administering the warnings.[23] However, police routinely deliver the *Miranda* warnings in a flat, perfunctory tone of voice to communicate that the warnings are merely a bureaucratic ritual. Although it might be inevitable that police would deliver *Miranda* warnings unenthusiastically, investigators whom we have interviewed say that they *consciously* recite the warnings in a manner intended to heighten the likelihood of eliciting a waiver. It is thus not surprising that police are so generally successful in obtaining waivers.[24]

C. Misrepresenting the Nature or Seriousness of the Offense

Once the suspect waives, police may misrepresent the nature or seriousness of the offense. They may, for example, tell a suspect that the murder victim is still alive, hoping that this will compel the suspect to talk. Or police may exaggerate the seriousness of the offense—overstating, for example, the amount of money embezzled—so that the suspect feels compelled to confess to a smaller role in the offense. Or the police may suggest that they are only interested in obtaining admissions to one crime, when in fact they are really investigating another crime. For example, in a recent case, *Colorado v. Spring*, federal agents interrogated a suspect on firearms charges and parlayed his confession into an additional, seemingly unrelated and unimportant, admission of first-degree murder.[25] Despite their pretense to the contrary, the federal agents were actually investigating the murder, not the firearms charge. This tactic was upheld by the Supreme Court.

D. Role Playing: Manipulative Appeals to Conscience

Effective interrogation often requires that the questioner feign different personality traits or act out a variety of roles.[26] The interrogator routinely projects sympathy, understanding, and compassion in order to play the role of the suspect's friend. The interrogator may also try to play the role of a brother or father figure, or even to act as a therapeutic or religious counselor to encourage the confession. The best-known role interrogators may act out is, of course, the good cop/bad cop routine, often played out by a single officer. While acting out these roles, the investigator importunes—sometimes relentlessly—the suspect to confess for the good of her case, her family, society, or conscience. These tactics generate an illusion of intimacy between the suspect and the officer while downplaying the adversarial aspects of interrogation.

The courts have routinely upheld the legitimacy of such techniques—which are among the police's most effective in inducing admissions—except when such role-playing or manipulative appeals to conscience can be construed as "coercive," as when, for example, an officer implies that God will punish the suspect for not confessing.[27]

E. Misrepresenting the Moral Seriousness of the Offense

Misrepresentation of the moral seriousness of an offense is at the heart of interrogation methods propounded by Inbau, Reid, and Buckley's influential police training manual.[28] Interrogating officials offer suspects excuses or moral justifications for their misconduct by providing the suspect with an external attribution of blame that will allow him to save face while confessing. Police may, for example, attempt to convince an alleged rapist that he was only trying to show the victim love or that she was really "asking for it"; or they may persuade an alleged embezzler that blame for her actions is attributable to low pay or poor working conditions. In *People v. Adams*, for example, the officer elicited the initial admission by convincing the suspect that it was the gun, not the suspect, that had done the actual shooting.[29] Widely upheld by the courts, this tactic is advertised by police training manuals and firms as one of their most effective.

F. The Use of Promises

The systematic persuasion—the wheedling, cajoling, coaxing, and importuning—employed to induce conversation and elicit admissions often involves, if only implicitly or indirectly, the use of promises. Although promises of leniency have been presumed to be coercive since 1897, courts continue to permit vague and indefinite promises.[30] The admissibility of a promise thus seems to turn on its specificity. For example, in *Miller v. Fenton*, the suspect was repeatedly told that he had mental problems and thus needed psychological treatment rather than punishment. Although this approach implicitly suggested a promise of leniency, the court upheld the validity of the resulting confession.[31]

Courts have also permitted officers to tell a suspect that his conscience will be relieved only if he confesses, or that they will inform the court of the suspect's cooperation, or that "a showing of remorse" will be a mitigating factor, or that they will help the suspect out in every way they can if he confesses.[32] Such promises are deceptive insofar as they create expectations that will not be met. Since interrogating officials are single-mindedly interested in obtaining admissions and confessions, they rarely feel obliged to uphold any of their promises.

G. Misrepresentations of Identity

A police agent may try to conceal his identity, pretending to be someone else, while interrogating a suspect. In *Leyra v. Denno*, the suspect was provided with a physician for painful sinus attacks he began to experience after several days of unsuccessful interrogation.[33] But the physician was really a police psychiatrist, who repeatedly assured the defendant that he had done no wrong and would be let off easily. The suspect subsequently confessed, but the Supreme Court ruled here that the confession was inadmissible. It would be equally impermissible for a police official or agent to pretend to be a suspect's lawyer or priest. However, in a very recent case, *Illinois v. Perkins*, a prison inmate, Perkins, admitted a murder to an undercover police officer who, posing as a returned escapee, had been placed in his cellblock.[34] The Rehnquist Court upheld the admissibility of the confession. Since Perkins was in jail for an offense unrelated to the murder to which he confessed, the Rehnquist Court said, Perkins was not, for *Miranda* purposes, "in custody." Nor, for the same reason, were his Sixth Amendment *Massiah* rights violated.[35] Thus, the profession or social group with which an undercover officer or agent identifies during the actual questioning may—as a result of professional disclosure rules or cultural norms—be more significant to the resulting legal judgment than the deceptive act itself.[36]

H. Fabricated Evidence

Police may confront the suspect with false evidence of his guilt. This may involve one or more of five gambits. One is to falsely inform the suspect that an accomplice has identified him. Another is to falsely state that existing physical evidence—such as fingerprints, bloodstains, or hair samples—confirm his guilt. Yet another is to assert that an eyewitness or the actual victim has identified and implicated him. Perhaps the most dramatic physical evidence ploy is to stage a line-up, in which a coached witness falsely identifies the suspect. Finally, one of the most common physical evidence ploys is to have the suspect take a lie-detector test and regardless of the results—which are scientifically unreliable and invalid in any event—inform the suspect that the polygraph confirms his guilt.[37] In the leading case on the use of police trickery, *Frazier v. Cupp*, the Supreme Court upheld the validity of falsely telling a suspect that his crime partner had confessed.[38]

THE CONSEQUENCES OF DECEPTION

Although lying is, as a general matter, considered immoral, virtually no one is prepared to forbid it categorically. The traditional case put to the absolutist is that of the murderer chasing a fleeing innocent victim, whose whereabouts are known by a third party. Should the third party sacrifice the innocent victim to the murderer for the cause of truth? Few of us would say that she should. We thus assume a utilitarian standard regarding deception. So, too, with respect to police interrogation.

Interrogatory deception is an exceedingly difficult issue, about which we share little collective feeling. How are we to balance our respect for truth and fairness with our powerful concern for public safety and the imposition of just deserts? We are always guided by underlying intuitions about the kind of community we want to foster and in which we want to live. Which is worse in the long run—the excesses of criminals or the excesses of authorities?

Few of us would countenance torture by police in the interests of those same values. One reason is that violence may produce false confessions. As Justice Jackson observed in his dissent in *Ashcraft*: ". . . [N]o officer of the law will resort to cruelty if truth is what he is seeking."[39] But that is only partly correct. Cruelty can also yield incontrovertible physical evidence. We reject torture for another reason—we find it uncivilized, conscience-shocking, unfair, so most of us are repelled by it. That leads to a third reason for opposing torture. If effective law enforcement requires public trust and cooperation, as the recent movement toward community-oriented policing suggests, police who torture can scarcely be expected to engender such confidence.

What about police deception? Does it lead to false confessions? Is it unfair? Does it undermine public confidence in the police? A recent and fascinating capital case in the Florida Court of Appeal, *Florida v. Cayward*, the facts of which are undisputed, is relevant to the above questions.[40] The defendant, a nineteen-year-old male, was suspected of sexually assaulting and smothering his five-year-old niece. Although he was suspected of the crime, the police felt they had too little evidence to charge him. So they interviewed him, eventually advised him of his rights, and obtained a written waiver.

Cayward maintained his innocence for about two hours. Then the police showed him two false reports, which they had fabricated with the knowledge of the state's attorney. Purportedly scientific, one report used Florida Department of Criminal Law Enforcement stationery; another used the stationery of Life Codes, Inc., a testing organization. The false reports established that his semen was found on the victim's underwear. Soon after, Cayward confessed.

Should this deception be considered as akin to lying to a murderer about the whereabouts of the victim? Or should police trickery, and especially the falsification of documents, be considered differently? We unsystematically put this hypothetical question to friends in Berkeley and asked about it in a discussion with scholars-in-residence at the Rockefeller Study Center in Bellagio, Italy. The answers, we discovered, revealed no common moral intuition. For some, the answer was clear—in either direction. "Of course the police should lie to catch the murdering rapist of a child," said one. "I don't want to live in a society where police are allowed to lie and to falsify evidence," said another. Most were ambivalent, and all were eager to know how the Florida court resolved the dilemma.

Citing *Frazier v. Cupp* and other cases, the court recognized "that police deception does not render a confession involuntary *per se*." Yet the court, deeply troubled by the police deception, distinguished between "verbal assertions and manufactured evidence." A "bright line" was drawn between the two on the following assumption: "It may well be that a suspect is more impressed and thereby more easily induced to confess when presented with tangible, official-looking reports as opposed to merely being told that some tests have implicated him."[41]

Although we do not know the accuracy of the conjecture, it assumes that false police assertions such as "Your fingerprints were found on the cash register" are rarely believed by suspects unless backed up by a false fingerprint report. But in these deception cases, we do not usually encounter prudent suspects who are skeptical of the police. Such suspects rarely, if ever, waive their constitutional rights to silence or to an attorney. As in *Cayward*, and many deception cases, the suspect, young or old, white or black, has naively waived his right to remain silent and to an attorney.

Would such a suspect disbelieve, for example, the following scenario? After two hours of questioning, the telephone rings. The detective answers, nods, looks serious, turns to the suspect and says: "We have just been informed by an independent laboratory that traces of your semen were found, by DNA tests, on the panties of the victim. What do you say to that?"

A verbal lie can be more or less convincing, depending upon the authority of the speaker, the manner of speaking, its contextual verisimilitude, and the gullibility of the listener. False documentation adds to verisimilitude, but a well-staged, carefully presented verbal lie can also convince. The decision in *Cayward*, however well-written and considered, is nevertheless bedeviled by the classic problem of determining whether Cayward's confession was "voluntary."

No *contested* confession, however, is ever voluntary in the sense of purging one's soul of guilt, as one would to a religious figure. "The principal value of confession may lie elsewhere, in its implicit reaffirmation of the moral order," writes Gerald M. Caplan. "The offender by his confession acknowledges that he is to blame, not the community."[42] That observation focuses on the offender. Sometimes that is true, sometimes it is not. Those who contest their confessions claim that they were unfairly pressured, and point to the tactics of the police. The claim is that the police violated the moral order by the use of unfair, shady, and thus wrongful tactics to elicit the confession. Had the police, for example, beaten a true confession out of Cayward, it would indeed seem perverse to regard his confession as a reaffirmation of the moral order.

If Cayward had been beaten, and had confessed, we would also be concerned that his confession was false. Assuming that all we know are the facts stated in the opinion, which say nothing of corroborating evidence or why Cayward was suspected, should we assume that his confession was necessarily true? However infrequent they may be, false confessions do occur. Moreover, they do not result only from physical abuse, threats of harm, or promises of leniency, as Fred Inbau and his associates have long maintained;[43] nor are they simply the result of police pressures that a fictionalized reasonable person would find "overbearing," as Joseph Grano's "mental freedom" test implies.[44] They may arise out of the manipulative tactics of influence and persuasion commonly taught in police seminars and practiced by police and used on Cayward.

Psychologists and others have recently begun to classify and analyze the logic and process of these false confessions,[45] which are among the leading causes of wrongful conviction.[46] Perhaps most interesting is the "coerced-internalized" false confession, which is elicited when the psychological pressures of interrogation cause an innocent person to temporarily internalize the message(s) of his or her interrogators and falsely believe himself to be guilty.[47] Although Cayward was probably factually guilty, he might have been innocent. Someone who is not altogether mature and mentally stable, as would almost certainly be true of a nineteen-year-old accused of smothering and raping his five-year-old niece, might also have a precarious and vague memory. When faced with fabricated, but supposedly incontrovertible, physical evidence of his guilt, he might falsely confess to a crime of which he has no recollection, as happened in the famous case of Peter Reilly,[48] and, more recently, in the Florida case of Tom Sawyer,[49] both of which were "coerced-internalized" false confessions.[50]

If Cayward was, in fact, guilty, as his confession suggests, the court was nevertheless willing to exclude it. Presumably, he will remain unpunished unless additional evidence can be produced. Characterizing the falsified evidence as an offense to "our traditional notions of due process of law," the Florida court was evidently alarmed by the *unfairness* of a system which allows police to "knowingly fabricate tangible documentation or physical evidence against an individual."[51] In addition to its "spontaneous distaste" for the conduct of the police, the court added a longer-range utilitarian consideration. Documents manufactured for such purposes, the court fears, may, because of their "potential of indefinite life and the facial appearance of authenticity,"[52] contaminate the entire criminal justice system. "A report falsified for interrogation purposes might well be retained and filed in police paperwork. Such reports have the potential of finding their way into the courtroom."[53] The court also worried that if false reports were allowed in evidence, police might be tempted to falsify all sorts of official documents "including warrants, orders and judgements," thereby undermining public respect for the authority and integrity of the judicial system.

Yet the slippery slope argument applies to lying as well as to falsification of documents. When police are permitted to lie in the interrogation context, why should they refrain from lying to judges when applying for warrants, from vio-lating internal police organization rules against lying, or from lying in the court-room? For example, an *Oakland Tribune* columnist, Alix Christie, recently received a letter from a science professor at the University of California at Berkeley who had served on an Alameda County (Oakland) murder jury. He was dismayed that a defendant, whom he believed to be guilty, had been acquit-ted because most of the jurors did not believe the police, even about how long it takes to drive from west to east Oakland. "The problem," writes Christie, "pre-dates Rodney King. It's one familiar to prosecutors fishing for jurors who don't fit the profile of people who distrust cops." She locates the problem in "the ugly fact that there are two Americas." In the first America, the one she was raised in, the police are the "good guys." In the other, police are viewed skeptically.

Police misconduct—and lying is ordinarily considered a form of miscon-duct—undermines public confidence and social cooperation, especially in the second America. People living in these areas often have had negative experiences with police, ranging from an aloof and legalistic policing "style" to corruption, and even to the sort of overt brutality that was captured on the videotape of the Rodney King beating in Los Angeles. Community-oriented policing is being implemented in a number of American police departments to improve trust and citizen cooperation by changing the attitudes of both police and public.

Police deception may thus engender a paradoxical outcome. Although affirmed in the interest of crime control values by its advocates like Fred Inbau—who, along with his co-author John Reid, has exerted a major influence on gen-erations of police interrogators—it may generate quite unanticipated conse-quences. Rarely do advocates of greater latitude for police to interrogate consider the effects of systematic lying on law enforcement's reputation for veracity. Police lying might not have mattered so much to police work in other times and places in American history. But today, when urban juries are increasingly composed of jurors disposed to be distrustful of police, deception by police during interroga-tion offers yet another reason for disbelieving law enforcement witnesses when they take the stand, thus reducing police effectiveness as controllers of crime.

Conservatives who lean toward crime control values do not countenance lying as a general matter. They approve of police deception as a necessity, mea-suring the cost of police deceit against the benefits of trickery for victims of crime and the safety of the general public. Police and prosecutors affirm deceit-ful interrogative practices not because they think these are admirable, but because they believe such tactics are necessary.[54]

The Florida police officers who fabricated evidence did so for the best of reasons. The victim was a five-year-old girl, and the crime was abhorrent and hard to prove. Nevertheless, the Florida court excluded the confession on due process grounds, arguing that police must be discouraged from fabricating false official documents. Many persons, but especially those who, like Fred Inbau, affirm the propriety of lying in the interrogatory context, tend to undervalue the significance of the long-term harms caused by such authorized deception: name-ly, that it tends to encourage further deceit, undermining the general norm against lying. And if it is true that the fabrication of documents "greatly lessens," as the Florida court says, "the respect the public has for the criminal justice system and for those sworn to uphold and enforce the law,"[55] doesn't that concern also apply to interrogatory lying?

There is an additional reason for opposing deceitful interrogation practices. It does happen that innocent people are convicted of crimes. Not as often, probably, as guilty people are set free, but it does happen. Should false evidence be presented, a suspect may confess in the belief that he will receive a lesser sentence. In a study in 1986, of wrongful conviction in felony cases, Ronald Huff and his colleagues conservatively estimated that nearly 6,000 false convictions occur every year in the United States.[56] Hugo Bedau and Michael Radelet, who subsequently studied 350 known miscarriages of justice in recent American history, identified false confessions as one of the leading sources of erroneous conviction of innocent individuals.[57]

There are no easy answers to these dilemmas, no easy lines to suggest when the need to keep police moral and honest brushes up against the imperatives of controlling crime. Phillip E. Johnson, who has proposed a thoughtful statutory replacement for the *Miranda* doctrine,[58] would not allow police to "intentionally misrepresent the amount of evidence against the suspect, or the nature and seriousness of the charges,"[59] as well as other, clearly more coercive tactics. But he would allow feigned sympathy or compassion, an appeal to conscience or values, and a statement to the suspect such as "A voluntary admission of guilt and sincere repentance may be given favorable consideration at the time of sentence."[60] Johnson states no formal principle for these distinctions, but does draw an intuitively sensible contrast between, on the one hand, outright *misrepresentations*, which might generalize to other venues and situations; and, on the other, *appeals* to self-interest or conscience, which seem to draw upon commonly held and morally acceptable values. If, however, as we have argued, rules for police conduct, and the values imparted through these rules, produce indirect, as well as direct, consequences for police practices and the culture of policing, Johnson's distinctions are persuasive. This resolution, we suggest, is quite different from the direction recently taken by the Rehnquist Court.

We have earlier argued that when courts allow police to deceive suspects for the good end of capturing criminals—even as, for example, in "sting" operations—they may be tempted to be untruthful when offering testimony. However we think we ought to resolve the problem of the ethics of deceptive interrogation, we need always to consider the unanticipated consequences of permitting police to engage in what would commonly be considered immoral conduct—such as falsifying evidence. The Supreme Court has moved in recent years to soften the control of police conduct in interrogation. In *Moran v. Burbine*, for example, the Court let stand a murder conviction even though the police had denied a lawyer—who had been requested by a third party, but without the suspect's knowledge, prior to his questioning—to the suspect during interrogation. The dissenters decried the "incommunicado questioning" and denounced the majority for having embraced "deception of the shabbiest kind."[61]

More recently, the notoriety of the Rodney King beating overshadowed the significance of the Rehnquist Court's most significant self-incrimination decision, *Arizona v. Fulminante*.[62] Here, a confession was obtained when a prison inmate, an ex-cop who was also an FBI informer, offered to protect Fulminante from prison violence, but only if he confessed to the murder of his daughter. In a sharply contested five-to-four opinion, the Court reversed the well-established doctrine that a coerced confession could never constitute "harmless error." Whether the ruling will be as important in *encouraging* police coercion of confessions as the King videotape will be in discouraging future street brutality remains to be seen. But in concert with other recent U.S. Supreme Court decisions that have cut back on the rights of defendants, the *Fulminante* decision may also send a message that police coercion is sometimes acceptable, and that a confession elicited by police deception will almost always be considered "voluntary."

NOTES

For helpful advice, criticism, and counsel, we would like to thank the following individuals: Albert Altschuler, Jack Greenberg, James Hahn, Sanford Kadish, Norman LaPera, Paul Mishkin, Robert Post, Peter Sarna, Jonathan Sither, Amy Toro, Jeremy Waldron, and, especially, Phillip Johnson.

1. Rothman & Neier, *India's Awful Prisons*, N.Y. Rev. Books, May 16, 1991, at 53-56.

2. Id. at 54.

3. *See* E. HOPKINS, OUR LAWLESS POLICE: A STUDY OF UNLAWFUL ENFORCEMENT (1931), and E. LAVINE, THE THIRD DEGREE: A DETAILED AND APPALLING EXPOSE OF POLICE BRUTALITY (1930).

4. "Confession at Gunpoint?" 20/20, ABC NEWS, March 29, 1991.

5. NATIONAL COMMISSION ON LAW OBSERVANCE AND ENFORCEMENT, LAWLESSNESS IN LAW ENFORCEMENT (1931).

6. Richard Leo, From Coercion to Deception: An Empirical Analysis of the Changing Nature of Modern Police Interrogation in America (paper presented at the Annual Meeting of the American Society of Criminology, Nov. 19-23, 1991).

7. *See* G. MARX, UNDERCOVER: POLICE SURVEILLANCE IN AMERICA (1988).

8. *See* Skolnick, *Deception by Police*, CRIMINAL JUSTICE ETHICS, Summer/Fall 1982, at 40-54.

9. Brown v. Mississippi, 297 U.S. 278 (1936).

10. Caplan, *Questioning Miranda*, 39 VANDERBILT LAW REVIEW 1417 (1985).

11. The Supreme Court's very recent ruling that coerced confessions may be "harmless error" will undermine this general rule. Arizona v. Fulminante, U.S. LEXIS 1854 (1991).

12. Chambers v. Florida, 309 U.S. 227 (1940).

13. 314 U.S. 219 (1941).

14. 322 U.S. 143 (1944).

15. *See* Rochin v. California, 342 U.S. 165 (1952), Spano v. New York, 360 U.S. 315 (1959), and Rogers v. Richmond, 365 U.S. 534 (1961).

16. Miranda v. Arizona, 384 U.S. 436 (1961).

17. Caplan, *supra* note 10, at 1422-23.

18. The state of Alaska requires, as a matter of state constitutional due process, that all custodial interrogations be electronically recorded. *See* Stephan v. State, 711 P.2d 1156 (1985).

19. Wald, et al., *Interrogations in New Haven: The Impact of Miranda*, 76 YALE L. J. 1519-1648 (1967), and N. MILNER, COURT AND LOCAL LAW ENFORCEMENT: THE IMPACT OF MIRANDA (1971).

20. Orozco v. Texas, 394 U.S. 324 (1969).

21. *See* Beckwith v. United States, 425 U.S. 341 (1976), Oregon v. Mathiason, 429 U.S. 492 (1977), and California v. Beheler, 463 U.S. 1121 (1983).

22. However, police may deceive an attorney who attempts to invoke a suspect's constitutional rights, as to whether the suspect will be interrogated, and the police do not have to inform the suspect that a third party has hired an attorney on his behalf. *People v. Moran*, 475 U.S. 412 (1986).

23. People v. Honeycutt, 570 P.2d 1050 (1977).

24. *See* O. STEPHENS, JR., THE SUPREME COURT AND CONFESSIONS OF GUILT 165-200 (1973) for a useful summary of studies assessing the impact of *Miranda* in New Haven, Los Angeles, Washington, D.C., Pittsburgh, Denver, and rural Wisconsin. These studies indicate that police obtain waivers from criminal suspects in most cases. Additionally, the Captain of the Criminal Investigation Division of the Oakland Police Department told one of the authors that detectives obtain waivers from criminal suspects in 85-90% of all cases involving interrogations.

25. Colorado v. Spring, 107 S.Ct.851 (1987).

26. Consider the following passage from R. Royal and S. Schutt, THE GENTLE ART OF INTERVIEWING AND INTERROGATION (1976): "To be truly proficient at interviewing or interrogation, one must possess the ability to portray a great variety of personality traits. The need to adjust character to harmonize with, or dominate, the many moods and traits of the subject is necessary. The interviewer/interrogator requires greater histrionic skill than the average actor. . . . The interviewer must be able to pretend anger, fear, joy, and numerous other emotions without affecting his judgment or revealing any personal emotion about the subject" (p.65).

27. People v. Adams, 143 Cal.App.3d 970 (1983).

28. F. INBAU, J. REID, & J. BUCKLEY, CRIMINAL INTERROGATION AND CONFESSIONS (1986).

29. People v. Adams, *supra* note 27.

30. Bram v. United States, 168 U.S. 532 (1897).

31. Miller v. Fenton, 796 F.2d 598 (1986).

32. Kaci & Rush, *At What Price Will We Obtain Confessions?* 71 JUDICATURE, 256-57 (1988).

33. Leyra v. Denno, 347 U.S. 556 (1954).

34. Illinois v. Perkins, 110 S.CT. 2394 (1990).

35. In Massiah v. United States, 377 U.S. 201 (1964), the U.S. Supreme Court held that post-indictment questioning of a defendant outside the presence of his lawyer violates the Sixth Amendment.

36. *See* Cohen, *Miranda and Police Deception in Interrogation: A Comment on Illinois v. Perkins*, CRIMINAL LAW BULLETIN 534-46 (1990).

37. *See* Skolnick, *Scientific Theory and Scientific Evidence: Analysis of Lie Detection*, 70 YALE LAW JOURNAL 694-728 (1961); and D. LYKKEN, A TREMOR IN THE BLOOD: USES AND ABUSES OF THE LIE DETECTOR (1981).

38. Frazier v. Cupp, 394 U.S. 731 (1969).

39. Ashcraft v. Tennessee, *supra* note 14, at 160.

40. Florida v. Cayward, 552 So.2d 971 (1989).

41. *Id.* at 977.

42. Caplan, *Miranda Revisited*, 93 YALE L.J. 1375 (1984).

43. F. INBAU, LIE-DETECTION AND CRIMINAL INTERROGATION (1942).

44. Grano, *Voluntariness, Free Will, and the Law of Confessions*, 65 VA. L. Rev. 859-945 (1979).

45. *See* Kassin & Wrightsman, *Confession Evidence*, in THE PSYCHOLOGY OF EVIDENCE AND TRIAL PROCEDURE (S. Kassin & L.Wrightsman eds. 1985). G. GUDJONSSON & N. CLARK, SUGGESTIBILITY IN POLICE INTERROGATION: A SOCIAL PSYCHO-LOGICAL MODEL (1985); Ofshe, *Coerced Confessions: The Logic of Seemingly Irrational Action*, 6 CULTIC STUD. J. 6-15 (1989); Gudjonsson, *The Psychology of False Confessions*, 57 MEDICO-LEGAL J. 93-110 (1989); R. Ofshe & R. Leo, The Social Psychology of Coerced-Internalized False Confessions (paper presented at the Annual Meetings of the American Sociological Association, August 23-27, 1991).

46. Bedau & Radelet, *Miscarriages of Justice in Potentially Capital Cases*, 40 STAN. L. Rev. 21-179 (1987).

47. Kassin & Wrightsman, *supra* note 45.

48. *See* J. BARTEL, A DEATH IN CANAAN, (1976); and D. CONNERY, GUILTY UNTIL PROVEN INNOCENT (1977).

49. State of Florida v. Tom Franklin Sawyer, 561 So.2d 278 (1990). *See also* Weiss, *Untrue Confessions*, MOTHER JONES, Sept., 1989, at 22-24 and 55-57.

50. Ofshe & Leo, *supra* note 45.

51. Florida v. Cayward, *supra* note 40, at 978.

52. *Id.*

53. *Id.*

54. Inbau, *Police Interrogation—A Practical Necessity*, 52 J. CRIM. L., CRIMINOLOGY, & POL. SCI. 421 (1961).

55. Florida v. Cayward, *supra* note 40, at 983.

56. Huff, Rattner & Sagarin, *Guilty Until Proven Innocent: Wrongful Conviction and Public Policy*, 32 CRIME & DELINQ. 518-44 (1986). *See also* Rattner, *Convicted But Innocent: Wrongful Conviction and the Criminal Justice System*, 12 L. & HUM. BEHAV. 283-93 (1988).

57. Bedau & Radelet, *supra* note 46.

58. P. JOHNSON, CRIMINAL PROCEDURE 540-50 (1988).

59. *Id.*, at 542.

60. *Id.*

61. Moran v. Burbine, 475 U.S. 412 (1986).

62. Arizona v. Fulminante, *supra* note 11.

DISCUSSION QUESTIONS

1. Differentiate between the various typologies of interrogatory deception. Which type do you think would be more problematic for an officer to engage in morally? Legally?

2. How does police deception differ from torture? Does police deception, especially in the interrogation phase, lead to false confessions? Explain.

3. What are the consequences of police deception?

CHAPTER 8

Ethical Dilemmas in Police Work

Joycelyn Pollock & Ronald Becker

There is a growing body of literature on the importance of teaching ethics in criminal justice curriculums (Kleinig, 1990; Pollock, 1994; Schmalleger and McKenrick, 1991; Silvester, 1990). Police ethics has received the most attention in the literature. One issue dealt with is where such teaching should be conducted. The focus of such debate is usually an argument over the benefits of the college classroom versus the police academy, but there is increasing recognition that both locales are important. Another discussion concerns whether teaching ethics is properly placed in an academy recruit class or as part of in-service training. Again, it is probably true that there is a need for a focused, guided discussion of ethical issues at both periods of a career in policing.

KEY CONCEPTS:
discretion
duty
gratuities
loyalty
police ethics
utilitarianism

Police ethics is particularly relevant, according to Kleinig (1990:4), because of the number of issues relevant to police, the discretionary nature of policing, the authority of police, the fact that they are not habitually moral, the crisis situations, the temptations and the peer pressure. The goals of police training typically include all aspects of how to perform tasks related to the job. More recently other information has been introduced, such as communication skills, multicultural understanding, and dealing with child abuse and the "battered woman syndrome." However, the role of the police in a free society and due process and ethical issues involved in investigation and enforcement often are not included in the training schedule.

In this chapter, ethics training for police officers will be the topic of discussion. Usually the content of such courses is developed as a combination of philosophy and discussion of ethical dilemmas that practitioners might face in the field. Swift, Houston and Anderson (1993), for instance, suggest that utilitarianism is the appropriate philosophical system because most officers (they also included correctional officers in their study) can identify with the concepts of utilitarianism and use them intuitively. Other authors also suggest exploring a philosophical foundation as well as practitioner issues as being an important part of the content for such a course (Kleinig, 1990; Schmalleger, 1990; Souryal, 1992).

The content of ethical dilemmas for police officers can be gleaned from newspapers, books in the field, and articles. Delattre's (1989) book, for instance, can be used as a source for a number of ethical dilemmas, as can Cohen and Feldberg (1991). Pollock (1994) provides dilemmas for police personnel as well as for corrections and other criminal justice professions. Pollock (1993) discusses a number of sources for police ethics and these can be used to develop other dilemmas.

Perusing the literature one can identify the following issues (although these by no means form an exhaustive list): gratuities, corruption, bribery, "shopping," whistleblowing and loyalty, undercover tactics, the use of deception, discretion, sleeping on duty, sex on duty and other misfeasance, deadly force, and brutality. Barker and Carter (1994) develop a typology of officer deviance including use of force, misconduct (violation of rules or laws) and corruption (gratuities and/or any misuse of position for expected reward). One might assume that these issues are the most problematic ethical issues in police work since they are what is primarily addressed in the literature. However, it may not necessarily be true that these issues are perceived by officers themselves as the most problematic. For example, although undercover tactics (i.e., deception) have received a great deal of attention in the literature, many officers are never faced with such issues because they are in patrol and not in criminal investigation. The issues of deadly force and brutality are certainly important, but they may not be day-to-day concerns for most officers who are rarely faced with such encounters. In addition, while most of the ethical issues mentioned thus far involve officer deviance, there are some ethical issues that do not involve misconduct. In fact, there may be situations in which neither decision that could be made by the officer is clearly wrong. Few attempts have been made to determine what ethical concerns are identified by the officers themselves. If such an attempt has been made in academy classrooms, the findings have not found their way into the literature.

One of the few instances in which officers were asked their views on ethical issues was a study done by Barker (1978). In this study he asked 50 officers in a small police department how many of their number participated in specific examples of unethical activity other than corruption. The categories were: "excessive force," "police perjury," "sex on duty," "drinking on duty" and "sleeping on duty." Barker also had them rank the perceived seriousness of such acts. Findings indicated that officers believed that sleeping on duty and engaging in sex while on duty were the most frequent forms of misconduct, and they were also rated as relatively less serious than other forms of unethical behavior. The police officers ranked the activities in the following way from most serious to least serious: drinking on duty, police perjury, sleeping on duty, sex on duty, brutality. Another measure of seriousness is in the officers' willingness to report another officer for the activity. In answer to this question, the officers respond-ed in the following way: 56 percent would always report drinking on duty; 28 percent would always report perjury; 19 percent would always report sex on duty; 14 percent would always report sleeping on duty; and 12 percent would always report brutality.

One might expect that the perceived extent and seriousness of various types of wrongdoing may vary from city to city. In an informal survey using the same choices as Barker's, one of the authors found that officers in a large city report-ed that their fellow officers engaged in significantly more drinking and less sex and brutality. It could also be that the changes are related to the time period in which the surveys were conducted because Barker's study took place in the late 1970s before officers were sensitized to the problem of police brutality.

Barker's study still does not fully explore what officers themselves perceive to be problematic issues because it uses a restricted list of activities. This chap-ter will discuss an approach to teaching ethics to an audience of police officers that allows class participants to submit their own ethical dilemmas and to ana-lyze these using a philosophical framework. The approach is premised on the assumption that officers will submit dilemmas that have relevance to them. Per-sonalizing course content and providing practitioners with a basic understanding of ethical analysis will hopefully help them to recognize ethical issues and resolve them.

Each of the authors has had the opportunity to teach ethics to police officers. As a pedagogical tool, one instructor utilized ethical dilemmas turned in by class participants as the basis for half the course content. The procedure operates as follows. First, the instructor defined the term *ethical dilemma* as: (1) a situation in which the officer did not know what the right course of action was, (2) a situ-ation in which the course of action the officer considered right was difficult to do, or (3) a situation in which the wrong course of action was very tempting. Then, the officers in each class were asked to write down a difficult ethical dilemma they had faced. This assignment took place after several hours of introductory material on ethics, morals and value systems, but before any issue-based mater-ial was presented, so officers were not yet focused on one or another specific type of dilemma (i.e., gratuities or brutality).

It is unclear whether officers reported ethical dilemmas according to fre-quency or seriousness or perhaps some other criteria. As mentioned previously, issues that pose the most serious ethical concerns, for example, use of deadly force and brutality, may be those that are least commonly faced. Officers may have identified an example of the most serious incident, the most recent incident or the incident most frequently presented to them. This exercise does present a useful way of obtaining relevant, realistic classroom material upon which to base a discussion of ethics.

Another exercise that was used in every class was to have the officers write their own code of ethics, under the restriction of limiting their code of ethics to one line. In other words, they were instructed to write down what they consid-ered the most important elements of a code for police officers or what makes a good police officer. These short one-sentence codes were collected and then read to the class, which analyzed the values expressed in each and identified the most frequently cited values. In all classes, police officers identified five common elements: (1) *legality* (enforcing and upholding the law); (2) *service* (protecting and serving the public); (3) *honesty and integrity;* (4) *loyalty;* and finally, (5) some version of the *Golden Rule* or respect for other persons. These five elements were mentioned in every class, though the relative rankings or emphasis given to each varied somewhat.

These concepts parallel closely the Code of Ethics promulgated by the International Chiefs of Police. Specifically, legality is represented by the phrase, "I will be exemplary in obeying the law and the regulations of my department," and service as, "my fundamental duty is to serve the community. . . ." Honesty and integrity is reflected in "Honest in thought and deed both in my personal and official life. . . ." The Golden Rule or some version of respect for other persons is exemplified in the lines in the Code that relate to never acting officiously or permitting personal feelings, prejudices or friendships, among other things, to influence decisions. Loyalty, in fact, is the only issue identified by officers with no direct parallel to the Code. Since it is a subject of concern for both officers and writers in the field of ethics, it is interesting that the Code has taken the opposite approach in a recent revision by specifically exhorting the duty to comply with investigations of wrongdoing in the phrase, "I will cooperate with all legally authorized agencies and their representatives in the pursuit of justice."

The five elements that officers viewed as important to a code of ethics were tied to the dilemmas they identified. *Legality* can be discussed in terms of discretion—what to do in particularly difficult situations in which no good solution presents itself and the law is not very helpful. *Service* is relevant to duty issues. These issues cover those instances in which it would be inconvenient or perceived as a waste of time to do a task that duty calls for. *Honesty* is related to whistleblowing and *loyalty* issues as well as temptations of taking money from a scene or accepting a bribe. Finally, the Golden Rule is related to all those incidents in which it is difficult to keep one's temper or treat people respectfully due to anger, the exigencies of the moment, or some other reason. These five elements comprise four categories of dilemmas.

The four categories are: (1) *discretion (legality)*, (2) *duty (service)*, (3) *honesty*, and (4) *loyalty*. The two most frequent categories of dilemmas reflected in the officers' submissions were loyalty versus whistleblowing and the use of discretion in difficult situations. In the remainder of this chapter, these dilemmas and the procedure used to analyze them will be discussed.

DISCRETION

Discretion can be defined as the power to make a choice. Obviously all ethical dilemmas involve making choices (e.g., whether to take a bribe). The situations categorized in this area, however, are within the purview of what is known as police discretion (e.g., whether to arrest, whether to ticket, what to do when faced with any altercation). Some of these dilemmas have not been readily identified as ethical issues in the literature. In these situations officers either felt uncomfortable about what the law or regulations required them to do, or they were sincerely confused as to what the appropriate course of action was.

Some incidents occur when the officer is faced with a choice of whether to enforce a law, or when the officer feels uncomfortable about enforcing it. Typically the law involved is relatively minor—a traffic citation, enforcing city warrants, or some other misdemeanor. The reason the officer hesitates or feels that the decision presents an ethical dilemma is because of situational elements (e.g., the age or poverty of the offender, or the perception that the person deserves a break). The following examples are representative. All are verbatim transcriptions of officers' submissions:

> Officer received a call regarding business holding a shoplifter. A 75-year-old female was being held for shoplifting needed medications. However, store insisted on filing charges on her.

> Kmart calls for a wagon call. You get there and find a 70-year-old lady arrested for trying to steal hearing aid batteries. She was on a fixed income and unable to purchase items. She even looks like your mother.

> While on patrol one day, I was dispatched to a disturbance at a gas station. Upon arrival I spotted a kid I saw in the neighborhood a lot. I knew this kid lived with his grandmother and that they were barely making ends meet. I had ran into problems before with the kid begging for money and washing people's windows at gas stations without being asked to. The gas station attendant wanted the child arrested for trespassing because he stated the child harasses the customers.

In these situations the offender is usually either poor and/or elderly. The stores often insist on prosecution, leaving the officer in a struggle between compassion and enforcing the law. In the next set of dilemmas or situations, there is no demanding complainant, but the officer feels strict legality may not serve the ends of justice, or at least feels torn about enforcing the law:

> Officer A was faced with arresting a person on a parole violation. Officer, while talking to family members, learned that parole violator had just started a new job, which was verified by employer. What should Officer A do? (Parole violation was for first DWI.)

> I arrested a lady with a baby for numerous traffic warrants. Do you take the baby to juvenile and her to jail, make arrangements for someone else to care for the baby, or just let her go and tell her to take care of the warrants on her own? She has no money and gave us no trouble.

> Riding with a partner we stopped a person in traffic for multiple violations, no insurance, no driver's license, no ID at all and who would face going to jail for traffic violations on Christmas Eve. Would you discourage your partner from taking him to jail?

The most numerous type of incidents involve women and/or families with children stopped for some sort of traffic violation. Some officers were very clear as to what criteria they used to guide their discretion, while others were more unsure about the ethical role of the police in traffic enforcement.

Another category of discretion dilemmas involved situations in which no law or policy may be involved, but the officer was still perplexed regarding how to resolve the situation. These situations were often family disputes in which a significant problem existed prior to interaction with a police officer. Here, the officer's dilemma arises from a sincere desire to do the right thing but not being sure what the right thing is. Referral sources in the community, while plentiful, are often unavailable or overused. The large number of these submitted dilemmas indicate that the officers perceive significant ethical issues in this area of policing. For most officers, it was not necessarily a question of doing something wrong, but rather of finding the best solution to a difficult problem.

> What do you do when called to a scene to transport and find some type of housing for an elderly parent whom the family no longer wants because of mental impairment, knowing that the family has used, in the past, the parent's resources as their mainstay?

> Officer A received call in regard to trespassing. Officer spoke with complainant at residence who wanted a female removed from his house. Female had a small child and was complainant's ex-girlfriend who had no family and no place to go.

This last dilemma is the single most frequent type of instance in this category. Typically boyfriends wanted girlfriends removed, girlfriends wanted boyfriends removed, parents wanted children removed, and husbands wanted wives removed, or vice versa. Police officers expressed the frustration inherent in having to deal with what are essentially difficult interpersonal problems, such as the examples below:

> You and your partner are dispatched to a disturbance at a low-income apartment complex. It involves a drunk husband and drunk wife calling the police for no reason. No crime has been committed. After being dispatched to the same apartment unit three or four times in one night, how should an officer resolve the situation? Arrest one or both for public intoxication inside their own residence? Unplug the phone? Continue to return every time they call?

> Officer A goes to a disturbance at a residence. It is his third time there. The problem is the same each time. Father gets drunk, he then tells his son, wife and kids to leave his home. The son refuses to take his family and leave. The real problem is the father being drunk and stupid, yet the father has a legal right to tell his son's family to leave. What should you do?

Some dilemmas arise because of a personal or professional relationship between the officer and the subject. Typically this involved stopping a speeding car and finding the driver to be another officer or responding to an altercation involving another officer or family member.

> You are on patrol, riding one man, at approx. 10 p.m. You and one other vehicle are stopped at a red light. The light changes and you and the other vehicle start driving. Suddenly you observe the other vehicle weaving from lane to lane. You turn on your lights and siren and after about an eight-block drive the vehicle finally pulls over. You exit your vehicle and find that not only is the driver very intoxicated, but he is also your first cousin. What should you do?

> Working a side job at a nightclub you notice a disturbance on the far side of the club. As you handle the problem, you discover that the instigator of the problem is an off-duty officer, who is extremely intoxicated, and refuses to follow your instructions. Also the other party involved, who is not an officer, is claiming that the officer assaulted him, although the other party does not know he is an officer.

> Officer A is on patrol. Suddenly he spots a vehicle traveling at a high rate of speed. Officer A stops the vehicle and finds out that the person is a law enforcement officer from a different agency. Officer A observes that he is highly intoxicated. What should he do?

By presenting these as dilemmas, officers indicate that they perceive that special treatment given to other officers is questionable even if they typically defend preferential treatment.

Discussions brought out from dilemmas concerning the use of discretion can be organized around the determination of which criteria may be considered ethical and which have less ethical support in guiding discretion. Because full enforcement is not always considered an option, officers use discretion in their decisionmaking. It is important for them to at least recognize the ethical issues involved in employing that discretion.

DUTY

Duty may involve situations in which there is a real question concerning what the duty of a police officer is in a certain situation. Duty may also involve those situations in which the officer knows that the job requires a particular action, but feels that action is either inconvenient or a waste of time. In the first situation, some of the examples of discretion given above may also apply to duty. For instance, in the case of a family altercation when a police officer responds and finds no crime has been committed, what is his or her duty? Is there or is there not a duty to try to resolve a volatile situation before it erupts into a crime? Some police officers believe they have a duty to help the poor and homeless find shelter, other officers see their job as being free from such responsibilities. This is the type of discussion that inevitably brings out differences of opinion among police officers and is linked to how they view their role in the community. It is also, of course, an ethical issue.

The other type of duty dilemma is more straightforward. Here, the officer knows there is a duty to perform a certain act. A frequent situation was the temptation (and evidently widespread practice) of either driving by an accident scene or avoiding it because it occurs near the end of a shift. There were also dilemmas involving repetitive 911 calls and the temptation to avoid them or respond to them halfheartedly. The following are examples:

> It is 10 minutes to off-duty time. You view an accident. Do you work the accident, even though you want to go home, or do you avoid the accident by sneaking around it?

> It is 10:30 p.m. and you are a late shift unit heading into the station when you notice a large traffic jam. As you near the scene you observe that it is an accident involving two cars and a fixed object. Do you stop and respond, or take the back way to the station?

> You get a disturbance call from the dispatcher at a certain location. You can see the location from inside a building you are in; and see that there is no disturbance at that location. Is it necessary to leave the building to respond to the call?

Another duty dilemma issue arose concerning the risk of contracting AIDS. Finally, there were miscellaneous duty issues, all under the general idea of using regular work hours to conduct personal business.

> You are involved in a situation where someone is injured and is in need of CPR. You know the injured person is a drug addict and a criminal. Do you perform CPR or not?

> To get in service after clearing a call or staying out of service to handle some personal business or affairs.

> An officer works a plainclothes assignment in a division where each squad is small and has its own supervisor. The officer's supervisor is off this day and the likelihood of being noticed leaving early is almost nonexistent. So why not cut out an hour and a half early when it won't be noticed? Your work will not be undone.

Discussion of duty issues in the classroom shows participants that not all police officers view duty in the same way. To move beyond a simple exchange of opinion, it is necessary to apply an ethical framework analysis that helps each officer understand that while his or her position may be justifiable to some extent and legal, it may have less ethical support than other positions.

HONESTY

Under the general heading of honesty, officers submitted dilemmas involving self-protection or enrichment, honesty versus the need to effect an arrest, and bribery. Many participants related dilemmas in which officers are confronted with temptations of money or other goods, typically "found" or at burglary scenes.

> Officer received a call to a robbery and on the way to the call he discovered a brown bag full of money. This officer was alone and no one saw him pick up the bag. The question is what to do with the bag, turn it in or keep it?

> Officer A and B are on the scene of a homicide involving a supposed drug dealer who is lying on the ground dead. No one is present except the officers, who then find $20,000 cash in suspect's pockets. Officer B insists that they should keep and split the money with each other.

> An officer is patrolling through an abandoned apartment complex when he observes a stack of lumber in the back of the complex to be used for remodeling. The officer is working on a project at home and could use a few pieces of the lumber. Nobody else is around. What should he do?

One interesting discussion device is to start with a dilemma using $20 "found" by a police officer and ask what the proper procedure is; then continue the discussion with larger amounts of money. While many officers would feel that it is a minor breach (if any at all) to keep the $20, at some point the amount of "found" money that is kept by the individual becomes perceived as unethical. The issue then becomes "is it the amount or the action" that should determine the ethical nature of the response.

Another type of dilemma involves officers trying to cover up their own wrongdoing by lying or not coming forward when they commit minor acts of wrongdoing. Given the number of dilemmas reported concerning small "fender-benders" with police cars, it may be surmised that the police parking lot is an insurer's nightmare.

> Officer had accident where there was no witnesses. Since it was an auto-fixed object, officer was at fault but he didn't want disciplinary action. The officer was deciding whether or not to suggest another car cut him off to explain how the accident occurred.

In another type of situation officers must either tell the truth and lose (or risk losing) an arrest, or misrepresent facts to save the arrest. While this is a popular topic in the literature, it was not a frequent dilemma submitted by officers.

> You stop somebody and check his pockets and find some dope. You had no probable cause to search him, but you did anyhow because you

> thought he might be holding. Do you find a reason to arrest him and then put in the report that you found the dope after the arrest so it won't get thrown out in court?

> Officer A sees a known crack dealer on a corner and searches him. He finds drugs, makes arrest and then lies about or makes up probable cause for the search in his report and in his courtroom testimony. Nobody knows but the officer and the suspect. The suspect did have the drug and he is a dealer in that neighborhood.

Bribery is a form of dishonesty that can be discussed under this category of dilemma. It can be defined as some reward for doing something illegal or for not doing something that is required. There were very few submissions from officers dealing with the issue of bribery. It may be that officers do not view it as a dilemma because they seldom receive opportunities, do not want to admit that it occurs, or may not consider it a dilemma because the occupational subculture is such that bribe-taking is clearly a serious violation and therefore there is no question as to the response to take when faced with such an opportunity.

> I was offered money for taking care of a ticket. Also offered money for giving information about a driver's license or license plate.

Loyalty

In situations or dilemmas involving loyalty versus whistleblowing, officers must decide what to do when faced with the wrongdoing of other police officers. The literature accurately reflects the saliency of this issue for police officers, given the frequency of this type of submission. Officers' dilemmas ran the gamut from seeing relatively minor wrongdoing (e.g., overtime misuses) to very serious violations (e.g., physical abuse of a suspect or the commission of another crime).

> On a winter afternoon Officers A and B are riding patrol in a rough area of town. Officer A spots a possible burglar and stops. After a brief chase the suspect is arrested. Officer B uses a little more force than necessary. Officer A does not agree, what does he do?

> You are on patrol. Your partner uses more force than you think needed when arresting a suspect and you are asked by the partner to lie about how much force was used if asked.

> Whether or not to tell a supervisor of another officer that you see verbally or physically abuse a citizen when it's not called for on a regular basis.

In fact, the only time abuse of force was mentioned at all was in this category of whether to report a fellow officer who used what was considered to be too much force. The third dilemma above illustrates, however, that the use of appropriate force may be in the eye of the beholder. Is the officer identifying the partner's action as problematic because of its nature, or because it is too frequent, or because it is uncalled for? When is it called for? Another set of issues involves observing or believing another officer has committed a crime.

> You are on patrol as you roll up on a possible narcotics transaction involving a known dope dealer. You make the block to set up on the buyer who is in a vehicle. By the time you make the block the buyer is rolling. You go to chase down the buyer and it takes you several blocks to catch up to him. In your mind he is trying to lose you. You manage to catch up to him about a mile away. It turns out the driver is an off-duty sheriff's deputy. What do you do?

> An officer is dispatched as a backup unit where an alarm is going off at a large jewelry store. He insists on doing the report listing items that were taken. A couple of days later you see him wearing items or showing off items he claims to have got a good deal on. These are items you saw in the store burglarized. What should you do?

Finally, there are dilemmas involving actions that may technically be crimes and often pose risks to other officers, but are not viewed to be as serious as buying drugs or stealing from the scene of a burglary. Several of these dilemmas again involve minor traffic accidents. Since officers get disciplined for driving errors, it is always a temptation to avoid responsibility.

> You are standing in a parking lot when you notice Officer A backing his car out of his parking space, he hits the car behind him, then drives off. A few seconds later the owner of the car comes out and asks you if you saw what happened. What should you do?

> One day while leaving the parking lot, my partner was driving and accidentally damaged a new patrol car which was parked next to us. We both got out of our patrol vehicle and observed the minor damage to the new vehicle. We both looked around but did not notice anyone else near. My partner told me he would report it to the sergeant at the end of the shift. However, the next day at roll call, the roll call sergeant asked if anyone knew how the new patrol car received the damage.

> Officer A sleeps on duty and doesn't run his calls. What should I (his partner) do?

> Officer A was an alcoholic and consumed alcohol very heavily on a day-to-day basis. Even while on duty, A was highly intoxicated. Joe Blow, a concerned citizen, who owned a liquor store in the beat, knew of A's situation and decided to call Officer B and advised him to talk to A about the problem before it gets out of hand. What should B do?

Since covering up for another officer is more risky now with the possibility of individual civil liability, it may be that fewer officers are willing to draw the "blue curtain." However, it is important to distinguish between reporting on a fellow officer because he or she did something wrong and telling the truth is the right thing to do, and coming forward or telling the truth in an official investigation in order to avoid being disciplined.

GRATUITIES

Gratuities is not a subject that emerges as an issue during the exercise involving the Code of Ethics; however, it is a subject that is hard to ignore in any law enforcement ethics class. It is represented in the policing literature and identified by lay people as a perennial problem among police (e.g., the infamous donut shop). Officers themselves often feel that there is nothing wrong with gratuities. One distinction that can be made in these dilemmas is between situations involving true gratuities (i.e., something given to all police as a policy) and gifts (i.e., something given to an individual in return for a specific action).

> Officer A is new to his beat. Where he worked before, he would stop by a local convenience store and get something to drink and pay for it. He has learned from past experiences that people always expect something in return. In this new beat he stops by the store. The clerk refuses to accept payment. Officer A explains that he would prefer to pay. The clerk, now upset, accuses officer of trying to be better than the others, and will tell his supervisor who also stops by. What does he do?

> Officer A stopped in a store in his beat and was offered anything he wanted in the store within reason: food, cigarettes, Skoal. And the worker offered him lottery tickets, which he may or may not have taken. After several days of going to the store, the worker tells the officer he sometimes has problems and could he give the worker his beeper number to call him if he has problems. The question is should the officer give his beeper number and feel obligated to call this person because he has gotten free articles?

> A guy's car had broken down on the freeway. As an officer on duty, I stopped. I took him home since he only lived a short distance away in my beat. It was early in the morning and the man was very appreciative. He wanted to buy me breakfast to show his appreciation so he offered me five dollars.

> Officer A is called to a burglar alarm at a Vietnamese business. Officer checks the building and finds that the Vietnamese family lives inside. Officer then checks the inside of the business and finds no sign of forced entry. Officer reassures the Vietnamese family that everything is alright. Vietnamese family then offers officer an envelope filled with unknown amount of cash. What should he do?

Discussion involving the ethics of gratuities can be hampered by defensiveness on the part of police participants, especially if the discussion takes place after lunch and many officers in the classroom have taken advantage of half-price or free meals in nearby restaurants. It is helpful to explore regional differences and clearly discuss definitions (i.e., the difference between gratuities and gifts) and the reason why gratuities to public servants is a problematic issue.

Now That We Have Them, What Do We Do With Them?

Descriptions of dilemmas submitted by officers indicate that they may view many relatively mundane issues as problematic. Decisions regarding whether to enforce a warrant or ticket, what to do in a domestic disturbance, and whether to leave early from an assignment are not perceived the same as police brutality or use of deception. Yet, it seems clear that if an ethics course for officers is to be relevant, it should cover these issues as well. The approach one should take in analyzing these dilemmas is up to the individual instructor. What follows is one way to utilize these dilemmas in a classroom.

As discussed previously, any class of police ethics must have a philosophical basis in order to move it beyond a mere "bull" session of opinions. While one may decide to simplify matters and only present one ethical framework, such as utilitarianism, and then use it to analyze ethical dilemmas, another approach may be to compare several ethical frameworks, such as utilitarianism, ethical formalism and religion.

After dilemmas are submitted, it is useful to group them together in some order so that similar dilemmas are discussed together. This exercise is similar to what was done above. One benefit of this approach is that officers realize they have similar concerns. The anonymity of the method ensures that officers have the opportunity to honestly address and describe the dilemmas they feel are most prevalent and important.

The first form of analysis is to determine at what level there is disagreement. One might ask the following questions: What does the law require? What does departmental policy require? What do personal ethics require? Interestingly, there is often heated discussion regarding legal definitions and policy mandates. This is why some ethics classes become training courses in such things as domestic violence laws and victim rights legislation. There may be agreement on whether there is an applicable law, but disagreement on departmental policy. There may be agreement on law and policy, but not on an ethical analysis. If there is an applicable law or policy and there is still an ethical concern whether to follow such law or policy, the issue of civil disobedience and duty becomes relevant. Can an officer be considered ethical if he or she follows a personal code of ethics that is contrary to a departmental directive? What if the departmental directive has no support from any ethical system? These are sensitive and important issues.

If there is no applicable law or departmental policy, then the discussion can quickly be directed to an ethical analysis of possible solutions. The instructor can direct discussion in at least two ways. First, participants can be assigned to groups and provided an ethical framework. Then group members can determine a solution that is justified by the ethical framework (i.e., utilitarianism, ethical formalism, ethics of care, etc.). Obviously, there has to be a basic understanding of these frameworks and it may be necessary to provide the groups with a quick review of previously presented material. Another approach is to ask the class what is the best solution to the dilemma and then analyze that solution using the ethical framework. For example, one of the previous dilemmas states:

> Officer received a call regarding a business holding a shoplifter. A 75-year-old female was being held for shoplifting needed medications. However, the store insisted on filing charges on her.

The first set of questions reveals the following. Is there an applicable law? Yes, and the woman obviously broke it. Is there an applicable departmental policy? Obviously the departmental policy would be to enforce the law, especially if there is a complainant wanting to press charges. Does this resolve the dilemma? For some officers it does. Some officers believe that their duty is to enforce the law, not mediate it. Therefore, in this situation, they merely respond to the event by enforcing the law. Other officers, however, would respond by saying there is still an ethical issue. It is these officers who identify this situation as a dilemma. Their solution may be to try to convince the storeowner to drop charges, perhaps even going so far as to pay for the items themselves. Is this their duty? There is obviously no professional duty that dictates such action, but some believe that personal ethics require a more complete response to the situation than merely acting as an agent of the law. The ethical frameworks are now applied to the possible solutions. Utilitarianism would be concerned with the relative costs and benefits of arrest versus some type of intervention. Ethical formalism would be concerned with duties. Ethics of care would focus on need (see Pollock, 1994, for a more complete discussion of some of these applications).

Another dilemma presented previously was the following:

> Officer A was an alcoholic and consumed alcohol very heavily on a day to day basis. Even while on duty A was highly intoxicated. Joe Blow, a concerned citizen, who owned a liquor store in the beat, knew of A's situation and decided to call Officer B and advised him to talk to A about the problem before it gets out of hand. What should B do?

Again, the first question is: Is there an applicable law? Public intoxication laws may be applicable. There certainly is an applicable departmental policy and a violation. What is the ethical issue? Personal loyalty versus whistleblowing. The appropriate solution for any individual officer may be discussed in terms of his or her own value system. Some officers place a higher value on loyalty than any other value, including integrity. Most balance loyalty against the severity of the wrongdoing. Alcohol use is considered less serious than illegal drug use. More officers would take action against an officer using illegal drugs than one abusing alcohol, despite the fact that the resultant effects on the officer may be similar. A discussion concerning this dilemma often involves the perceived unfairness of an administrative response. For example, while other types of professionals may be censured for alcohol problems, police officers often lose their jobs and their career. This can be tied in to an application of utilitarianism. What are the relative costs and benefits associated with turning the officer in, talking to the officer or doing nothing? An application of ethical formalism would be concerned with the duty of the officer with knowledge of the problem. (See Cohen and Feldberg, 1991, for a more complete discussion of similar issues.)

Such discussion will hopefully show that some decisions have little or no ethical rationale. In addition, some rationales for actions can only be described as egoist or primarily self-serving. Officers are seldom forced to present ethical rationales for their decisions. Some do not like the experience. Yet others have indicated that all police officers could benefit from such experience and it "reminds them of why they entered the law enforcement profession in the first place."

CONCLUSION

This chapter presented the premise that the best ethics course for police officers is one that is relevant to them. One way to achieve that is to utilize their own dilemmas in guiding the discussion of ethics. Most of these dilemmas fall into particular types of categories. The frequency of examples concerning more mundane issues indicates that the literature on police ethics may have missed some important, albeit less "juicy," issues of police ethics. Such topics as what to do with an elderly shoplifter, whether to enforce an outstanding warrant for a poor mother or whether to report a minor fender-bender during a shift may not be the stuff of "Dirty Harry" movies, but they are experienced by many police officers nonetheless. The method of analysis presented can be utilized for various types of ethical dilemmas, and the benefit of such analysis is that it gives police officers the tools to identify and resolve their own ethical dilemmas.

REFERENCES

Barker, Thomas (1994a). "Peer Group Support for Police Occupational Deviance." In T. Barker and D. Carter (eds.), *Police Deviance, 3d Edition*. Cincinnati, OH: Anderson Publishing Co., pp. 45-57.

Barker, Thomas (1994b). "A Typology of Police Deviance." In T. Barker and D. Carter (eds.), *Police Deviance, 3d Edition*. Cincinnati, OH: Anderson Publishing Co., pp. 3-12.

Barker, Thomas (1978). "An Empirical Study of Police Deviance Other Than Corruption," *Journal of Police Science and Administration* 6, 3:264-272.

Barker, Thomas and David Carter (1994). *Police Deviance, 3d Edition*. Cincinnati, OH: Anderson Publishing Co.

Canons of Police Ethics (1992). International Association of Chiefs of Police, Arlington, VA.

Carter, David (1994). "Theoretical Dimensions in the Abuse of Authority by Police Officers." In T. Barker and D. Carter (eds.), *Police Deviance, 3d Edition*. Cincinnati, OH: Anderson Publishing Co., pp. 269-290.

Carter, David and Darrel Stephens (1994). "Police Ethics, Integrity, and Off-Duty Behavior: Policy Issues of Officer Conduct." In T. Barker and D. Carter (eds.), *Police Deviance, 3d Edition*. Cincinnati, OH: Anderson Publishing Co., pp. 29-44.

Cohen, Howard (1985). "A Dilemma for Discretion." In W. Heffernan and T. Stroup (eds.), *Police Ethics: Hard Choices in Law Enforcement*. New York: John Jay Press, pp. 69-82.

Cohen, Howard and Michael Feldberg (1991). *Power and Restraint: The Moral Dimension of Police Work*. New York: Praeger Press.

Delaney, H.R. (1990). "Toward a Police Professional Ethic." In F. Schmalleger (ed.), *Ethics in Criminal Justice: A Justice Professional Reader*. Bristol, Indiana: Wyndham Hall Press, pp. 78-94.

Delattre, Edwin J. (1989). *Character and Cops: Ethics in Policing*. Lanham, MD: AEI Press.

Doyle, James (1985). "Police Discretion, Legality, and Morality." In W. Heffernan and T. Stroup (eds.), *Police Ethics: Hard Choices in Law Enforcement*. New York: John Jay Press, pp. 47-69.

Heffernan, William (1985). "The Police and the Rules of Office." In W. Heffernan and T. Stroup (eds.), *Police Ethics: Hard Choices in Law Enforcement*. New York: John Jay Press, pp. 3-25.

Heffernan, William and Timothy Stroup (eds.) (1985). *Police Ethics: Hard Choices in Law Enforcement*. New York: John Jay Press.

Kleinig, John (1990). "Teaching and Learning Police Ethics: Competing and Complementary Approaches." *Journal of Criminal Justice* 18:1-18.

Metz, Harold (1990). "An Ethical Model for Law Enforcement Administrators." In F. Schmalleger (ed.), *Ethics in Criminal Justice: A Justice Professional Reader*. Bristol, Indiana: Wyndham Hall Press, p. 95-102.

Pollock, Joycelyn (1993). "Ethics and the Criminal Justice Curriculum," *Journal of Criminal Justice Education* 4, 2:377-391.

Pollock, Joycelyn (1994). *Ethics in Crime and Justice: Dilemmas and Decisions, 2nd Edition*. Belmont, CA: Wadsworth Publishing.

Schmalleger, Frank (ed.) (1990). *Ethics in Criminal Justice: A Justice Professional Reader*. Bristol, Indiana: Wyndham Hall Press.

Schmalleger, Frank and Robert McKenrick (1991). *Criminal Justice Ethics: An Annotated Bibliography*. Westport, CT: Greenwood Press.

Sherman, Lawrence (1982). "Learning Police Ethics," *Criminal Justice Ethics* 1, 1:10-19.

Silvester, Deanna (1990). "Ethics and Privatization in Criminal Justice: Does Education Have a Role to Play?" *Journal of Criminal Justice* 18:65-70.

Souryal, Sam (1992). *Ethics in Criminal Justice: In Search of the Truth.* Cincinnati, OH: Anderson Publishing Co.

Souryal, Sam and Dennis Potts (1993). "What Am I Supposed to Fall Back On? Cultural Literacy in Criminal Justice Ethics," *Journal of Criminal Justice Education* 4:15-41.

Swift, Andrew, James Houston and Robin Anderson (1993). "Cops, Hacks and the Greater Good." Presented at the Academy of Criminal Justice Sciences, Kansas City, Missouri, March 1993.

Wren, Thomas (1985). "Whistle-Blowing and Loyalty to One's Friends." In W. Heffernan and T. Stroup (eds.), *Police Ethics: Hard Choices in Law Enforcement.* New York: John Jay Press, pp. 26-46.

DISCUSSION QUESTIONS

1. If you were a police officer, what would you consider to be the five most important elements that should be included in a police code of ethics? List and describe each category.

2. Of all the categories listed in the text—discretion, duty, honesty and loyalty—which do you think is the most important? Explain your answer. Which do you think is the least important? Explain your answer.

3. What are the dangers of accepting even minor gratuities such as free cups of coffee, discounts or free tickets to sporting or entertainment events? Can the acceptance of gratuities contribute to more serious problems in policing?

4. To what extent should a police department strive to minimize discretion? How can a department minimize or structure police discretion? Do officers welcome limits on their discretion? Why or why not?

EXERCISE 1:

Section II: Ethical Issues in Policing

DIFFERENT CHOICES, EQUAL PROTECTION?

"You folks need to settle your differences and get along," Sergeant Waddell mumbles as he leaves the apartment with you trailing behind him. The sergeant, a 30-year veteran, switches on the ignition of the cruiser and continues, half-talking to you and half-talking to himself.

"I don't know what the world's coming to! Two men living together like that. It just ain't natural. It's tough enough dealing with the Saturday night husband-and-wife drunks without having to try and calm down the likes of them. They like to call themselves gay, but from the looks of that smaller one, it don't look like he was having too gay of a time! Looked like the bigger feller whipped up on him. Besides, with him being thin like that, I wouldn't be surprised if he didn't have AIDS. I'll tell you one thing. I was glad to get out of there. Who knows what kind of germs was in their apartment?" Lighting a cigarette, he turns to you. "I bet they didn't teach you how to deal with those kind of people in college."

You pause before you respond, not wanting to offend the sergeant, who is also your training officer. "We were taught that it would be difficult and challenging when dealing with the homosexual community, because of AIDS and our own biases and prejudices, as well as a lot of myths that are going around."

"Myths, my ass," Sergeant Waddell interrupts. "That AIDS disease will kill you stone-cold dead. I don't trust the government. You can't tell me you can't catch that stuff from mosquitos either. Who knows how you can catch it? All I know is I want to wash my hands."

From Larry S. Miller and Michael Braswell, *Human Relations and Police Work*, 4th ed. (Prospect Heights, IL: Waveland Press), 1997. Reprinted with permission.

"Well, I would agree that there are a lot of questions," you reply. "But our professors always reminded us that every citizen was entitled to equal opportunity under the law, regardless of their sexual preferences. I was taught that I was to treat them professionally, just as in any domestic disturbance. It seems to me that we should have done something besides just telling them to quiet down and get along with each other. I mean, we should have arrested the big guy just like we would have done if it was a spousal abuse case."

Turning into McDonalds, the sergeant turns once more to you, "Simpson, you're a good kid and I believe you will make a fine officer. But you need to remember that the classroom is one thing and the real world is another. I don't hate those kind of people, but they made their own bed and now they'll have to lie in it. I don't know what else we could have done. They weren't married and, even if they were, I don't believe it's legal in this state. We couldn't take the little guy to a spousal abuse shelter, they'd laugh their asses off at us. And I don't think that domestic violence law covers people like that anyway. Why don't you go order us a couple of black coffees to go while I wash my hands?"

Waiting for the coffee, you reflect on Waddell's words. He is a respected veteran police officer and you understand his uneasiness. You felt it, too. You also remember the look of fear and helplessness on the face of the battered guy, Eddie, who called the police. One part of you wanted to go back and check on him and do something, even if it meant arresting the other guy for domestic violence. Another part of you wanted to stay on Sergeant Waddell's good side. After all, he is your training officer. What are you going to do?

Questions:

1. What police ethics might this new recruit be torn between? Explain.

2. How might a department with stricter objectives or codes of conduct have influenced the behavior of the officers? Explain.

3. Address this case from the three ethical models of utilitarianism, deontology and peacemaking. Which perspective do you feel would be most helpful in this instance? Why?

4. Research the local laws of your area and report back to the class. Are homosexual relationships covered by the local laws in your area? How might this information affect the officers' behavior?

> A man can only do what he can do. But if he does that each day he can sleep at night and do it again the next day.
>
> —Albert Schweitzer

SECTION III

Ethics and the Courts

It has been argued that while our criminal justice system is not perfect, it does yield a kind of "rough justice." No one is guilty of exactly the crime for which they are convicted, and no one receives exactly the penalty they deserve, but the majority of people do receive a disposition that approximates justice.

This view is probably accurate, but it is also somewhat troubling. While it is an eminently pragmatic approach, one may question the extent to which justice can be "approximated." One can also question the process by which this approximation is achieved. When defense attorneys and prosecutors struggle against each other in the adversary process, is truth the likely outcome, or just a lucky possibility? Is the process any more agreeable when there is little real argument, just a negotiation over charge and sentence recommendation?

This is hardly the process one would design to find the right punishment to fit the crime or the criminal. But in whose hands should such decisions be placed? The legislature can attempt to ensure greater consistency through determinate sentencing, but such efforts often result in higher penalties than judicial discretion would yield. And in this period of prison overcrowding, what is the correct use of incarceration? One is forced to juxtapose a moral obligation to minimize prison costs that serve to shortchange state health, education, and welfare programs, with an equally important obligation to protect the community from crime.

The decisions that defense attorneys, prosecutors, judges, and legislators must make are difficult ones, requiring a balancing of sound ethical judgments with the pragmatic realities of their positions. To assist their students in dealing with these problems, law schools provide instruction in professional ethics. This is normally achieved by requiring students to complete a course that addresses the practicing attorney's obligations to the client, to the bar, and to the court. Questions have been raised, however, about the utility of requiring a single isolated ethics course, as opposed to integrating a concern with ethics into the general curriculum. While the former provides more intense and focused study, the latter encourages the incorporation of ethical concerns into every aspect of law. This incorporation may be a more effective means of instilling high standards, because many ethical dilemmas seem to be a direct result of the conflicting obligations inherent in the practice of law.

THE PRACTICE OF LAW

CHAPTER 9

Pure Legal Advocates and Moral Agents: Two Concepts of a Lawyer in an Adversary System

Elliot D. Cohen

It is sometimes asked if a good lawyer in an adversary system also can be a good person. We must first notice that there are two different senses of the term *good* employed in this question. In its first occurrence, good may be taken in its instrumental sense to mean, roughly, *effective*. In its second occurrence, *good* may be taken in its moral sense to mean *morally good*. Thus the question is whether an effective lawyer also can be a morally good person. And the latter question, it is clear, can be answered only if we have some idea of what we mean by a morally good person, and by an effective lawyer.

KEY CONCEPTS:

moral agent

moral autonomy

moral courage

moral respectability

pure legal advocate

Accordingly, in this paper I shall first outline what we take to be salient marks of a morally good person. Second, I shall examine one sense of a lawyer, what we call the *pure legal advocate concept*, in which a good lawyer does *not* satisfy our criteria of a morally good person. Third, I shall examine a further concept of a lawyer, what might be called the *moral agent concept*, according to which a good lawyer is, *ipso facto*, a morally good person. Fourth, I shall show how the moral agent concept of a lawyer may be brought to bear on the American Bar Association's *Code of Professional Responsibility*. Fifth, in the light of my analysis of the Code, I shall examine the ABA's current code of ethics, the *Model Rules of Professional Conduct*. Sixth, I shall answer some possible objections to applying the moral agent concept.

Elliott D. Cohen, "Pure Legal Advocates and Moral Agents: Two Concepts of a Lawyer in an Adversary System," (as appeared in *Criminal Justice Ethics*, Volume 4, Number 1 [Winter/Spring 1985] pp. 38-59). Reprinted by permission of the Institute for Criminal Justice Ethics, 899 Tenth Avenue, New York, NY 10019-1029.

Morally Good Persons

Following one tradition, let us say that a morally good person is a person who, through exercise and training, has cultivated certain morally desirable traits of character, the latter traits being constituted by dispositions to act, think, and feel in certain ways, under certain conditions, which are *themselves* morally desirable.[1] What traits of character in particular are morally desirable and to what extent and in what combinations they must be cultivated for a person to be morally good are admittedly no settled matters. Still, there are some traits which at least most of us would countenance as being important, if not essential, ingredients of the morally good personality. It is such traits of character with which I shall be concerned, particularly those among them which seem to be the most relevant to legal practice.

What then are some such characteristic marks of a morally good person?

1. We would not ordinarily countenance a person as being morally good if we believed that he was not a *just* person, that is, if we thought that he was not disposed to treat others justly. There are, however, two senses of *just* and *unjust* in which a person may be said to treat others justly or unjustly.

   First, a person may be said to treat others justly when, in distributing some good or service among them, she observes the principle of treating relevantly similar cases in a similar fashion; and she may be said to treat others *unjustly* in this sense, when she violates this principle. For example, a physician who consistently distributes medical service among the ill on the basis of medical need would, *ceteris paribus,* be acting justly in this sense; whereas one who distributes such service without regard to medical needs, but instead with regard to race or religion, would, in this sense, be acting unjustly. This is so because we typically regard medical need as the controlling factor in distributing health care; whereas race and religion appear to be quite irrelevant in such a context.

   We may, however, be said to treat others justly when we are respectful of their legal and moral rights, or when we give to them what they rightfully deserve; and we may be said to treat others unjustly when we intrude upon their legal or moral rights, or when we treat them in ways in which they do not deserve to be treated. For example, one acts justly, in this sense, when he keeps an agreement with an individual who has the right to insist upon its being kept; or a judge acts justly, in this sense, when he hands down a well-deserved punishment to a legal offender; whereas a person perpetrates an injustice upon another, in this sense, when he fails to uphold a binding agreement or when he inflicts injury upon an innocent party.[2]

   Let us say, then, that the just person is one who is disposed to treat others justly in *both* of the above senses. That is, she tends to be consistent in her treatment of others—she does not normally make biased or arbitrary exceptions. But she is also the sort of person who respects individual rights and can usually be counted upon to make good her obligations to others.

2. Being morally good also would appear to require being *truthful*. By *truthful person* is meant one who is in the habit of asserting things only if he *believes* them to be true. Thus he is in the habit of asserting things with the intention of *informing* his hearers, and not deceiving them, about the truth. An *untruthful* person, on the other hand, is in the habit of asserting things which she *disbelieves;* and this she does with the intention of deceiving her hearers about the truth.[3] Moreover, the untruthful person may deceive not merely through her spoken word, but also by other means. She may, for example, leave false clues or simply remain silent where such measures are calculated to mislead as to the truth.[4] This is not to suggest that such tactics are never justified; it is rather to say that, when they constitute the rule instead of the exception, the person in question has fallen below that level of truthfulness which we should normally require of a morally good person.

3. Being a morally good person also would seem to demand at least *some* measure of *moral courage*. Indeed, it would appear that a person could not be just or truthful if he did not have any such measure; for it often takes courage to be honest or to do what is just. By a *morally* courageous person, we mean a person who is disposed toward doing what he thinks is morally right even when he believes that his doing so means, or is likely to mean, his suffering some substantial hardship. As Aristotle suggests, it is "the mark of a brave man to face things that are, and seem, terrible for a man, because it is noble to do so and disgraceful not to do so."[5]

   And, therefore, we can say, along with Aristotle, that a person who endures hardship just for the sake of some reward—such as fame or fortune—or for the sake of avoiding some punishment—such as public disfavor or legal sanctions—is not acting truly courageously in this sense, for he acts not because it is morally right to do so, but to gain a reward or avoid a punishment.[6]

4. The moral quality of a person is no doubt often revealed through her monetary habits. Indeed, for some individuals, the making of money constitutes an end in itself for which they willfully transgress the bounds of morally permissible conduct—for example, the pimp, the drug dealer, the thief, and the hit man. And some—those whom we characterize as stingy, miserly, tight—cling to their money with such tenacity that they would sooner allow great inequities to occur than surrender a dollar.

The morally good person, on the other hand, would appear to be one who has developed *morally respectable* monetary habits. Such a person Aristotle calls a *liberal* person, one who, he states, "will both give and spend the right amounts and on the right objects, alike in small things and in great, and that with pleasure; he will also take the right amounts and from the right sources."[7] Following Aristotle, let us say then that a morally good person must also be, to some degree, a *liberal* person.

5. We also should expect a morally good person to be *benevolent.* By this we mean that she is disposed to do good for others when she is reasonably situated, and to do no harm. And the concern she has for the well-being of others does not arise from some ulterior motive but rather *for its own sake.* Furthermore, she is disposed toward *feeling* certain ways under certain conditions—for example, feeling sorrow over another's misfortune or taking pleasure in another's good fortune or in helping another.[8]

   It is not supposed, however, that in order to be a morally good person one must be disposed toward benefiting others at great sacrifice to oneself; nor is it supposed that such a person must go very far to benefit or feel sympathetic toward those who do not stand in any concrete personal relation, such as friendship or kinship. Still, a person who does not go an inch to benefit *anyone*—unless justice demands it—and who sympathizes with no one is perhaps at most a minimally good person. But one who intentionally harms others, as a matter of course, with pleasure or without regret, cannot normally be regarded as being benevolent. Indeed, such is a mark of a malevolent or morally base person.

6. So too would we expect to find *trustworthiness* in a morally good person. That is, we should expect such a person to be in a habit of keeping the confidences and agreements which he freely accepts or enters upon. Indeed, the person who breaks faith for no good reason is not just being dishonest; he is also being a "traitor" or a "double-crosser."

   This, however, is not to suppose that an individual must *never* breach a trust if he is to be a morally good person. There are undoubtedly some extenuating circumstances in which breaking a trust would be the morally right thing to do—as when keeping it involves working some greater injustice upon someone than that involved in breaking it.[9] Nor is it to be supposed that trustworthiness is a *sufficient* condition of being morally good. There may be loyalty among thieves, for instance, but we should not, for that reason alone, take their lot to be morally good.

7. A morally good person, I would suggest, is one who is regularly disposed to do her *own* moral thinking—that is, to come to her own decisions about moral issues on the basis of her own moral principles; and then, in turn, to *act* upon her considered judgment. Kant expressed this fact by saying that the will of a morally good person (that is, a morally good will) is one which is determined "autonomously."[10] Following his usage, let us say then that a morally good person is a person who possesses *moral autonomy.*

Being such a person is undoubtedly no easy matter, for moral decisions are frequently difficult ones to make. For instance, in cases of conflict between one's moral principles, one must weigh one principle against another and then "strike a moral balance"—as, for instance, in a case where keeping a promise involves inflicting harm upon another; or when, in determining the value of the consequences of an act, one must balance the good consequences against the bad ones. And such determinations are clearly no mere matter of logical deduction. All that one reasonably can be expected to do in such cases is to try one's level best. But it is a mark of a morally autonomous person, and thus of a morally good person, that he actually *makes* such an earnest effort.

Keeping the foregoing criteria of a morally good person in mind, let us now turn to an analysis of lawyers.

THE PURE LEGAL ADVOCATE CONCEPT

Following one traditional usage, we can say that the concept of a lawyer is a *functional* concept—that is, it may be defined in terms of the function or role which a lawyer *qua* lawyer is supposed to perform, in an analogous manner, in which a watchdog may be defined in terms of its function of guarding property, or in which a carpenter's hammer may be defined in terms of *its* function of driving in nails. Hence, just as a good (effective) watchdog may be defined as a dog that performs well the function of guarding property, so too may a good (effective) lawyer be defined as a person who performs well the function or role of a lawyer.[11] What, then, we may ask, *is* the function or role of a lawyer?

One sense of *lawyer* is that in which the role of a lawyer is restricted to that of the client's legal advocate, and in which a good lawyer is thus conceived as being *simply* an effective legal advocate. This sense, which we shall hereafter call the *pure legal advocate concept,* is exemplified in the classic statement made by Lord Brougham when he defended Queen Caroline against George IV in their divorce case before the House of Lords. He states:

> An advocate, in discharge of his duty, knows but one person in all the world, and that person is his client. To save that client by all means and expedients, and at all hazards and costs to other persons, and, amongst them, to himself, is his first and only duty.[12]

The pure legal advocate concept is also more recently suggested by Canon 15 of the ABA *Canons of Professional Ethics,* which states that

> the lawyer owes "entire devotion to the interest of the client, warm zeal in the maintenance and defense of his rights and the exertion of his utmost learning and ability," to the end that nothing be taken or be withheld from him, save by the rules of law, legally applied.[13]

This concept is also suggested, among other places, in *The Ethics of Advocacy* by Charles P. Curtis.[14]

Given the pure legal advocate concept, it is easy for one to conclude that the necessary and sufficient mark of a good lawyer is her tendency to win cases by all legal means. For, as was said, this concept supposes that a good lawyer is simply an effective legal advocate; and it is easy to suppose that the necessary and sufficient mark of an effective legal advocate is her tendency to win cases legally. A good lawyer hence emerges as a legal technician skillful in manipulating legal rules for the advancement of her clients' legal interests; in this sense, the good lawyer is no different than a skillful chess player able to manipulate the rules of chess to win *his* game.

Furthermore, given this concept, a lawyer may, and indeed is required, to do certain kinds of things on behalf of his client which would ordinarily be regarded as being morally objectionable. In such instances all that matters, so far as lawyering is concerned, is that such acts are legal means of advancing the client's legal interests. For instance, a defense attorney in a rape case may cross-examine the prosecutrix, whom he knows to be telling the truth, about her chastity for purposes of casting doubt upon her truthful testimony. Or, he may permit his client to take the stand knowing well that the client will perjure himself. Or, a lawyer in a civil case may invoke a legal technicality (for example, the statute of limitations) on behalf of his client to defeat a just cause against him. Or, a corporate lawyer on a continuing retainer may represent a client who seeks to keep a factory in operation which creates a public health hazard by emitting harmful pollutants into the air.[15]

However, some who countenance the pure legal advocate concept— namely, those sometimes referred to as rule utilitarians—hold that such immoralities as the above-mentioned ones are the necessary evils of maintaining an adversary system which itself does the greatest good. The working assumption here is that the adversarial form of legal administration, wherein two zealous advocates are pitted against each other before an impartial judge, constitutes the best-known way of maximizing truth and justice; and that, furthermore, this system works best when lawyers disregard their personal moral convictions and thereby restrict their professional activities to the zealous legal representation of their clients.[16]

If the rule utilitarian is correct, then lawyering, so conceived, can be said to be a morally justified function, notwithstanding that, on that view, a lawyer may be required to engage in conduct which, by common standards, is morally objectionable. Thus, when seen in this light, the lawyer emerges as a promoter of the highly prized ends of justice and truth, and as an individual who, because of her service to society, is worthy of praise and admiration. Indeed, she begins to seem like a morally good person.

Nevertheless, I want to suggest that the appearance is deceiving, that, on the contrary, the lawyer, so conceived, will inevitably fall short of our marks of a morally good person. Moreover, I want to suggest that, as a result of such shortcomings, there is substantial disutility in the pure legal advocate concept of lawyering which its utilitarian exponents rarely take into account in their utilitarian justification of it.

Let me emphasize that I am supposing, along with Aristotle, that it takes exercise and training to cultivate the character traits of a morally good person: one is not simply born with them.[17] My claim is, accordingly, that the legal function as construed under the pure legal advocate concept, with its emphasis on suppression of the individual lawyer's personal moral convictions, does not allow for the cultivation of these traits and is, in fact, quite conducive to their corresponding vices.

Furthermore, I am supposing that a lawyer cannot easily detach his professional life from his private life and thereby cannot easily be one sort of person with one set of values in the one life, and a quite different sort with quite different values in the other life.[18]

The latter supposition is justified by the substantial amount of empirical evidence that now exists correlating the personality traits of individuals with their specific vocations.[19] One ambiguity, however, is whether individual vocations influence personality traits,[20] or personality traits influence choice of vocation, or some combination of both; for any one of these hypotheses would explain the correlation.

Some studies have supported the hypothesis that personality traits influence choice of profession—that is, that people with certain personalities are attracted to certain professions to satisfy their individual needs.[21] But even *if* this hypothesis is true, and the other above-mentioned hypotheses are false, it is clear that the kind of person found in a profession will remain a function of the way the profession itself is conceived. Specifically, on the hypothesis in question: We would expect the personalities of those choosing careers in law to depend upon their conception of a lawyer. But, if I am correct, then legal practice as construed on the pure legal advocate model could seem attractive only to those individuals who would feel comfortable in a professional climate which discourages, rather than promotes, the personality traits of a morally good person as here understood.

Moral Shortcomings of the Pure Legal Advocate

1. It appears that a lawyer, on the pure legal advocate concept, inevitably will fall short of being a *just* person. For, although she does not violate the principle of treating relevantly similar cases similarly when she gives special preference to her client—inasmuch as being a client would appear to be a *relevant* dissimilarity for the purposes of an adversary system—she does, indeed, work injustices through the violation of the *moral rights* of individuals. For on this concept the lawyer's fundamental professional obligation is to do whatever she can, within legal limits, to advance the legal interests of her clients. But from this basic obligation there derives a more specific one which, contra Kant, may be expressed thus: "Whenever legally possible, treat others not as ends but as means toward winning your case."

    For example, the criminal defense lawyer is thereby authorized to knowingly destroy the testimony of an innocent rape victim to get an acquittal for his client; and a civil lawyer is authorized to knowingly deprive another of what he rightfully deserves by invoking the statute of limitations for the purpose of furthering his client's interests. But we shall concur with Kant that lawyers, like anyone else, have a duty to treat others with the respect which they, as persons, have a right to insist upon.

2. Nor will the pure legal advocate meet the mark of *truthfulness*. For, from her cardinal obligation there derives the secondary obligation of being *un*truthful where doing so can legally contribute toward winning the case. An example of a lawyer who complies with this obligation is one who remains silent when she knows that her client has, under oath, lied to the court. The lawyer, by wittingly saying nothing, engages in deceptive behavior—she contributes to the court's being deceived as to the truth—and is on that count *herself* guilty of being untruthful. Indeed, scrupulous adherence to this obligation could hardly support anything but an untruthful habit.

3. Nor does the concept in question support *moral courage*. For, according to it, the personal moral convictions of a lawyer are irrelevant to his function and should not serve as reasons for zealous representation of clients, or for any sacrifices—of time, money, reputation, and the like—which he may make on their behalf. Indeed, if he is to do his job well, then he must get into the habit of *not* being influenced by his moral outlook. Rather, any sacrifice he may make should be for the sake of obtaining a legal victory, be it a moral one or not. It is plausible to suppose, however, that where

morality takes a back seat, ulterior motives such as the self-aggran-dizement obtained through winning will serve as the primary motivation.

4. Nor does the pure legal advocate concept support *liberality;* for the pure legal advocate, through her unconcern with the moral charac-ter of her clients and the purposes for which they hire her, acquires the habit of taking money from dishonorable individuals for unsa-vory purposes. She thus emerges as a professional who can be hired, for a good sum, to do the dirty work of a villain or a scoundrel. Indeed, she then begins to seem more like a hired assas-sin than like the liberal person whom Aristotle had in view. The high-priced corporate lawyer who wittingly helps her corporate client to market a dangerous product provides us with one example of such a lawyer; and the high-priced criminal lawyer who special-izes in defending mass murderers is another.

5. Furthermore, the pure legal advocate concept does not appear to sat-isfy the minimum condition of *benevolence*—that is, the nonmalevo-lence expected of a morally good person. For, from his primary obligation there derives the secondary obligation to employ even such means to forward a client's interests as are injurious to others, so long, of course, as they are legal. But this also means that a lawyer must learn to put off sympathetic feelings which a benevo-lent person would normally have. In particular, he must get used to working injury upon others without having any strong feelings of guilt, sorrow, or regret, for, to be sure, such feelings could serve only to interfere with the execution of his basic obligation to his client. The result is thus a callous attitude in his dealings with oth-ers. As Charles Curtis puts it, the lawyer "is required to treat oth-ers as if they were barbarians and enemies."[22] And, notwithstand-ing the benefits the lawyer may confer upon his clients, we should not want to call such a person benevolent.

6. Prima facie, it appears that the morally desirable character trait of *trustworthiness* derives strong support from the pure legal advocate concept. For, indeed, it appears that a lawyer cannot put on the most effective representation of her client's interests unless she is also prepared to hold in confidence the secrets entrusted to her by her client. A problem with this view, however, arises in the case in which there is a conflict between a lawyer's obligation to keep her client's confidence and some other *moral* obligation—for instance, that of not harming innocent persons. In such a case, the restricted lawyer is required to keep her client's confidence so long as it is legally possible and in her client's best interest to do so. Her con-

sidered judgment as to what is, under the circumstances, morally best is then quite irrelevant. But it is a mark of a morally good person to choose what she thinks is, all things considered, the *morally right* thing to do in such a situation. Hence, whereas a morally good person sees his obligation to keep confidences as one among several moral principles which may at times override one another, the pure legal advocate sees *her* professional obligation to keep her clients' confidences as binding upon her independently of the moral propriety of doing so in any particular case.

In any event, even *if* it is admitted that the pure legal advocate concept reinforces trustworthiness which, *in itself,* is a morally good trait, this still does not show that the good lawyer, on this conception, can be a morally good person. For, as we have seen, there are *further* requisites of a morally good life.

7. I have suggested that an important quality of a morally good person is that he has *moral autonomy.* However, the pure legal advocate concept offers no stimulus to the cultivation of this trait. For, as we have seen, the pure legal advocate inhabits a world in which his moral judgment is quite beside the point. If morality is relevant, it is so at the level of the judge or the legislator, but it is quite outside the purview of the lawyer's function. The lawyer must know the law and must know that he owes his undivided allegiance to his client. Given the latter, he can easily accommodate himself to the requirements of the law. His decisions are, in effect, made *for him* by the system he serves. He is more like a cog in a machine and less like a person. But the moral world is inhabited by *persons*—that is, individuals who autonomously confront their moral responsibilities; so that, for a lawyer who has grown comfortable with passing the buck of moral responsibility, there is little hope of his aspiring to the morally good life.

THE MORAL AGENT CONCEPT

If I am correct, then it appears that the pure legal advocate who scrupulously adheres to her restricted role, far from being a morally good person, will be given ample opportunity for becoming—if she is not already—quite the opposite. For she will thereby be placed in a professional climate conducive to her being unjust instead of just; untruthful instead of truthful; unmotivated by a moral outlook instead of morally courageous; illiberal instead of liberal; callous instead of benevolent; morally irresponsible instead of morally autonomous. In short, she will fall well below the minimum standards of a morally good person.

But if all this is right, then there will, it seems, be a good deal of *disutility* in the pure legal advocate concept which, indeed, any utilitarian exponent of it ought to consider in computing its overall balance of utility. For it appears that such personality traits as those mentioned above, when associated with our concept of a lawyer, can serve only to bring disrespect upon the legal profession and, by association, upon the legal system as a whole. And this low regard may well lead to a commonplace view of the adversary system as a haven for the guilty and the wicked and as something of which the innocent and the morally good ought to steer clear. It can very well serve to discourage persons of strong moral character from entering the legal profession.[23] It is also quite plausible that pure legal advocates who, by virtue of their knowledge of, and relation to, the law, are uniquely situated to contribute to needed changes in unjust laws, will disconcern themselves with such moral reformation. Moreover, add to these the disutility involved in the unsavory acts performed by pure legal advocates on behalf of their clients in the normal course of discharging their professional obligations— the injuries thereby done to individual litigants as well as to others—and there is at least a strong prima facie case for abandoning the adversary system entirely in favor of a different model (an inquisitorial model for instance) or for adopting a concept of a lawyer in an adversary system which avoids these disutilities.

Fortunately, there *is* a further concept of a lawyer which, while *not* abandoning the adversarial approach, serves to avoid much of the disutility mentioned above.

This further sense, hereafter called the *moral agent concept,* is exemplified, for example, in the remarks on advocacy made by Lord Chief Justice Cockburn, in the presence of Lord Brougham, at a dinner given in honor of M. Berryer on November 8, 1864. He stated:

> My noble and learned friend, Lord Brougham, whose words are the words of wisdom, said that an advocate should be fearless in carrying out the interests of his client: but I couple that with this qualification and this restriction—that the arms which he wields are to be the arms of the warrior and not of the assassin. It is his duty to strive to accomplish the interest of his clients *per fas,* but not *per nefas;* it is his duty, to the utmost of his power, to seek to reconcile the interests he is bound to maintain, and the duty it is incumbent upon him to discharge, with the eternal and immutable interests of truth and justice.[24]

The moral agent concept was also expressed, more recently, by John Noonan when he remarked that:

> a lawyer should not impose his conscience on his client; neither can he accept his client's decision and remain entirely free from all moral responsibility, subject only to the restraints of the criminal law. The framework of the adversary system provides only the first set of guidelines for a lawyer's conduct. He is also a human being and cannot submerge his humanity by playing a technician's role.[25]

And this concept is suggested elsewhere by Richard Wasserstrom, Jeremy Bentham, and *The Report of the Joint Conference on Professional Responsibility*.[26]

Given the moral agent concept, we may no longer say that the good lawyer is *simply* the effective legal advocate; he is, rather, one who is effective in *morally as well as legally* advocating his client's cause. Hence, one cannot infer from this concept that the good lawyer is one who tends to win his cases. For, on this concept, he is not merely a good legal technician; he is also one who conducts himself in the manner of a *morally good person*—that is, as a person with morally desirable character traits.

It is evident, however, that a lawyer cannot so conduct herself unless she also subscribes to the *moral principles* to which a morally good person would subscribe were she to participate in an adversarial process. If our analysis of a morally good person is supposed, then such principles would need to be ones supportive of the personality traits set forth in that analysis. To wit, from these character traits we may derive a corresponding set of moral principles which are adjusted to an adversarial context. I suggest the following formulations, although other similar formulations are possible:

- Treat others as ends in themselves and not as mere means to winning cases. (Principle of Individual Justice)

- Treat clients and other professional relations who are relatively similar in a similar fashion. (Principle of Distributive Justice)

- Do not deliberately engage in behavior apt to deceive the court as to the truth. (Principle of Truthfulness)

- Be willing, if necessary, to make reasonable personal sacrifices— of time, money, popularity, and so on—for what you justifiably believe to be a morally good cause. (Principle of Moral Courage)

- Do not give money to, or accept money from, clients for wrongful purposes or in wrongful amounts. (Principle of Liberality)

- Avoid harming others in the process of representing your client. (Principle of Nonmalevolence)

- Be loyal to your client and do not betray his confidences. (Principle of Trustworthiness)

- Make your *own* moral decisions to the best of your ability and act consistently upon them. (Principle of Moral Autonomy)

We can say that the above principles, or ones like them, at least in part *constitute or define* the moral agent concept of a lawyer; for they are principles to which a lawyer's conduct must to some extent conform if he is to function not simply as a legal advocate but also as a morally good person.

I am *not* suggesting that these principles are unconditional ones. Indeed, to say so would be unrealistic since they will inevitably come into conflict with each other when applied to specific contexts, thereby making it impossible for the lawyer to satisfy all principles at once. (That is, in order to be truthful, a lawyer may need to betray a client's trust, and conversely.) Rather, what I am suggesting is that such principles impose upon a lawyer *conditional*—or prima facie—obligations which, in cases of conflict, must be weighed, one against the other, by the lawyer in question in the context in question.

Let me offer an example which will illustrate the difference between applying, in conflict situations, the above multi-principle model and the pure legal advocate model. In *Lawyers' Ethics in an Adversary System,* Monroe Freedman cites the following:

> In a recent case in Lake Pleasant, New York, a defendant in a murder case told his lawyers about two other people he had killed and where their bodies had been hidden. The lawyers went there, observed the bodies, and took photographs of them. They did not, however, inform the authorities about the bodies until several months later, when their clients had confessed to those crimes. In addition to withholding the information from police and prosecutors, one of the attorneys denied information to one of the victims' parents, who came to him in the course of seeking his missing daughter.[27]

According to Freedman, the lawyers in the above-cited case were simply discharging their *unconditional* professional obligation to represent their clients' legal interests. However, if the moral agent concept is supposed, then it is clear that the above lawyers could have revealed where the bodies were buried. Admittedly, according to the Principle of Trustworthiness, a lawyer has a (prima facie) obligation to keep his client's confidences. But, he also has further (prima facie) obligations such as those of Truthfulness, Individual Justice, and Nonmalevolence. I think that a plausible case can be made that the latter principles were sacrificed to some extent by the lawyers in the Lake Pleasant case at least insofar as their treatment of the relatives of the deceased was concerned. And it is plausible, I believe, to argue that the moral weight of the latter principles, taken collectively, outweighed that of the Principle of Trustworthiness taken by itself in the situation in question. This need *not* have been what the lawyers in the cited case should have finally decided to be the correct balancing of principles. The point I want to make is rather that the lawyers *did have* in the first place, on the conception in question, the *moral autonomy* (as legitimized by our Principle of Moral Autonomy) to make such a judgment on the matter. It is just such moral autonomy—with its weighing of competing moral principles, one against the other—that the pure legal advocate concept disallows.

Of course, if lawyers are allowed such autonomy, there arises the difficulty of providing *criteria* for arbitrating between conflicting principles. This difficulty, we have seen, does not arise on the pure legal advocate model since the pure legal advocate is, in effect, insulated from making moral trade-offs by her unconditional allegiance to her client's legal interests.

One normative view regarding how a lawyer, in accordance with the moral agent concept, might go about solving moral dilemmas takes the form of a "pure" utilitarianism. According to such an ethic, all eight of our principles are to be understood as receiving their ultimate justification from the principle of utility. Hence, in case of conflict the final court of appeal will be the principle of utility itself.

I do not think, however, that such a basis for solving lawyers' moral dilemmas would be adequate. My objection is that which has traditionally been made against utilitarian ethics which are not tempered by justice considerations. Suppose, for example, a criminal lawyer is defending an influential politician accused of rape. Suppose also that the politician admits his guilt to his attorney but nevertheless informs her of his intention to testify under oath (to that which is false) that the defendant first made sexual advances toward him. Now suppose that the politician in question is in the process of bringing about a change in taxation which would mean substantial tax reductions for millions of Americans, and that furthermore, these efforts would most likely be defeated if the politician in question were convicted of rape. On the pure utilitarian criterion, it would appear that the attorney in question would be committed to allowing the politician to perjure himself notwithstanding the defeat of the true rape claim; for the greatest good would (*ex hypothesi*) be served by allowing the politician to escape the charge of rape through his perjured testimony. But in such a case it would seem unjust (by the Principle of Individual Justice) to sacrifice the well-being of the truthful rape victim for the tax reduction. Indeed, in doing so, the lawyer would arguably be committing a grossly immoral act. But, if so, the principle of utility untempered by some principle(s) of justice—such as the Principle of Individual Justice or the Principle of Distributive Justice—would be an inadequate criterion for settling lawyers' moral dilemmas.

A modified utilitarian approach would be to construct a meta-level rule telling lawyers which principle is to receive priority in cases of conflict. The meta-level rule is then to be justified on the basis of the utility of having such a rule. For example, it could be held that the greatest good is ultimately served by requiring lawyers, as a matter of course, to give priority to truthfulness over nonmalevolence.

I do not think, however, that such a position would be tenable. First, like rule utilitarianism in general, it leads to a kind of rule worship where lawyers are asked to abide by a rule even in contexts where the greatest good would not be served by subscribing to it or in which justice considerations would seem to proscribe acting in accordance with it. Furthermore, the view in question is inconsistent with the Principle of Moral Autonomy[,] which legitimizes a lawyer's acting according to his own considered moral judgments. Indeed, in one of its forms—the one in which the Principle of Trustworthiness is unconditionally ranked above all other principles—this view would seem to be extensionally equivalent to the pure legal advocate model according to which a lawyer is asked to ignore his personal moral convictions.

How then is a lawyer, on the moral agent concept, to resolve [antinomies] arising between these principles? Although I do not see any formula for doing so, this is not to suggest that one resolution is as respectable as any other. For one thing, there is a difference between the ethical judgment of a lawyer who is *factually enlightened* and one that is not. For example, the judgment of a lawyer who allows trustworthiness to override harm in a particular case without adequate knowledge of the nature and extent of the harm is less respectable than the judgment of a lawyer who takes account of such facts.

Still, once the facts are known a decision must be made in their light; and I think it would be intellectually dishonest to suggest that there is some principle(s) from which we may logically deduce our decision. Principles take us just so far, leaving the final verdict in our hands.

It is the lack of clear, noncontroversial criteria for resolving moral dilemmas, and the ensuing feeling that ethics is, in the end, a matter of "fiat" or "personal preference," that may make some feel uncomfortable about giving lawyers moral autonomy. However, it should be kept in mind by those who worry about the "gray" areas of ethics that the making of ethical decisions is already an accepted and unavoidable part of the role of *some* officials in our legal system. For example, given the "open-textured" quality of legal rules and precedents themselves, judges often need to rely upon their own *moral* evaluations in deciding whether a given set of facts falls under a given legal rule or precedent.[28] But if judges can handle their moral problems—and I believe that, in general, they *do* handle them—then there appears to be less reason to fear that lawyers cannot or will not handle *their* moral problems.

THE MORAL AGENT CONCEPT AND THE ABA CODE OF PROFESSIONAL RESPONSIBILITY

In his classical formulation of a natural law jurisprudence, St. Thomas Aquinas distinguishes between certain basic moral principles, those which he calls *general* principles of natural law and certain *secondary* ones; the latter being more specific deductions from the former. For example, he tells us that "One must not kill" is a secondary principle deducible from "One should do harm to no man." Moreover, such secondary principles, he maintains, assume the status of *human laws* provided that they are enforced by the state.[29]

I think Aquinas's distinction between general and secondary principles of natural law is instructive for our purposes; for, *if* we construe the legal profession on the moral agent concept, then we might say that our eight principles constitute certain general "natural laws" of legal practice—*natural* in the sense that they are at least in part *definitive* of the lawyer's role—from which more specific moral principles can be deduced.[30] Moreover, an examination of the ABA *Code of Professional Responsibility* reveals that some such deductions have indeed assumed the force of law.

What follows is a listing of some, although not all, corollaries of our general principles as they occur in the Code.[31] In the light of this list, I shall suggest certain revisions required in the Code if it is to adequately support the moral agent concept of a lawyer. I shall then, in the next part of this paper, use these revisions as a basis for criticizing the ABA's current code of ethics, the *Model Rules of Professional Responsibility.*

It will be noted that some of the principles listed below are prefixed by "EC" (*ethical consideration*), whereas others are prefixed by "DR" (*disciplinary rule*). The former are "aspirational in character" and are "intended to provide guidance, but their violation is not intended to result in disciplinary action." The disciplinary rules, on the other hand, state the "minimum level of conduct below which no lawyer can fall without being subject to disciplinary action." I think, however, that it would be unsound to infer, from the fact that violations of DRs are subject to disciplinary action whereas violations of ECs are not, that the CRs are somehow more important to legal practice. At least this inference would be unsound from the point of view of the moral agent conception which stresses aspirational aspects of morality as well as ground-floor duties. Moreover, it should be noted that some states actually consider the ECs to be obligatory in character.[32]

Individual Justice

DR 7-105(A) A lawyer shall not present, participate in presenting, or threaten to present criminal charges solely to obtain an advantage in a civil matter.

DR 4-101(B)(3) Except when permitted under DR 4-101(C),[33] a lawyer shall not knowingly use a confidence or secret of his client for the advantage of himself or of a third person, unless the client consents after full disclosure.

Distributive Justice

DR 8-101(A)(2) A lawyer who holds a public office shall not use his public position to influence, or attempt to influence, a tribunal to act in favor of himself or of a client.

DR 5-105(A) A lawyer shall decline proffered employment if the exercise of his independent professional judgment in behalf of a client will be or is likely to be adversely affected by the acceptance of the proffered employment, except to the extent permitted under DR 5-105(C).[34]

DR 5-105(B) A lawyer shall not continue multiple employment if the exercise of his independent professional judgment in behalf of a client will be or is likely to be adversely affected by his representation of another client, except to the extent permitted under DR 5-105(C).

Truthfulness

DR 7-102(A)(3)-(7) In his representation of a client a lawyer shall not (3) conceal or knowingly fail to disclose that which he is required by law to reveal; (4) knowingly use perjured testimony or false evidence; (5) knowingly make a false statement of law or fact; (6) participate in the creation or preservation of evidence when he knows or it is obvious that the evidence is false; (7) counsel or assist his client in conduct that the lawyer knows to be illegal or fraudulent.

DR 7-102(B)(1) A lawyer who receives information clearly establishing that his client has, in the course of the representation, perpetrated a fraud upon a person or tribunal shall promptly call upon his client to rectify the same, and *if his client refuses or is unable to do so, he shall reveal the fraud to the affected person or tribunal.*[35]

Moral Courage

EC 2-27 Regardless of his personal feelings, a lawyer should not decline representation because a client or a cause is unpopular or community reaction is adverse.

EC 2-25 Every lawyer, regardless of professional prominence or professional workload, should find time to participate in serving the disadvantaged. The rendition of free legal services to those unable to pay reasonable fees continues to be an obligation of each lawyer. . . .

Liberality

DR 2-106(A) A lawyer shall not enter into an agreement for, charge, or collect an illegal or clearly excessive fee.

DR 7-109(C) A lawyer shall not pay, offer to pay, or acquiesce in the payment of compensation to a witness contingent upon the content of his testimony or the outcome of the case. . . .

Nonmalevolence

DR 7-102(A)(1) In his representation of a client, a lawyer shall not file a suit, assert a position, conduct a defense, delay a trial, or take other action on behalf of his client when he knows or when it is obvious that such action would serve *merely* to harass or maliciously injure another.[36]

EC 7-10 The duty of a lawyer to represent his client with zeal does not militate against his concurrent obligation to treat with consideration all persons involved in the process and to avoid the infliction of *needless* harm.[37]

Trustworthiness

> **DR 4-101(B)(1)-(2)** Except when permitted under DR 4-101(C),[38] a lawyer shall not knowingly (1) reveal a confidence or secret of his client; (2) use a confidence or secret of his client to the disadvantage of the client.

> **DR 7-101(A)(1)** A lawyer shall not intentionally fail to seek the lawful objectives of his client through reasonably available means permitted by law and the disciplinary rules, except as provided by DR7-101(B).

> **DR 7-101(B)** A lawyer does not violate this disciplinary rule, however, by acceding to reasonable requests of opposing counsel which do not prejudice the rights of his client, by being punctual in fulfilling all professional commitments, by avoiding offensive tactics, or by treating with courtesy and consideration all persons involved in the legal process.

It may appear, from a brief study of the above rules and considerations, that the moral agent concept is well entrenched in the Code. I do not believe, however, that this is quite right; for, although secondary precepts drawn from our general principles can be found in significant numbers, the principle of moral autonomy, which legitimizes trade-offs between principles where conflicts arise, is not unequivocally visible.

Consider DR 7-102(B)(1), cited above under Truthfulness. The italicized portion suggests that the lawyer's allegiance to his client is not so unconditional after all. However, this clause was amended as of March 1, 1974, by the ABA to include the further proviso "except when the information is protected as a privileged communication."[39] Thus amended, the lawyer is disallowed the autonomy to reveal such frauds even when, in a given context, he considers the obligation of truthfulness to override that of confidentiality.

In recognition of such autonomy, the rule in question might be revised along the following lines:

> **DR 7-102(B)(1) (Revised)** A lawyer who receives information clearly establishing that his client has, in the course of representation, perpetrated a fraud upon a person or tribunal shall promptly call upon his client to rectify the same, and if his client refuses or is unable to do so, he shall reveal the fraud to the affected person or tribunal *except* when the information is protected as a privileged communication *and* the lawyer sincerely believes, after careful consideration of the relevant facts, that, notwithstanding the perpetration of the fraud, the disclosure of such privileged information in such cases would be morally wrong.

The above revision seems to me to present a compromise between the version of the rule as amended in 1974 and the earlier formulation. For, like the

1974 rule, it recognizes a lawyer's obligation of confidentiality; and, like the earlier versions, it recognizes an obligation of truthfulness. But, unlike both versions, it gives a lawyer the autonomy to make trade-offs between these two obligations when conflicts arise. In short, this revision recognizes that neither truthfulness nor confidentiality is absolute; that one can, on occasion, give way to the other.

For example, if a complainant in a rape case confidentially informed her lawyer that she had falsely denied under oath her former unchastity in order to protect her reputation as well as the prospects of winning her case, the lawyer might be hard put to disclose such privileged information to the court. On the other hand, if a defendant in a rape case confidentially informed his lawyer of his having falsely denied under oath that he even *saw* the prosecutrix on the night of the alleged rape, then the lawyer might be hard put *not* to reveal the information *even if* privileged. In the former case, the fraudulent testimony would not completely destroy the prospects of an informed verdict; in the latter case, though, the fraudulent testimony would greatly impede the search for truth if not corrected. As such, a lawyer might allow confidentiality to be overridden by truthfulness in the latter case although not in the former case. My proposed formulation of DR 7-102(B)(1) at least has the virtue of recognizing such possibilities.

Consider EC 7-10, cited above under Nonmalevolence. It asserts two "concurrent" duties—namely, the duty of a lawyer to represent her client with zeal and her duty to treat others with consideration and to avoid the infliction of "needless harm." But what harm is to be termed "needless" for purposes of this consideration?

One response is that "needless" harms are those which are not necessary for the purpose of advancing the client's legal concerns. This understanding would, it seems to me, be consistent with the Code's use of "merely" in DR 7-102(A)(1); for actions which serve "*merely* to harass or maliciously injure another" do not serve also to advance legal interests. When so understood, however, EC 7-10 is tantamount to saying that lawyers should not harm others *if* this is not in the client's legal interest. But what if it *is* in the client's legal interest to harm another? On the present understanding, and in the absence of any further proviso, the lawyer would apparently be bound by her obligation to her client.

If EC 7-10 is to unequivocally recognize two "concurrent" obligations—one proscribing harming others and the other prescribing zealous advocacy—it will need to be reformulated. But, clearly, once two such obligations are recognized, the possibility of conflict between them arises—a possibility which does not occur when the proscription is only against "needless" harms as above understood and not against harms in general. Moreover, the resolution of such conflicts calls for lawyers' moral autonomy—that is, a lawyer must then attempt to make reasonable trade-offs between these obligations when they conflict. In short, the lawyer becomes a moral agent confronted with moral dilemmas.

To bring EC 7-10 into line with the moral agent concept, I would accordingly suggest something like the following reformulation:

> **EC 7-10 (Revised)** In his representation of a client, a lawyer should not engage in conduct, even if in his client's best legal interest, when, upon careful consideration of relevant facts and likelihoods, he sincerely believes that, notwithstanding his obligation to his client, the seriousness of the harm which would thereby ensue to others would render his so acting morally untenable.

The above formulation, unlike the former one, recognizes two concurrent obligations which can at times conflict; furthermore, it gives the individual lawyer the *moral autonomy* to rationally resolve such dilemmas.

Once EC 7-10 is so revised, I would have no objection to DR 7-102(A)(1). This could then be understood as an unconditional proscription of harmful acts serving no legal interest—which is as it should be on the present conception. It would obviously be untenable, however, to set forth a DR which *un*conditionally proscribed *all* harmful acts!

Consider, too, secondary precepts of trustworthiness—in particular, DR 7-101(A)(1). It states that the exceptions to a lawyer's zealous advocacy for her client's lawful objectives are provided for by DR 7-101(B), which runs as follows:

> **DR 7-101(B)** In his representation of a client, a lawyer may (1) where permissible, exercise his professional judgment to waive or fail to assert a right or position of his client; (2) refuse to aid or participate in conduct that he believes to be unlawful, even though there is some support for an argument that the conduct is legal.

The first clause of the above rule gives the lawyer the personal autonomy to refuse to assert a position opted for by her client. However, it is not clear that this autonomy extends to *moral* disputes, for EC 7-9 states the following:

> **EC 7-9** In the exercise of his professional judgment on those decisions which are for his determination in the handling of a legal matter, a lawyer should always act in a manner consistent with the best interests of his client. However, when an action in the best interest of his client seems to him to be unjust, he may ask his client for permission to forego such action.

Presumably, DR 7-101(B)(1) must refer to matters concerning the best interest of the client, although not to moral ones; for, according to EC 7-9, a lawyer caught up in a moral dilemma may *ask* the client to forego the course of action in question; but this is other than to actually "waive or fail to assert a right or position of his client."

It appears, then, that to bring the code into line with the moral agent concept, a further "morals" proviso is needed for DR 7-101(B). I suggest something like the following:

> **DR 7-101(B)(3)** In his representation of a client, a lawyer may refuse to aid or participate in conduct that he sincerely believes, after careful reflection on the relevant facts, to be unjust or otherwise morally wrong notwithstanding his obligation to seek the lawful objectives of his client.

Similarly, revisions along the following lines are needed in EC 7-9:

> **EC 7-9 (Revised)** In the exercise of his professional judgment on those issues which are for his determination in the handling of a legal matter, a lawyer should typically act in a manner consistent with the best interests of his client. However, in those cases where he sincerely believes, after careful reflection on the relevant facts, that an action in the best interest of his client is unjust or otherwise immoral, he should inform his client of the same and forego such action.[40]

Finally, to bring the moral agent concept into clear focus, I would suggest adding to the Code a general ethical consideration regarding lawyers' moral autonomy. It may, perhaps, read as follows:

> A cardinal duty of a lawyer is to zealously represent his clients' interests within the bounds of the law; but it must also be kept in view that a lawyer, as a servant of such values as truth and justice, is also a moral agent with a duty to *morally* uphold the legal interests of his clients. A lawyer should never allow his role as advocate to blind him to his own sense of propriety.

The foregoing suggestions are not intended to cover all the changes in the Code which would need to be made *if* it were to adequately support the moral agent concept. They are, however, ones which seem to me to be necessary ones. In general, these changes would aim at increasing lawyers' moral autonomy within the parameters of an adversarial process. Without such autonomy, the other moral principles reflected in the Code—other than that of Trustworthiness—would be without force. Where the obligation to zealously pursue the client's legal interests conflicts with other principles—such as Nonmalevolence and Truthfulness, as well as the secondary principles thereof—the lawyer, on the unrevised formulation of the Code, is entitled to pay only lip service to them.

One issue, however, is whether such lawyer autonomy *ought,* in the first place, to be codified—that is, built into a code of legal ethics. After all, it might be argued, a code of legal ethics needs to be enforceable if it is to be efficacious in controlling lawyers' conduct; and the discretionary approach would tend to make such enforceability either difficult or impossible.

There are several responses to the above argument. First, codifying lawyer autonomy in the manner here suggested is not tantamount to giving a lawyer a license to do *whatever* she thinks (rightly or wrongly) is morally indicated. A lawyer's increased moral autonomy will still be circumscribed around *other* legal realities. For example, it would not be permissible for a lawyer who has moral autonomy to counsel a client to commit perjury or to intentionally present false testimony to a tribunal *even if* she thought, with all sincerity, that there were overriding moral reasons—say, utilitarian ones—for doing so. Indeed, such a lawyer who failed to recognize the limits of her authority would still find herself subject to disciplinary action.

Second, it would be an oversimplification of the situation to suppose that the *specific* disciplinary rules which incorporate moral autonomy would be rendered totally unenforceable. Although it is true that a lawyer who exercises his moral discretion, where permitted by a disciplinary rule, could not be subject to disciplinary action for doing so, it is false to suppose that disciplinary action could not be taken against him on *other* grounds. For example, my revised version of DR 7-102(B)(1) permits a lawyer moral discretion about revealing frauds perpetrated upon a person or tribunal by his client. But this does not mean that a lawyer can, for example, accept additional fees from a client in return for withholding information about his perjurious testimony. Indeed, such conduct would still constitute a violation of DR 7-102(B)(1), as revised, and it would be subject to disciplinary action. To this extent DR 7-102(B)(1) would retain some measure of enforceability. And the same thing could be said, *mutatis mutandis*, about the discretionary authority conferred upon a lawyer by my DR 7-101(B)(3).

Third, not all the suggested revisions I have made pertain to disciplinary rules. Some—such as those of EC 7-10, EC 7-9, and my suggestion for a general ethical consideration about lawyers' moral autonomy—have instead been concerned with ethical considerations. And, strictly speaking, ethical considerations are not always supposed to be *enforceable;* yet they still do provide important guidelines of lawyers' professional conduct no less than the disciplinary rules, which *are* always supposed to be enforceable.

Fourth, the latter consideration raises a question about the primary purpose of a code of professional ethics. Even *if* a significant measure of enforceability is lost by codifying lawyers' moral autonomy, I do not believe that the raison d'etre of the Code will be sacrificed. It is plausible to argue that the *primary* purpose of a code of professional ethics is to *guide* professionals' actions. It is only when this primary function breaks down that issues of enforcement even arise.[41] To be sure, the imposition of sanctions for noncompliance may serve to strengthen the motive of conformity to the rules as announced. But this is not the *only* way to encourage such conformity. The cultivation of an *internalized* sense of professional responsibility is still another.[42]

A further objection to codifying the moral agent concept might be put as follows. Lawyers, like anyone else, are fallible in their moral judgments. Hence, instead of placing the burden of moral decisionmaking in their hands, it would seem more of a solution to protect the rights of litigants and other affected parties by instituting appropriate laws, thereby providing new legal boundaries to which the lawyer must conform her advocacy. In this way, a lawyer may be free to concentrate her efforts on the zealous defense of her client's interests *within the bounds of the law* without the added headache of moral decisionmaking.

The above argument, in my estimation, makes a valid point. Our laws *should* strive as much as possible to protect the rights of litigants and other affected parties. But it errs when it supposes that the expansion of law in this direction will serve to eliminate moral dilemmas in legal practice. A similar fallacy has, it seems to me, occurred in reasoning concerning the role of a judge. I have in mind here what has sometimes been called "formalism," "conceptualism," or "mechanical jurisprudence"—that is, the belief that by formulating general rules, the need to exercise discretion when applying them to particular cases may be eliminated. But, as I have suggested earlier,[43] the "open-textured" nature of such rules makes unavoidable the exercise of discretion when subsuming particular cases under them; and, indeed, such discretion can be, and frequently is, of a *moral* character. Similarly, it would be mistaken to suppose that by formulating general rules concerning the rights of litigants and affected others the lawyer may be relieved of the need to exercise moral discretion in the course of complying with those rules. For *their* "open-textured" character will still leave space for moral dilemmas. In short, moral problems are inevitable in legal practice; hence a lawyer might as well be given the autonomy to intelligently address them, rather than ignoring them, transferring them to other lawyers by withdrawing from morally perplexing cases, or otherwise attempting to avoid them. As shall be suggested in the following discussion, the ABA in its recent move to revise the Code has explicitly acknowledged the limited capacity of general rules to dictate moral outcomes, and therewith the need for moral discretion on the part of lawyers.

THE MORAL AGENT CONCEPT AND THE ABA MODEL RULES OF PROFESSIONAL CONDUCT

The ABA has recently adopted its *Model Rules of Professional Conduct.*[44] This document constitutes an attempt at a comprehensive revamping of the 1969 Code.

One salient change is in its format. The Model Rules, unlike the Code, do not distinguish between ethical considerations and disciplinary rules. Rather, all the new rules are taken to be obligatory and much of what appears in the ECs of the Code is incorporated into the rules themselves or into *comments* on the rules which contain explanations of, and rationales behind, the rules.[45]

The Model Rules, I believe, represent an important step in the direction of the moral agent concept. Indeed, the Preamble provides a clear suggestion of this concept:

> Virtually all difficult ethical problems arise from conflicts between a lawyer's responsibilities to clients, to the legal system and to the lawyer's own interest in remaining an upright person while earning a satisfactory living. The Rules of Professional Conduct prescribe terms

for resolving such conflicts. Within the framework of these Rules many difficult issues of professional discretion can arise. Such issues must be resolved through the exercise of sensitive professional and moral judgment guided by the basic principles underlying the Rules.

And, again, the late Robert J. Kutak, Chairman of the ABA Commission on Evaluation of Professional Standards, in commenting on the discussion draft of the Rules, asserted that

an implicit theme running through the draft is the recognition that a certain measure of professional discretion is required on the part of a lawyer confronted with ethical choices among competing values. No rules that honestly attempt to grapple with the dilemmas of ethical choice can dictate in every case what the proper choice must be. But codes and rules can—and, we believe, the discussion draft does—compel the reasoned exercise of that choice.[46]

However, notwithstanding such recognition of lawyers' moral autonomy, I believe that much of what I have said about the 1969 Code can be said, *mutatis mutandis*, about the current Model Rules. For example, Rule 3.3(a)(2), regarding "Candor toward the Tribunal," makes it obligatory for a lawyer to disclose a client's perjury to the court should the client himself refuse to do so.[47]

Now Rule 3.3(a)(2) has, I think, the virtue of recognizing unequivocally that the bond of lawyer-client confidentiality is not an absolute. In this respect, it represents a significant advance beyond DR 7-102(B)(1) as amended by the ABA in 1974 (although the amended form was only adopted by some, not all, states).[48] However, it seems to me that 3.3(a)(2) does not go quite far enough when it supposes that candor toward the tribunal must, in *all* cases of perjury (or at best in all such cases not falling under a constitutional requirement),[49] override lawyer-client confidentiality. And, in this regard, I believe that my revised version of DR 7-102(B)(1), suggested earlier,[50] is instructive. For, as there noted, it provides the lawyer with the *autonomy* to balance truthfulness against trustworthiness *in the context in which the conflict arises*. Rule 3.3(a)(2) does not allow the lawyer any such discretion. But, as Kutak himself admitted, "no rules that honestly attempt to grapple with the dilemmas of ethical choice can dictate in every case what the proper choice must be."

Rule 1.2 of the Model Rules addresses the scope of the lawyer's authority in handling his client's case. According to this rule, "The client has ultimate authority to determine the purposes to be served by legal representation, within the limits imposed by law and the lawyer's professional obligations."[51]

But what is a lawyer to do if a client insists upon pursuing objectives or means which, although legal, are morally undesirable? What if, for instance, the client's unscrupulous tactics will have "material adverse effect" upon a third party? Apparently, the lawyer will be unauthorized by the rule in question to follow her own moral conscience, for a lawyer "should defer to a client regarding such questions as . . . concern for third persons who might be adversely affected."[52] I submit that my reformulations of DR 7-101(B) and EC 7-9, suggested earlier,[53] at least have the virtue of allowing a lawyer, in such cases, to follow her own moral conscience.

Rule 4.4, concerning "Respect for Rights of Third Persons," says that

> In representing a client a lawyer shall not use means that have no substantial purpose other than to embarrass, delay, or burden a third person. . . .

However, in this rule, "no other substantial purpose" appears to be functioning in a similar way in which "merely" and "needless" function, respectively, in DR 7-102(A)(1) and EC 7-10.[54] For, presumably, a means employed by a lawyer which served to advance a client's legal interests but which also served to cause significant harm to a third person *would have* a substantial purpose other than the harm incurred; and, as such, the conduct in question would be permissible under Rule 4.4 and perhaps mandated by Rule 1.2—should the client insist upon such a course of action. But I believe that a rule which adequately reflects the moral agent concept would proscribe such conduct if the lawyer considered the resulting harm to be of such seriousness as to render the course of action morally untenable. In this regard, my earlier reformulation of EC 7-10[55] is instructive.

There has been much controversy generated in the ABA House of Delegates surrounding the correct formulation of Rule 1.6 of the Model Rules, which pertains to "Confidentiality of Information." The earlier 1981 draft of this rule proposed by the Kutak Commission allowed lawyers a good deal of discretion in revealing confidential information. For instance, it permitted—but did not require—a lawyer to reveal confidential information "to prevent the client from committing a criminal or fraudulent act that the lawyer believes is likely to result in death or substantial bodily harm, or substantial injury to financial interest or property of another"; as well as "to rectify the consequences of a client's criminal or fraudulent act in the commission of which the lawyer's services had been used."[56]

Now, this formulation of Rule 1.6, as proposed by the Kutak Commission, clearly recognizes the prima facie character of Trustworthiness as well as the importance of the Principle of Autonomy, which gives lawyers authority to balance competing moral claims in the specific contexts in which they arise—other things being equal. In this regard, the rule in question goes a considerable distance toward exemplifying the moral agent concept of a lawyer.

However, the Kutak Commission's formulation of Rule 1.6 did not survive intact; and the amended version of Rule 1.6 which was finally approved by the ABA House of Delegates in August, 1983, "eliminated much of the discretion to reveal client confidences that the proposed rule would have given."[57] The approved version of Rule 1.6 permits a lawyer to reveal confidential information which the lawyer reasonably believes necessary to "prevent the client from committing a criminal act that the lawyer believes is likely to result in imminent death or substantial bodily harm." Therein, the earlier reference to "fraudulent acts"— in addition to criminal ones—is dropped; the autonomy to reveal confidential information for purposes of preventing "substantial injury to financial interest or property of another" is no longer recognized; and such autonomy for purposes of "rectifying the consequences of a client's criminal or fraudulent act in the commission of which the lawyer's services had been used" is not recognized.

Nor does the approved version of Rule 1.6 represent any significant advance upon the 1969 Code, so far as the moral agent concept is concerned.[58] In fact, Rule 1.6 as amended would seem to be *inconsistent* with Rule 3.3, which makes it obligatory for a lawyer to reveal to a tribunal information pointing to a client's perjury; for, given the confidential nature of any such information, Rule 1.6, as amended, would seem to require that such information *not* be revealed.[59]

One way of resolving this apparent inconsistency would be to *dis*allow a lawyer to reveal a client's perjured testimony. But another way to resolve it would be to unequivocally acknowledge the prima facie or conditional status of confidentiality. And this would be tantamount to granting lawyers the autonomy to balance, in context, confidentiality against other competing values—namely, truthfulness as well as other principles constitutive of the moral agent concept. The Kutak Commission's formulation of Rule 1.6 has, in my estimation, cast its vote in the latter direction; and it at least has the virtue of being consistent with Rule 3.3.

Rule 6.1 on "Pro Bono [Public] Service" holds that a lawyer has a responsibility to "render public interest legal service." This responsibility, it states, may be discharged by:

> providing professional service at no fee or a reduced fee to persons of limited means or to public service or charitable groups or organizations, by service in activities for improving the law, the legal system or the legal profession, and by financial support for organizations that provide legal services to persons of limited means.

Prima facie, the above rule appears to have made an advance toward the moral agent concept, especially insofar as it supports the principles of Moral Courage and Liberality. However, in the Comment on this rule, it is stated explicitly that the responsibility in question "is not intended to be enforced through disciplinary process." The upshot of this has been to render the new rule equivalent in effect to EC 2-25 of the 1969 Code, which also recognized such a responsibility. (In fact, EC 2-25 has been incorporated directly into the Comment provided for Rule 6.1.) This is so because the only possible practical difference between Rule 6.1 and EC 2-25 could be in terms of enforceability. But Rule 6.1 is intended to be no more enforced than the old EC—which, of course, was not enforced. Therefore, it does not truly constitute an advance toward the moral agent concept.

It should be remarked, however, that the earlier draft of the Model Rules proposed by the Kutak Commission did *not*, in its Comment on Rule 6.1, state that the responsibility it creates "is not intended to be enforced by disciplinary process." Had this version of 6.1 survived intact—which it did not—it would have constituted a significant move in the direction of the moral agent concept.

The foregoing remarks on the Model Rules, as well as those on the Code, have not been intended as a thoroughgoing critique. They do, however, point to some key places in the Model Rules where more attention should be focused *if* such rules are to more adequately reflect the moral agent concept. A crucial question, obviously, is whether such a concept, as here characterized, is the appropriate route to travel.

I have already argued that the alternative to the moral agent concept—that is, the pure legal advocate concept—can have unwelcome effects upon the moral character of lawyers and that this, in turn, can have a significant measure of social disutility which *any* utilitarian calculus (whether this calculus be "pure" or mixed with deontological considerations) should consider. Yet there are also arguments *against* this conception. I will now discuss what seem to be to be two very common ones.

THE MORAL AGENT CONCEPT: SOME ARGUMENTS AGAINST IT ANSWERED

According to one argument, if lawyers are given the autonomy to break confidences with clients in those situations in which they judge further serious moral principles to be overriding, then the obligation lawyers have to keep their clients' confidences will be destroyed. As a result, clients will cease to confide in their lawyers and thus will withhold information necessary for an adequate defense of their legal interests. The final result will then be the demise of the adversary system itself and its accompanying benefits. For example, according to Monroe Freedman,

> the adversary system, within which the lawyer functions, contemplates that the lawyer frequently will learn from the client information that is highly incriminating and may even learn, as in the Lake Pleasant case, that the client has in fact committed serious crimes. In such a case, if the attorney were required to divulge that information, the obligation of confidentiality would be destroyed, and with it, the adversary system itself.[60]

First, the argument in question rests upon the unfounded assumption that the obligation of confidentiality will be destroyed if lawyers are allowed to take exception to it in serious moral conflicts. That is, because lawyers in general are allowed to make such exceptions does not mean that they will no longer see themselves as being under an obligation to keep their clients' confidences. To argue thus is like arguing that if certain exceptions to the proscription against killing are permitted—such as self-defense—then people will no longer see themselves as having a duty not to kill others. The fall down the slippery slope does not necessarily occur.

Second, those who advance the argument in question do not provide adequate evidence to support the claim that clients in general will cease to confide in their lawyers if they are not given an unconditional guarantee by their lawyers that all information conveyed, no matter what, will be taken confidentially. Indeed, even such intimate bonds as friendship, to which the lawyer-client relation has sometimes been compared,[61] have their moral limits. We do not typically expect our friends to surrender their moral integrity for our security. Yet that fact does not serve to destroy the bond of trust existing in such a relation. The claim that the bond of trust existing between lawyer and client will be destroyed if lawyers are given their moral autonomy appears to be equally as unfounded.

Third, even if it is admitted that according lawyers such moral autonomy will cause *some* clients, even some innocent ones, to omit information necessary for their adequate defense, this fact does not entail that the problem will be so widespread and serious as to lead to the destruction of the adversary system. It must also be kept in mind that an unconditional bond of confidentiality also generates difficulties. (Consider, for example, those resulting from the lawyers' actions in the Lake Pleasant case.) Moreover, there are favorable consequences of according lawyers moral autonomy which must also be taken into account. Thus, for example, Bentham suggests that one such consequence would be "that a guilty person will not in general be able to derive quite so much assistance from his law advisor, in the way of concerting a false defense, as he may do at present.[62]

In short, there is simply no clear proof that the effects of according lawyers the autonomy to take moral exception to the confidentiality principle would be so dramatic as to destroy the adversary system.

It is sometimes argued that, if lawyers were permitted the power of accepting or refusing employment or of retaining or withdrawing from cases, according to their personal moral judgments as to the guilt of a party or as to the goodness of a cause, then the role of the judge would be usurped; the lawyer, in effect, would become the judge. And this could, in turn, present serious moral difficulties, particularly for defendants in criminal cases. For there it may be argued that, if an individual defendant seems guilty enough, then no criminal lawyer will take his case, and, as such, he will be deprived of his constitutional right to counsel and to his day in court. Moreover, it is often difficult for a criminal lawyer to withdraw from a case he has already undertaken without leaving the impression that his ex-client is guilty. And, of course, it is always possible that a person who seems guilty is not *actually* guilty.[63]

I do think, however, that the above argument succeeds in destroying the moral agent concept. For one thing, it depends upon the untenable assumption that if the moral agent concept is generally accepted, then *no* criminal lawyer will defend seemingly guilty individuals. It is more realistic to suppose that, no matter *what* concept is adopted, there will always be *someone* to take up such a cause.

But more importantly, the argument appears to be attacking a straw man. For there is no inconsistency between a criminal lawyer's defending an apparently guilty client and her accepting the moral agent concept. None of our eight moral principles constituting that concept would, in fact, militate against her doing so. Indeed, it appears that an adequate understanding of our principle of distributive justice would demand that criminal lawyers *not* allow individuals, no matter how guilty they might *seem* to be, to be deprived of their constitutional right to counsel. Moreover, it often takes *moral courage* to represent clients who have come under public disfavor (see EC 2-27). Hence, the moral agent concept appears to support criminal lawyers' defense of the guilty rather than to proscribe it.

Nor do I think that there is any solid support for the claim that, if lawyers accept the moral agent concept with its insistence upon lawyers' moral autonomy, the role of the judge will be usurped by the lawyer. For such autonomy is not tantamount to license. The autonomous lawyer is still his client's advocate; it is his job to defend his client's legal interests and to present them in the clearest and most forceful light. But he must accomplish this task within the parameters of morality—that is, without forfeiting his moral integrity. It is not at all clear, therefore, why such a conception must lead to usurpation of the judge's role by the lawyer.

CONCLUDING REMARKS

Again we return to the question whether a good lawyer, in an adversary system, can be a morally good person. In answering this, a great deal depends upon our concept of a lawyer. For it is our full conception of the role of a professional which sets the parameters on the kind of personality compatible with that role and which serves to shape the personalities of its participants accordingly, or to invite those sorts who would fit it. I do not mean to suggest by this that there are not currently practicing lawyers who fit our criteria of morally good persons. This would be an absurd suggestion. Yet it is, I think, probable that most of these individuals have adopted the moral agent concept in some form or other.

If the legal profession is to move further in the direction of the moral agent concept, some changes must be made in its understanding. I have suggested, for example, some ways in which the *Code of Professional Responsibility* could be revamped in this direction. Indeed, the *Model Rules of Professional Conduct* now embraced by the ABA seems to me to be, in some respects, an initial step in this direction.

But it will, I submit, take more than the revamping of the Code in order to fully institute the moral agent concept. The spirit of this concept will need to be *internalized,* as well, through the appropriate education. Above all, law schools and prelaw curricula will need to provide prospective lawyers with the facilities for cultivating an understanding of, and sensitivity to, moral problems. For the lawyer's ability to deal sensibly with such moral problems is an essential part of his professional function. It is beyond the scope of this paper to outline in detail what such curricula would consist of, but they would, undoubtedly, include diverse courses in applied ethics and legal philosophy.[64]

Presently, the legal profession is, I think, on a course toward the moral agent concept. Conceptual shifts of this magnitude, however, do not spring up full-blown overnight; they take time and occur in stages. But, to be sure, it is a process worth nurturing, not just for the good of the legal profession itself, but for the good of all of us, whom the profession so vitally serves.[65]

NOTES

1. See Aristotle, *Nicomachean Ethics,* Bk. II. All quotations in this paper from *Aristotle's Ethics* are from 9 *The Works of Aristotle* (W.D. Ross ed. 1963).

2. Compare Joel Feinberg's distinction between "comparative" and "noncomparative" senses of justice in his *Social Philosophy* 98-99 (1973). Compare also John Stuart Mill's discussion of justice in his *Utilitarianism* ch. 5.

3. See Chisholm & Feehan, "The Intent to Deceive," 74 *Journal of Philosophy* 143-59 (1977).

4. Compare C. Fried, *Right and Wrong* 57-58 (1978).

5. Aristotle, *supra* note 1, at 1117a16.

6. Id. at 1116a15-b3.

7. Id. at 1120b29-31.

8. Compare H. Sidgwick, *The Methods of Ethics* 238-39 (1962); compare also A. Smith, *The Theory of Moral Sentiments* 345 (1966).

9. Compare, e.g., the discussion of justified violations to the rule of confidentiality between a physician and his patient in T.L. Beauchamp & J.F. Childress, *Principles of Biomedical Ethics* 214-17 (1979).

10. I. Kant, *Groundwork of the Metaphysic of Morals* 98-99 (H.J. Paton Trans. 1964).

11. A person can admittedly perform the function of a lawyer without actually *being* a lawyer, in an analogous manner in which a rock can serve the function of a hammer without actually being a hammer. Further conditions must also be satisfied—for example, a lawyer must have gone to law school and passed the bar. For this complication in the analysis of functional concepts—which is here ignored for the sake of simplicity—see G.H. von Wright, *The Varieties of Goodness* 20-22 (1968).

12. M.H. Freedman, *Lawyers' Ethics in an Adversary System* 9 (1975).

13. American Bar Association, *Canons of Professional Ethics* (1908).

14. See Curtis, "The Ethics of Advocacy," 4 *Stanford Law Review* 3-23 (1951).

15. The cited examples appear, respectively, in Freedman, *supra* note 12 at ch. 4, esp. 48-49; Freedman, "Professional Responsibility of the Criminal Defense Lawyer: The Three Hardest Questions," 64 *Michigan Law Review* 1474-78 (1966); Fried, "The Lawyer as Friend: The Moral Foundations of the Lawyer-Client Relations," 85 *Yale Law Journal* 1064 (1976); Wasserstrom, "Lawyers as Professionals: Some Moral Issues," 5 *Human Relations* 8 (1975).

16. "Are there no limits (short of violating criminal laws and rules of court) to the partisan zeal that an attorney should exert on behalf of a client who may be a murderer, a rapist, a drug pusher, or a despoiler of the environment? Is the lawyer never to make a conscientious judgment about the impact of the client's conduct on the public interest and to temper the zealousness of his or her representation accordingly? I believe that the adversary system is itself in the highest public interest...and that it is, therefore, inconsistent with the public interest to

direct lawyers to be less than zealous in their roles as partisan advocates in an adversary system." Freedman, "Are There Public Interest Limits on Lawyers' Advocacy?" 2 *Journal of the Legal Prof.* 47 (1977).

17. Aristotle, *supra* note 1 at 1103a15-b1.

18. Compare Richard Wasserstrom's suggestion that the behavior engaged in by the Watergate lawyers on behalf of Richard Nixon—lying to the public, dissembling, stonewalling, tape-recording conversations, playing dirty tricks, etc.—was "the likely if not inevitable consequence of their legal acculturation," *supra* note 15 at 15.

19. For example, *see generally,* "Factors and Theories of Career Development," in B. Shertzer & S. Stone, *Fundamentals of Guidance* ch. 12 (1981).

20. See, e.g., the discussions of studies on the influence of vocations upon personality traits in Komarovsky & Sargent, "Research into Subcultural Influences upon Personality," in *Culture and Personality* 145-48 (S.S. Sargent and M.W. Smith eds. 1949).

21. See, e.g., Teevan, "Personality Correlates of Undergraduate Fields of Specialization," 18 *Journal of Consulting Psychology* 212-14 (1954).

22. Curtis, *supra* note 14 at 5.

23. See Teevan, *supra* note 21.

24. Costigan, "The Full Remarks on Advocacy of Lord Brougham and Lord Chief Justice Cockburn at the Dinner to M. Berryer on November 8, 1864," 19 *California Law Review* 523 (1931).

25. Noonan, "The Purpose of Advocacy and the Limits of Confidentiality," 64 *Michigan Law Review* 1492 (1966).

26. See, respectively, Wasserstrom, *supra* note 15; J. Bentham, "Rationale of Judicial Evidence," bk. 9, ch. 5, in 7 *The Works of Jeremy Bentham* (J. Bowring ed. 1843); American Bar Association and the Association of American Law Schools, "Professional Responsibility: Report of the Joint Conference," 44 *A.B.A. Journal* 1161 (1958).

27. M. Freedman, *supra* note 12 at 1.

28. Compare Jones, "Legal Realism and Natural Law," in *The Nature of Law* (M.P. Golding ed. 1966).

29. See St. Thomas Aquinas, Summa Theological, 1. 11., Q. 94, a. 6; Q. 91, a. 3.

30. If we do say this, then we will be countenancing a "natural law" conception of lawyering resembling in its essentials a "natural law" conception of law. For just as the latter conception denies any separation between law and morality, such a conception of lawyering denies any separation between *legal practice* and morality. We could, perhaps, also carry the analogy with jurisprudence further and suggest that the pure legal advocate conception of a lawyer establishes for legal practice a "legal positivist" conception which maintains a separation (conceptually) between legal practice and morality in a similar way in which "legal positivist" conceptions of law maintain a separation (conceptually) between law and morality.

31. All rules listed are from the *American Bar Association, Code of Professional Responsibliity* (1969), hereinafter cited as A.B.A. CODE. Their classification under the eight principles, however, is my own.

32. See the *Prelminary Statement* to the A.B.A. Code.

33. According to DR 4-101(C)(1)-(4), a lawyer may reveal "(1) confidences or secrets with the consent of the client or clients affected, but only after a full disclosure to them; (2) confidences or secrets when permitted under Disciplinary Rules or required by law or court orders; (3) the intention of his client to commit a crime and the information necessary to prevent the crime; (4) confidences or secrets necessary to establish or collect his fee or to defend himself or his employees or associates against an accusation of wrongful conduct." A.B.A. Code.

34. DR 5-105(C) states: "In the situations covered by DR 5-105 (A) and (B), a lawyer may represent multiple clients if . . . he can adequately represent the interests of each and if each consents to the representation after a full disclosure of the possible effects of such representation on the exercise of his independent professional judgment on behalf of each." A.B.A. Code.

35. The italics are mine.

36. The italics are mine.

37. The italics are mine.

38. See A.B.A. Code, *supra* note 33.

39. See M. Freedman, *supra* note 12 at 257-59.

40. The provision that a lawyer should inform his client of his decision to forego the action in question seems to me to follow from our Principle of Individual Justice as well as that of Trustworthiness.

41. Compare H.L.A. Hart's discussion of the criminal law and its sanctions in *The Concept of Law* 38-39 (1961).

42. This concept is discussed briefly later; see p. 50 of [article in original journal].

43. See p. 50 of [article in original journal].

44. American Bar Association, Model Rules of Professional Conduct, reprinted in 52 U.S.L.W. 1-27 (Aug. 16, 1983) (No. 7). Final approval of the Model Rules came at the Annual Meeting of the American Bar Association, Atlanta, July 28, 1983–August 4, 1983.

45. It should be noted that the Ethical Considerations proposed in the preceding part of this paper could well be incorporated into the commentary format followed by the Model Rules. Hence, these proposals continue to be relevant notwithstanding the A.B.A.'s decision to omit Ethical Considerations as such from their ethical code. I owe this point to Professor William Heffernan.

46. R.J. Kutak, 66 *American Bar Association Journal* 48 (1980).

47. It should, however, be noted that although, according to Rule 3.3, the obligation to disclose a client's perjury also applies to criminal defense lawyers, this obligation is "qualified by constitutional provisions for due process and the right to counsel in criminal cases." This means that, in some jurisdictions, such a lawyer may, notwithstanding this obligation, be required to "present an accused as a witness if the accused wishes to testify, even if counsel knows the testimony will be false." See the parts of the Comment accompanying Rule 3.3 which are entitled "Constitutional Requirements," "Refusing to Offer Proof Believed to be False," and "Perjury by a Criminal Defendant."

48. See the discussion of this amendment, at p. 50 of [article in original journal].

49. See note 47 above.

50. See id.

51. Comment, Rule 1.2, Model Rules.

52. Id.

53. See p. 51 of [article in original journal].

54. See *Nonmalevolence,* p. 49 of [article in original journal].

55. See p. 51 of [article in original journal].

56. *American Bar Association Commission on Evaluation of Professional Standards, Final Draft of The Model Rules of Professional Conduct* Rule 1.6 (1981).

57. "Midyear Meeting of American Bar Association," 51 *U.S.L.W.* 2489 (Feb. 22, 1983).

58. Compare DR 4-101(C) of the Code as cited in note 33 above.

59. See the discussion concerning consistency in the report on the "Midyear Meeting of the American Bar Association," *supra* note 56 at 2491.

60. M. Freedman, *supra* note 12 at 5.

61. See e.g., Fried *supra* note 15.

62. Compare generally, M. Freedman, *supra* note 12.

63. Compare generally, M. Freedman, *supra* note 12.

64. Investigations of this sort are already in progress. See e.g., The Council for Philosophical Studies, S. Gorovitz & B. Miller, *Professional Responsibility in the Law: A Curriculum Report from the Institute on Law & Ethics* (Summer 1977). (The Center for Philosophy and Public Policy at the University of Maryland has also recently announced the availability of a model course on "Ethics and the Legal Profession" prepared by Professor David Luban. A copy can be obtained by sending $2.50 for postage and handling to Maryland Courses, Center for Philosophy and Public Policy, Woods 0123, University of Maryland, College Park, MD 20742.)

65. I am thankful to Professor Walter Probert and Judge Charles Smith for their assistance in obtaining important references. I am also thankful to Gale Spieler Cohen and an anonymous referee of *Criminal Justice Ethics* for their contribution to some of the ideas contained herein.

DISCUSSION QUESTIONS

1. Do you feel that the adversary system, with two legal advocates pitted against each other, constitutes the best way of maximizing truth and justice? Why or why not?

2. Do you feel that it would make a difference if lawyers' moral autonomy were codified (that is, built into a code of legal ethics)? Explain your answer in detail.

3. Explain in detail the strengths and weaknesses of Cohen's pure legal advocate concept and moral agent concept. List some advantages and disadvantages of each.

4. Do you agree with Cohen that not promising complete confidentiality to clients would have no negative effects?

CASE STUDY

Chapter 9:
Pure Legal
Advocates and
Moral Agents:
Two Concepts
of a Lawyer
in an Adversary
System

CHILD RAPIST

You are an Assistant District Attorney in a small circuit court region. The region consists of three counties with an average population of 80,000 people per county. The community you serve is primarily composed of middle-class people with middle-class values. Having come from a large city, you were particularly impressed with the small town atmosphere and easy way of life.

The District Attorney General hired you straight out of law school two years ago. You felt that a job with the D.A.'s office would be an excellent opportunity to gain needed experience and develop a reputation as a good lawyer. Your ambition is to enter the political arena and perhaps run for State Representative in a couple of years. You have stressed a "law and order" image in order to accomplish your career ambitions.

As you prepare to look over the court docket for tomorrow's cases, your secretary advises you that Sheriff's Investigator John Wainwright is waiting to see you. "John, come in. I was going to call you about our burglary case tomorrow. You didn't have to come over here in person today."

"Thanks Bill, but I need to talk with you about another matter. You know, we arrested a young man by the name of Fred Granger a couple of days ago for rape and I wanted to fill you in on some details," the investigator begins.

"Yes, I was at the arraignment, remember?" you jokingly respond. Fred Granger is a 22-year-old white male who works in a nearby factory. He has a high school education and no prior felony arrests or convictions, but does have a previous conviction for DUI two years ago and one for possession of marijuana

---

From Michael Braswell, Tyler Fletcher and Larry S. Miller, *Human Relations and Corrections,* 4th ed. (Prospect Heights, IL: Waveland Press), 1997. Reprinted with permission.

three years ago. He has been charged with the rape of a 13-year-old girl under state code 37-1-2702:

> Any adult who carnally knows a child under the age of fourteen by sexual intercourse shall be guilty of the capital offense of rape. The punishment for same shall be not less than ten years nor more than thirty years in the state penitentiary without parole. It shall be no defense that the child consented to the act or that the defendant was ignorant of the age of the child.

The punishment for this offense is no different than for the crime of forcible rape in your state. Fred Granger was arrested on a complaint from the parents of a thirteen year old girl named Debbie. It seems Fred picked Debbie up for a date, went to the lake and had sexual intercourse with her. It was a clear violation of the law and an apparently easy conviction since Fred admitted to arresting officers that he had sex with Debbie.

"So, what information do you have for me, John?" you ask.

"We've obtained statements from everyone involved. This is basically what went down. Fred knew Debbie's sister, Nina, who is twenty years old. Fred and Nina had gone out before on a couple of dates in the past and have had intercourse. It seems Nina and her younger sister, Debbie, have the reputation of being "easy." Anyway, Fred called Nina for a date and Nina wasn't at home. Debbie answered the phone and started flirting with Fred. Fred asked Debbie if she wanted to go with him to the lake and Debbie agreed. Debbie apparently wore a very revealing bathing suit and 'came on' to Fred. They had intercourse and Fred dropped Debbie back home. Debbie's parents inquired about her activities for the day and Debbie told them everything, even about the sex. That's when we got the call. Fred states that he thought Debbie was over eighteen and that Debbie consented to having sex with him. Debbie supports this story. Both of them were drinking beer at the lake," the investigator continued.

"Yes, well, I see. But, it's no defense for Fred to be ignorant of her actual age and no defense for him that Debbie consented. He probably got her drunk anyway. The law is clear on this matter," you advise.

"Yes, I know. But this Debbie has a reputation of being very promiscuous. She is very open about the fact that she consented. She now says she's in love with Fred. Needless to say, her parents aren't very happy about her attitude, but they seem to have very little control over her or her sister. In addition, anyone can look at Debbie and make a mistake about her age." The investigator pulls out and shows you a recent photograph of Debbie.

The photograph surprises you. You had not previously seen the victim but from the photography Debbie looks well over twenty years old.

"Hey, she does look twenty," you respond. "She certainly would have fooled me."

"Yeah. Anyone could have made that mistake," the investigator replies.

Looking over the statements that the investigator brought, you begin to feel uneasy about the case. In the legal sense, Fred is a criminal. He violated the state law. He has no legal defense. The girl is under fourteen which means she cannot testify that she consented. The fact that she has had intercourse before cannot be used as a defense for Fred. It seems to be an open and shut case. Fred is looking at ten to thirty years with no chance of parole. Even if he got the minimum ten years, it is still a stiff punishment for ignorance. You decide to call on the District Attorney General for advice.

"Yes, Bill. I see why you are concerned. It seems to me you have three options here. One, you could *nolle prosequi* the case (a formal entry on the record by the prosecuting attorney that he will not prosecute the case further). Two, you could reduce charges through a plea bargain agreement. Or, three, you could prosecute to the fullest extent of the law. It's basically a choice between legal ethics and personal ethics. Legal ethics would dictate that you prosecute to the fullest. A crime by statutes has been committed and you are sworn to uphold the law. In that sense, it would not be legally ethical for you to *nolle prosequi* or plea bargain when you have such a strong case. And, if you did, it might affect your political career. The news media and the public would not take your letting a 'child rapist' off without comment. On the other hand, your personal ethics dictate that this Fred fellow is not a typical criminal. He's guilty of stupidity maybe. But, apparently when you look at Debbie, you can see why. If you prosecuted the case, the jury might see Debbie the way Fred saw her and acquit him. But that is a big chance to take. Juries are unpredictable and you can't bring up the fact that she 'looks' of age. I don't know Bill. It's your decision. I'll back you on whatever you decide."

Questions:

1. Examine this case in terms of the moral agent and the legal agent. Compare and contrast the two in terms of the decision that the prosecuting attorney must make.

2. Develop a position in regard to what you would do if you were the prosecuting attorney. Explain your reasoning. What do you think would be the most likely outcome of this case?

CHAPTER 10

Why Prosecutors Misbehave

Bennett L. Gershman

The duties of the prosecuting attorney were well-stated in the classic opinion of Justice Sutherland 50 years ago.[1] The interest of the prosecutor, he wrote, "is not that he shall win a case, but that justice shall be done. As such, he is in a peculiar and very definite sense the servant of the law, the twofold aim of which is that guilt shall not escape or innocence suffer. He may prosecute with earnestness and vigor— indeed, he should do so. But, while he may strike hard blows, he is not at liberty to strike foul ones."[2]

Despite this admonition, prosecutors continue to strike "foul blows," perpetuating a disease which began long before Justice Sutherland's oft-quoted opinion. Indeed instances of prosecutorial misconduct were reported at least as far back as 1897,[3] and as recently as the latest volume of the *Supreme Court Reporter.*[4] The span between these cases is replete with innumerable instances of improper conduct of the prosecutor, much of which defies belief.

One of the leading examples of outrageous conduct by a prosecutor is *Miller v. Pate,*[5] where the prosecutor concealed from the jury in a murder case the fact that a pair of undershorts with red stains on it, a crucial piece of evidence, were stained not by blood but by paint. Equally startling is *United States v. Perry,*[6] where the prosecutor, in his summation, commented on the fact that the "defendants and their counsel are completely unable to explain away their guilt."[7] Similarly, in *Dubose v. State,*[8] the prosecutor argued to the jury: "Now, not one sentence, not one scintilla of evidence, not one word in any way did this defendant or these attorneys challenge the credibility of the complaining witness."[9] At a

> **KEY CONCEPTS:**
>
> courtroom misconduct
>
> forensic misconduct
>
> harmless error doctrine
>
> oral advocacy
>
> prosecutorial misconduct

time when it should be clear that constitutional and ethical standards prevent prosecutors from behaving this way,[10] we ought to question why prosecutors so frequently engage in such conduct.

Much of the above misconduct occurs in a courtroom. The terms "courtroom" or "forensic misconduct" have never been precisely defined. One commentator describes courtroom misconduct as those "types of misconduct which involve efforts to influence the jury through various sorts of inadmissible evidence."[11] Another commentator suggests that forensic misconduct "may be generally defined as any activity by the prosecutor which tends to divert the jury from making its determination of guilt or innocence by weighing the legally admitted evidence in the manner prescribed by law."[12] For purposes of this analysis, the latter definition applies, as it encompasses a broader array of behavior which can be classed as misconduct. As will be seen, prosecutorial misconduct can occur even without the use of inadmissible evidence.

This article will address two aspects of the problem of courtroom misconduct. First, it will discuss why prosecutors engage in courtroom misconduct, and then why our present system offers little incentive to a prosecutor to change his behavior.

WHY MISCONDUCT OCCURS

Intuition tells us that the reason so much courtroom misconduct by the prosecutor[13] occurs is quite simple: it works. From my ten years of experience as a prosecutor, I would hypothesize that most prosecutors deny that misconduct is helpful in winning a case. Indeed, there is a strong philosophical argument that prosecutorial misconduct corrupts the judicial system, thereby robbing it of its legitimacy. In this regard, one would probably be hard pressed to find a prosecutor who would even mention that he would consider the thought of some form of misconduct.

Nonetheless, all of this talk is merely academic, because, as we know, if only from the thousands of cases in the reports, courtroom misconduct does occur. If the prosecutor did not believe it would be effective to stretch his argument to the ethical limit and then risk going beyond that ethical limit, he would not take the risk.

Intuition aside, however, several studies have shown the importance of oral advocacy in the courtroom, as well as the effect produced by such conduct. For example, the student of trial advocacy often is told of the importance of the opening statement. Prosecutors would undoubtedly agree that the opening statement is indeed crucial. In a University of Kansas study,[14] the importance of the opening statement was confirmed. From this study, the authors concluded that, in the course of any given trial,[15] the jurors were affected most by the first strong presentation which they saw. This finding leads to the conclusion that if a prosecutor were to present a particularly strong opening argument, the jury would favor the prosecution throughout the trial. Alternatively, if the prosecutor were to provide a weak opening statement, followed by a strong opening statement by the defense, then, according to the authors, the jury would favor the defense during the trial. It thus becomes evident that the prosecutor will be best served by making the strongest opening argument possible, and thereby [assisting] the jury in gaining a better insight into what they are about to hear and see. The opportunity for the prosecutor to influence the jury at this point in the trial is considerable, and virtually all prosecutors would probably attempt to use this opportunity to their advantage, even if the circumstances do not call for lengthy or dramatic opening remarks.[16]

An additional aspect of the prosecutor's power over the jury is suggested in a University of North Carolina study.[17] This study found that the more arguments counsel raises with respect to the different substantive arguments offered, the more the jury will believe in that party's case. Moreover, this study found that there is not necessarily a correlation between the amount of objective information in the communication and the persuasiveness of the presentation.

For the trial attorney, then, this study clearly points to the advantage of raising as many issues as possible at trial. For the prosecutor, the two studies taken together would dictate an "action packed" opening statement, containing as many arguments that can be mustered, even those which might be irrelevant or unnecessary to convince the jury of the defendant's guilt. The second study would also dictate the same strategy for the closing argument. Consequently, a prosecutor who, through use of these techniques, attempts to assure that the jury knows his case may, despite violating ethical standards to seek justice,[18] be "rewarded" with a guilty verdict. Thus, one begins to perceive the incentive that leads the prosecutor to misbehave in the courtroom.[19]

Similar incentives can be seen with respect to the complex problem of controlling evidence to which the jury may have access. It is common knowledge that, in the course of any trial, statements frequently are made by the attorneys or witnesses, despite the fact these statements may not be admissible as evidence. Following such a statement, the trial judge may, at the request of opposing counsel, instruct the jury to disregard what they have heard. Most trial lawyers, if they are candid, will agree that it is virtually impossible for jurors realistically to disregard these inadmissible statements. Studies here again demonstrate that our intuition is correct and that this evidence often is considered by jurors in reaching a verdict.

For example, an interesting study conducted at the University of Washington[20] tested the effects of inadmissible evidence on the decisions of jurors. The authors of the test designed a variety of scenarios whereby some jurors heard about an incriminating piece of evidence while other jurors did not. The study found that the effect of the inadmissible evidence was directly correlated to the strength of the prosecutor's case. The authors of the study reported that when the prosecutor presented a weak case, the inadmissible evidence did in fact prejudice the jurors. Furthermore, the judge's admonition to the jurors to disregard certain evidence did not have the same effect as when the evidence had not been mentioned at all. It had a prejudicial impact anyway.

However, the study also indicated that when there was a strong prosecution case, the inadmissible evidence had little, if any, effect.[21] Nonetheless, the most significant conclusion from the study is that inadmissible evidence had its most prejudicial impact when there was little other evidence on which the jury could base a decision. In this situation, "the controversial evidence becomes quite salient in the jurors' minds."[22]

Finally, with respect to inadmissible evidence and stricken testimony, even if one were to reject all of the studies discussed, it is still clear that although "stricken testimony may tend to be rejected in open discussion, it does have an impact, perhaps even an unconscious one, on the individual juror's judgment."[23] As with previously discussed points, this factor—the unconscious effect of stricken testimony or evidence—will generally not be lost on the prosecutor who is in tune with the psychology of the jury.

The applicability of these studies to this analysis, then, is quite clear. Faced with a difficult case in which there may be a problem of proof, a prosecutor might be tempted to sway the jury by adverting to a matter which might be highly prejudicial. In this connection, another study[24] has suggested that the jury will more likely consider inadmissible evidence that favors the defendant rather than inadmissible evidence that favors conviction.[25]

Despite this factor of "defense favoritism," it is again evident that a prosecutor may find it rewarding to misconduct himself in the courtroom. Of course, a prosecutor who adopts the unethical norm and improperly allows jurors to hear inadmissible proof runs the risk of jeopardizing any resulting conviction. In a situation where the prosecutor feels there is a weak case, however, a subsequent reversal is not a particularly effective sanction when a conviction might have been difficult to achieve in the first place. Consequently, an unethical courtroom "trick" can be a very attractive idea to the prosecutor who feels he must win.[26] Additionally, there is always the possibility of another conviction even after an appellate reversal. Indeed, while a large number of cases are dismissed following remand by an appellate court, nearly one half of reversals still result in some type of conviction.[27] Therefore, a prosecutor can still succeed in obtaining a conviction even after his misconduct led to a reversal.

An additional problem in the area of prosecutor-jury interaction is the prosecutor's prestige; since the prosecutor represents the "government," jurors are more likely to believe him.[28] Put simply, prosecutors "are the good guys of the legal system,"[29] and because they have such glamour, they often may be tempted to use this advantage in an unethical manner. This presents a problem for the prosecutor in that the "average citizen may often forgive, yea urge prosecutors on in ethical indiscretions, for the end, convictions of criminals, certainly justifies in the public eye any means necessary."[30] Consequently, unless the prosecutor is a person of high integrity and is able to uphold the highest moral standards, the problem of courtroom misconduct inevitably will be tolerated by the public.

Moreover, when considering the problems facing the prosecutor, one also must consider the tremendous stress under which the prosecutor labors on a daily basis. Besides the stressful conditions faced by the ordinary courtroom litigator,[31] prosecuting attorneys, particularly those in large metropolitan areas, are faced with huge and very demanding caseloads. As a result of case volume and time demands, prosecutors may not be able to take advantage of opportunities to relax and recover from the constant onslaught their emotions face every day in the courtroom."[32]

Under these highly stressful conditions, it is understandable that a prosecutor occasionally may find it difficult to face these everyday pressures and to resist temptations to behave unethically. It is not unreasonable to suggest that the conditions under which the prosecutor works can have a profound effect on his attempt to maintain high moral and ethical standards. Having established this hypothesis, one can see yet another reason why courtroom misconduct may occur.

WHY MISCONDUCT CONTINUES

Having demonstrated that courtroom misconduct may in many instances be highly effective, the question arises as to why such practices continue in our judicial system. A number of reasons may account for this phenomenon. Perhaps the most significant reason for the continued presence of prosecutorial misconduct is the harmless error doctrine. Under this doctrine, an appellate court can affirm a conviction despite the presence of serious misconduct during the trial. As Justice Traynor once stated, the "practical objective of tests of harmless error is to conserve judicial resources by enabling appellate courts to cleanse the judicial process of prejudicial error without becoming mired in harmless error."[33]

Although the definition advanced by Justice Traynor portrays the harmless error doctrine as having a more desirable consequence, this desirability is undermined when the prosecutor is able to misconduct himself without fear of sanction. Additionally, since every case is different, what constitutes harmless error in one case may be reversible error in another. Consequently, harmless error determinations do not offer any significant precedents by which prosecutors can judge the status of their behavior.

By way of illustration, consider two cases in which the prosecutor implicitly told the jury of his personal belief in the defendant's guilt. In one case, the prosecutor stated, "I have never tried a case where the evidence was so clear and convincing."[34] In the other case, the prosecutor told the jury that he did not try cases unless he was sure of them.[35] In the first case the conviction was affirmed, while in the second case the conviction was reversed. Interestingly, the court in the first case affirmed the conviction despite its belief that the "prosecutor's remarks were totally out of order."[36] Accordingly, despite making comments which were "totally out of order," the prosecutor did not suffer any penalty.

Contrasting these two cases presents clear evidence of what is perhaps the worst derivative effect of the harmless error rule. The problem is that the stronger the prosecutor's case, the more misconduct he can commit without being reversed. Indeed, in the [*People v.*] *Shields* case, the court stated that "the guilt of the defendant was clearly established not only beyond a reasonable doubt, but well beyond any conceivable doubt."[37] For purposes of our analysis, it is clear that by deciding as they do, courts often provide little discouragement to a prosecutor who believes, and rightly so, that he does not have to be as careful about his conduct when he has a strong case. The relation of this factor to the amount of courtroom misconduct cannot be ignored.

Neither can one ignore the essential absurdity of a harmless error determination. To apply the harmless error rule, appellate judges attempt to evaluate how various evidentiary items or instances of prosecutorial misconduct may have affected the jury's verdict. Although it may be relatively simple in some cases to determine whether improper conduct during a trial was harmless, there are many instances when such an analysis cannot properly be made but nevertheless is made. For example, consider the situation when an appellate court is divided on whether or not a given error was harmless. In *United States v. Antonelli Fireworks Co.,*[38] two judges (including Judge Learned Hand) believed that the prosecutor's error was harmless. Yet, Judge Frank, the third judge sitting in the case, completely disagreed, writing a scathing dissent nearly three times the length of the majority opinion. One wonders how harmless error can be fairly applied when there is such a significant difference of opinion among highly respected members of a court as to the extent of harmfulness of trial errors. Perhaps even more interesting is the Supreme Court's reversal of the Court of Appeals for the Second Circuit's unanimous finding of harmless error in *United States v. Berger.*[39] As noted, *Berger* now represents the classic statement of the scope of the prosecutor's duties. Yet, in his majority opinion for the Second Circuit, Judge Learned Hand found the prosecutor's misconduct harmless.

The implications of these contradictory decisions are significant, for they demonstrate the utter failure of appellate courts to provide incentives for the prosecutor to control his behavior. If misconduct can be excused even when reasonable judges differ as to the extent of harm caused by such misbehavior, then very little guidance is given to a prosecutor to assist him in determining the propriety of his actions. Clearly, without such guidance, the potential for misconduct significantly increases.

The *Shields* case presents yet another factor which suggests why the prosecutor has only a limited incentive to avoid misconduct. In *Shields,* the court refused to review certain "potentially inflammatory statements" made by the prosecutor because of the failure of the defense to object.[40] Although this approach has not been uniformly applied by all courts, the implications of this technique to reject a defendant's claim are considerable. Most important, it encourages prosecutors to make remarks that they know are objectionable in the hope that defense counsel will not object. This situation recalls the previous discussion, which dealt with the effect of inadmissible evidence on jurors. Defense counsel here is in a difficult predicament. If he does not object, he ordinarily waives any appealable issue in the event of conviction. If he does object, he highlights to the jury the fact that the prosecutor has just done something which some jurors may feel is so damaging to the defendant that the defense does not want it brought out.

The dilemma of the defense attorney in this situation is confirmed by a Duke University study.[41] In that study, jurors learned of various pieces of evidence which were ruled inadmissible. The study found that when the judge admonished the jury to disregard the evidence, the bias created by that evidence was not significantly reduced.[42] Consequently, when a prejudicial remark is made by the prosecutor, defense counsel must act carefully to avoid damaging his client's case. In short, the prosecutor has yet another weapon, in this instance an arguably unfair aspect of the appellate process, which requires preservation of an appealable issue.[43]

A final point when analyzing why prosecutorial misconduct persists is the unavailability or inadequacy of penalties visited upon the prosecutor personally in the event of misconduct. Punishment in our legal system comes in varying degrees. An appellate court can punish a prosecutor by simply cautioning him not to act in the same manner again, reversing his case, or, in some cases, identifying by name the prosecutor who misconducted himself.[44] Even these punishments, however, may not be sufficient to dissuade prosecutors from acting improperly. One noteworthy case[45] describes a prosecutor who appeared before the appellate court on a misconduct issue for the third time, each instance in a different case.

Perhaps the ultimate reason for the ineffectiveness of the judicial system in curbing prosecutorial misconduct is that prosecutors are not personally liable for their misconduct. In *Imbler v. Pachtman*,[46] the Supreme Court held that "in initiating a prosecution and in presenting the state's case, the prosecutor is immune from a civil suit for damages under Section 1983."[47] Furthermore, prosecutors have absolute rather than a more limited, qualified, immunity. Thus, during the course of a trial, the prosecutor is absolutely shielded from any civil liability which might arise due to his misconduct, even if that misconduct was performed with malice.

There is clearly a need for some level of immunity to be accorded all government officials. Without such immunity, much of what is normally done by officials in authority might not be performed out of fear that their practices are later deemed harmful or improper. Granting prosecutors a certain level of immunity is reasonable. Allowing prosecutors to be completely shielded from civil liability in the event of misconduct, however, provides no deterrent to courtroom misconduct.

CONCLUSION

This analysis was undertaken to determine why the issue of misconduct seems so prevalent in the criminal trial. For the prosecutor, the temptation to cross over the allowable ethical limit must often be irresistible because of the distinct advantages that such misconduct creates in assisting the prosecutor to win his case by effectively influencing the jury. Most prosecutors must inevitably be subject to this temptation. It takes a constant effort on the part of every prosecutor to maintain the high moral standards which are necessary to avoid such temptations.

Despite the frequent occurrences of courtroom misconduct, appellate courts have not provided significant incentives to the prosecutor to avoid misconduct. It is not until the courts decide to take a stricter, more consistent approach to this problem that inroads will be made in the effort to end it. One solution might be to impose civil liability on the prosecutor who misconducts himself with malice. Although this will not solve the problem, it might be a step in the right direction.

NOTES

1. Berger v. United States, 295 U.S. 78 (1935).

2. Id. at 88.

3. See Dunlop v. United States, 165 U.S. 486 (1897), where the prosecutor, in an obscenity case, argued to the jury "I do not believe that there are twelve men that could be gathered by the venire of this court . . ., except where they were bought and perjured in advance, whose verdict I would not be willing to take. . . ." Id. at 498. Following this remark defense counsel objected, and the court held that statement to be improper.

4. See Caldwell v. Mississippi, 105 S. Ct. 2633 (1985) (improper argument to capital sentencing jury); United States v. Young, 105 S. Ct. 1038 (1985) (improper argument but not plain error).

5. 386 U.S. 1 (1967). In this case, the Supreme Court overturned the defendant's conviction after the Court of Appeals for the Seventh Circuit had upheld it. The Court noted that the prosecutor "deliberately misrepresented the truth" and that such behavior would not be tolerated under the Fourteenth Amendment. Id. at 67. [sic]

6. 643 F.2d 38 (2d Cir. 1981).

7. Id. at 51.

8. 531 S.W.2d 330 (Texas 1975).

9. Id. at 331. The court noted that the argument was clearly a comment on the failure of the defendant to testify at trial.

10. See Griffin v. California, 380 U.S. 609 (1965), where the Supreme Court applied the Fifth Amendment to the states under the Fourteenth Amendment.

11. Alschuler, "Courtroom Misconduct by Prosecutors and Trial Judges," 50 *Texas Law Review* 627, 633 (1972).

12. Note, "The Nature and Function of Forensic Misconduct in the Prosecution of a Criminal Case," 54 *Colorado Law Review* 946, 949 (1954).

13. Of course, there is also a significant amount of defense misconduct which takes place. In this respect, for an interesting article which takes a different approach than this article, see Kamm, "The Case for the Prosecutor," 13 U. Tol. L. Rev. 331 (1982), where the author notes that "courts carefully nurture the defendant's rights while cavalierly ignoring the rights of the people."

14. Pyszczynski, "The Effects of Opening Statement on Mock Jurors' Verdicts in a Simulated Criminal Trial," II J. *Journal of Applied Social Psychology* 301 (1981).

15. All of the cited studies include within the report a caveat about the value of the study when applied to a "real world" case. Nonetheless, they are still worthwhile for the purpose of this analysis.

16. In some jurisdictions, attorneys may often use the voir dire to accomplish the goal of early influence of the jury.

17. Calder, "The Relation of Cognitive and Memorial Processes to Persuasion in a Simulated Jury Trial," 4 *Journal of Applied Social Psychology* 62 (1974).

18. See Model Code of Professional Responsibility EC 7-13 (1980) ("The duty of the prosecutor is to seek justice.").

19. Of course, this may apply to other attorneys as well.

20. Sue, S., R.E. Smith, and C. Caldwell, "The Effects of Inadmissible Evidence on the Decisions of Simulated Jurors—A Moral Dilemma," 3 *Journal of Applied Social Psychology* 345 (1973).

21. Perhaps lending validity to application of the harmless error doctrine, which will be discussed later in this article.

22. Sue, note 20 *supra* at 351.

23. Hastie, *Inside the Jury* 232 (1983).

24. Thompson, "Inadmissible Evidence and Jury Verdicts," 40 *Journal of Personality & Social Psychology* 453 (1981).

25. The author did note that the defendant in the test case was very sympathetic and that the results may have been different with a less sympathetic defendant.

26. Of course, this begs the question: "Is there a prosecutor who would take a case to trial and then feel that he didn't have to win?" It is hoped that, in such a situation, trial would never be an option. Rather, one would hope for an early dismissal of the charges.

27. Roper, "Does Procedural Due Process Make a Difference?" 65 *Judicature* 136 (1981). This article suggests that the rate of nearly 50 percent of acquittals following reversal is proof that due process is a viable means for legitimatizing the judiciary. While this is true, the fact remains that there is still a 50 percent conviction rate after reversal, thereby giving many prosecutors a second chance to convict after their original misconduct.

28. See People v. McCoy, 220 N.W. 2d 456 (Mich. 1974), where the prosecutor, in attempt to bolster his case, told the jury that "the Detroit Police Department, the detectives in the Homicide Bureau, these detectives you see in court today, and myself from the prosecutor's office, we don't bring cases unless we're sure, unless we're positive." Id. at 460. [sic]

29. Emmons, "Morality and Ethics—A Prosecutor's View," *Advanced Criminal Trial Tactics* 393-407 (P.L.I. 1977).

30. Id.

31. For an interesting article on the topic, see Zimmerman, "Stress and the Trial Lawyer," 9 *Litigation* 4, 37-42 (1983).

32. For example, the Zimmerman article suggests time off from work and "celebration" with family and friends to effectively induce relaxation.

33. R. Traynor, *The Riddle of Harmless Error* 81 (1970).

34. People v. Shields, 58 A.D.2d 94, 96 (N.Y.), aff'd. 46 N.Y.2d 764 (1977).

35. People v. McCoy, 220 N.W.2d 456 (Mich. 1974).

36. Shields, 58 A.D.2d at 97.

37. Id. at 99.

38. 155 F.2d 631 (2d Cir. 1946).

39. 73 F.2d 278 (1934), rev'd, 295 U.S. 78 (1935).

40. Shields, 58 A.D.2d at 97.

41. Wolf, "Effects of Inadmissible Evidence and Level of Judicial Admonishment to Disregard on the Judgments of Mock Jurors," 7 *Journal of Applied Social Psychology* 205 (1977).

42. Additionally of note is the fact that if the judge rules the evidence [inadmissible] and did not admonish the jury, then the biasing effect of the evidence was eliminated. The authors of the study concluded that by being told not to consider certain evidence, the jurors felt a loss of freedom and that to retain their freedom, they considered it anyway. The psychological term for this effect is called reactance.

43. Of course, this does not mean that appeals should always be allowed, even in the absence of an appealable issue. Rather, one should confine the availability of these appeals to the narrow circumstances discussed.

44. See United States v. Burse, 531 F.2d 1151 (2d Cir. 1976), where the court named the prosecutor in the body of its opinion.

45. United States v. Drummond, 481 F.2d 62 (2d Cir. 1973).

46. 424 U.S. 409 (1976).

47. Id. at 431, 42 U.S.C. 1983 authorizes civil actions against state officials who violate civil rights "under color of state law."

DISCUSSION QUESTIONS

1. If you were a prosecutor, do you feel it would be ethical to engage purposely in courtroom misconduct to win a case? Why or why not?

2. If you were a juror and were asked to disregard stricken testimony, do you feel you could still be objective in the case? Explain.

3. Explain both the advantages and disadvantages of the harmless error doctrine as related to prosecutors.

4. Do you feel it is more acceptable for prosecutors to demonstrate misconduct in felony trials than in misdemeanor trials? Discuss your position.

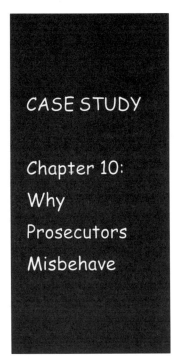

CASE STUDY

Chapter 10:
Why
Prosecutors
Misbehave

JUSTICE OR POLITICS

You have been district attorney for 12 years and a prosecuting attorney for almost 25 years. You know you are good with people—all kinds of people. That is why you keep getting elected and that is why you are the favorite to win the state assembly. As district attorney for Middleview County, you have backed up your tough talk about making "the time fit the crime" for violent offenders. You have "talked the talk and walked the walk." In fact, you have a perfect record concerning first-degree murder cases. You have won them all and in every case the offender has received the death penalty.

Sipping a cup of coffee, you stretch back in your leather chair and consider the case before you. Elroy Dudley, or "the Dude" as he is known in Middleview County, is one "bad" piece of work. Forty-five years old, Elroy has a long history of physically assaulting men and women. You have sent Elroy to state prison on two previous charges, where he has served a total of 10 years. After he finished his last sentence, it was just six weeks before Elroy was involved in a bar room brawl where a man was killed. Apparently, "the Dude" tried to pick up someone else's escort. Shortly thereafter, six to eight men were involved in a free for all. Several people were stabbed and several shots were fired. The deceased, one Red "Big Red" Smith, was stabbed once in the heart. The people in your county were really afraid of Elroy and had been afraid of Big Red as well. Young and old, male and female, all seemed to feel relief. They also voiced their opinion regarding the wish that "the Dude" had met a similar fate.

Finishing the last of your coffee and drumming your finger on the open folder, you consider your options. A lot is riding on this case. If you handle it right, you could walk into that state seat blindfolded. There is no direct evidence connecting Elroy to Big Red's death, but he was a central figure in the brawl. Elroy was also a threat to the community. You are certain you could get several of the other "lowlifes" to implicate Elroy with a little coaxing. You aren't certain that Elroy killed Big Red, but there is no doubt he was capable. And his personal history of violence speaks for itself. If you could put "the Dude" on death row, you would be doing yourself and everybody else in Middleview County a favor. Everyone but Elroy and anyone who cares for him.

Questions:

1. Examine this case in terms of utilitarian and deontological perspectives.

2. Explain what type of misconduct the attorney is contemplating in this instance. What types of misconduct may be permissible under these circumstances?

3. What position would you take in this case? What do you think would be the most probable outcome of this case?

CHAPTER 11

The Lawyer as Liar

H. Richard Uviller

However defended we may have become against the ancient and still prevalent obloquy heaped upon our profession, we must all feel aggrieved to some extent by our low repute. The appropriate response is not, however, to rail against the popular image makers, to protest the insulting "lawyer jokes," or to share the scorn our friends gently acknowledge to us. Rather, we should ask ourselves from time to time, why are we so persistently, so generally, so angrily scorned? Could there be any truth behind the image we are projecting? I propose to take a close look at one of the most corrosive of the stereotypes pasted on us: *the lawyer as liar*.

> **KEY CONCEPTS:**
>
> Code of Professional Responsibilities
>
> lawyer-client relationship
>
> lawyer-to-lawyer relationship

The Code of Professional Responsibility commands truthfulness from the lawyer. The general language of DR 7-102(A)(5) goes like this: "In his representation of a client, a lawyer shall not knowingly make a false statement of law or fact." It sounds pretty sweeping, but in its setting it might be read to govern only statements made to courts. The ABA Model Rule 3,4(a)(1), expressly derived from DR 7-102(A)(5), is more explicit in this limitation, providing: "A lawyer shall not knowingly make a false statement of material fact or law to a tribunal."

Considerable thought has been given in the bar and among academic commentators to the meaning of the injunction with respect to courtroom behavior. Is the lawyer obliged to correct a judge's misapprehension when the judge announces that she is disposed to extend leniency to the lawyer's client in view of the defendant's spotless record? What is the lawyer's obligation in arguing the incredibility of an important adverse witness [whom] the lawyer has good reason to believe told the complete truth? And that perennial favorite, what should the lawyer tell the judge is the reason he seeks to withdraw as counsel for a client who cannot be dissuaded from taking the stand to lie in his own defense?

H. Richard Uviller, "The Lawyer as Liar," (as appeared in *Criminal Justice Ethics*, Volume 13, Number 2 [Summer/Fall 1994] pp. 2, 102-105. Reprinted by permission of the Institute for Criminal Justice Ethics, 899 Tenth Avenue, New York, NY 10019-1029.

While to some the questions regarding the ethical duty of courtroom candor are many and weighty, I do not propose to rehearse the well-known literature on this aspect of the lawyer's obligation to speak the truth. To me, it is obvious that DR 7-102 of the Code means precisely what it clearly and unequivocally says: at least when a lawyer addresses the court, *make no false statements of law or fact*. As long as we can still distinguish a false statement from a true one, I see no need to belabor the point.

But DR 1-102(A)(4) is set in a much more general canon dealing with the "integrity" of the profession. That provision declares that "[a] lawyer shall not engage in conduct involving dishonesty, fraud, deceit, or misrepresentation."[1] I should like to consider three extra-cathedral aspects of a lawyer's interactions— coming, I believe, within the purview of this provision—in which the reputation of the Bar is diminished by lawyers' disregard for the ethical obligation of honesty. The applications I mean to touch upon here are: the lawyer's relations with clients, with each other, and with the public at large. While data are scarce, it is my strong impression that the import of this ethical obligation is so widely unknown, misread, or ignored that we all suffer.[2]

The Lawyer-Client Relationship

Many practicing and academic lawyers agree that [the lawyer-client] relationship is the bedrock of the profession of law. Shrouded by a virtually impenetrable privilege, the communications between the lawyer and client acquire an aura that is almost holy. Dedication, fidelity, and zeal are marks of religious devotion. Many would say these are also the defining qualities of a lawyer's professional service. And considerable support for this view may be gleaned from the Code of Professional Responsibility. Specific disciplinary rules require the lawyer to address the client's business zealously while guarding all confidences and secrets communicated within the sacred relationship. More broadly, the entire code is largely premised on the fiduciary obligations of counsel to a private client.

Yet, despite an array of provisions addressed to the lawyer-client interaction, there is little in the Code of Professional Responsibility specifically enjoining the lawyer to speak fully and honestly to the client. Of the Disciplinary Rules, only DR 9-102(B)(1) requires that the lawyer "[p]romptly notify a client of the receipt of his funds, securities, or other properties." The advisory Ethical Considerations are more explicit. EC 7-8 says that a lawyer "should exert his best efforts to insure that decisions of his client are made only after the client has been informed of relevant considerations." EC 9-2 provides that "a lawyer should fully and promptly inform his client of material developments in the matters being handled for the client." The Model Rules of Professional Conduct are considerably better. Rule 1.4 provides:

(a) A lawyer shall keep a client reasonably informed about the status of a matter and promptly comply with reasonable requests for information.

(b) A lawyer shall explain a matter to the extent reasonably necessary to permit the client to make informed decisions regarding the representation.

Though elevating the precept from an Ethical Consideration to a Rule is a notable improvement over the Code, the Rule is somewhat less than ideal. I do not worry too much that the formulation lacks a direct command of truthfulness; I regard that as firmly implicit. Rather, it is clear that these provisions relate only to the rather narrow subjects of the "status of a matter" and information necessary to allow the client to decide whether or not to retain the lawyer. As far as appears, the Rule simply says nothing regarding the many other communications from lawyers to clients—work performed, facts learned, even the applicable law need not be fully or accurately conveyed under this Rule.

There are surely occasions where even the most virtuous lawyer may wish to be free of the obligation of strict candor to the client. For example, the lawyer might disapprove of a client's projected scheme for any of a number of nonlegal reasons: unsound business judgment, bad public relations, unwise assessment of key people. In such circumstances, where ordinary, friendly counsel is unavailing, the temptation is almost irresistible to couch one's judgment in legal terms. Exaggerating the legal risks, even expressing false uncertainty of consequences to dissuade the client from taking ill-advised action must be a common recourse for even the ethically minded, well-intentioned lawyer. And when used to promote the client's interest—as seen by the lawyer—such misstatements are hardly thought to be an abuse of the relationship. Indeed, I have heard lawyers express with some pride how the legal counseling relationship can be skillfully employed to save clients from their own ill-conceived plans.

Perhaps one of the major areas where lawyers may be tempted to color the truth is in the negotiation of a settlement, civil or criminal. Certainly, this is the activity that has called for most of the printer's ink spilled in the general area of professional dissimulation. For reasons of convinced dedication or, perhaps, for reasons of personal convenience or economic advantage, a lawyer may wish to influence his or her client to accept a proffered settlement offer. "I've had a hundred clients in your position," a lawyer may say, overstating the fact, "and I can tell you that the plea the DA is offering here is a better deal than most people in your circumstances get." Or the lawyer may say, "I've dealt with this insurance lawyer before, and when he says this is the highest offer his client will make in a case like this, he means he is ready to go to trial, and, as I've told you before, we have serious problems before a jury on a claim like this." Or the lawyer may say, "The judge told me this is the best offer we're going to get. If we don't take it, this judge will sit on the trial and, believe me, juries eat out of her hand; she can charge us right out of court."

There are, of course, few data from the clients themselves regarding this sort of representation from counsel. Although in some studies clients report grievances against their lawyers in terms of "deception," the specifics are usually of the order of "stringing him along," boosting fees, or dodging phone calls.[3] Understandably, most clients do not know of the lawyer's misstatements simply because the client has no other avenue of information. If the lawyer says her adversary is bluffing, the client can hardly prove the contrary; if the lawyer says two associates worked on the memo for fourteen hours, the client cannot know that only one did it in seven. In one article, however, a professor reports that, in a small sample of lawyers interviewed, she obtained information on a variety of deceptive billing practices.[4] No one that I know of has come up with the empirical data to support a general theory of falsification, but from hunch and anecdote, we all suspect strongly that many lawyers misrepresent their knowledge and experience to gain a client's confidence, exaggerate the complexity of work or the demands of skill to justify their fees, and, quite probably, purport to convey information from courts and adversaries to support the course of action they advise.

From reported decisions, we learn little of the dimensions of the problem. The vast bulk of cases that reach the reporters concerning lawyer dishonesty are clear cases of embezzlement, fraud, and theft. The subtler forms of misrepresentation rarely find their way into the grievance process. Over the years, however, there have been a few in which lawyers were suspended for false billing statements and neglect of the client's interest, covered by false reports. In these relatively rare decisions, courts have generally reaffirmed the lawyer's duty of candor toward a client.

Despite the temptations, despite lapsed lawyers who cannot foreswear client manipulation, I cannot believe that most good lawyers do not take as a fundamental tenet of principle that all communications with a client must be scrupulously truthful, that a lawyer must appraise alternatives, make predictions, and couch advice in honest analysis, carefully expressed. At least, I am fairly confident that the honorable bar would gladly proclaim such a tenet, and regret their few, necessary deviations from it. How can a relationship of mutual trust be built on anything less?

The picture is complicated somewhat by the complex client. Lawyers sometimes represent a client composed of multiple or hierarchical units. The managerial officer, let us suppose, consults the lawyer, but is reluctant to allow other corporate officers or personnel in on the subject of the consultation. Obedience to the wishes of the client's representative might require the lawyer to represent her service (in a bill, let us say) in a way that would mislead other components of the corporate client—other officers, the billing department, or the Board of Directors. Even here, where some part of the complex client has requested it, it is hard to see how the lawyer can misstate the nature of the services performed when the only purpose thereof is to throw some component of the complex client off the scent.

All that is needed is an institutional commitment to this universally accepted principle. Why should the Code not include a declaration that a false statement of fact or law to a client, however well-intentioned, is unprofessional? And pending such a remedy for a glaring omission, why should not lawyers in their retainer contracts promise clients a completely honest appraisal? And why should not malpractice actions lie for a failure of counsel to render a scrupulously honest opinion?

LAWYER-TO-LAWYER RELATIONSHIPS

This is a much more difficult, complex area than the relatively straightforward powerset of counselor-counselee. Here, we encounter the old adversary interaction between peers. Where professional ethics have been largely defined in terms of duties to the client, it is hard to find a precept that requires the lawyer to deal honestly with the client's adversary. In fact, in civil practice lore (unlike criminal practice), it is widely accepted that lawyers never trust an adversary's representation. Indeed, so deeply imbedded in practice is this principle of mutual suspicion, that I have been told that honesty would be a *disservice* to the client since it would be routinely discounted by a sophisticated adversary as puffing.[5]

Yet even the skepticism characteristic of an adversary stance may be tempered by respect. If lawyers here, like the barristers in the mother country, came to value personal honor above the transitory interests of a client, could they not take the word of one another without undermining their adversary position? Support for this radical notion may be found in the dealings between public prosecutors and defense counsel on the criminal side. Many judges and lawyers have told me that, notwithstanding their often bitter adversary representations to one another, if a prosecutor tells defense counsel that she is ready to recommend a sentence of three-to-six on a guilty plea, the defendant's lawyer will likely tell his client he can bank on it. So, too, if a defense lawyer tells the prosecutor, "This time I think you may have a genuine mis-identification," most prosecutors will go back and give the case another hard look. It is simply a different ethic, grown up by usage in many jurisdictions. It survives very nicely with a full-blown adversary system and pervasive lawyer-to-lawyer negotiation.

Outside the litigation context, it should be even easier to convert to an ethic of mutual professional respect. Lawyers can obviously serve their clients more effectively if they feel they can get an accurate picture of the beliefs and opinions from which the other parties are operating. Why have we taken our adversary tradition to the point of customary dissimulation?

One is tempted to suppose that without the supervening ethic of class that until recently pervaded the British Bar, the lawyer's adversarial role breeds a confrontational mentality. As Daniel Boorstin has effectively demonstrated, the American national experience has endowed us with a national character of frontier values.[6] American lawyers, then, embrace the individualistic image peculiar to our frontier character. Rejecting the communitarian ethic of collegiality in favor of the competitive, showdown, fight-to-win self-definition, we lawyers tend to think trust—even of one's peers—is for suckers.

I have sometimes forced a rueful laugh from friends and former students in practice by pointing out how every litigation team I have ever encountered had told me that they were the only virtuous litigators; all their adversaries were shameless, unscrupulous and deceitful. But it is true. Litigation in particular—both courtroom and pre-trial—certainly breeds that team mentality more appropriate to athletic contests than professional engagement. But I suspect the same xenophobia may be found in all subsets where lawyers must deal with lawyers representing parties of somewhat differing interests.[7] I have seen it myself in those happily few, happily minor matters where I have received legal service. Some small business between coop partners and the lawyers start stirring up antagonism: a hint of litigation, a veiled challenge of conflicting interest, a small snide comment on the other lawyer's client. I had to step in and say, "Cut it out. I can smell what you guys are up to and I do not like it. I will not let you put us at odds."

But I digress. I mean to suggest only that out of this Wyatt Earp, American image of the lawyer-champion comes the ethic of mutual suspicion and distrust. I am sure the practicing bar, if they notice it at all, quickly defend their own misrepresentations as responsive and self-protective. No one wants to be the first patsy; it is not good for business, for one thing. For another, there is the matter of pride. Though many lawyers justly boast of a lively public spirit and a general good-guy persona, I fear that many would blanche at the proposal that they speak nothing but the truth to one another. Something must be done to change this attitude. It is bad for them, bad for clients, and bad for the honor of the profession.

THE LAWYER'S DUTY TO THE PUBLIC AT LARGE

For some lawyers, public and private, occasions arise on which they discover that the public, through the news media, are eager to hear from them. For many, the spotlight, the demand for their words, is irresistible. For others, a public statement in support of the client seems to advance or defend the interests of the client. These occasions are sensitive moments, both for the attorneys involved and for the image they project of the profession.

In general, I see nothing wrong with public statements by lawyers for either side. I do, however, believe that the content of such public statements must be carefully weighed. And indeed the Code of Professional Responsibility demands no less. DR 7-107 contains a number of very specific restrictions on the contents of public statements that a participating lawyer may make. DR 7-107(A) is directed primarily at prosecution lawyers, allowing them only to state the investigation is in progress plus matters of public record; they may also warn of dangers or request public assistance. Paragraph (B), however, is directed at lawyers on both sides of criminal cases (and appears limited to criminal cases). Among other forbidden subjects, the section prohibits public statements expressing "[a]ny opinion as to the guilt or innocence of the accused, the evidence, or the merits of the case."[8]

Has there ever been an explicit rule more honored in the breach? My purpose here is not to decry the growing custom in high-visibility cases for lawyers to take on the role of public relations spokespersons. If a lawyer were truthfully to issue a statement on the projected defense of an indicted client, thereby countering the published allegations of the accusatory instrument (amplified, perhaps, by comments of police or prosecutors), I would have no serious quarrel with the release. Inasmuch as it did not express the personal *opinion* of the lawyer on these matters, I doubt if it would run afoul of DR 7-107(B) either. But when the lawyer's public declaration includes false statements of fact or ill-founded opinions—e.g., "My client is the victim of a political vendetta!"; "The evidence in this case will totally vindicate my client!" or the like—I see an ethical problem of a different order of magnitude. How many times has the public seen a brave and defiant defense collapse into a guilty plea, the lawyer's fierce averrals of wronged innocence of no greater interest than yesterday's news?

But the lie has done its damage. It helps confirm the public image of the lawyer's word as less trustworthy than the claims of a hired tout. With each personal endorsement, lawyers reduce the credence the public accords to what lawyers say. Talk about blind disregard for long-run interests! Apart from every other consideration—from Disciplinary Rules to *ad hoc* "gag orders"—all lawyers should be enjoined from issuing any false or misleading information concerning a pending case or matter entrusted to their professional care. And that injunction should not be dissolved by any claim of short-term advancement of the client's cause.

A PROPOSAL

Perhaps one reason DR 1-102(A)(4) is virtually invisible on the ethical landscape is its unfortunate wording. While only a moment's reflection is needed to see that a false statement to a client or colleague during negotiations is "conduct involving dishonesty, etc.," I fear the provision is cited only where *conduct* like theft or forgery is the subject. While verbal misrepresentation might figure in the charge, it is more likely to be a deceitful representation in a letter to the client or other document than a mere *oral* statement.

To focus my proposal, I will try to formulate the sort of ethical imperative that I believe should govern all professional communications of lawyers—and in what I hope is unmistakable language.

> In every instance in which a lawyer, in the course of professional performance, communicates with other persons, including but not limited to clients, parties, witnesses, colleagues, adversaries, courts, and the general public, the lawyer must communicate truthfully on every material matter.
>
> By truthful communication is meant: (a) a declaration of fact in strict accord with facts either known to the lawyer or reasonably inferred from other facts and circumstances known to the lawyer, or (b) statements of opinion honestly based on reliable information and sincerely believed by the lawyer to be the lawyer's best judgment, or (c) the reasonably complete and accurate transmission of a communication originating elsewhere.

> By material matter is meant: matters of substance touching on the subject of representation, the merits of any cause, the progress or prospects of the cause, or any other matter upon which persons may be reasonably expected to rely in forming judgments or deciding upon action.
>
> Nothing in this rule shall be construed to require a lawyer to communicate with any person on any matter.

In brief, I would demand that every lawyer, when speaking in a professional role, must truthfully convey facts, law, and opinions and must transmit accurately the statements of others on all matters of consequence. I say nothing of the duty to ascertain pertinent facts, nor the responsibility to acquire knowledge, experience, and acumen in the formulation of professional opinions. It seems to be the general obligations of zeal and competence expressed in Canons 6 and 7 of the Code of Professional Responsibility simply and eloquently treat these matters. And obviously nothing in my formulation even hints at an ethical obligation to disclose anything, especially outside the confidential relationship. As indicated above, some provisions counsel the lawyer to speak in order to keep a client fully advised while other important restrictions bid the lawyer hold his [or her] peace. My formulation suggests no realignment of those obligations. I say only that in those situations where for one reason or another, founded in duty or discretion, a lawyer chooses to make a statement, [he or] she should be scrupulous regarding the accuracy of its contents.

I do not urge this unequivocal professional commitment to truth telling from any absolute ethical imperative. In fact, I am convinced that purely moral considerations do not invariably command strict honesty. Nor do I urge this precept simply to enhance the lawyer's practical clout. It may be that the interests of efficiency dictate a policy of candor, but I do not rely on that pragmatic judgment for there are surely those who would argue that the most efficient system is the one that has developed. So, if the policy I recommend is justified by neither a theory of natural moral law nor pragmatic realism, where cometh its justification?

I am not sure I have a satisfactory answer for that question. I do believe lawyers occupy an influential position in the affairs of government, commerce, and the private lives of the people. And I believe lawyers are well-equipped by trained faculties of reasoning and educated knowledge of law. But I believe that their contribution is not maximized by these skills alone. I believe the position of moral rectitude is also a powerful implement. Not only does it enhance the capacity for moral suasion, but it signifies an important element of disinterest, of detachment, of objectivity. Thus, for a lawyer convincingly to announce, "When I speak, I am ethically bound to tell the truth regardless of the implications," is to fortify the word of the lawyer and to affirm that professionalism is a virtue above partisan considerations. And that, to me, justly accords with the nature of our calling, both in dignity and in efficacy.

NOTES

1. This provision is reproduced *verbatim* in the ABA MODEL RULES OF PROFESSIONAL CONDUCT, Rule 8.4(c).

2. Richard K. Burke, in an article, *"Truth in Lawyering: An Essay on Lying and Deceit in the Practice of Law*, 38 ARK. L. REV 1 (1984), referring to DR 1-102(A)(3)(4) and Rule 8.4, has this to say:

    > [T]he effectiveness of this general and broad prohibition of misconduct has been, to say the least, de minimis. For years we have "winked, blinked, and nodded" at blatant, if not outrageous, lying and deception in pleading, negotiating, investigating, testifying, and bargaining. In almost every aspect of our professional practice we have come to accept, in fact to expect, a certain amount of lying and deception.

3. Lerman, *Lying to Clients*, 138 U. PA. L. Rev. 659 (1990).

4. *Id.*

5. Professor Walter W. Steele notes that routine misrepresentation in negotiation is justified by lawyers as part of a zealous defense, and that the convention of deceit is "inherent in negotiation," *Deceptive Negotiating and High-Toned Morality*, 39 VAND. L. REV. 1387 (1966). *See also* Wetlaufer, *The Ethics of Lying in Negotiations*, 75 IOWA L. REV. 1219 (1990).

6. D. BOORSTIN, THE AMERICANS: THE NATIONAL EXPERIENCE (1965).

7. Professor Walter W. Steele, *supra* note 5: As practiced by many attorneys, deception is the spirit of negotiation. Negotiating lawyers misstate facts, willfully mislead by manipulating known facts, or fail to correct an opponent's ignorance or misconception about matters central to the negotiation.

8. Rule 3.6 of the MODEL RULES is virtually identical.

DISCUSSION QUESTIONS

1. What are the three relationships in which a lawyer is typically engaged? Explain the difficulties associated with each one.

2. Explain DR 1-102(A)(4), the canon of integrity. How might this be a difficult proposal to uphold, given the dynamics of the adversarial system?

3. What ethical imperative does Uviller formulate to govern the professional communications of lawyers? Debate the pros and cons of his proposition. How would it affect each of the relationships alluded to earlier?

SENTENCING

Criminal Sentencing: Honesty, Prediction, Discrimination and Ethics

Lawrence F. Travis III

Sentencing is the decision of what to do with the person convicted of a criminal offense. Traditionally, we have responded to criminality by imposing a punishment on the criminal. Von Hirsch defined criminal punishment as, "the infliction by the state of consequences normally considered unpleasant, on a person in response to his having been convicted of a crime" (1976:34). Graeme Newman simply states, "Punishment must, above all else, be painful" (1983:6). For our purposes then, criminal punishment is the purposeful infliction of pain on a person as a result of a criminal conviction.

There is an element of reflex in punishment. That is, when we are harmed by someone or something, we tend to strike back in reaction. Mackie (1982) traced the origins of criminal punishments to such reflex responses. Criminal punishment is, at least partly, a return of harm for harm, or wrong for wrong. Yet there is an old saying that two wrongs don't make a right.

> KEY CONCEPTS:
> desert
> deterrence
> false negative
> false positive
> incapacitation
> prediction
> punishment
> sentencing
> treatment
> utilitarianism

Others, like Garland (1990) argue that punishment, whatever its origins, is also a product of social structure and cultural values. Who we punish, when we punish and how we punish are determined by the role of punishment in society. Further, punishment itself affects social values in a number of important ways. These include defining what is improper behavior, building a sense of togetherness among the law-abiding, and supporting our beliefs about the nature of humankind and society.

If ethics is the study of morality and what is right or wrong, it is likely that no aspect of the criminal justice process is more amenable to ethical examination than sentencing. By committing a crime, the offender has wronged society. By punishing, society arguably "wrongs" the offender. The purpose of this paper is to examine the question: how can punishment be justified? Following that, we will briefly explore three ethical issues that remain even if punishment itself is accepted.

While we do not normally apply the saying about "two wrongs not making a right" to the question of criminal punishment, it seems apropos. How can we justify the purposeful infliction of pain, even on those convicted of crimes? What factors make punishment right and whether we should punish are interrelated questions. The answers to these questions depend upon how punishment is defined.

THE PURPOSE OF CRIMINAL PUNISHMENT

Should we punish? This question is so basic that it is often unasked and unanswered. Yet, when, whom and how we punish are contingent on why we punish. We tend to believe that criminals should be punished. The wrong they do by committing crimes demands a punitive response. We often disagree, however, on why crime requires punishment. Traditionally, four reasons for punishment have been advanced: deterrence, incapacitation, treatment and desert.

Deterrence

Deterrence supports punishment as an example of what awaits law breakers. This example is expected to convince would-be offenders to avoid criminal behavior. Deterrence is based on a conception of human beings as rational and guided by a pleasure principle. That is, humans do things that please them and avoid things that hurt them. Further, they weigh the likely consequences of their behavior and choose activities accordingly (Paternoster, 1987).

In order for a punishment to deter, two conditions must be met. First, the penalty must be severe enough so that the pain of the punishment exceeds the benefit of the crime. For example, a $50 fine for theft of $100 would not deter because the crime results in a "net gain" of $50. Second, the penalty must be imposed. If the criminal is unlikely to be caught and/or punished, the threat of the penalty is not likely to be "real." The lower the chance of punishment, the greater the chance of crime.

Deterrence works on two levels. General deterrence applies when the offender is punished so that others will be afraid to commit crimes. Thus the purpose of the punishment is to deter the general public from crime. Specific deterrence occurs when the penalty is designed to convince the particular offender not to commit another crime in the future.

As a justification for punishment, deterrence emphasizes the needs of the collective over those of the individual. The purpose of punishment is to control future crime. A deterrence rationale would allow the imposition of a severe penalty for a minor offense if that penalty would prevent a large enough number of future offenses. For example, a $10,000 fine for a $10 theft could be justified under deterrence if it would prevent at least 1,000 such thefts. Research to date does not indicate that we are very effective at deterrence (Paternoster, 1987; Sherman et al., 1997).

Incapacitation

Like deterrence, incapacitation is a justification for criminal punishment based on the promise of reducing future crime. In contrast to deterrence, however, incapacitation supports penalties that prevent offenders from having the chance to commit new crimes. While deterrence seeks to convince offenders that crime will not pay, incapacitation seeks to limit the offender's ability to commit a new crime.

One reason to incarcerate a convicted offender is that, at least while in prison, that person is not able to harm society by committing more crimes. The primary problem with incapacitation as a justification for punishment is our inability to accurately predict who is likely to commit future crimes (Visher, 1987). Research to date seems to indicate that incapacitative penalties entail a significant increase in prison population (Greenwood, 1982; Van Dine, Conrad & Dinitz, 1979). To be sure that dangerous offenders are "locked up," we must also incarcerate relatively large numbers of nondangerous offenders (Sherman et al., 1997).

Treatment

Another justification for punishment is to allow for the treatment or rehabilitation of criminal offenders. This philosophy assumes that crime is caused by a variety of reasons, such as poverty, discrimination or individual pathology. Punishments are designed to change the offender's need or desire to commit crime. Like deterrence and incapacitation, the ultimate goal of treatment is a reduction in future crime. Unlike the other two rationales, however, treatment emphasizes the individual offender (Cullen & Gilbert, 1982).

Studies of the effects of treatment suggest that most programs currently available are not very effective (Bailey, 1966; Martinson, 1974; Sherman et al., 1997). Efforts to treat criminal offenders continue, and many programs show promise of effectiveness with some types of offenders (Gendreau, Little & Coggin, 1995; Gendreau & Ross, 1987; Van Voorhis, 1987). As with the prediction problems of incapacitation, treatment attempts are limited by our ability to design and implement effective programs matched to suitable types of offenders.

Desert

A final rationale for criminal punishment is desert, also sometimes called "retribution." This justification for punishment is the only one of the four that is "backward-looking." Unlike deterrence, incapacitation or treatment, a desert rationale does not seek to reduce future crime. Rather, desert is based on the idea that the offender deserves to be punished as a result of committing a crime.

As a justification for punishment, desert places limits of both who may be punished, and the degree to which someone may be punished. Desert requires that penalties be imposed only on those who have committed a crime. Further, a desert rationale requires that the punishment be commensurate with (proportional to) the severity of the crime committed. In these ways, desert may be considered to emphasize the interests of the individual offender over those of the collective (i.e., society).

UTILITARIANISM VERSUS EQUITY

These four rationales and their varying emphases on the individual or collective interests in punishment highlight the ethical dilemma identified by Packer (1966). The core issue involves the role of social utility in punishment. Utility means the benefit, or the "good," expected as a result of punishment. Those who support punishment on the basis of the good it will produce emphasize a utilitarian rationale. In contrast, those who support punishment regardless of effects, based on a notion that crime deserves punishment, emphasize equity or fairness.

In brief, we can say that deterrence, incapacitation and treatment are utilitarian purposes of punishment. Desert is nonutilitarian. Only the desert principle supports the imposition of punishment regardless of effects. The other rationales depend upon some good resulting from the penalty.

If someone is convicted of a crime, should they be punished? If no one else will know that the crime went unpunished and the offender will not commit another crime in the future, there is no reason to punish under a deterrence rationale. No one will be deterred by the penalty. Similarly, given that the offender will not commit a new crime, there is no need to incapacitate or treat the offender. Thus, utilitarian purposes cannot support the imposition of a penalty in this case.

Yet, most of us will be uncomfortable with allowing a criminal to escape punishment. At base, most of us support a desert rationale for punishment. Someone who has broken the law has "earned" or deserves a punishment. Because those who do not commit a crime are not rewarded for law-abiding behavior, those who violate the law should be punished. This seems only fair, or equitable.

Mackie (1982) referred to this as the "paradox of retribution." By this he meant that it is not possible to explain or develop a desert rationale within a reasonable system of moral thought, yet it is also not possible to eliminate desert from our moral thinking. Retribution does not make sense. Desert suggests that wrongful acts should be punished but offers no reason for punishment. Mackie resolves the paradox by saying that punishment is essentially a reflex based on emotions. We react to things and people who hurt us by hurting them in return.

Given this emotional need to harm those who harm us, we will punish criminals without regard for possible beneficial effects of punishment. As punishment became institutionalized in society, jurists and philosophers developed more rational justifications for punishment based on utilitarian notions (Garland, 1990). These notions may explain particular punishments and the selection of specific offenders for punishment, but they do not explain why we punish. It is likely that we punish because punishment seems "right." Just as good deeds should be rewarded, bad ones should be punished. People should receive rewards and punishments for their good and bad behavior. This conception of reward and punishment as earned is the core of the concept of equity.

If Mackie's assessment is correct, it means that we will punish criminals routinely without regard to the effects of punishment. Nonetheless, we would like the two wrongs of crime and punishment to make some sort of right—to produce some good. We are not satisfied with a system of penalties that merely reacts to behavior. We want to influence the future. Thus, most criminal sentences involve a mix of equity and utilitarian justifications.

It is these utilitarian purposes of punishment that raise the ethical dilemma of sentencing as a balance between the needs of the collective and those of the individual. During the 1970s, retribution or desert experienced a renaissance (Cullen & Gilbert, 1982). This renaissance defined retribution as a limiting factor in punishment (Fogel, 1975; Frankel, 1972; Twentieth Century Fund, 1976; Von Hirsch, 1976).

The resurgence of desert was directed at fairness in criminal punishments. Proponents of desert-based sentencing were concerned with what they perceived as unfair disparities in criminal punishments. Under the laws of most states, it was possible for offenders convicted of the same offense to receive widely different penalties. One person convicted of burglary might be placed in prison while another might receive probation. Reliance on a desert rationale would narrow this range of penalties, ensuring that similar offenders convicted of similar crimes would experience similar penalties.

Desert would lead to more equitable punishment. Supporters of desert felt that it was unjust to punish similar people differently, as each had "earned" the same penalty. It was also wrong to impose a very harsh penalty on someone in order to deter others, or to prevent a possible future offense by the person. Desert required that the offender be guilty of the offense for which punishment was imposed, and that the offense, not the offender, was the subject of punishment.

At the level of fairness to the individual offender, general deterrence and collective incapacitation (Visher, 1987)—by which everyone convicted of the same offense receives the same sentence in hopes of reducing general levels of future crime—are less troublesome than individual predictions. If everyone convicted of an offense receives a similar punishment, whether for incapacitative or general deterrent purposes, individual fairness in terms of equivalent penalties is achieved. If these penalties are excessive in comparison to the seriousness of the crime (all burglars receive a term of life imprisonment, for example) while the sentences are equal, they are not equitable. The harm of the punishment exceeds the harm of the crime.

Equity, in terms of retribution is both an explanation of punishment and a limit on punishment. We will punish criminals because they have earned a penalty. We can only punish guilty criminals, and only in proportion to the seriousness of their crime. Von Hirsch and Hanrahan (1979) proposed a "modified just deserts" sentencing rationale that includes these two dimensions of equity. They argued that desert justifies the imposition of a penalty, and sets the outer limits of the punishment. Within these limits, however, utilitarian considerations could be used to allow different penalties to be imposed on offenders convicted of the same offense. Thus, burglary may deserve imprisonment of between one and three years. The sentencing judge would be able to impose a three-year term for incapacitation or treatment or deterrence, but would not be allowed to impose more than the upper limit. So too, the judge could impose a one-year term for the burglary, but not a term less than one year, because burglary deserves at least that level of punishment.

THE PRACTICE OF PUNISHMENT

Punishment is firmly established in our culture and our history. It seems safe to say that we will continue to punish criminals in the future, just as we have punished them in the past. The core dilemma in punishment is trying to achieve a balance between considerations of equity, which are at the base of punishment, and desires for utility that can be realized through punishment. Over time, and across different types of offenders and offenses, this balance shifts. At any time the practice of punishment reflects the current balance between concern for the interests of the individual as expressed in terms of equity, and concerns for the needs of society expressed in terms of utility. The ethical question remains constant, however. That question is: Under what circumstances is the state justified in applying how much punishment to individuals?

Is there ever a time when it would be all right to impose the death penalty on someone convicted of theft? Should prison crowding (and the expense of prisons) justify reducing the prison term of a violent offender? As these questions illustrate, sentencing involves the fundamental issue of individual interests versus societal needs. The ethical problem exists in our attempts to determine the "right" balance of the two.

CONTEMPORARY ETHICAL CONCERNS IN SENTENCING

Leaving aside the question of whether we should punish, there are several important ethical considerations in contemporary sentencing. That is, assuming our current system of criminal punishment achieves an acceptable balance between concern for individual interests and social needs, this system contains some ethical dilemmas. Among the most important considerations are those dealing with honesty in the sentencing of criminals, the role of prediction in the allocation of criminal penalties, and the problem of discriminatory punishment.

Honesty About Punishment

Persons sentenced to prison in state courts in 1994 were expected to serve less than 40 percent of the prison term imposed by the judge (Langan & Brown, 1997:4). Of those receiving their first release from state prison on a violent offense conviction in 1994, the average offender has served less than one-half of the original prison term. The sentences announced in court are often quite different from the penalties served by convicted offenders. There is growing pressure for criminal justice officials to be more honest about sentencing practices. Recent federal legislation includes incentives to promote "truth in sentencing." A goal of the "truth in sentencing" movement is to ensure that violent offenders serve at least 85 percent of the prison terms they receive from the court.

Several current practices lead to the mistruths in sentencing. Most states award or allow inmates to earn "good time." Good time is a reduction in the length of sentence given for good behavior in the institution. It is common for such reductions to be in the one-third to one-half range, so that a sentence of nine years, if all good time is applied, becomes a term of four and one-half to six years. Discretionary release on parole also affects time served. An inmate sentenced to 10 years might be paroled after serving only three. Even most of those who receive life sentences are expected to be released at some point (Beck & Greenfeld, 1995:2).

Critics of this "dishonesty" in sentencing contend that current practices are wrong. Early release of offenders undermines the deterrent effect of the law and fails to provide adequate protection to the public (incapacitation). In addition to these negative effects on potential utilitarian benefits of punishment, critics also make the point that it is wrong to mislead the public. When citizens learn that offenders are not being punished as they had expected, critics contend, the citizens lose respect for the law and question the integrity of the criminal justice system.

The question of honesty in sentencing is complicated. Assuming truth in sentencing is desirable, how can we achieve such honesty? One solution is to simply keep offenders incarcerated for longer periods of time. The problem, of course, is that in doing so we must increase the harm of the punishment relative to past practice, and we must somehow find ways to pay for the increased prison population. Another solution is to lower court-imposed sentences to terms that are closer to what prisoners typically serve. This solution faces the political problem of appearing to lessen the seriousness with which we view crimes, and the perception that criminal justice agents have become "soft on crime." A third, and perhaps most common solution, is to combine the two by increasing the time served by violent offenders while reducing sentences for nonviolent offenders. Of course, as with any compromise, this third solution has the strengths and weaknesses of the first two. It is not clear that the compromise solves the dilemma of dishonesty in sentencing.

One of the pressing issues in sentencing today is how to achieve truth in sentencing. Whatever strategy is selected, we must be aware of the implications of changes in punishment for the balance between individual interests and social needs. If we opt to compromise, then we must reexamine the distribution of punishments. What crimes ought to receive more punishment than they presently do, and which crimes should receive less? If we change the distribution of punishment, what other effects might this have on fairness in punishment?

Prediction in Punishment

A second contemporary (and continuing) ethical issue in sentencing concerns the role of prediction in the assignment of criminal penalties. Clear and O'Leary (1983:35-38) recognized the central role of prediction in all aspects of criminal justice. Society expects its criminal justice apparatus to protect it from crime, and part of this protection involves the identification of risk and taking steps to minimize the chance of future crimes. The assignment of criminal penalties involves the prediction of future criminality and an assessment of the likely harm of that future crime. Indeed, one reason to increase terms for violent offenders and decrease the punishment of nonviolent offenders is because violent crimes are more damaging and, thus, justice system agents have a greater interest in preventing violent crimes.

In any attempt to predict "dangerousness" among a population of offenders, two types of error are possible. An offender who does not pose a risk of future crime may be erroneously predicted to be dangerous. This type of error is called a "false positive" because the offender was falsely (erroneously) predicted to be positive for danger. Conversely, an offender who actually poses a danger of future crime may be erroneously predicted to be "safe." This type of error is called a "false negative" because the offender was falsely (erroneously) predicted to be negative for danger.

False positives are subjected to greater levels of punishment than they need or deserve based on their actual dangerousness. Because they are predicted to be dangerous, we will incapacitate them or subject them to more severe sanctions to ensure specific deterrence or treatment. False negatives are punished less than they need or deserve based on their actual dangerousness. Because they are predicted to be safe, we return them to society quickly and allow them to commit additional crimes.

If we accept prediction as an appropriate consideration in sentencing, the use of differential sanctions is ethically justifiable based on the need to protect society. Yet, it remains wrong to subject a nondangerous offender to more severe punishment. Similarly, it is wrong not to punish more severely an offender who is actually dangerous. Both false positives and false negatives are treated unfairly, and both errors place increased burdens on society.

We currently do not have total accuracy in our predictions, so we make both kinds of errors. In practice, false positives occur about seven times for every true positive. Further, we correctly predict only about half of the truly dangerous offenders, so that our false negative rate is roughly equal to our true negative rate (Wenk, Robison & Smith, 1972). That is, we make many mistakes.

An alternative solution to this dilemma, of course, is to impose harsher penalties on all offenders, as if they were all dangerous. This would lead to "fair" punishment in that everyone receives a similar penalty, but it is a very expensive policy. Also, critics argue that such a policy is unethical since it subjects all offenders to more severe punishment when most do not deserve it.

Even if we could achieve complete accuracy in our predictions of future crime, the ethical question remains: Should we punish people for crimes they have not yet committed? If I knew you were going to break the speed limit next week, should I collect a fine from you today? If I do, what should I do next week when I catch you speeding? That is, by sentencing based on a prediction, have we allowed the offender to "pre-pay" for crime, so that when the crime actually occurs, there is no punishment after the crime? Must we wait for someone to actually commit an offense before we punish? Suppose we predict that someone will commit a murder. If we incarcerate them now, they do not have the chance to commit the murder, and so the crime never occurs. Since the crime never occurred, do we have a right to imprison the predicted offender?

Concern about repeat offenders and career criminals raises the issue of prediction. Recent attention to "three strikes and you're out" laws illustrates the point. These laws impose long prison sentences on those convicted of their third felony offense. The logic behind such laws is that three-time losers are dangerous and need to be incapacitated. Many states have passed or are considering such laws. The ethical issues around prediction in sentencing are complicated, and do not disappear even if we manage to achieve completely accurate predictions. We must still decide the balance between individual interests and community needs. Does the community's need for safety outweigh the individual's interest in liberty if we predict that the individual will eventually commit a crime? Under what circumstances might the community's needs be more important? Under what circumstances is the individual's interest in liberty most important?

Discrimination in Sentencing

The purpose of prediction is to discriminate between those offenders who require more punishment and those who can be safely given less punishment. A related ethical concern is how the predictive system achieves this discrimination.

It is possible that errors in prediction are not random but that they result in differential punishment for some persons as opposed to others. The data concerning the characteristics of persons receiving severe sanctions indicates that sentencing decisions are disproportionate. Males, minority group members, young adults and the poor are more likely to receive harsh sentences than females, older adults, whites and the more affluent (Petersilia, 1983; Visher, 1983). The third ethical issue in contemporary sentencing concerns discrimination in the assignment of criminal penalties.

Klein, Turner and Petersilia (1988) reported that criminal sentences in California were based more on the seriousness of the offense, prior criminal record of the offender, and justice process variables than on race. The fact remains, however, that the ethically acceptable factors that predict future crime and explain sentence severity—prior record, criminal justice history and offense seriousness—appear to be related to sex, race, age and social class. The conclusion that these factors are more determinative of punishment than race or sex does not necessarily mean that sentencing decisions do not discriminate.

The problem of the relationships between race, sex, socioeconomic status, age and the factors that explain sentences are complex. Race, for example, may be related to unemployment because of societal discrimination. In turn, unemployment may be related to involvement in crime and criminal justice processing decisions (bail, probation and parole supervision, and the like), which in turn are related to future criminality. Punishments based on the likelihood of future criminality as predicted from prior record or criminal justice history will reflect the effects of race, sex and social class. However, because the sentencing decision relies only on prior criminal record and criminal justice history, the effect of race, sex and class may be hidden from those making the punishment decision.

A related issue concerns definitions of offense seriousness. The war on drugs provides an excellent example. Under federal sentencing rules, offenses involving crack cocaine were treated more severely than those involving powder cocaine. Racial differences in the use of these drugs (blacks were more likely to use crack; whites more likely to use powder cocaine) resulted in disproportionate sentencing of cocaine offenders as black offenders more often received prison terms, and received longer terms than white offenders. So too, an emphasis on certain types of drug offense, such as street sales versus possession, produces racial differences in punishment (Barnes & Kingsnorth, 1996).

The ethical problem here is akin to that faced by automobile insurance underwriters. Punishments based on predictions of future crime treat some individual offenders unfairly, just as does blanket assignment of certain groups of drivers to "high-risk" classes for insurance. Treatment of different kinds of criminal behavior as more serious is like assigning different insurance rates based on the type of automobile driven, not the skill of the driver. At what point, if ever, does this unfair treatment of individual offenders (or drivers) render the assignment process unethical? Is crack cocaine use more serious than powder cocaine use? If it is, how concerned should we be over racial differences in preference for types of drugs? When, if ever, is discrimination ethically acceptable?

CONCLUSIONS

An examination of the ethics of criminal sentencing raises many questions, but provides few answers. The answers are judgment calls that depend upon the individual doing the judging. A central determinant of how one may resolve these ethical issues is the resolution of the conflict between utility and equity. If the interests of the individual predominate, one is likely to support a desert (or possibly treatment) justification for punishment and oppose most predictive efforts. Similarly, one is likely to opt for truth in sentencing by reducing sentences imposed to more closely match time currently served, and to oppose prediction in sentencing and be very cautious about potential discrimination resulting from laws and practices. On the other hand, if one emphasizes utility, it is likely that they will support prediction, solve the truth in sentencing problem by increasing penalties (at least for more serious offenses) and be less concerned about potential discriminatory effects of laws and practices.

This difference in perspective is reflected in how one views errors of prediction. If false positive errors are more troubling than false negative errors, there is a greater concern for equity than utility. If false negative errors are more troublesome, it evidences a greater concern for public safety. Those who emphasize community protection are usually willing to accept false positive errors, arguing that is not unjust to punish them more severely than their actual risk would warrant.

Each of us may very well answer the questions about sentencing differently. In essence, these are all ethical questions that require us to think about what is right or wrong with sentencing and criminal punishment. The ethics of sentencing can be stated as a question of justice. We need to determine what are just punishments, and how sentences can be imposed justly. As Von Hirsch states, "While people will disagree about what justice requires, our assumption of the primacy of justice is vital because it alters the terms of the debate. One cannot, on this assumption, defend any scheme for dealing with convicted criminals solely by pointing to its usefulness in controlling crime: one is compelled to inquire whether that scheme is a just one and why" (1976:5).

REFERENCES

Bailey, W. (1966). "Correctional Outcome: An Evaluation of 100 Reports," *Journal of Criminal Law, Criminology & Police Science* 57:153-160.

Barnes, C. & R. Kingsnorth (1996). "Race, Drug, and Criminal Sentencing: Hidden Effects of the Criminal Law," *Journal of Criminal Justice* 24, 1:39-55.

Beck, A. & L. Greenfeld (1995). *Violent Offenders in State Prison: Sentences and Time Served*. Washington, DC: Bureau of Justice Statistics.

Clear, T. & V. O'Leary (1983). *Controlling the Offender in the Community*. Lexington, MA: Lexington Books.

Cullen, F.T. & K.E. Gilbert (1982). *Reaffirming Rehabilitation.* Cincinnati: Anderson.

Fogel, D. (1979). *"We Are the Living Proof..." The Justice Model for Corrections,* 2nd ed. Cincinnati: Anderson.

Frankel, M. (1972). *Criminal Sentences: Law Without Order.* New York: Hill & Wang.

Garland, D. (1990). *Punishment and Modern Society.* Chicago: University of Chicago Press.

Gendreau, P. & R. Ross (1987). "Revivification of Rehabilitation: Evidence from the 1980s," *Justice Quarterly* 4, 3:349-407.

Gendreau, P., T. Little & C. Coggin (1995). *A Meta-Analysis of the Predictors of Adult Offender Recidivism: What Works!* St. John, Canada: Univ. of New Brunswick.

Greenwood, P. (1982). *Selective Incapacitation.* Santa Monica, CA: RAND.

Klein, S., S. Turner & J. Petersilia (1988). *Racial Equity in Sentencing.* Santa Monica, CA: RAND.

Langan, P. & J. Brown (1997). *Felony Sentences in State Courts, 1994.* Washington, DC: Bureau of Justice Statistics.

Mackie, J. (1982). "Morality and the Retributive Emotions," *Criminal Justice Ethics* 1, 1:3-10.

Martinson, R. (1974). "What Works?," *The Public Interest* (Spring):22.

Newman, G. (1983). *Just and Painful.* New York: Macmillan.

Packer, H. (1966). *The Limits of the Criminal Sanction.* Stanford, CA: Stanford University Press.

Paternoster, R. (1987). "The Deterrent Effect of the Perceived Certainty and Severity of Punishment: A Review of the Evidence and Issues," *Justice Quarterly* 4, 2:173-217.

Petersilia, J. (1983). *Racial Disparities in the Criminal Justice System.* Santa Monica: RAND.

Sherman, L., D. Gottfredson, D. MacKenzie, J. Eck, P. Reuter & S. Bushway (1997). *Preventing Crime: What Works, What Doesn't, What's Promising.* Washington, DC: National Institute of Justice.

Twentieth Century Fund Task Force on Criminal Sentencing (1976). *Fair and Certain Punishment.* New York: McGraw-Hill.

Van Dine, S., J. Conrad & S. Dinitz (1979). "The Incapacitation of the Chronic Thug," *Journal of Criminal Law & Criminology* 65:535.

Van Voorhis, P. (1987). "Correctional Effectiveness: The High Cost of Ignoring Success," *Federal Probation* 51, 1:56-62.

Visher, C. (1987). "Incapacitation and Crime Control: Does a 'Lock 'em Up Strategy Reduce Crime?," *Justice Quarterly* 4, 4:513-543.

Visher, C. (1983). "Gender, Police Arrest Decisions and Notions of Chivalry," *Criminology* 21, 1:5-28.

Von Hirsch, A. (1976). *Doing Justice.* New York: Hill & Wang.

Von Hirsch, A. & K. Hanrahan (1979). *The Question of Parole.* Cambridge, MA: Ballinger.

Wenk, E., J. Robison & G. Smith (1972). "Can Violence be Predicted?," *Crime and Delinquency* 18, 3:393-402.

DISCUSSION QUESTIONS

1. Should criminal punishments be based on predictions of crime? If so, what types of errors would we expect to make with such predictors?

2. Why do sentencing decisions discriminate against certain groups, and what should be done to minimize discrimination?

3. Compare and contrast the four traditional purposes of criminal punishment and explain some advantages and disadvantages that may be found in each case.

CASE STUDY

Chapter 12: Criminal Sentencing: Honesty, Prediction, Discrimination and Ethics

THE COURT AND CHILD ABUSE

As a lawyer you enjoyed private practice. However, after ten years of successful practice, you decided to enter public service and politics. You and your family realize that public service does not have the financial rewards of a private practice, but your ten-year law practice solidified your financial situation. Over the years you made some important personal connections and a good name for yourself. On your first attempt at public service, you were elected county prosecutor. Being a prosecutor was a different kind of law practice; your new job was to convict people in the name of the state instead of defending them. Of the variety of cases you prosecuted, some naturally stirred your interests and work capacity more than others. Because you were a family man, the crime of child abuse was one of the crimes that always seemed to make you press harder. You always attempted to prosecute abusive parents to the full extent of the law and have their children removed to a nonthreatening environment. Trials for this offense always proved to be an emotional experience for you.

Your career as county prosecutor progressed rapidly. Eventually, you were appointed a family court judge, a position which again proved to be a different world. You now had to evaluate facts objectively, rather than approaching the case primarily from a prosecutor's or defense lawyer's point of view. Your first case of child abuse as judge was a very difficult experience. The family was very prominent in the community. The police discovered the abuse as a result of a family disturbance call. The abuse had apparently been taking place for a short time, and because of the family's community standing, had been covered

From Michael Braswell, Tyler Fletcher and Larry S. Miller, *Human Relations and Corrections,* 4th ed. (Prospect Heights, IL: Waveland Press), 1997. Reprinted with permission.

up. The abuse seemed to have resulted from marital problems which had led both parents to heavy drinking. During an argument between the couple, their seven-year-old son interrupted them. They had since focused and projected their problems onto the child. The actual physical abuse was usually a belt strap across the back of the young boy. The psychological damage to the youth as a result of his parents' behavior was, of course, impossible to measure.

You are not the county prosecutor or defense attorney now. You are the judge and you must try to do what is best for all concerned, especially the boy. Should you take him out of his home or not? If you do, you will be taking him away from the place he lives and his natural parents. His parents are in the financial position to do a great deal for their son where a government agency could not. More importantly, the boy does love his parents and seems to want to stay with them. On the other hand, if you do not remove him from the home, he could be subjected to even more severe abuse. Hopefully, the court experience might open the eyes of the parents to their need for professional help in solving their problems and child abuse tendencies, but there is no way to be sure. Do you take the child out of his home or do you let the parents keep custody and hope that the child will not be subjected to further abuse?

Questions:

1. Explain the concepts of false positive and false negative in terms of the decision to remove the boy from his home.

2. How might the mere experience of court change the behavior of the parents? What is this classical concept in criminal justice called?

3. Think of creative sentencing tactics that may be more effective on the underlying problem in this situation.

CHAPTER 13

Myth that Punishment Can Fit the Crime

Harold E. Pepinsky & Paul Jesilow

The class was a graduate seminar in "Philosophical Issues of Law and Social Control." The teacher had just finished the introductory lecture, filling three blackboards with a proof in symbolic logic that there is no adequate justification for punishment.

A student asked, "What would you do if a man raped your daughter?"

"I'd try to reason with him."

"What if you couldn't reason with him?"

"I'd kill the sonuvabitch."

—State University of New York
at Albany, 1976

KEY CONCEPTS:

certainty

punishment

retribution

severity

swiftness

You may recall how Shylock lost his case in Shakespeare's *Merchant of Venice*. He had contracted to receive a pound of flesh if a borrower defaulted on a loan, and the court ruled in favor of Shylock's claim to the flesh after the borrower's default. Portia ordered a final judgment: yes, Shylock was entitled to his pound of flesh, but no more. If he cut out the slightest fraction more than a pound, or if so much as a single drop of blood fell out of the wound, Shylock would be in breach of the agreement and hence criminally liable for harm done. The court agreed, and Shylock was forced to abandon his quest for justice in favor of mercy.

During the past decade, many in the American criminological community have been driven to Shylock's position. On one hand, they accept as fact that taking pounds of flesh from offenders neither rehabilitates them nor reduces crime. On the other hand, they figure a social contract has to be upheld, and that anyone who breaches the contract by breaking the law must be made to suffer in due measure by a just society. Lawyer/criminologist Andrew von Hirsch has coined the term "just deserts" to refer to this ultimate rationale for punishment of offenders. The punishment should fit the crime—no more, no less.

The classical notion of retribution is known as *lex talionis*, or "an eye for an eye." If I blind someone in one eye and am blinded in turn, that is justice. But, the equation will not precisely fit. If, for instance, I blind my victim without warning, then the victim suffers after the event, but not before. If I am then sentenced to be blinded in return, I suffer anticipation of the event as well. It is like taking a drop of blood along with the pound of flesh. Harm under one set of circumstances is bound to include elements that harm under other circumstances lacks. One reason some theologians postulate that vengeance must be left in God's hands and not given over to mere mortals is that, in the final analysis, we are incapable of constructing an equation that takes all circumstances and types of harm into account.

Punishment for crime is generally far less straightforward even than taking an eye for an eye. The most common form of punishment we use today is length of incarceration, but few of our prisoners are punished for confining others. Most are there for taking property without the owners' permission. French historian Michel Foucault has pointed out what a remarkable achievement it has been for Americans to decide that harm can be measured in days, months and years. The human obsession for rationality drives people to think lives are interchangeable with machine parts whose cost and productive value can be quantified. So now the cost of a burglary can be measured against the length of time we deny a person's freedom. But when clearly thought about, "How many years of a person's liberty equals the value of a lost television set?" has to be seen as an absurd question. The same applies to laying offenses along a scale of punishment. If you send your daughter to her room for 10 minutes for breaking a 50-cent tumbler in a fit of anger, would you send her to her room for 13 days, 21 hours and 20 minutes to uphold moral principle and teach her a lesson if she broke a $1,000 antique vase? You might well show your anger and demand that she help mend the vase as well as possible, but that bid for accountability and responsibility would scarcely be retributive—and would hardly be punitive at all.

British criminologist Leslie Wilkins has carried the problem a step further by noting that crimes are not punished; offenders are. Attribution theorists like psychologist Joanne Joseph Moore have been studying how people assess the culpability of defendants. They find, for example, that jurors weigh a number of characteristics of victims and offenders. In the theft of a television, it would matter whether the jurors thought that the victim was an unattractive character who might have angered the offender, or whether the offender was thought to be a basically respectable person who came under an accomplice's evil influence, or whether the defendant seemed to smile rather than show remorse when the victim testified. Our criminal law recognizes some of this complexity, beginning with the requirement for most offenses not only that the defendant be found to have committed a wrongful act, but be found to have intended it. The law also allows other grounds for finding defendants not guilty, or for aggravating or mitigating offenses. Going further, sociologists Victoria Swigert and Ronald Farrell find that defendants charged with criminal homicide in an Eastern city were most likely to be convicted of first-degree murder rather than of lesser offenses if their physical appearance corresponded to the local psychiatric category, "normal primitive." Try as they might, human beings seem to be incapable of judging people by judging acts alone, and their predispositions affect their decisions of how much harm a defendant has done and how long he or she should suffer for it.

Twenty years ago, sociologists Thorsten Sellin and Marvin Wolfgang put together a scale of seriousness of offenses from rankings that judges, police and students gave to a set of crimes. Other researchers have since found that different categories of people produce much the same scale, both in the United States and in Canada. The problem is that real criminal cases entail real defendants and real complainants, so that in practice, those who assess offenses have room to feel considerable justification for concluding that one theft of $100 worth of property from a dwelling is more serious than another. Had Shylock been a surgeon trying to excise a one-pound tumor from a patient who objected on religious grounds, Portia might even have argued Shylock's case.

It is one thing to say that offenders ought to be given their just deserts. It is quite another to figure out what just deserts are.

Guidelines used by sentencing judges in various jurisdictions take several variables into account, including legal seriousness of offense charged, prior record, employment status and bail status of the defendant. These guidelines have been found to predict whether defendants will be sent to jail with about 80 percent accuracy. It is harder to predict how long a jail sentence will be imposed or what form or length of community supervision will be given. Meanwhile, experienced defendants report bewilderment over getting off when they have done something serious and being severely sentenced when their guilt is questionable or their offense trivial. Cases are legion of codefendants receiving widely disparate sentences.

A common exercise among those who teach criminal justice courses is to give students hypothetical cases and ask them to decide which sentence should be imposed. The sentences asked for not only vary widely among students both for each case and across cases, but many times exceed the limits the law allows.

Consensus about what punishment offenders deserve is limited in our society. This is not too surprising. The variety of offenses covered by penal codes is staggering, and the variety of circumstances of defendants' cases are greater still. Consensus would require that crime witnesses react with equal horror. It would require that witnesses readily cooperate in giving full information. More to the point, it would require substantial acknowledgment from about two million Americans currently serving sentences behind bars or in the community that they got their due, and all these views would have to coincide with penalties provided by law if the state were to embody retributive justice.

The problem goes further. Since, as we have seen, crime is so common among Americans, there is often dissensus as to whether punishment is deserved at all. For example, it is well documented that most middle-aged Americans have at least experimented with marijuana, and that a substantial number of otherwise respectable Americans use it regularly. Possession of small amounts of the drug is completely legal only in Alaska, finable in some states, and remains a major felony punishable by years in prison in others. Cultivation of the plant for sale is a crime in all American jurisdictions, and yet a large and growing number of farmers—who would never use the drug themselves—have turned to cultivating this profitable cash crop. Some honest, hard-working growers are quite upset about criminals who try to steal from them, although of course they are in no position to ask for police protection or to take out insurance. Some people think those who are involved in the sale and distribution of marijuana ought to be lined up against a wall and shot. How on earth is consensus to be achieved?

A number of writers propose that so-called crimes without victims, like those involving marijuana, ought to be decriminalized or even legalized. That in itself, however, would not solve the problem for other crimes. How many people can candidly say that they, or their nearest-and-dearest, never stole (perhaps equipment or food from work) or vandalized (perhaps kicked a vending machine or "toilet papered" a house) or assaulted (perhaps got in a minor scuffle) or trespassed or lied for personal gain? These are the kinds of offenses that dominate criminal court dockets. How severely would we punish ourselves for our own crimes?

Consensus on punishment requires that criminals be truly extraordinary. They must do that which people generally find intolerable, practically unimaginable. We have little trouble agreeing that the crimes of John Wayne Gacy, Steven Judy or Charles Manson are outrageous, and although we may differ over the death penalty, we agree that their transgressions call for an extreme sanction. There is a consensus that burying young men in one's garden, or raping and strangling an unknown woman and murdering children, or hanging and stabbing a pregnant woman in a ritual is beyond our wildest fantasies. If a major city were to reserve punishment for something like the worst offender of the month, popular consensus might be achieved that a punishment constituted just deserts.

CONTROLLING PUNISHMENT

To fit the crime, punishment not only needs to have a certain level, but needs to be swift and sure. If punishment is long delayed, the connection between it and the offense becomes strained. Retribution is an expression of moral outrage, of the passion of the moment over wrong done. It makes little sense to punish someone who has long been behaving properly for a transgression long past. That is the reason that statutes of limitation cut off prosecution for all but the most serious crimes after some time has elapsed.

Criminal justice officials cannot help but be guided by conscience and are inclined to believe in the justice of what they have done. If suddenly called upon to punish offenders more severely, they will do so more selectively and with greater deliberation. If called upon to punish more often, they will temper their severity. If called upon to speed up punishment, they will show more leniency and discharge more suspects, or punish without taking evidence of innocence into account.

These patterns are well documented. In the eighteenth century, for example, the British Parliament made a number of offenses punishable by death. As the courts faced imposing death sentences in more kinds of crimes, informal settlement of cases rose to prominence, and most of those sentenced to death were reprieved. In the early 1970s, Governor Nelson Rockefeller sponsored legislation in New York State that mandated life sentences for those selling illicit drugs. Under the law, charges could not be reduced once defendants had been indicted. So, police were less inclined to charge suspects with sale of drugs, prosecutors were more likely to charge defendants with a lesser offense like simple possession of drugs, defendants had little incentive to refrain from requesting jury trials that added to the judicial backlog, and conviction rates among those going to trial dropped as juries proved reluctant to convict on such serious charges. On the other hand, when penalties have been substantially reduced, as in Nebraska for possession of marijuana in the early 1970s, arrests and convictions have surged before settling down at a new plateau.

Since the 1950s, the Dutch have concentrated on increasing the likelihood that defendants brought to trial would get convicted. Convictions have increased, but, in the process, delays in getting to trial are at the point at which many defendants seem to drop out of the system, and the severity of sentence has dropped to the point where it can be measured in days rather than months or years. The average daily convict population has remained roughly constant, at about 20 or 22 per 100,000 population, the lowest known rate in the world.

In a study of experimental programs to reduce trial delay, political scientist Mary Lee Luskin found that punishment decreased by six days for every 10 days' shortening of the time between the initial charging and the final court disposition. And as those who have been to traffic court—where "justice" is swift—can attest, penalties are not only light, but pleas of innocence are likely to be ignored in the rush of business; the innocent are nearly as subject to punishment as the guilty.

Suppose we want to make punishment both swift and sure while closely controlling its severity. The problem of making these three elements of punishment coincide is similar to trying to hold the south poles of three electromagnets together. If you increase the electrical energy going through any of the magnets, it will tend to push the other magnets away. If you clamp down hard, you may be able to hold the magnets together awhile, but as your hand tires they are likely to slip. In criminal justice, increasing the energy and attention devoted to any of the three elements of punishment will make the other two slip out of control.

As the current is turned down toward zero, holding the magnets together becomes relatively effortless. Similarly, a small criminal justice force with practically no crime to respond to will be in a good position to respond swiftly, surely, and with measured severity to crimes that it handles. They will be able to devote singular attention to each offense. As rare and peculiar events, offenses will meet popular consensus that they are intolerable. Hence, citizens will more readily collaborate with law enforcement forces to put evidence together and to identify offenders. When the offender is brought to trial, the likelihood of conviction will be high, and consensus will be forthcoming on the punishment the clear and distinctive deviant deserves.

If criminal justice officials are to make punishment swiftly and surely fit crimes, criminal justice must be a small and largely superfluous force in a practically crime-free society. If more resources are put into the criminal justice system of a society with a high crime rate, the system will further break down and fail even more dismally to provide a just response to crime. This is exactly what has happened in the United States. As we have added personnel and money to an already large criminal justice force, we have been confronted with a system that fills prisons with too severely punished minor offenders, manifestly fails to respond to most offenses, prolongs trial and punishment in cluttered courts, and is capricious about whom is punished and for how long.

IMPLICATIONS FOR CRIME CONTROL

Some advocates of retribution do not care whether punishment prevents crime. They argue that a citizenry deserves to have offenders punished regardless of whether punishment offers more than the satisfaction of moral indignation. If current attempts to build up law enforcement are only made to satisfy moral indignation, they are unjustified. Public dissatisfaction with delays, uncertainty and improper severity will more than offset the desire for revenge.

Retribution can be thought to prevent crime, however. The state that shows itself capable of making punishments fit crimes can be assumed to earn public respect for its authority, and by extension, to earn public respect for its laws. A people who respect the state and its law can be expected to behave lawfully.

From another perspective, swift, sure punishment of controlled severity can be expected to deter people—both from committing a first offense and from committing additional crimes. It is important to recognize a key distinction between punishing for retribution and punishing for deterrence. For retribution, punishment is to be proportional to harm done by offenders; for deterrence, punishment is to cost offenders just more than they gain by committing offenses. At extremes, offenders who killed simply to take 10 cents from their victims might be executed for the sake of retribution, and fined 11 cents to achieve deterrence. As Italian nobleman Cesare Beccaria wrote in the eighteenth century, a system designed to deter crime will generally impose far less severe punishments than one designed to achieve retribution. Since heavier punishments delay and reduce certainty of punishment, they impair its power to deter.

Still, consensus on light punishment is no easier to achieve with a massive criminal justice system; and a system that deters through punishment should have hardly any crime left to punish. From the perspective of deterrence, it is a sign of failure that a system that already punishes plentifully should be called upon to punish still more in order to prevent crime.

If anything, American criminal justice seems to play a role in promoting disrespect for law and order. Various independent estimates reach a common conclusion: Imprisoning growing numbers of offenders has at best a marginal effect on crime rates, since so many people fill the void by starting lives of crime. It may be that repressive criminal justice systems here and elsewhere (as in Argentina, Chile, the Soviet Union and South Africa) reflect or cause popular brutality. The fact remains that societies in which punishment is extensive have large and intractable problems of crime and violence. Societies that generate punishment generate crime, while relatively peaceful societies (the Netherlands and Japan, for example) find less pressure to punish.

There are more fundamental forces than criminal justice that enable people to live together peacefully. If we can slow down people's response to disputes so that they have time to act with greater deliberation and accommodation to needs of offenders and victims alike, there will be more of a chance that the punishment will fit the crime.

DISCUSSION QUESTIONS

1. If it is true that it is a myth that the punishment can fit the crime, what would you consider a better form of punishment than we currently have? If you think there is none, give your reasons and cite specific examples in which you feel our system has been or will be successful.

2. Distinguish between punishing for retribution and punishing for deterrence. What are the ramifications of the two different systems of punishment? Is one more effective than the other? Explain your reasoning.

CHAPTER 14

A Life for a Life?
Opinion and Debate

Robert Johnson

Most Americans support the death penalty for the crime of murder. The threat of execution, they believe, scares potential killers straight and hence saves the innocent lives they would have taken. At a deeper, more visceral level, how-ever, most people simply want murderers to be paid back for their crimes. Deterrence is gravy. The main course is retributive justice, leavened with revenge: A life for a life.

Few murderers have been executed recent-ly, but that is changing. Legal appeals are run-ning out for hundreds of condemned prisoners. At least one jurist has greeted this trend with impatient approval. "Enough is enough on these appeals," said Texas Judge Michael McSpad-den. "It's time to enforce the laws." Speaking of one notorious resident of Texas' death row, McSpadden vowed: "We will do it as soon as possible. I'm not going to give him one day longer." His brethren on the Supreme Court appear to be of similar mind, demanding, with a hint of irony, "a presumption of finality" in these cases. The message from the High Court, says editorialist Colman McCarthy, is that the Justices are "tired of capital punishment cases, that it is time for the states to get on with them."

KEY CONCEPTS:

death penalty

Golden Rule

lex talionis

life imprisonment

retribution

Should the states indeed decide to "go for it," to quote McCarthy, the result will be an avalanche of executions. Justice Department calculations suggest that executions could occur at a rate as high as three per week. Even death penalty foes like Henry Schwarzschild, who, as head of the ACLU death penalty task force, is prone to underestimate in these matters, fears an execution a week. Whichever estimate you believe, a morbid pace of executions would be main-

Reprinted with permission of the Academy of Criminal Justice Sciences. Robert Johnson, "A Life for a Life?" and Ernest van den Haag "Reply" (1984). *Justice Quarterly* 1(4):569-580.

tained for years—there are more than 1,400 prisoners awaiting execution. Nothing remotely similar to this has happened since the Great Depression, an era that is notable for its harsh justice.

Admittedly, an execution or so a week pales in comparison to the thousands of executions which have recently taken place in countries like China and Iran, where the rate of state killings of criminals may reach as high as 1,000 a month. But in these countries the issue is terror, not justice. Law is a cover for rule by brute force and even, on occasion, mob violence. Life, even innocent life, is considered cheap and is further cheapened by executions. In contrast, our concern is for justice under law and our preeminent value is humaneness, emphasizing the value of human life, including the lives of those guilty of atrocious crimes. Our humanitarian values thus compel us to reexamine our commitment to the death penalty and to consider less drastic ways of punishing our worst criminals.

MURDERERS ARE PEOPLE, TOO

An execution is always a tragic ending to human life. The belief that the person put to death has committed a terrible crime and in some abstract sense may deserve to die does not change this fact. Yet many people ignore the tragic side of the death penalty. They have no empathy or fellow feeling for those who kill. Some, for instance, see murderers as so many anonymous crime statistics. For others, murderers are monsters, animals, or some species of psychopath. These jaundiced views, moreover, are not restricted to an uninformed and vindictive segment of the populace. Walter Berns, a scholar and advocate of the death penalty, openly mocked Supreme Court Justice Brennan for contending that "Even the vilest criminal remains a human being possessed of human dignity." It was only a few years back that the Chief Justice of Georgia's Supreme Court likened murderers to mad dogs. That must still unsettle the 100 or so condemned prisoners (kennelled?) on Georgia's death row and subject to his rulings on their appeals. An editorialist in Alabama sounded a similar theme when he described execution as "an act approaching judicial euthanasia," a merciful gesture putting brutish criminals out of their (our?) misery. William Raspberry, a syndicated columnist, summed up this point of view when he observed that "It is possible for a criminal to commit acts so heinous as to place himself outside the category of human, to render him subject to extermination as one might exterminate a mad dog, without consideration of how the animal came to contract rabies in the first place."

For most people, then, executing murderers is not seen as killing fellow human beings. By executing murderers we disown them, wash our hands of them, punish them as only monsters should be punished: violently, with utter disregard for their humanity. We seek a life for a life because there is no middle ground with monsters, no extenuation, mitigation, or mercy. Their lives do not reflect error, foible, or fate; they embody evil and malevolence. With them, fire must be met with fire, violence must beget violence, all accounts must be closed, irrevocably.

These sentiments are widely and even fervently held today, but they are wrong nonetheless. Murderers are dangerously flawed human beings—they are not creatures beyond comprehension or control. Their violence is not a specter or disease that afflicts them without rhyme or reason, nor is it merely a convenient vehicle for ugly passions. Rather, their violence is an adaptation to bleak and often brutal lives. "There is nothing as internal as pain," states convicted killer Jack Abbott, who speaks from experience, "especially human pain. The catalog of suffering it would take to record the intricacies of pain that led to the manifestation of an act of . . . murder would be very melancholy to relate." Abbott's violence and that of most violent men is ultimately spawned by the hostility and abuse of others, and it feeds on low self-confidence and fractured self-esteem. Paradoxically, their violence is a twisted form of self-defense that serves only to confirm the feelings of weakness and vulnerability that provoke it in the first place. When their violence claims innocent victims, it signals not a triumph of nerve but a loss of control. Violence is thus a human failing, and it must be punished accordingly.

Why not simply execute murderers and be done with them? Granted they are human beings, but they are still dangerous. Besides, a hard life may make violence understandable, but it doesn't give anyone the right to harm or kill another person. Nobody put a gun to their heads and forced them to kill; they chose to kill their victims, and they deserve a punishment that fits their crime.

A KILLING BY ANY OTHER NAME

How do we decide what punishment fits the crime of murder, particularly the premeditated and often heinous murders that people think of when they call for the death penalty? *Lex talionis*—retaliation in kind, an eye for an eye—is perhaps the most cogent moral principle that can be invoked, in the abstract, to support the death penalty for the crime of murder. This principle is, according to philosopher Jeffrey Reiman, "the law enforcement arm of the Golden Rule." People should be treated the way they treat others. "Treating others as you would have them treat you," explains Reiman, "means treating others as equal in worth to you. . . . Treating people as they have actually treated others enforces the Golden Rule," but only up to a point, at least in an imperfect world in which access to the human and material resources which promote the development of personhood is decidedly unequal. As psychiatrist Willard Gaylin tells us, the impoverished lives of violent men typically place them beyond the Golden Rule.

> To be totally unaccepted, to be totally unloved—indeed, to be almost totally disapproved—either requires the rejection of one's self (an intolerable situation) or a total dissociation from the judging individual. Such total dissociation is dangerous, however, when we are required to live in a social community. Surely the kind of . . . brutality that is evidenced in the newspapers every day, in which a street-

mugger hits a random woman over the head with a lead pipe as a convenient means of gaining the $6 in her purse, implies more than just
the need for $6. It suggests that the concept of identity has been
destroyed, or never developed; that the person now feels so "other" that
he is no longer within the framework of identification necessary for
introjection of a value system. Such behavior is beyond the Golden Rule,
for that implies the identity of personhood between the other and you.
Obviously, it is more analogous to the squashing of a bug approaching
your picnic table. To give up on one's self is to give up on one's own personal value, and ultimately to give up on a sense of values.

Does enforcing the equal worth of persons hold out the prospect of justice for
these offenders? Does it take account of the forces that shape their lives? Is it not
disingenuous to claim that violent men in effect choose to be subjected to violence in return, a claim that pays tribute to a personhood we violate or ignore
until the juncture of punishment, at which point we "honor" them with yet
another indignity? Paradoxically, violent men live by a Golden Rule of sorts,
with others cast as agents and targets of violence. For them, the Golden Rule
boils down to "might makes right," and it is on the basis of this primitive retributive notion that they will understand the death penalty.

Moreover, even if the Golden Rule does apply to these offenders, it has a different meaning when invoked by individuals and institutions. When person A
hits person B in a fit of anger, person B, now angry, responds in kind. It may
not be advisable for B to do so, but it is understandable, given his anger, and just,
given what has been done to him. Person A deserves a taste of his own medicine and person B, who is not obligated to be a saint, can justifiably give it to
him. But the equation is different when the state enters the picture. The state
redresses harms long after they have occurred; passions have subsided and cooler heads are meant to prevail. (Person B might also act dispassionately and long
after the offense, but this, as criminologist Graeme Newman's analysis of the history of punishment makes painfully clear, is not the typical instance of person-
to-person retribution). The dynamics of the offense must be considered and
weighed in assessing a just penalty, and a panoply of sanctions can be used to
achieve this end. Objectivity and compassion are expected to operate. So is the
generous side of the Golden Rule—the notion that one can be a model of correct
conduct not by matching harm with harm but by showing both the offender and
society that there is a better way to solve problems.

Delegating the administration of justice to the state was meant to make us
more civilized, to end blood feuds and raise our punishments to a level of mature,
compassionate discourse. Surely neither "eye for an eye" justice nor the Golden
Rule requires that we, through the state, replicate crimes under color of law. One
would hope that we are not enjoined by any notion of justice to compete with
criminals to see who can mete out the worst harms. And surely "retributive justice," as it is called in academe, does not condone violence when there are equitable and humane alternatives to punish the offender and protect the society.

Thus, while it is true that murderers must be paid back for what they have done to their victims, this must be done in a way that is just and proper and not simply an imitation of their violence. This point is obvious as it applies to other crimes, including other violent crimes. No one seriously entertains the notion of robbing robbers, mugging muggers, or raping rapists, even if this is, strictly speaking, what these offenders deserve. Instead, these criminals are imprisoned for periods of time that are believed to produce suffering equivalent to, or commensurate with, the suffering wrought by their crimes.[1] We settle for something on the order of "eye for an eye" justice in the hope that the penalty, which balances such values as justice and mercy, won't be worse than the crime it punishes. We also hope that the penalty of imprisonment might at least on occasion prove constructively painful—that criminals might come out of prison better persons than when they went in. By using prison we aim to administer a civilized and potentially civilizing punishment in line with Plato's dictum: "Judgment by sentence of law is never inflicted for harm's sake. Its normal effect is one of two; it makes him that suffers it a better man, or, failing that, less of a wretch. . . ."[2]

The idea that we should kill killers has always had a fairly wide following, however. Indeed, support for the death penalty goes far beyond the laws presently on our books. It is a sad fact, for instance, that public opinion supports the death penalty for all manner of murders, including some that lack premeditation. Why this retributive passion?

One reason why it may be easy to contemplate executing murderers is simply that a killing can be imitated literally and discreetly by agents of the state. Justice can be rendered with decorum. This is certainly not the case with other serious crimes such as rapes, robberies, or even burglaries. State sponsored sodomy of rapists, for instance, is hard to envision, and presumably even harder to carry out. One imagines—and hopes—there would be fewer volunteers to carry out this punishment than is presently the case for executions. Volunteer executioners speak about "doing one's duty," however onerous and thankless the task, in the name of law and justice. They even appear on television talk shows and are well received by audiences! One is tempted to think of them as admirable citizens, working as they do without recompense in the war against crime. This temptation can be easily resisted in the case of other punishments ostensibly warranted by retributive justice—rape for the rapist being an excellent example—where the punishment's affinity with criminal violence is easier to see.

Another reason we execute murderers with few qualms, and occasionally with enthusiasm, is that these offenders are readily seen as monsters, and of course one can't equivocate with monsters. If ever violence warranted counterviolence, it would be with these creatures! But it is vital to recognize that killing killers is really no different from visiting any other crime upon its author. The fact that lesser offenders, including rapists, robbers, and even burglars, have been executed in the past doesn't change this point. It simply indicates that we were less discriminating in our use of the term "monster," and allowed murderers to define justice for the whole mélange of entities that came under that label.

Put bluntly, an execution is a premeditated killing, no more and no less. Fittingly, it is often preceded by trials in which, according to criminologist Stephen Gettinger, an inadequate defense is "the single outstanding characteristic" of capital defendants who, as a result, appear in court as "creatures beyond comprehension, virtually gagged and masked in preparation for the execution chamber." Death row confinement culminates the preparatory process. Here, in Camus' analysis and in my own research, we learn that the condemned suffer a "living death." They are literally dehumanized—alive as bodies but, in varying degrees, dead as persons—and curiously reminiscent of the dehumanized monsters that haunt our imagination.

Their executioners experience a parallel though less extreme fate; they suffer a limited and essentially symbolic form of dehumanization in which they relinquish their personhood and become instruments of the death penalty's violence. "It is a paradox of bureaucratically administered violence," as I have observed elsewhere, "that men must be dehumanized—dead as persons—to play their roles as killers and victims." The executions themselves bear this out. As any witness to one will attest, an execution is a methodical and chilling affair, as much a violation of a person's humanity as a murder. In fact, among the most shocking murders are those characterized as "execution-style slayings," a comparison that highlights the cold-blooded and dehumanizing character of executions for everyone involved. It is irrelevant that an execution is carried out in antiseptic surroundings and after extended legal appeals. Society may convert a killing into a bureaucratic event or procedure, but it cannot thereby change its nature.

A Life for a Life

Murderers treat their victims like objects to be violated and discarded, but we as a society must not fashion our punishments after their acts. (Indeed, at the heart of the Eighth Amendment ban against "cruel and unusual punishments" is the prohibition of punishments which "deny the dignity of man.") Instead, murderers, like other criminals, must be punished as human beings who deserve to suffer in a way that is commensurate with the harm they have caused. Thus, their punishment must approximate death and yet respect their humanity by treating them as full-blooded persons and not as mere physical objects.

This means lengthy prison terms for murderers. When we sentence criminals to prison we demand a painful suspension of their lives—a temporary death, if you will—until they are deemed worthy of return to the society of the living.[3] But how long is enough? At what point does a prison term inflict enough pain to pay back the murderer for his crime?

The answer varies. The context in which the crime occurs, for example, is a critical factor in assessing punishment. Sentences presently take account of some specific contextual factors, such as duress or the presence or absence of explicit prior intent. But more general and often crucial contextual factors (such as those raised by Gaylin, above, relating to the brutalization of the human spirit) are rarely, if ever, considered in any systematic way. Sensibilities also come into play. Pain is a subjective experience, and what constitutes sufficient pain will depend on the capacity of the person who inflicts or authorizes punishment to empathize with the criminal. This presents a serious problem in the case of murder, since few of us are able to empathize with murderers. Yet, if we are unable to put ourselves in their shoes, unable to feel for them, we are unable to develop a sense of their suffering and hence unable to determine when they have suffered enough.

In fact, in the absence of empathy, there is no limit to the pain one can inflict, since by definition the pain affects someone for whom one feels nothing and whom one naturally assumes feels nothing himself. This means that we imagine we are dealing with cold-blooded felons, the extreme case of which is the monster, who are impervious to pain and hence must be punished according to a scale of suffering far in excess of what we would apply to ourselves or others like us. We may even believe that there is no really adequate punishment. It is perhaps for this reason that we can bandy about prison terms of 5, 10, 20, 40 or (in states like Texas) literally thousands of years as though they were civilized, even "soft," penalties.

Perhaps a way out of this dilemma is to relate prison sentences to our own life experiences. A four-year sentence for instance, sounds like a snap, a travesty of justice in the case of murder. But imagine spending the whole of one's high school years, including summers, separated from loved ones and confined for the greater part of each day to a cage. A 10-year sentence would take up one's entire grade school term (including summers), plus two full years for good measure. For the average American who is middle-aged, a 30- or 40-year sentence comes close to obliterating any life at all. Though a true life sentence falls short of execution, surely no criminal deserves a harsher fate than this!

The majority of murderers can point to a host of mitigating circumstances in their lives and in their crimes (though, as noted above, only some of them are presently recognized in law). One must hope that, for them, serving sentences of no more than ten years would be sufficient punishment. Some are more culpable and would no doubt deserve longer sentences; a few might marshall an impressive array of exonerating conditions and warrant shorter terms of confinement. Our worst murderers, those "monsters" we presently consign to the death chamber because their actions seem to place them beyond the bounds of human decency, would of course be eligible for lengthy prison terms, including a natural or true life sentence.

True life sentences are only rarely meted out in our courts, and never with explicit recognition that this sentence—in which the offender is slated to spend his entire remaining life in prison—is in fact a kind of death penalty. True life prisoners remain physically alive and in the company of other convicts and guards; they are treated as human beings and remain members, however marginal, of the human community. They can forge a life of sorts behind bars, but one organized on existential lines and etched in suffering, for, at a profoundly human level they experience a civil death, the death of freedom. The prison is their cemetery, a 6-foot by 9-foot cell their tomb. Their freedom is interred in the name of justice. They are consigned to mark the passage of their lives in the prison's peculiar dead time, which serves no larger human purpose and confers few rewards. In effect, they give their civil lives in return for the natural lives they have taken. A true life sentence, then, can and should be used as a practical moral alternative to the death penalty, a civilized and potentially even civilizing application of the Golden Rule in the extreme case of cold-blooded and unmitigated murder.

Perhaps the primary objection to this proposal during these hard economic times is the price tag. We've all heard about the cost of new prison construction, which can run in the neighborhood of $60,000 per cell, and about per capita confinement costs of anywhere from $5,000 to $25,000 a year. True life sentences would presumably cost a fortune in new cell construction and in bills incurred to keep men confined for 40 or more years at a time, depending upon average prisoner longevity. One can readily envision, for example, a tab of some $600,000 per prisoner sentenced to a life term. One is likely to think that, if nothing else, executions are humane for taxpayers.

But the actual cost of true life sentences would fall considerably short of these estimates and would roughly parallel the cost of executions. We won't have to build new cells for true life prisoners. These prisoners would be confined under any sentencing scheme, whether on death rows or in standard maximum security prisons. When crowding is a problem, less serious offenders can be released to make room for murderers, a policy that seems eminently sensible. Moreover, "The actual out-of-pocket costs to keep a man alive in any prison," as criminologist John Conrad has observed, "is less than $5,000 per year."[4] In states like Texas, where confinement costs are low, it is much cheaper still. A true life term, calculated as a 40-year sentence of imprisonment, would cost taxpayers no more than $200,000 per prisoner in states like New York and California, and would cost considerably less in other states. While these costs are quite high, they compare favorable with the cost of death sentences, which require complicated trials, lengthy appeals, years of special custodial housing for the condemned, and elaborate ritual killings. There are, in other words, no bargain punishments for murder. Neither executions nor life sentences come cheap.

Beyond the matter of cost, some people will balk at the idea of a true life sentence because they don't believe prison is punishment. They refuse to subsidize the lives of luxury to which country club prisons are presumed to accustom the convicts. This cynical but widely held view is seriously misleading. A prison joke has it that the country club prison is much like the Loch Ness monster: There are sporadic citizen sightings but no scientific confirmations. Prisons are costly to operate, but little of this money is spent on convict sustenance, let alone the amenities of life. For instance, in New York, a state noted for a progressive penal system, a prisoner's meal bill comes to under two dollars a day! Some country club! In point of fact, prisons are spartan environments. A lifetime in prison is a lifetime of suffering and privation.

Other objections to this proposal relate to public safety. After all, dead prisoners pose no threats, whereas life prisoners appear to be at least potential dangers to the community. For all intents and purposes, however, true life prisoners are punished and incapacitated for life. Maximum security prison walls (as distinct from the notoriously permeable fences that enclose medium and minimum security prisons) virtually assure that society has nothing more to fear from these prisoners.[5] Nor are they a special threat to other prisoners or guards. Most lifers, in fact, are compliant prisoners; those who are more troublesome can be segregated from the main prison population. Finally, the presence of life prisoners may indirectly promote public safety by discouraging at least some other prisoners from their criminal ways, if for no other reason than that lifers stand as flesh-and-blood testaments to the wages of violent crime.

A true life sentence is an awesome judgment, but unlike a death sentence it need not destroy the prisoner or impart a legacy of irreversible mistakes. A life sentence is a painful punishment but it can be borne with dignity. It can also be changed. New evidence may alter a verdict or indicate a lesser sentence; substantial and enduring changes of character may, in extraordinary cases, permit the resurrection of a few of these prisoners, for example by means of special pardons. New evidence is only rarely discovered, of course, and pardons are even harder to come by, but at least avenues of mercy and redress remain open to us in our search for justice.

A true life sentence should replace execution as our most severe penalty. A civil life for a natural life is punishment enough—for our worst murderers, who must pay dearly for their crimes, and for the society which must take cold comfort in the administration of that punishment.

NOTES

1. Imprisonment bears a superficial resemblance to the kidnapping situation, but there are intrinsic and important differences. There are always some programs and ameliorative resources in prison, as well as activities such as work, which can have reformative value. More fundamentally, there is the longstanding belief that the "pains of imprisonment" can be constructive in the same sense that the "pains" of monastic life can be constructive and result in an improvement of the inmate's character.

2. No civilizing consequences even remotely attach to killings or executions, at least in the modern mind. Ironically, Plato did envision executions in his Republic. He saw crime as a kind of disease which contaminated and tortured its host; the serious and incurable criminal would be released from his earthly bondage by execution, a punishment which was presumed to make him "less of a wretch." Philippe Aries tells us that other notions of death prevalent before the 20th century, particularly those associated with a forgiving God and a congenial afterlife, made a foreseen death a "tame" and desirable arrangement. Here, too, execution might be conceived as a blessing of sorts, allowing the criminal to come to terms with his Maker. In our secular age, where men are neither believed possessed by criminal demons of one sort or another nor the confident beneficiaries of a guaranteed afterlife, the benefits of death cannot be invoked to defend the death penalty.

3. Interestingly, prisoners until fairly recently were viewed as the legal equivalent of dead men. They were "civilities mortuus," and their estates, if they had any, were "administered like that of dead men."

4. Higher estimates of confinement costs incorrectly attribute overhead expenses—that is, the fixed costs of running prisons independent of who is in them and how many people are in them—to individual prisoners. They also discount one unique economic aspect of life sentence prisoners' confinement, noted by Conrad: "Most lifers tend to be employed, sooner or later, on productive jobs, which may eliminate the cost of keeping them altogether.

5. To be sure, convicts sometimes escape from maximum security prisons. The rate of such escapes is, however, quite low. Even less common are escapes from prison that are accompanied by violent crimes against the public. We are reminded by van den Haag that prisons are costly, in the main, "because they are too secure."

A LIFE FOR A LIFE?
REPLY

Ernest van den Haag

"A Life for a Life" often asserts what it asserts vaguely and without evidence, or argument, so as to leave me rather baffled. Nonetheless, I shall confine myself to replying to the points against the death penalty made therein, since I have presented my arguments for the death penalty elsewhere.[1]

Professor Johnson complains about the "morbid pace of executions"—three a week—which he predicts on the basis of reports from anonymous Justice Department informants. He does not say what a healthy pace of executions would be. At the current (non-morbid?) pace most persons sentenced to death will die of old age.

"In the absence of empathy" Professor Johnson writes, "there is no limit to the pain one can inflict, since, by definition the pain affects someone for whom one feels nothing and whom [sic] one naturally assumes feels nothing himself." I know of no evidence indicating that in the "absence of empathy there is no limit to the pain one can inflict," nor do I know how that absence is established. There is no evidence for Professor Johnson's view that those who favor the death penalty typically have no empathy with murderers. Couldn't it be that execution is thought necessary, despite empathy? Or because of it? Does Professor Johnson confuse empathy with sympathy? Even so, did Melville's Captain Vere lack sympathy for Billy Budd, whom he had executed for what amounted, at most, to negligent manslaughter?

The suggestion that empathy sets limits to the infliction of pain is plainly wrong. Sadists like to inflict pain because they feel empathy, not because they don't—that is, after all, why they inflict pain on people, and not on furniture. Further, why does one "naturally" assume that anyone for whom one feels no empathy would "feel nothing himself?" One would have to be quite confused to confuse one's lack of empathy with someone else's pain with the other person's not feeling pain. I have never known anyone who lacks empathy with the pain of others to deny that others feel pain. No evidence is offered. Incidentally, Professor Johnson's view, that those who favor the death penalty believe that murderers to be executed feel no pain, contradicts his prior assertion, that those who favor the death penalty want murderers to be executed because of vindictiveness. If they "naturally" assume that murderers do not suffer, how are they vindictive?

It is difficult to cope with this style of argument. Nevertheless let me try to extract what specifics I can find and consider them *seriatim.*

"Murderers are people, too" Professor Johnson writes, but the death penalty dehumanizes them by showing "utter disregard for their humanity." We are not told why execution is inconsistent with regard to humanity. By definition? such as: "to execute someone is to disregard his humanity?" If so, the definition strikes me as circular and impossible to confuse with an argument.

Philosophers, such as Immanuel Kant, G.F.W. Hegel and many others, have argued that their humanity, their human dignity, not only permits, but actually demands, that murderers be executed and that not to do so would deny the human dignity, the humanity, of murderers. Kant may be wrong. I believe he is. But he offered an argument. Professor Johnson does not. He merely asserts that execution shows "utter disregard" for the murderer's "humanity" and does not tell us why, as though assertion were argument.[2] This is reiterated throughout. We are told that "men must be dehumanized to execute or be executed," but we are not told wherein this means anything other than that Professor Johnson disapproves of executions. He complains that they are "methodical and chilling." Would he want them to be spontaneous and warm? or to be public festivals, as in the past?

According to Professor Johnson, advocates of the death penalty believe that "murderers are beyond comprehension or control." He does not tell what proportion of retentionists hold this silly belief or how he found out. I favor the death penalty and believe that murderers can be comprehended. But I do not believe that "*tout comprendre c'est tout pardonner,*" Mme. de Stael (and Professor Johnson?) notwithstanding. I can also believe that most would-be murderers can be controlled, best by the threat of the death penalty. Finally, I believe that knocking down strawmen is not a helpful way of arguing the cause of abolition, or any other.

Professor Johnson has Jack Abbott, a convicted killer, "who speaks from experience," testify that "violence . . . is ultimately spawned by the hostility and abuse of others. . . ." I suspect that Abbott's testimony is a mite self-serving. Professor Johnson apparently does not. Anyway, he endorses Abbott's view, with psychological speculations suggesting that murderers murder because they have not been loved enough and suffer from "fractured self-esteem." This should mitigate their punishment. Surely, some well-loved people do murder (or is murdering itself the evidence for "fractured self-esteem?") and some unloved people do not. How does Professor Johnson's explanation apply to mafiosi, leading a close and rich family life? Or to murderers who murdered because they love someone not otherwise attainable? Professor Johnson's explanation hardly explains much. But even if explanatory, as it probably is for some murders, how would it mitigate, or reduce, the murderer's responsibility for his crime? Causation is not compulsion. If a court finds that the murderer could, but did not choose to, control his act—else he could not be found guilty—why does Professor Johnson think that "fractured self-esteem"—if it were the cause—is the same as lack of control? How does a cause become an excuse?

Professor Johnson writes that "delegating . . . justice to the state was meant to raise our punishments to a level of mature compassionate discourse" ("discourse" leaves me confounded, but let that go) which would exclude the death penalty. The premise is wrong, and the conclusion does not follow. The history of punishment does not suggest that delegation to the state was meant to reduce them. Nor did it. Reductions did occur in the last 200 years, for reasons independent of delegation to the state.

At any rate it is a *petitio principii* to argue that the death penalty should be abolished because we were meant to be "mature and compassionate." What Professor Johnson has to show is that maturity, or compassion, require abolition of the death penalty. He merely asserts it.

Further on, Professor Johnson argues that, since the *lex talionis* cannot determine punishment for many crimes, such as rape, or fraud, it should not determine the punishment for murder. Why not? If we can't feed everybody, does it follow that we should not feed anybody? There are arguments against the *lex talionis.* This is not one.

Professor Johnson calls an execution a "premeditated killing." It is. But he neglects to mention that it differs from premeditated murder by being a lawful punishment for a crime. That, indeed, is the difference between crimes, including premeditated murder, and punishments, including executions. The physical characteristics of crimes and punishments may well be identical. Crimes differ from punishments in their social characteristics. Professor Johnson writes in a footnote that imprisonment differs from kidnapping because of the "ameliorative resources" of prisons. These are contingent. The essential difference is that kidnapping is a crime—unlawful imprisonment—and lawful imprisonment is the punishment for it, regardless of "ameliorative resources."

Professor Johnson suggests that some term of imprisonment is enough or, anyway, nicer, as a punishment for murder. I have dealt with this matter elsewhere.[3] He also tries to persuade us that even life imprisonment would be cheaper than the death penalty. His comparison is based on two common errors. First, he compares the marginal cost of imprisonment with the average cost of the death penalty. (See his footnote 4.) A correct comparison is of the two marginal costs or of the two average costs. Second, he assumes that there will be more trial costs for death penalty cases than for life imprisonment cases, because the death penalty leads to more appeals. Since life prisoners spend their time on *habeas corpus* appeals, I doubt this.

Finally, Professor Johnson argues that "life prisoners may indirectly promote public safety . . . [since they] stand as flesh and blood testaments to the wages of violent crime." I agree. Life imprisonment may have deterrent effects. Why wouldn't the death penalty? "A life sentence" Professor Johnson goes on ". . . can be borne with dignity." Sure, and why can a death sentence not be borne with dignity? We are not told.

Rereading Professor Johnson, I gather that he opposes the death penalty and suppose that he has good reasons. Someday I hope to learn what they are.

NOTES

1. E. van den Haag and J.P. Conrad *The Death Penalty: A Debate*, Plenum Publishing Corp., NY (1983).

2. Professor Johnson also suggests that murderers are unlikely to appreciate that they are executed for the sake of their human dignity. This is often true. But Kant thought so too, and Professor Johnson does not address his argument.

3. E. van den Haag, *loc. cit.*

DISCUSSION QUESTIONS

1. Do you agree with van den Haag's statement that understanding why a person does something does not pardon him or her from that act? Why?

2. Explain why you think that either Johnson or van den Haag has the strongest argument for his position. Who has the more convincing argument and why?

3. Discuss your position on the death penalty and explain your reasoning in detail.

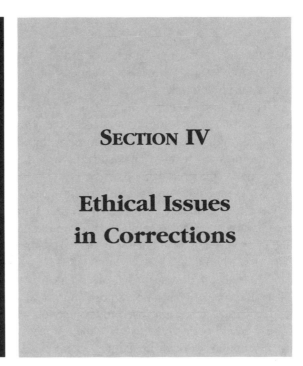

> What lies behind us and what lies before us are tiny matters compared to what lies within us.
>
> —Ralph Waldo Emerson

SECTION IV

Ethical Issues in Corrections

Can offenders be corrected by encouraging them to behave more ethically? By teaching them how to recognize and analyze moral dilemmas? While few would argue that this practice alone will dissuade many people from crime, it is equally clear that an ability to assess the harmfulness of one's acts and to anticipate consequences may be a prerequisite to moral and law-abiding conduct. Given that ability, one can then specify the skills and contexts likely to encourage ethical conduct.

Correctional staffs inside and outside institutional boundaries also need to know how to assess moral dilemmas and how to behave in an ethical fashion. Too often, situational factors work against this objective as well.

Many correctional institutions are plagued by high staff turnover, which means that a high percentage of guards are rookies. These individuals must confront a population of offenders housed in crowded circumstances, inmates whose chief objective is to do their time with as little discomfort as possible. Prison inmates are generally quite interested in paying off guards to improve their living circumstances, to turn a blind eye to various institutional infractions and/or to bring illicit substances or weapons into the institution. Because these inmates may know as much about running the institution as some of the guards, it is often very easy for correctional officers to become dependent on inmates for assistance in doing their jobs, only to find that inmates expect something in return.

Probation and parole officers face different but related problems. The "burned out" probation or parole officer may be as reluctant to supervise his clients as the "burned out" police officer is to answer calls. Or misuse of authority might mean that a probationer or parolee is harassed by his supervisor. Discrimination results when the conditions of release are enforced differently against certain offenders.

The ultimate power of the probation or parole officer is the ability to initiate revocation proceedings that can send the offender to prison. The challenge is to use this authority in the same manner as the ethical police officer employs his coercive power—with an understanding of humanity but with a willingness to intervene for the greater good.

While probation and parole officers have worked hard to establish themselves as professionals, correctional officers have had greater difficulty in this regard, largely because the positions often require little in the way of education and offer very low pay. For many persons, working as a correctional officer is only an interim job.

The Federal Bureau of Prisons offers a notable exception to this pattern. There, the correctional officer's position is viewed as the entry point on a career ladder. This practice, employed in conjunction with the conscientious screening of new employees and the use of a management scheme that serves to discourage corruption, works to make the federal prison system an environment more likely to promote high ethical standards.

CHAPTER 15

Keeping an Eye on the Keeper: Prison Corruption and its Control

Bernard J. McCarthy

This chapter examines the problem of prison corruption and its control as one form of ethical misconduct in institutional correctional systems. Historically, prison corruption has been a persistent and pervasive feature of corrections, periodically erupting in the form of scandals brought to our attention by the press. In recent years, major prison scandals have been reported in Alabama, California, Delaware, Hawaii, Illinois, New York, Pennsylvania and Tennessee. Organized crime, large-scale street gangs and the general avarice of prison employees have been behind a number of these scandals. Other than media reports, little is known about the problem. This informational deficiency is related to a larger problem in corrections: the failure to systematically examine the impact of staff behavior on the correctional process. However, the significance of this problem (i.e., employee behavior) should not be underestimated. The critical role played by employees in the correctional enterprise has been noted by correctional practitioners and prison reformers:

> [It] is obvious, too, that the best security which society can have, that suitable punishments will be inflicted in a suitable manner, must arise from the character of the men to whom the government of the prison is entrusted (Boston Prison Discipline Society, 1827:18).

KEY CONCEPTS:

anticorruption policy

corruption

corruption through default

corruption through friendship

corruption through reciprocity

malfeasance

material accommodations

misfeasance

nonfeasance

power accommodations

status accommodations

Sykes's "pains of imprisonment"

Adapted from Bernard J. McCarthy, "Keeping an Eye on the Keeper: Prison Corruption and Its Control," *The Prison Journal,* Volume 64, Number 2 [Fall/Winter 1984] pp. 113-125.

In 1870, the Reverend James Woodworth, Secretary of the California Prison Commission, stated:

> Until it [prison guard reform] is accomplished, nothing is accomplished. When this work is done, everything will be done, for all the details of a reformed prison discipline are wrapped up in this supreme effort, as oak is in the acorn (Fogel, 1979:69).

Jessica Mitford reported in a critical study of prisons:

> The character and mentality of the keepers may be of more importance in understanding prisons than the character and mentality of the kept (Reid, 1981:211).

Generally, in the area of public service, the integrity of government workers has been viewed as a significant factor in the effective and efficient operation of government. In criminal justice there exists a voluminous literature on police corruption, yet this subject represents one of the least understood areas in corrections. This paper will focus on one dimension of employee behavior in an institutional setting: staff corruption. In this paper we will examine the forms, functions and impact of corrupt practices on the correctional process.

Corrupt practices in prison range from simple acts of theft and pilferage to large-scale criminal conspiracies (e.g., drug trafficking, counterfeiting rings, sale of paroles, etc.). These forms of correctional malpractice may be directed at inmates, employees, the state and the general community.

The potential impact of such practices may be great. In terms of its impact on the criminal justice system, corrupt practices undermine and erode respect for the justice system by both offenders and the general public and lead to the selective nullification of the "pains of imprisonment" (i.e., the correctional process for certain offenders). For example, offenders may be able to arrange the purchase of paroles and pardons or drastically improve their standard of living in custody. Corrupt practices may also lead to a breakdown in the control structure of the organization and to the demoralization of correctional workers. The existence of corrupt practices also undermines the impact of correctional programs designed to change offenders. The importation of drugs into a prison may completely undo the efforts of maintaining a drug-free facility.

Within corrections, the incentives for corrupt behavior are many. From the offenders' perspective, they have everything to gain (i.e., the so-called pains of imprisonment may be neutralized or their release from custody secured) and very little to lose. From the employees' perspective, corrupt practices represent a lucrative, albeit illicit, way to supplement one's income (usually without significant risk). In one recent investigation nicknamed "Operation Bad Fellas," U.S Bureau of Prison correctional officers were charged with smuggling heroin, marijuana, steroids, Italian food, vodka, wine, vitamins, clothing and electronic equipment into a federal correctional facility in New York City. Bribes received by staff ranged from $100 to $1,000 per delivery (Suro, 1997).

This paper examines the problem of staff corruption within a prison system and addresses three basic questions:

1. What is corruption, and what forms does it take in an institutional setting?

2. What factors appear to be associated with its relative incidence?

3. What steps should be taken to control the problem?

DEFINING CORRUPTION IN A CORRECTIONAL ENVIRONMENT

In the correctional literature, the concept of corruption has been used frequently, usually referring to a general adulteration of the formal goals of the correctional process (Rothman, 1971; Sykes, 1956, 1958). The literature on corruption, particularly police corruption, provides a much narrower definition, which aids researchers interested in studying the problem (see Kleinig, 1996). For the purposes of this paper, however, corruption is defined more specifically as the intentional violation of organizational norms (i.e., rules and regulations) by public employees for personal material gain.

This definition was formulated on the basis of a review of the corruption literature, particularly the literature on police corruption. As one might expect, there exist varying definitions and corresponding approaches to the study of corruption (Heidenheimer, 1970). In the research on police corruption, most studies appear to use what has been referred to as a public-office-centered definition of corruption (Simpson, 1978). The public-office-centered definition views corruption as essentially a violation of organizational norms by a public servant for personal gain (Heidenheimer, 1970). Examples of this approach may be found in the writings of Sherman (1974), Meyer (1976), Goldstein (1977), Barker (1977) and Kleinig (1996). This approach has been adopted in this paper. Corruption occurs when a public servant (prison employee) violates organizational rules and regulations for his or her own personal material gain.

In operationalizing this definition of corruption, certain conditions must be satisfied before an act can be defined as corrupt. First, the action must involve individuals who function as employees. Second, the offense must be in violation of the formal rules of the organization. Third, the offense must involve an employee receiving some personal material gain for the misuse of one's office. These conditions clearly distinguish corrupt behavior from other forms of staff misconduct, such as excessive use of force. A standard definition of corruption, consistent with the general literature, is critical in building an information base regarding corrupt practices in corrections and for comparative purposes with the larger criminal justice system.

TYPES OF PRISON CORRUPTION

Unlike the literature on police corruption, very little is known regarding the types of corrupt practices experienced by correctional agencies. In addressing this problem, McCarthy (1981) examined the official records of an internal affairs unit of a state department of corrections.

The internal affairs unit had the responsibility for investigating all allegations of misconduct by staff or inmates. Cases compiled by this unit were content-analyzed to determine the range and types of corrupt practices experienced by this agency. Admittedly, this information source provides a limited view of the problem because it is based on official statistics. However, as researchers in the field of police corruption have suggested, the records of the internal affairs unit represent one of the best available sources of information for examining this topic (Meyer, 1976; Sherman, 1979).

This review of the case files identified several types of corrupt conduct: theft, trafficking in contraband, embezzlement, misuse of authority, and a residual or miscellaneous category.

Theft generally involved reports of items reported as stolen from inmates during frisks and cell searches (drugs, money, jewelry), visitors who were being processed for visiting, and staff members. This form of misconduct was generally committed by low-level staff (e.g., correctional officers) and was opportunistic in nature.

Trafficking in contraband involved staff members conspiring with inmates and civilians to smuggle contraband (drugs, alcohol, money, steroids, food and weapons) into correctional facilities for money, drugs or services (usually of a sexual nature). The organization of this activity varied considerably. Some were large-scale conspiracies involving street gangs or organized crime officials on both the inside and the outside. Others were individuals acting on their own.

An act of embezzlement was defined as systematically converting state property to one's own use. This offense was differentiated from theft, which tended to occur in single events that were opportunistic in nature. This offense involved employees, sometimes with the help of inmates, systematically stealing money or materials from state accounts (inmate canteens or employee credit unions) and from warehouses.

Misuse of authority is a general category involving the intentional misuse of discretion for personal material gain. This form of corruption consisted of three basic offenses directed against inmates: the acceptance of gratuities from inmates for special consideration in obtaining legitimate prison privileges (e.g., payoffs to receive choice cells or job assignments); the acceptance of gratuities for special consideration in obtaining or protecting illicit prison activities (e.g., allowing illegal drug sales or gambling); and the mistreatment or extortion of inmates by staff for personal material gain (e.g., threatening to punish or otherwise harm an inmate if a payment is not forthcoming).

THE ROLE OF DISCRETION

All forms of corruption involve the misuse of discretion by public employees. The role played by discretion in corrections is significant. Correctional officials are provided with a broad mandate by law to develop and administer correctional agencies. This broad authority extends to devising rules, regulations and procedures designed to control and otherwise handle offenders under custody. Corruption occurs when officials misuse this discretionary power for personal material gain. At a general level, three forms of discretionary misconduct can be identified: misfeasance, malfeasance and nonfeasance.

For the purpose of understanding the relationship between corrupt practices and the misuse of authority, the different forms of corruption have been sorted into the three categories of discretionary misconduct (see Table 15.1).

Misfeasance refers to the improper performance of some act that an official may lawfully do (*Black's Law Dictionary*, 1968). Offenses in corrections that fall into this category include the acceptance of gratuities for special privileges or preferential treatment (e.g., assignment to honor blocks, access to phone calls), the selective application of formal rewards and punishments to inmates for a fee, the sale of paroles or other forms of releases, and the misuse or misappropriation of state resources for one's own personal gain. All these acts involve an employee misusing the lawful authority vested in his or her office for personal gain.

Corrupt practices falling into the category of misfeasance are directed at improving the living conditions of inmates and, as a result, they reduce the deprivations associated with imprisonment. The misuse of lawful authority appears to be in an area in which line staff have the greatest opportunities to maximize their personal gain (especially in supplementing their income through the commission of illicit acts), because the nature of their work permits them the greatest influence over routine prisoner conditions.

Malfeasance refers to direct misconduct or wrongful conduct by a public official or employee, as opposed to the improper use of legitimate power or authority (*Black's Law Dictionary*, 1968). Corrupt practices that fall in this category involve primarily criminal acts and include theft; embezzlement; trafficking in contraband; extortion; exploitation of inmates or their families for money, goods and services; protection rackets; assisting escapes (as opposed to arranging paroles or sentence communications); and engaging in criminal conspiracies with inmates for such purposes as forgery, drug sales and counterfeiting.

Acts of malfeasance appear to represent more aggressive and serious acts by staff to supplement their incomes. This type of offense is similar to the grass eater/meat eater distinction found in studies of police corruption (Knapp Commission, 1973). Meat eaters are viewed as aggressively exploiting every possible situation for personal gain. Grass eaters, on the other hand, take whatever comes their way. For instance, a meat eater might sell drugs in prison, while a grass eater might respond to an inmate's request for drugs.

Table 15.1
Pattern of Corruption by Type of Decision

Corrupt Acts by Discretionary Decisions	Officials Involved
Misfeasance	
Provide Preferential Treatment and Special Privileges	Line Staff
Selective Application of Rewards and Punishments	Line Staff
Forms of Legitimate Release	Administrators
Misappropriation of Resources	Administrators
Malfeasance	
Trafficking	Line Staff
Extortion/Exploitation	Line Staff
Protection Rackets	Line Staff
Embezzlement/Theft	Line Staff & Administrators
Criminal Conspiracies	Line Staff
Nonfeasance	
Failure to Enforce Regulations	Line Staff
Cover Ups	Administrators & Line Staff

The last category is nonfeasance. This refers to the failure to act according to one's responsibilities, or the omission of an act that an official ought to perform (*Black's Law Dictionary*, 1968). McKorkle (1970) has suggested that nonfeasance is more responsible for corrupting correctional officers than malfeasance. Two types of corrupt practices appear to be involved in this type of decision: first, selectively ignoring inmate violations of institutional rules, such as permitting inmates to engage in sexual activities with visitors or looking the other way when marijuana or other drugs are smuggled into the facility by visitors in return for payment; and second, the failure to report or stop other employees involved in misconduct. This second practice might typically consist of a low-level employee not informing on a fellow officer or superior because of an implied or direct promise of personal gain, such as promotion or transfer. In other cases an administrator may fail to stop staff misconduct for fear of public scandal and possible loss of position.

FACTORS ASSOCIATED WITH CORRUPTION

In a U.S. Department of Justice study on municipal corruption (1978), two factors were identified as influencing the degree of corruption experienced by a particular governmental agency: the opportunities for corruption and the incentives to make use of those opportunities (Gardiner and Lyman, 1978). In the following section, these two factors will be examined within the context of a prison environment.

A third factor identified by other studies of public corruption was politics (Gardiner, 1970; Sherman, 1978). Sherman suggests that a leading explanation for police corruption was the capture of the department by the political environment. Corrections is not immune from the power of politics. Correctional programs at the state and local level are influenced by the political process, particularly in terms of the appointment of administrative staff and the allocation of resources.

THE ROLE OF OPPORTUNITIES

Three forces on prison systems directly affect the incentives and opportunities for corruption. One, the trend to incarcerate criminals, has led to unprecedented levels of crowding in state prison systems. Two, career criminals are receiving longer sentences as the public sentiment toward punishment continues to harden (e.g., "three strikes and you're out" laws) and these long-term offenders are making up a larger percentage of the inmate population. Three, citizen attitudes toward the treatment of prisoners has led to a toughening of programs directed at prison inmates (e.g., chain gangs, the introduction of tobacco-free prisons and the elimination of amenities like recreation and college-level educational programs). These forces increase the deprivations associated with imprisonment and provide extra incentive to inmates to attempt to mitigate or neutralize the pains of imprisonment.

The opportunities for corruption arise from the tremendous amounts of discretionary authority allocated by the legislature to correctional officials. As Costikyan has noted, "Corruption is always where the discretionary power resides" (1974:20). In the prison, employees—particularly low-level ones (e.g., correction officers, counselors, and other line workers)—are responsible for monitoring and controlling virtually all inmate behavior. These officials constantly make low-visibility discretionary decisions that reward positive behavior and penalize negative behavior. These decisions directly affect the day-to-day living conditions experienced by inmates under custody.

In a prison environment, staff members, armed with a limited arsenal of formal rewards and punishments, are given the task of controlling a reluctant, resistant and sometimes hostile inmate population. Special privileges in the form of extra television time, phone calls, job assignments, cell changes, conjugal visits, transfers and furloughs may be used to reward positive behavior. Punishments, in the form of withdrawal of privileges, transfers or various forms of deprivation (cell restriction to solitary confinement and loss of good time), are used to control inmates.

The way that staff members apply these rewards and punishments has both short-term and long-term consequences for inmates and their experiences in the correctional system. Accordingly, when one considers the conditions of confinement, one recognizes the many incentives and pressures for inmates to attempt to corrupt staff as one means of improving their living conditions or for staff to exploit their power. Individuals sentenced to prison are subjected to various levels of deprivations, commonly referred to as "pains of imprisonment," which affect both the physical and psychological state of the individuals. Sykes defined these pains of imprisonment as the deprivation of liberty, goods and services, heterosexual relations, autonomy and security (Sykes, 1958). In dealing with these "pains" associated with confinement, inmates make various adaptations to their immediate environment to help soften its psychological and physical impact. One of the techniques that they use is the corruption of correctional employees as a means of neutralizing or improving their conditions of confinement (for example, through the smuggling of drugs, food, radios or money, or the purchase of privileges).

In her journalistic study of an inmate incarcerated in a maximum-security prison, Sheehan made the following comment regarding the motivation of inmates in prison:

> Most men in the prison are in prison precisely because they were not willing to go without on the street. They are no more willing to go without in prison, so they hustle to afford what they cannot afford to buy (1978:9).

Hustling usually brings the inmates and/or confederates into situations in which they need the cooperation of a staff member, either to overlook an infraction, perform a favor or smuggle in some item. As such, the incentives or pressures for inmates to influence the reward and punishment structure through corruption are enormous. Gardiner and Lyman underscore this point when they state: "Corruption can only occur when officials have an opportunity to exercise their authority in ways which would lead others to want to pay for favorable treatment" (1978:141).

INCENTIVES FOR CORRUPTION

The incentives for employees to take advantage of the power associated with their position in an institutional setting are many. They range from structural and organizational characteristics or prison management to individual factors (e.g., honesty of staff, the financial needs of employees, etc.).

A major incentive for corrupt practices results from defects in the prison organization's control structure. The prison, which is essentially a coercive organization, formally bases its control on the use of coercive power (Etzioni, 1964:59). However, correctional employees, particularly line staff, find that there are limits to the degree of compliance achieved through the use of coercive power (Cloward, 1960; Sykes, 1958). In order to do the job successfully, coercive power must be supplemented with informal exchange relations with inmates. These informal control practices are utilized by staff for control purposes and are responsible for the smooth functioning of the institution and for maintaining an uneasy peace (Cloward, 1960; Irwin, 1980; Sykes, 1958). As Sykes pointed out almost 30 years ago:

> The custodians (guards) . . . are under strong pressure to compromise with their captives for it is a paradox that they can insure their dominance only by allowing it to be corrupted. Only by tolerating violations of minor rules and regulations can the guard secure compliance in the major areas of the custodial regime (1956:158).

According to Sykes, three factors are responsible for undermining the formal control structure of the prison: (1) friendships with inmates, (2) reciprocal relationships, and (3) defaults. Each of these factors develops at the line-staff level as a function of long-term and close working associations between guard and inmate in a closed setting. Irwin (1980), in a contemporary update, cited corrupt favoritism as a significant factor in the day-to-day management of the prison.

Corruption through friendship evolves from the close contact that prisoners and guards share in their daily interactions. In many cases, they get to know one another as individuals, and friendships may develop. These friendships may, in turn, affect how staff members use their authority. Corruption through reciprocity occurs as an indirect consequence of the exchange relations that develop between inmates and staff: "You do something for me, I'll do something for you." Corruption through default occurs when staff members (e.g., cellblock officers) begin to rely on inmates to assist them with their duties, such as report writing and cell checks. In time, the employee depends on the inmates for their assistance in satisfactorily performing his or her duties.

Cloward (1960) also pointed out how defects in the prison organization's control apparatus lead staff members to develop informal means of control through the development of various accommodations between the keepers and the kept.

Material accommodations occur when staff provide certain inmates with access to forbidden goods and services or contraband in return for their cooperation. Cloward provides an example of this when he quotes an inmate explaining how he makes home brew.

> You go to make arrangements with the mess sergeant. He gets the ingredients and when we're in business . . . it's one of those you do this for me and I'll do this for you sort of thing. . . . The sergeant has to feed 1,500 men. It don't look good if he goofs. He wants the job done right. Now we're the ones who do the work, the cooking and all of that. So the sergeant, he says, okay you can make a little drink. But see to it that you get that food on the lines or the deal's off (1960:7).

Power accommodations occur when selected inmates are provided with access to restricted information, such as the date and time of an impending shakedown (search of cells) or access to key correctional personnel. Frequently, these take the form of reciprocal relationships in which valuable information is exchanged by both staff and inmates. Inmates inform on one another, and staff in turn may disclose administration plans regarding such activities as the time and place of cell searches.

Status accommodations result when staff provide special deference to certain inmates. According to Cloward:

> The right guy . . . seems to be left alone (by staff) in spite of conspic-
> uous deviance from official values, and this mark of untouchability
> results in high status among his peers (1960:40).

The cumulative effect of these accommodations may predispose certain correctional employees to take advantage of their situation and attempt to materially benefit from their working relationships with inmates, staff and contractors.

Another factor that complicates matters is the type and quality of persons recruited and hired to work in correctional facilities. Frequently the quality of the work force is uneven and sometimes substandard because of low pay and poor working conditions. These individuals are placed in situations in which they are given considerable discretionary authority (without much training in its use) in a setting in which the visibility of their actions is quite low. When this occurs, the probability of corrupt practices increases. Another factor that provides an incentive for corruption is the impact of politics. If the selection and promotion of employees are influenced by politics, employee decisions may benefit the political party in power.

CONTROLLING CORRUPTION

First of all, it must be recognized that corruption is a regular feature of government processes. The problem of corruption can probably never be eradicated; however, certain steps may be taken to control the problem (Gardiner, 1970:93). In this section, we will examine several strategies that a correctional administrator may adopt to address the problem of corruption within a correctional agency.

A first step in dealing with the problem of corruption is to develop and enforce an anticorruption policy. This policy should define what the agency means by corruption as well as specify the penalties associated with such practices. [See Ward and McCormack (1978) for an example of developing an anticorruption policy for police departments.] Once this policy has been formulated, it should be disseminated to the employees of the department. Training should also be provided to employees regarding the nature, causes, impact and consequences of corrupt practices. For deterrence to work, these policies must be enforced.

Second, the correctional agency should develop a proactive mechanism to detect and investigate corrupt practices. This includes the establishment of an internal affairs unit and a process that encourages employees, inmates, and civilians to report allegations of staff misconduct. A whistle-blower hotline is used by many states to deal with governmental misconduct and this can be extended to prison systems. In addition, the use of routine and special audit procedures on a random basis will ensure the proper expenditure of funds. In one state, state-level investigators randomly target prisons and conduct interdiction investigations to search for contraband. Inmates, staff and civilians are subject to searches and drug testing, including a drug detection system known as Ionscan. In one year these searches resulted in the seizure of a large quantity of drugs (cocaine, crack cocaine and marijuana) and weapons, including 13 firearms and 280 rounds of ammunition in one state system (Florida Department of Corrections, 1997).

Third, correctional administrators should attempt to improve management practices in the prison. This internal reform is directed at improving the control of the organization. In prior studies of corruption, where leadership and control were weak, the potential for corruption increased (Gardiner, 1970). Management must take affirmative steps toward reducing the opportunities for corruption. One step in this direction is to structure the use of discretion and make the visibility of low-level decisionmakers more public. Guidelines for the use of discretionary rewards and punishments should be public. For example, specific criteria and a review process should be established to review cell changes, job assignments and transfers or temporary releases. These decisions should be periodically reviewed by supervisors to ensure the accountability of decisionmakers. Internal reform should also include screening of employees in order to improve their overall quality. Selection procedures should be upgraded to include psychological testing and formal preservice training designed to screen out questionable employees. Also, simple police checks of an individual's background could be expanded by requiring in-depth background investigations of prospective employees. Some states are finding that members of street gangs are applying for jobs as correctional officers to assist in the expansion of the gang's power inside prisons. Routine investigations have also found that individuals with felony convictions and even escapees have been hired as correctional employees.

Also, the working conditions of employees should be improved. Improving wage scales, enlarging job responsibilities and broadening employee participation in decisionmaking, as well as increasing efforts toward professionalization by creating opportunities for preservice and in-service training and advancement on the basis of merit, are reforms that would enhance the quality of correctional employees.

A fourth and final recommendation addresses the political environment. A correctional administrator has little control over political and community attitudes, but one should take steps to insulate his or her employees from external pressure placed on them. By requiring merit selection and promotion of employees, a correctional administrator reduces the impact of political interference in the operation of the agency.

In sum, controlling corruption requires a commitment by correctional administrators to improve and upgrade the general correctional environment (particularly the working conditions for staff), to protect employees from political pressures and to replace a tendency toward complacency, with a concern for accountability. Opportunities for corruption must be identified and addressed and the risks taken by persons predisposed to misconduct must be increased. It is doubtful that corrupt practices can be eliminated but they can be reduced and controlled.

REFERENCES

Barker, Thomas (1977). "Social Definitions of Police Corruption," *Criminal Justice Review* 1 (Fall): 101-110.

Black's Law Dictionary (1968). St. Paul, MN: West Publishing Co.

Boston Prison Discipline Society (1826-1854) (1972). Reprint of 1st-29th Annual Report. Montclair, NJ: Patterson-Smith.

Clark, J.P., & Richard C. Hollinger (1981). Theft by Employees in Work Organizations. Minneapolis: University of Minnesota. Cited in *Criminal Justice Abstracts* 1(March):19.

Cloward, R. (1960). *Theoretical Studies in the Social Organization of the Prison*. Social Science Research Council.

Costikyan, E.N. (1974). "The Locus of Corruption." In *Theft of the City: Readings on Corruption in Urban America*, by J.A. Gardiner & D. J. Olsen (eds.). Bloomington: Indiana University Press.

Crouch, Ben (ed.) (1980). *The Keepers: Prison Guards and Contemporary Corrections*. Springfield, IL: Charles C Thomas.

Davis, Kenneth C. (1960). *Discretionary Justice: A Preliminary Inquiry*. Baton Rouge: Louisiana State University Press.

Duchaine, N. (1979). *The Literature of Police Corruption*. Vol. II. New York: John Jay Press.

Duffee, D. (1974). "The Correction Officer Subculture and Organizational Change," *Journal of Research in Crime and Delinquency* 2:155-172.

Etzioni, Amitai (1964). *Modern Organizations*. Englewood Cliffs, NJ: Prentice-Hall.

Florida Department of Corrections, Office of the Inspector General Annual Report, 1997.

Fogel, David (1979). *"We Are the Living Proof:" The Justice Model for Corrections*. Cincinnati, OH: Anderson Publishing Co.

Gardiner, J.A. (1970). *The Politics of Corruption*. New York: The Russell Sage Foundation.

Gardiner, J.A., & T.R. Lyman (1978). *Decisions for Sale, Corruption and Reform in Land Use and Building Regulations*. New York: Praeger Publishers.

Goldstein, H. (1977). *Policing in a Free Society*. Cambridge, MA: Ballinger Publishing Co.

Heidenheimer, Arnold (1970). *Political Corruption: Readings in Comparative Analysis*. New York: Holt, Rinehart & Winston.

Irwin, John (1980). *Prisons in Turmoil*. Boston: Little, Brown & Co.

Kleinig, J. (1996). *The Ethics of Policing*. New York: Cambridge University Press.

Knapp, W. (1973). *Knapp Commission on Police Corruption*. New York: Brazilier.

Lombardo, Lucien X. (1989). *Guards Imprisoned: Correctional Officers at Work*. Cincinnati, OH: Anderson Publishing Co.

Lyman, T., T. Fletcher & J. Gardiner (1978). *Prevention, Detection and Correction of Corruption in Local Government*. Washington, DC: U.S. Government Printing Office.

McCarthy, B.J. (1981). "Exploratory Study in Corruption in Corrections." Ph.D. dissertation, The Florida State University.

McKorkle, L. (1970). "Guard-Inmate Relationships." In *The Sociology of Punishment and Control*, N. Johnston et al. (eds.), New York: John Wiley and Sons.

Meyer, J.D. (1976). "Definitional and Etiological Issues in Police Corruption: An Assessment and Synthesis of Competing Perspectives." *Journal of Police Science and Police Administration* 4:46-55.

Mitford, Jessica (1973). *Kind and Usual Punishment*. Cited in Reid, S.T., *The Correctional System*. New York: Holt, Rinehart & Winston, 1981.

Rothman, D. (1971). *The Discovery of the Asylum: Social Order in the New Republic*. Boston: Little, Brown & Co.

Sheehan, S. (1978). *A Prison and a Prisoner*. Boston: Mifflin Co.

Sherman, L. (1974). *Police Corruption: A Sociological Perspective*. New York: Anchor Books.

_____ (1978). *Scandal and Reform, Controlling Police Corruption*. Berkeley: University of California Press.

_____ (1979). "Obtaining Access to Police Internal Affairs Files." *Criminal Law Bulletin* 15 September-October: 449-461.

Simpson, Anthony (1978). *The Literature of Police Corruption*. New York: John Jay Press.

Suro, Robert (1997). "Officials Wonder if Bribery Arrests at Federal Prison are Isolated or Trend." *The Washington Post*, June 1, 1997, A08.

Sykes, G. (1956). "The Corruption of Authority and Rehabilitation," *Social Forces* 34:157-162.

_____ (1958). *The Society of Captives: A Study of a Maximum Security Prison*. Princeton, NJ: Princeton University Press.

Ward, R., & R. McCormack (1979). *An Anti-Corruption Manual for Administrators in Law Enforcement*. New York: The John Jay Press.

DISCUSSION QUESTIONS

1. What kinds of motivations might a correctional officer have for engaging in corruption? Are some forms of corruption worse than others? Explain.

2. Is corruption an unavoidable result of discretion? Discuss your response in detail.

3. Can correctional officers be expected to have moral careers comparable to other criminal justice professionals? How might those careers differ from those already discussed?

CHAPTER 16

Ethical Issues in Probation, Parole and Community Corrections

John T. Whitehead

INTRODUCTION

It is no accident that more movies and television shows are made about police officers than about probation and parole officers. Because probation and parole are not as dramatic as policing, the ethical issues in probation, parole and other types of community correctional pro-grams are somewhat more ordinary. Probation and parole officers simply do not have the opportunities to become involved in dramatic matters such as the drug bust and corruption involving some police officers in large cities.

This does not mean that there are no ethi-cal issues in probation and parole. It just means that the issues are usually less dramatic and more subtle. This chapter will discuss some of the problems that can arise in probation and parole work, including ethical issues concern-ing intensive supervision, electronic monitoring and house arrest.

KEY CONCEPTS:

community service

parole

probation

whistle-blowing

Before delving into the ethical issues in community corrections, it may be helpful to state some assumptions. In this chapter it is assumed that there are cer-tain values to guide ethical choices, such as truth, honesty, fairness, hard work and consideration for others. For this discussion, it does not matter whether these values are considered moral absolutes or simply mutually agreed upon conven-tions. Whatever their sources, the following discussion assumes such values exist and that most individuals subscribe to them. For example, it is assumed that it is ethical for probation and parole employees to put in a full day's work for a full day's pay. Employees who do less are considered to be acting unethically.

THE MISSION OF PROBATION AND PAROLE

The major ethical issue in probation and parole is the definition of the mission of community supervision. This refers to deciding on the purpose or objective of supervision.

Traditionally the mission of probation and parole supervision has been described as some combination of assistance and control, treatment and security, or service and surveillance (Studt, 1973). In other words, officers are supposed to provide services to offenders while also monitoring them so that the community is protected from new crimes.

In the last few years, a number of voices have been calling for corrections to revert back to a very punishment-oriented philosophy. It is not unusual to hear calls for spartan prisons with few or no amenities for prisoners. Critics have voiced their opposition to television (both cable and regular broadcast programming), weightlifting and athletics as needless frills that prisoners, by virtue of their crimes, simply do not deserve. Extremists call for the reinstatement of chain gangs, while slightly less strident souls simply suggest hard labor for all prisoners to keep them busy and to punish them for their transgressions.

The community corrections corollary to this would be stringent supervision: frequent reporting, curfews, work or community service requirements, fines, supervision fees and drug testing. These measures would make probation and parole as punitive as possible. The mission would be punishment, pure and simple. The role of the officer would be to make sure that the punishment is being delivered.

Just as prison extremists urge the return of chain gangs, probation-parole extremists urge several harsh changes for community supervision offenders. One is the wearing of insignia to mark one's status as an offender. Offenders would wear shirts or vests or license plates proclaiming their status as an offender (e.g., "drunk driver," "shoplifter," etc.) to the world as they shop at the mall or drive down the street. Society would mark offenders with a "scarlet letter": "D" for drunk driver or "S" for shoplifter, just as puritan New England branded the Hester Prynnes of its day for adultery. (This issue will be considered further in a later section concerning acceptable penal content.)

The new penology (Feeley & Simon, 1992) takes a less strident stance and argues that probation and parole should be efficient monitors of the conditions of supervision. If an offender fails to follow the conditions of supervision, then the officer should be swift to report the failure to the court or the parole board. Sufficiently serious or frequent violations would land the offender in prison. Ironically, failure becomes success in this model. Whereas old-fashioned officers who aimed for the rehabilitation of offenders would consider recidivism (new crimes) a failure of supervision, new penology officers would consider a new crime a success as long as it is noted and used to get the offender back into prison. Here the officer claims that one is doing one's job because signs of continuing criminal tendencies are used to get the offender off the street. The objective is to classify offenders into various categories of risk and to place them into the proper risk-management response. There is no pretense of trying to rehabilitate or cure the offender.

One of the most hopeful philosophies of probation and parole is the restorative justice model. This model of criminal justice is concerned with reparation to the victim and involvement of the victim in the criminal justice process, remorse and accountability for offenders, and peace and justice for the community (Bazemore & Maloney, 1994; Bazemore & Umbreit, 1995). This model argues that neither punishment nor treatment alone is effective in changing offenders or restoring the victim or the community to its pre-crime state. Instead, the model focuses on reparation, restitution, dialogue and negotiation in order to restore the victim and the community to its pre-crime state. The model involves both a micro dimension (offender reparation and restitution to the victim[s]) and a macro dimension (a community responsibility for crime control and the need for order and safety in the community).

One ethical issue underlying these reconceptualizations of the mission of probation and parole is the question of what society owes the offender. The easy answer is that society owes the offender nothing. The criminal has broken the law and he or she must pay his or her debt to society. This view is congruent with the current popularity of neoclassical theories of criminal behavior that emphasize free will and accountability (see, for example, Wilson, 1983). Offenders are seen as choosing crime and as responsible for their actions. The only questions are the determination of the debt the offender must pay to society and the control of the offender so new crimes are prevented. Thus, the focus is on retribution, deterrence and incapacitation. There is little or no emphasis on assistance to the offender.

Positivist theories of crime, on the other hand, contend that crime is not so simple. Biological, psychological and sociological factors explain criminal behavior (Lilly, Cullen & Ball, 1989). Human behavior reflects all sorts of influences, ranging from genetic makeup to parental upbringing to the availability of educational and job opportunities. Positivist perspectives imply that society has a responsibility to assist the offender because societal factors have contributed to the criminal behavior. Thus, there is a direct link between positivist perspectives and programs to assist offenders in prison and in the community.

The peacemaking perspective outlined in an earlier chapter in this book suggests that all of us have a responsibility to the offender. The principles of caring and connectedness imply that we cannot just ignore offenders but that our common humanity is the basis for remembering that offenders are like us and want and deserve humane treatment and assistance.

The ethical question is this: Can society embrace a neoclassical perspective—assume offenders are totally free and responsible—and simply ignore any consideration of assistance to offenders? Or does society have some obligation to help offenders to some degree?

One answer to this question is that society does have a duty to provide assistance to offenders but that probation and parole should not attempt such a task. Embracing this solution, Rosecrance (1986) argues that other community agencies should provide assistance to offenders and that probation should be limited to investigations and monitoring of court-imposed sentence conditions. Much of the monitoring would be computer-assisted.

Rosecrance argues this drastic solution for several reasons. First, research and his own probation experience have convinced him that organizational priorities typically take precedence over concern for the needs of the offender. Both line officers and supervisors are generally more concerned with appearing effective rather than with actually having some impact on clients. As a result, reports of supposedly effective programs must be viewed skeptically. The effectiveness may well reflect organizational manipulations rather than true reformation of offenders. Second, offenders and officers come from different social worlds. As a result, neither party trusts the other and communication between the two often deteriorates into "patent mendacity" (Rosecrance, 1986:28). Third, if service means counseling or therapy, officers often have no particular expertise in these areas (Rosecrance, 1986). In fact, officers who attempt counseling may harm offender psyches (Dietrich, 1979).

Research on intensive supervision, however, suggests that Rosecrance is wrong. A number of studies on intensive supervision have shown that there is "solid empirical evidence that ordering offenders into treatment and requiring them to participate reduces recidivism [new crimes]" (Petersilia, 1997:187). In one study, recidivism was reduced by 20-30 percent (Petersilia & Turner, 1993).

In light of these studies, it can be argued that the ethical course of action is to provide treatment programs because they both assist the offender and also reduce new crimes. Providing treatment is also consistent with Kant's categorical imperative to treat people as subjects and with peacemaking's precept of caring.

A related consideration that many people forget is the state's obligation to the correctional worker to provide a humane working environment. Even if criminals are seen as deserving only warehouse prisons and some police-like form of probation and parole, some consideration must be given to the employee. What sort of individual would want to work in sparse and spartan prisons? What sort of individual would choose to be a probation or parole officer if the job required only punishment-oriented activities? Because research has indicated that probation officers value a sense of personal accomplishment from involvement with offenders (Whitehead, 1989), any proposal to divorce officers from assistance tasks raises the specter of alienating a substantial number of line officers.

Thus, recent writing on the mission of probation and parole and calls for spartan prisons and punitive probation and parole raise important ethical considerations. Does society have any obligation to provide assistance to offenders? Does the introduction of increased emphasis on controlling offenders result in a work environment that would have negative consequences for officers? These are questions that need attention.

THE EFFECTIVENESS OF COMMUNITY CORRECTIONS

Considerable research has accumulated on the issue of whether probation is effective. A brief review of this research will be presented. Then there will be a consideration of the ethical implications of the effectiveness research.

A 1985 report triggered much of the attention to the question of probation effectiveness. That report, the RAND Report (Petersilia et al., 1985), found that two counties in California had considerable difficulty with felons placed on probation; 65 percent of the felons studied were rearrested within 40 months and one-third were incarcerated. The report received national attention and caused many to think that probation was a miserable failure. The report was a major factor in the subsequent move to reform probation by developing stricter measures (such as intensive supervision, house arrest and electronic monitoring programs) for probationers.

There were several problems with the RAND report, however, that did not receive adequate attention. One problem was that the dramatic failure rates noted in the report may have been unique to the two California counties studied. Studies of felony probation in other jurisdictions have shown varying failure rates from quite low to about as high as those found in Los Angeles and Alameda counties (Geerken & Hayes, 1993). Another fact ignored in the report was that most probationers are misdemeanor offenders who do quite well on probation.

An ethical question raised by the report is whether workers—officers and managerial personnel alike—are not doing the jobs that they should be doing. If workers and whole agencies are derelict in their responsibilities, ethical irresponsibility on the part of line officers may be the root problem behind the ineffectiveness.

Several factors point to worker malfeasance as contributing to probation ineffectiveness. A unique study on probation undertaken by the General Accounting Office (1976) found that about 60 percent of the court-ordered conditions of sentence were *not* enforced by probation departments. More disturbing was that only 38 percent of the case folders examined had written treatment plans. In other words, in the majority of cases, officers were not even taking the trouble to sit down and write out a set of objectives for the offenders they were supervising. This is equivalent to a college professor not bothering to write a syllabus for a course, having no plan of action for the semester. An in-depth study of parole officers by McCleary found that parole officers "like the rest of us, are interested in doing as little work as possible" (1978:43). McCleary found that parole officers spent much of their time in outside pursuits such as getting a master's degree or running a restaurant. This left less time for their work with parolees.

In short, if community supervision is ineffective, part of the reason may be that officers—and the managers who supervise them—are not doing their jobs. Thus workers may not be living up to the ethical standard of putting in a full day's work for a full day's pay.

Alternatively, the problem may be that we simply do not really know what to do to help probationers and parolees stay away from crime. Criminology is far from complete agreement on a theory or set of theories about why individuals commit crime or on proven strategies to rehabilitate offenders. Some theories focus on the individual deficits of offenders, others on societal ills, and still others criticize society for defining certain actions as criminal and ignoring other equally harmful actions (Lilly, Cullen & Ball, 1989). Although progress has been made in refining theories about the causes of crime and what are appropriate interventions, criminologists are still exploring both of these issues for better answers. Still another part of the answer involves a clearer definition of the mission of probation and parole so officers have a clear role to perform.

ACCEPTABLE PENAL CONTENT

In the discussion of the mission of probation and parole, it was noted that extremists argue that some offenders should wear shirts or bumper stickers marking them as drunk drivers, shoplifters or whatever crime the person has been convicted of. In a thought-provoking piece, von Hirsch (1990) notes the ethical concern that any such innovations not insult or demean offenders but satisfy the standard of acceptable penal content:[1]

> Acceptable penal content, then, is the idea that a sanction should be devised so that its intended penal deprivations are those that can be administered in a manner that is clearly consistent with the offender's dignity. If the penal deprivation includes a given imposition, X, then one must ask whether that can be undergone by offenders in a reasonably self-possessed fashion. Unless one is confident that it can, it should not be a part of the sanction. (von Hirsch, 1990:167)

Thus, von Hirsch is opposed to T-shirts for offenders or bumper stickers that make drunk drivers advertise their offense because there "is no way a person can, with dignity, go about in public with a sign admitting himself or herself to be a moral pariah" (1990:168). Similarly, he would be opposed to chain gangs because it is not possible to undergo such a measure with any sense of dignity.

Proponents of identifying labels for offenders would argue that they enhance the punishment value of community corrections. Such marks make probation or parole tougher rather than a lenient "slap on the wrist." Supporters would also argue that there may be deterrent value in the measures. It is embarrassing to wear such markings and this could serve to deter others from drunk driving or whatever offense results in the added penalty.

Von Hirsch also relates the concept of acceptable penal content to home visits. Traditionally, probation and parole officers have made unannounced home visits to check on offenders and to offer assistance and counseling. Von Hirsch approves of such visits

> only as a mechanism to help enforce another sanction that *does* meet our suggested standard of acceptable penal content. . . . It is not plausible to assert that, without any other need for it, the punishment for a given type of crime should be that state agents will periodically snoop into one's home. (von Hirsch, 1990:169)

INTENSIVE SUPERVISION ISSUES

For the last decade reformers have advocated intensive supervision as a way to improve regular probation and parole supervision. Giving officers smaller caseloads so that they can provide closer supervision—more frequent contacts—has been supported for both crime control and rehabilitation goals. Intensive supervision raises some ethical concerns.

The major concern about intensive supervision can be labeled a "truth in advertising" issue. Intensive supervision has been promoted as the cure for the failure of traditional probation to decrease the recidivism of felony offenders. The major problem with this claim is that it is simply not true. A major evaluation of several intensive supervision programs concluded that there were no differences between intensive and routine supervision programs (Petersilia, Peterson & Turner, 1992). Many offenders do benefit from the programs, but intensive supervision is not a panacea or cure-all for the ills of ordinary probation. Also, as noted above, it appears that treatment components rather than control components may be related to offender success (Petersilia, 1997). Second, the programs divert some offenders from prison but not as many as had been anticipated. Many of the offenders placed into intensive supervision programs would have gone into regular probation if the intensive programs were not available. One study estimated that only one-half of the offenders placed into the program studied would have gone to prison if the program had not been available to judges (Whitehead, Miller & Myers, 1995). Third, ironically, intensive supervision programs can and do operate to *increase* prison populations. The more intensive monitoring involved in these programs (e.g., urinalysis testing) can lead to the detection of illegal drug use or other offenses, which can result in violations. Therefore, offenders on intensive supervision face a higher risk of being detected for behaviors that will send them to prison than do offenders on regular supervision (see Clear & Braga, 1995). Fourth, although intensive supervision can be less expensive than prison, it is more expensive than ordinary supervision.

The ethical issue is whether to continue to promote intensive supervision as a means to reduce recidivism and to reduce prison populations when in fact intensive supervision fails to achieve the dramatic results many had promised. Probably the most honest summary statement about intensive supervision is that it can serve as a probation enhancement. It can make probation tougher than it used to be. This, however, is a much less dramatic claim than was originally made. One wonders if such a reduced claim will be enough to keep intensive supervision popular.

Another concern is that both punitive and risk-control conditions of intensive supervision "are applied across-the-board without much attention to the individual circumstances of the case" (Clear & Hardyman, 1990:54). For example, every intensive supervision offender may be subject to urinalysis checks for drug use even though many have never shown any indication of drug use. This can create a problem of discovering that an offender is adjusting positively on supervision except for recreational marijuana use. The dilemma, then, is how to react to the drug violation. A violation and incarceration would be an ironic twist to the stated intent of many programs to divert offenders from prison. A likely scenario is that "the probation officer is forced to play a type of game—warning the offender and noting the violation but trying to avoid action unless something else happens in the case" (Clear & Hardyman, 1990:54). Such game-playing is hardly new (see McCleary, 1978, for example), but it cannot be avoided in face of the fiscal fact that the "resources simply do not exist to carry out all the threats made in the ISPs [intensive supervision programs] . . ." (Clear & Hardyman, 1990:54).

Another ethical concern is the contention that electronic monitoring is an insidious invasion of the privacy of the home—a principle enshrined in the Fourth Amendment. Corbett and Marx argue that electronic monitoring destroys the privacy of the home:

> Figuratively, prisons have been dismantled, and each individual cell has been reassembled in private homes. Once homes start to serve as modular prisons and bedrooms as cells, what will become of our cherished notion of "home"? If privacy is obliterated *legally* in prison and if EM [electronic monitoring] provides the functional equivalent of prison at home, privacy rights for home confinees and family members are potentially jeopardized. (1991:409)

In short, there are some serious problems surrounding intensive supervision, house arrest and electronic monitoring. To expect that recent interventions are correctional cure-alls is to invite unnecessary disillusionment.

Officer Concerns in Intensive Supervision Programs

A frequently ignored consideration in the development of intensive programs is what impact such programs will have on the line personnel. Several scenarios are foreseeable. One is popular acceptance by workers. Given the greater role clarity inherent in the recent intensive supervision programs, compared to the role ambiguity and role conflict frequently found in traditional probation, positive worker attitudes are a distinct possibility. Another possible scenario, however, is initial euphoria followed by more negative attitudes. Given the expectations of line officers to monitor offenders 24 hours per day, seven days a week, officers may temporarily experience the special aura of an exciting innovation only to sink into a depression occasioned by unrealistic expectations. Who wants to be on call all hours of the night every day of the week?

Due to the fiscal constraints on state and local government, it is very possible that officers in intensive supervision programs will be called on to perform such Herculean tasks without the resources for backups and relief. Physicians can join group practice arrangements to find some relief from never-ending demands, but the officers in these new programs will not have that luxury. There are too many state and local governments experiencing financial exigency to warrant optimism about the resources that will be allocated to correctional programs.

Another possible reaction of line officers is that officers assigned regular probation caseloads may resent the special status and pay of intensive supervision officers. Regular officers may become envious about the reduced caseloads of intensive officers, especially if officers with regular caseloads suspect that the intensive supervision officers' caseloads show little or no difference in risk levels compared to the regular probationers (Clear & Hardyman, 1990).

Evaluations of intensive supervision in Georgia, Illinois and New Jersey have reported positive reactions of line personnel (Tonry, 1990). One partial inquiry into the effects of home confinement on a nonrepresentative sample of federal probation officers showed that the officers did not report widespread negative impacts even though overtime was routine (Beck, Klein-Saffran & Wooten, 1990). These findings suggest that negative effects on workers are not a necessary by-product of recent innovations. More research needs to be conducted, however, before firm conclusions are drawn, especially in light of the fact that corrections employment has proven to be conducive to stress and burnout (Whitehead, 1989; Williamson, 1990).

A more specific problem that intermediate punishments may pose for correctional workers is role conflict: "a tension between his control function and his casework function, having to be both a policeman and a social worker" (Morris & Tonry, 1990:183). The enforcement of the conditions of intermediate punishments, such as urinalysis checks for drug use, necessarily places the officer in the role of an enforcer because there "is no way in which effective, regular, but unpredictable urine testing . . . can be made other than as a police-type function" (Morris & Tonry, 1990:185).

One way to resolve this is through team supervision of offenders placed on intermediate punishments. With this approach, one team member emphasizes the enforcement of the conditions of the sanction and the other provides assistance. Another possible resolution is closer cooperation with local police (Morris & Tonry, 1990). Whatever approach is attempted, however, the basic conflict needs to be addressed.

Offender Concerns

Another concern is the reaction of offenders to community supervision programs. Although many assume that offenders would automatically prefer intensive supervision, house arrest or electronic monitoring to prison, research in Oregon found that one-quarter of the offenders there chose prison over intensive supervision (Petersilia, 1990). Byrne interprets this finding to mean that "some offenders would rather *interrupt* their lifestyle (via incarceration) than deal with attempts to *change* it (via compliance with probation conditions)" (1990:23). A more recent study found some offenders opting for prison over community supervision in order to avoid financial conditions such as restitution orders (Jones, 1996). Cynics or conservatives may wonder who really cares what offenders think, but probation officers know from experience that the attitude of the offender affects, at the very least, the quality of the supervision experience for officers.

From another perspective, there is concern that class bias may affect decisions regarding which offenders are selected for these programs. Some offenders may not have a private residence and thus would be ineligible for house arrest. Some offenders may not be able to afford the supervision fees associated with either intensive supervision or house arrest, especially if those fees are high enough to offset the costs of expensive electronic monitoring equipment. Consequently, "there may well be a tendency to apply house arrest and electronic monitoring to the more privileged and to deny it to the indigent" (Morris & Tonry, 1990:217-218). In effect, this could lead to a dual system of sanctions: incarceration for the poor and alternatives for the wealthy.

PRIVATIZATION

Another ethical issue is whether states should privatize probation and parole services or continue to keep them public. (This topic is also considered in the chapter on ethical issues and prison.)

Proponents of privatization argue several benefits for turning over various governmental services to private corporations. One alleged benefit is the reduction of operating costs. Proponents claim that private enterprise can do things more efficiently and less expensively than the government. Government operation is equated with waste and inefficiency. Some of this is attributed to the civil service system, which guarantees job tenure except in extreme circumstances when jobs are abolished. Civil service workers are not under the same pressures as workers in private industry, who must consistently show a profit.

Opponents of privatization argue that government agencies *can* be efficient and effective. According to this perspective, government offices can adopt efficiency- and effectiveness-enhancing strategies just as do privately run agencies.

Perhaps the main argument against privatization is whether it is appropriate for government to turn over functions as basic as the correctional supervision of offenders to private businesses. Many question whether the symbolic task of punishing offenders should be handed over to workers who wear uniforms that say "Brand X Corrections" rather than the "State of ___" (American Bar Association, 1986). The most dramatic example of this would be for "Brand X Corrections" to carry out capital punishment. Should the state surrender the symbolism of the state executing an offender? Less dramatically, is it right for the state to contract out prison operations that involve the deprivation of liberty and serious disciplinary measures such as solitary confinement? Set against this context, is it ethical to allow a private company to operate a probation or parole operation that involves the very important decision of whether to allow an offender to remain in the community or be revoked for a violation and sent to prison? Or does the deprivation of liberty involve a basic right that ought not to be relinquished by the government?

Another concern with regard to privatization is whether the profit motive can debase corrections. For example, would private probation or parole agencies be under pressure to keep clients under supervision beyond an appropriate release time so as to keep caseloads and reimbursements high? Would private agencies try to pay their employees fair salaries or would profit pressures work to minimize salaries and benefits for officers? Would private agencies try to cut services for offenders (counseling, drug treatment) to a minimum?

In the nineteenth century, the profit motive did operate to cause significant problems in many state prison systems. In one juvenile system, for example, boys were leased out to private contractors for their labor. Hardworking boys would be kept under supervision longer than necessary because the contractor did not want to lose their productivity (Pisciotta, 1982).

A more recent example of the profit motive perhaps having a negative effect occurred in Texas in 1997. Guards in a Texas jail were videotaped apparently shooting offenders with stun guns, kicking offenders in the groin, allowing dogs to bite the offenders and making offenders crawl on their hands and knees. These guards were Texas jailers supervising Missouri offenders who had been sent to excess jail space in Texas because of overcrowding in Missouri—at a charge of $40 per day per offender to the state of Missouri (MSNBC, August 19, 1997). This situation is sort of an in-between area between public and private enterprise, in which one state offers a service to another state for a profit. Arguably, the profit motive influenced Texas officials to be lax in their training and/or supervision to the extent that this brutality occurred.

One response to such problems is spelling out a private agency's responsibilities to offenders in a carefully devised contract and then monitoring the implementation of the contract. If state inspectors enforce the contract conditions, then problems can be prevented or quickly resolved. If a private agency does not resolve any problems, they are in violation of the contract and the agency can be dropped. Opponents of privatization argue that there is a problem with this argument. If the state wants to end a contract, there may not be another service provider willing and able to step in and take over the contracted service. At the very least, it would take some time for another company to be ready to step in and provide the needed service.

Still another problem with privatization is that private agencies can be overly selective of the clients (offenders) they want to manage. Private agencies in corrections and in areas such as welfare (for example, training public assistance clients to become job-ready) have been criticized for picking the most capable clients (Rosin, 1997). The criticism is that these individuals may have been able to succeed on probation or in getting off of public assistance with little or no help. Statistics showing them to be success stories are thereby misleading. Private agencies have selected the individuals most likely to succeed and ignored the individuals most in need of intervention. The state was left to deal with the more difficult cases.

In summary, proponents of privatization argue that private agencies can provide needed services such as probation and parole supervision more effectively and efficiently than the government has done in the past. Opponents argue that government agencies can themselves become more effective and efficient. Opponents also contend that there can be serious problems with privatization. They question whether it is right to allow the state to give away the highly symbolic function of depriving citizens of their freedom and supervising the deprivation of liberty.

Supervision of Sex Offenders

In 1997, a California law took effect mandating that several classes of convicted sexual offenders be given injections of medroxyprogesterone acetate (Depo-Provera) as a condition of parole. Among others, the law targeted anyone who was convicted of molesting a child under age 13 (Turk, 1997). This law and similar measures, such as requiring a woman convicted of child abuse to be implanted with Norplant (a birth control device), raise several ethical issues.

A basic issue is whether it is permissible for the state to deprive an offender of the right to procreate. (The drug acts as a birth control device for women but not for men.) Another issue is whether it is ethical to force the drug on offenders whose molesting problem is not necessarily related to their hormones. For example, the behavior of some sex offenders may be related to an alcohol problem and the drug may actually have no effect. This is important, given the possible side effects of any drug. Even a drug that has no known side effects at present may be found to have harmful side effects at a point later in time.

Still another issue is that such draconian measures may be counterproductive. Kear-Colwell and Pollock (1997), for example, argue that confrontational therapy may be antitherapeutic as opposed to motivational therapy. Although confrontational strategies may impress the public with the appearance that the state is doing something to control sex offenders, such harsh measures may in fact be failing to address the underlying causes of sex offending and, thus, not serving the community.

Use of Volunteers

Several ethical issues arise in the use of volunteers in probation and parole. The basic ethical issue is whether it is responsible to use volunteers. If volunteers are sought merely to save a government agency from hiring needed probation or parole officers, some people (e.g., officers and their unions) would argue that this represents an unethical use of volunteers, and that offenders, officers and society are being shortchanged. According to this argument, offenders are not receiving the professional supervision and assistance they need; officers (actually would-be officers) are denied jobs because volunteers are being used instead of hiring additional officers; and, finally, society is not getting the effective supervision it wants.

On the other hand, if volunteers are being used for tasks that officers cannot and should not be doing, then there is a valid use for volunteers. An example of this type of volunteer activity is the establishment of a one-to-one relationship with the offender. Here the volunteer acts as a "big brother or sister" or friend in relation to the offender. Officers do not have the time to establish such personal relationships with offenders, nor would it be proper for officers to do so, given their authority over offenders. Because such one-to-one relationships are the most frequent volunteer assignments (Shields, Chapman & Wingard, 1983), it appears that many volunteers are being used properly.

The critical issue is whether volunteers are doing what additional officers would be doing or whether they are making unique contributions to the department. A complicating issue is the fiscal fact that many probation and parole departments must proceed with reduced funding. Los Angeles County Probation, for example, lost approximately one-third of its staff due to voter-approved cost-cutting. As a result, caseloads doubled. One part of the department's response to this crisis was to use more than 1,000 volunteers to provide a number of services (Nidorf, 1996). Ideally, a sufficient number of paid officers should be budgeted for every department in the country. Realistically, many government bodies are facing financial limitations and are not funding the number of officer positions that are needed. In such circumstances, volunteers may allow a department to provide services it otherwise could not provide.

CORRUPTION

Like police officers and prison guards, probation and parole officers can become involved in corruption. They can take money from clients improperly or they can sexually harass clients. It appears that such problems have not been as widespread in community corrections as in policing, but such problems do sometimes occur.

Sometimes the problem is easy to resolve. An officer in one agency was pocketing the fine and restitution money he was collecting from offenders. The agency discovered the problem and changed its collection system from having the individual officer collect such monies to having a cashier's office do so. Offenders would go to the cashier's office to make payments and get a written receipt. Officers and supervisors would receive a printout each week detailing payments and outstanding balances. The new system removed any possibility of individual officers pilfering payments.

Finding a solution to corruption, however, is not always so direct. Managers must be vigilant to detect corruption, yet they must also foster a sense of trust among their employees.

Summary

Although community corrections is not as dramatic as policing, this chapter has shown that ethical problems do arise. One of the principal ethical issues is the question of the purpose or mission of probation, parole and other types of community corrections. Many are calling for punitive approaches to the supervision of offenders. Others, such as those in the peacemaking school, remind us that religious strands in the American tradition teach us to respect the humanity of offenders even when it appears that such offenders have done horrible deeds and seem to no longer merit humane treatment. This very basic conflict of ideas is prominent in probation and parole—and it affects other issues such as privatization and corruption. As the new century unfolds, it will be important to watch how states and counties decide to answer such questions about the supervision of offenders in the community.

References

American Bar Association (1986). *Section of Criminal Justice, Report to the House of Delegates.* Chicago: American Bar Association.

Bazemore, G. & Maloney, D. (1994). "Rehabilitating Community Service: Toward Restorative Service Sanctions in a Balanced Justice System," *Federal Probation*, 58 (1): 24-35.

Bazemore, G. & Umbreit, M. (1995). "Rethinking the Sanctioning Function in Juvenile Court: Retributive or Restorative Responses to Youth Crime," *Crime and Delinquency*, 41: 296-316.

Beck, J.L., Klein-Saffran, J. & Wooten, H.B. (1990). "Home Confinement and the Use of Electronic Monitoring with Federal Parolees," *Federal Probation*, 54 (4): 22-31.

Byrne, J.M. (1990). "The Future of Intensive Probation Supervision and the New Intermediate Sanctions," *Crime and Delinquency*, 36: 6-41.

Clear, T.R. & Braga, A.A. (1995). "Community Corrections." In J.Q. Wilson & J. Petersilia (Eds.), *Crime* (pp. 421-444). San Francisco: Institute for Contemporary Studies.

Clear, T.R. & Hardyman, P.L. (1990). "The New Intensive Supervision Movement," *Crime and Delinquency*, 36: 42-60.

Corbett, R. & Marx, G.T. (1991). "No Soul in the New Machine: Technofallacies in the Electronic Monitoring Movement," *Justice Quarterly*, 8: 399-414.

Dietrich, S.G. (1979). "The Probation Officer as Therapist," *Federal Probation*, 43 (2): 14-19.

Feeley, M. & Simon, J. (1992). "The New Penology: Notes on the Emerging Strategy of Corrections and Its Implications," *Criminology*, 30: 449-474.

Geerken, M. & Hayes, H. (1993). "Probation and Parole: Public Risks and the Future of Incarceration Alternatives," *Criminology*, 31: 549-564.

General Accounting Office (1976). *State and County Probation Systems in Crisis*. Washington, DC: U.S. Government Printing Office.

Jones, M. (1996). "Voluntary Revocations and the "Elect-to-Serve" Option in North Carolina Probation," *Crime and Delinquency*, 42: 36-49.

Kear-Colwell, J. & Pollock, P. (1997). "Motivation or Confrontation: Which Approach to the Child Sex Offender?," *Criminal Justice & Behavior*, 24: 20-33.

Lilly, J.R., Cullen, F.T., & Ball, R.A. (1989). *Criminological Theory: Context and Consequences*. Newbury Park, CA: Sage.

McCleary, R. (1978). *Dangerous Men: The Sociology of Parole*. Beverly Hills, CA: Sage.

Morris, N. & Tonry, M. (1990). *Between Prison and Probation: Intermediate Punishments in a Rational Sentencing System*. New York: Oxford University.

MSNBC, August 1997.

Nidorf, B.J. (1996). "Surviving in a 'Lock Them Up' Era," *Federal Probation*, 60 (1): 4-10.

Petersilia, J. (1990). "Conditions that Permit Intensive Supervision Programs to Survive," *Crime and Delinquency*, 36: 126-145.

Petersilia, J. (1997). "Probation in the United States." In M. Tonry (Ed.), *Crime and Justice: A Review of Research* (Vol. 22) (pp. 149-200). Chicago: University of Chicago Press.

Petersilia, J., Turner, S., Kahan, J., & Peterson, J. (1985). *Granting Felons Probation: Public Risks and Alternatives*. Santa Monica, CA: RAND.

Petersilia, J., Peterson, J., & Turner, S. (1992). *Intensive Probation and Parole: Research Findings and Policy Implications*. Santa Monica, CA: RAND.

Petersilia, J. & Turner, S. (1993). "Intensive Probation and Parole." In M. Tonry (Ed.), *Crime and Justice: A Review of Research* (Vol. 17) (pp. 281-336). Chicago: University of Chicago Press.

Pisciotta, A.W. (1982). "Saving the Children: The Promise and Practice of *Parens Patriae*, 1838-98," *Crime and Delinquency*, 28: 410-425.

Rosecrance, J. (1986). "Probation Supervision: Mission Impossible," *Federal Probation*, 50, 1: 25-31.

Rosin, H. (1997). "About Face: The Appearance of Welfare Success," *New Republic*, 217 (August, 4): 16-19.

Shields, P.M., Chapman, C.W., & Wingard, D.R. (1983). "Using Volunteers in Adult Probation," *Federal Probation*, 46, 2: 57-64.

Studt, E. (1973). *Surveillance and Service in Parole: A Report of the Parole Action Study*. Washington, DC: National Institute of Corrections.

Tonry, M. (1990). "Stated and Latent Functions of ISP," *Crime and Delinquency*, 36: 174-191.

Turk, C. (1997). "Kinder Cut: A Limited Defense of Chemical Castration," *New Republic*, 217 (8: August 25, 1997): 12-13.

von Hirsch, A. (1990). "The Ethics of Community-Based Sanctions." *Crime and Delinquency* 36: 162-173.

Whitehead, J. T. (1989). *Burnout in Probation and Corrections*. New York: Praeger.

Whitehead, J.T. (1992). "Control and the Use of Technology in Community Supervision." In P.J. Benekos & A.V. Merlo (Eds.), *Corrections: Dilemmas and Directions*. Cincinnati, OH: Anderson.

Whitehead, J.T., Miller, L.S., & Myers, L.B. (1995). 'The Diversionary Effectiveness of Intensive Supervision and Community Corrections Programs." In J.O. Smykla & W.L. Selke (Eds.), *Intermediate Sanctions: Sentencing in the 1990s* (pp. 135-151). Cincinnati, OH: Anderson.

Williamson, H.E. (1990). *The Corrections Profession*. Newbury Park, CA: Sage.

Wilson, J.Q. (1983). *Thinking about Crime*. Revised edition. New York: Vintage Books.

NOTE

1. Much of the material in this section on acceptable penal content and the following section on intensive supervision issues is a revision of an earlier analysis of community corrections written for a chapter in a different book (Whitehead, 1992).

DISCUSSION QUESTIONS

1. What do you think is the mission of community corrections? Give reasons for your choice?

2. Discuss the privatization of correctional services. What are some of the arguments for and against privatization?

3. An ethical issue when considering the job of the probation/parole officer is what, if anything, society owes the offender. Can society embrace a neo-classical perspective, assume offenders are totally free and responsible, and simply ignore any consideration of assistance to offenders? Or does society have some obligation to help offenders to some degree? How does White-head feel about this issue? What is your opinion? Explain.

4. Considering Whitehead's discussion of whistle-blowing, what would you do if you knew that one officer was going home two hours early every day? What would it take to make you "blow the whistle," or do you feel it is not your responsibility? Explain.

5. How much involvement should victims have in judgments related to their offender (e.g., parole release)? How can their involvement lead to unequal treatment of offenders?

CHAPTER 17

Ethics and Prison: Selected Issues

John T. Whitehead

INTRODUCTION

Prisons are a source of fascination for us all. Although prisons are intended to repel us, they seem to be a source of mysterious interest. Moviemakers have capitalized on this interest with countless movies set in real or fictitious prisons, especially traditional "Big House" prisons such as Sing Sing or Walla Walla. Another testimony to the uncanny attractiveness of prisons is the conversion of Alcatraz, the former disciplinary prison of the federal prison system, to a museum where tourists can walk around and even be locked in a cell for a few minutes of imaginary incarceration.

This chapter will examine some of the ethical issues about prison. It will discuss prison composition, discrimination, prison conditions, treatment, victimization, elderly offenders, women in prison, and privatization. Guard corruption will not be considered because McCarthy discussed that issue in Chapter 15.

KEY CONCEPTS:

discrimination

elderly offenders

prison composition

prison conditions

privatization

treatment

victimization

WHO BELONGS IN PRISON?

A basic ethical question about prison is who belongs there? What kinds of offenders deserve to be sentenced to prison? A number of critics contend that many of the people sent to prison do not need to be there. According to these critics, these prisoners are neither violent nor career criminals, and most citizens do not really want such people incarcerated. Irwin and Austin (1997:58-59), for example, give 1992 prison admission statistics that show that only 27 percent of prison admittees that year were admitted to prison for a violent crime conviction. Like other prison critics (see, for example, Tonry, 1995), Irwin and Austin note with alarm the increased use of prison for drug crimes (1997:27-28).

Conservatives, on the other hand, applaud the growth in the prison population. DiIulio, for example, argues that average citizens want prisons to be used and that prison incapacitates and saves money: "'prison pays' for most prisoners: it costs society about twice as much to let a prisoner roam the streets in search of fresh victims as it does to keep him locked up for a year" (DiIulio, 1995: 41). DiIulio (1994) also argues that greater use of incarcerative sentences will reduce crime in our nation's crime-ridden neighborhoods.

A complete analysis of this issue is beyond the scope of this chapter,[1] but some consideration is necessary. First, critics of increased incarceration fail to mention several crucial points about prison/prisoner statistics. For example, critics often fail to note that approximately 15 percent of the offenders admitted to prison each year are admitted for burglary (Maguire & Pastore, 1996:567). Although prison critics conventionally label burglary as a "property" crime, many citizens regard this crime as a much more serious crime than other property crimes such as shoplifting. Burglary involves trespass into one's personal space (one's "castle" or home) and it also involves a very real potential for violence. Either the burglar or the victim may have a weapon at hand and resort to using it. A qualitative indicator of the seriousness with which some people regard burglary is the criminal law allowance of deadly force against burglary in at least one state (see, e.g., Alabama Code, 13A-3-23). Another connection of burglary to violent crime is that many burglars are looking for guns (Wright & Decker, 1994:144). Clearly, there is some probability that these guns will be fenced or otherwise transferred to other criminals directly engaged in violent crime. Second, many of the "nonviolent" offenders admitted to prison in any year were repeat offenders and/or offenders who had been under community supervision of some sort. In 1991, for example, 45.9 percent of all state prisoners were either probation or parole violators at the time of their admission to prison (Cohen, 1995). In 1992 parole violators represented 29 percent of prison admissions (Maguire & Pastore, 1996:567). Thus, it is misleading to argue that only 27 percent of new admissions to prison are violent when another 15 percent are burglars and another 29 percent are repeat offenders (parole violators).

Also, in giving *admission* statistics critics may overlook *composition* statistics. For example, in both 1992 and 1993 almost one-half (48%) of the prisoners in state prisons were in prison for a violent crime (Beck & Gillard, 1995). Another 11 percent were in prison for burglary. Thus, approximately six out of 10 prisoners were in prison for either burglary or a violent crime.

In addition, drug offenders may be more threatening than Irwin and Austin consider them to be. One investigation found that many crack users were involved in both crack dealing and other crime. Inciardi and his colleagues (1993) studied serious delinquents in Miami at the start of the crack epidemic in the mid-1980s. They found that more than one-half of the crack users in their sample were dealers and 18 percent were "dealers plus" (i.e., they also manufactured, smuggled or wholesaled the drug). More importantly, these dealers were far from innocent, recreational purveyors: "Degree of crack-market participation was also related to earlier and greater general crime involvement, *including violent crime* (emphasis in the original) (Inciardi, Horowitz & Pottieger, 1993:178). Further, a number of studies "have shown that lethal violence is used commonly by drug traffickers in the pursuit of their economic interests" (Brownstein, Spunt, Crimmins & Langley, 1995:475).

On the other hand, prison proponents also omit or fail to emphasize some important points about prison composition. For example, the contention that the average citizen wants criminals incarcerated (see, for example, DiIulio, 1995) is only partially correct. There is substantial agreement in the literature that the public is not as punitive as surmised but rather still wants rehabilitation and will opt for nonincarcerative sentences for many offenders. When asked in 1995 whether the government should "make a greater effort these days [to] rehabilitate criminals who commit violent crimes or punish and put away criminals who commit violent crimes," 26 percent of the respondents in one public opinion poll favored rehabilitation and another 12 percent favored *both* rehabilitation and punishment (Maguire & Pastore, 1996:177). When asked whether they thought violent criminals could "be rehabilitated given early intervention with the right program," 14 percent of the sample thought most could be rehabilitated and 45 percent thought that some could be rehabilitated (Maguire & Pastore, 1996:177). Research in California found that citizens did indeed initially express a preference for prison for 25 hypothetical cases varying from petty theft to rape. After being informed of costs and alternatives to incarceration, however, these same citizens wanted only 27 percent of the hypothetical offenders to be incarcerated (DiMascio, 1995). Recent research in Ohio showed that on a global measure of support 88 percent of the sample favored a "three strikes and you're out" law. On more specific measures, however, only 17 percent of the respondents favored life sentences; most favored sentences of five to 15 years in prison. Thus, it is safe to say that "underneath more punitive global attitudes, in specific situations the American public tends to be less punitive and to favor a more diversified response to crime than simply locking up offenders . . ." (Applegate et al., 1996:519).

Similarly, the matter of incapacitation is much more complex than many prison proponents portray. Spelman (1994) found that collective incapacitation is at best a "gamble" that "may pay off" (p. 289) and that the effect of selective incapacitation is at best—and under ideal conditions—only 4 to 8 percent (p. 289). This led Spelman to caution that "the crime problem can never be substantially reduced through incapacitation alone" (1994:312). Instead,

> [C]riminal justice policies that deter and rehabilitate individual offenders; broader-based policies aimed at ameliorating continuing social problems such as chronic poverty and unemployment, teenage pregnancy and child abuse, and the like; and entirely different approaches aimed at reducing the number of criminal opportunities rather than just the number of criminals, all deserve continued attention. (Spelman, 1994:312)

In summary, the debate about who should go to prison is often clouded by partisan positions that fail to consider some important pieces of information. Critics of prison tend to overemphasize the use of prison for nonviolent offenders. Proponents oversell the alleged benefits of prison and ignore polling research that indicates the public's willingness to use nonincarcerative options. Hopefully, a peacemaking approach mindful of as much clarity as possible will help to resolve the debate.

DISCRIMINATION IN SENTENCING

A more specific concern in the larger question of prison composition has been alleged discrimination in sentencing to prisons. In 1992, for example, 54 percent of all prison admissions were African-Americans (Maguire & Pastore, 1996). Further, African-Americans make up 12 percent of the general population but 31 percent of federal prisoners and 51 percent of state prisoners (Mumola & Beck, 1997; Walker, Spohn & DeLone, 1996).

The overrepresentation of African-Americans in prisons is nothing new. This group made up 30 percent of the prison population in 1940, more than 40 percent in 1980 (Walker, Spohn & DeLone 1996), 46 percent in 1985 and 49 percent in 1990 (Mumola & Beck, 1997). However, one aspect of the problem that *is* new is the increased number of African-Americans incarcerated for drug offenses (Mumola & Beck, 1997). Several observers argue that police "target minority communities—where drug dealing is more visible and where it is thus easier for the police to make arrests—and tend to give less attention to drug activities in other neighborhoods" (Walker, Spohn & DeLone, 1996:209).

A few cautions are in order. Drug offenders may be more threatening than some of the critics of the incarceration of drug offenders consider them to be. As noted in the previous section, use may also mean involvement in drug dealing, criminal activity and violence (including lethal violence) (Brownstein et al., 1995; Inciardi, Horowitz & Pottieger, 1993).

These observations are not meant to justify discriminatory policing and/or sentencing of African-American drug offenders. They are simply offered to show that there is some reason for society to be concerned about drug offending, no matter which racial or ethnic group is involved.

It would seem that the ethical course of action is to pursue a drug policy that treats all races the same. It would also seem that any drug policy should not discriminate or give the *appearance* of discrimination. At the very least, our nation's drug policy has failed on the latter account. A number of observers have judged the drug war to violate the appearance of impartial handling. Steps need to be taken to correct that appearance. If the famous O.J. Simpson murder trial said anything, it is that how the criminal justice system treats African-Americans is clearly under scrutiny and even the perception of bias can have harmful consequences. Continuing the recent drug policy runs the risk of alienating still further minority members who are already substantially alienated.

PRISON CONDITIONS: CODDLING OR TOUGHNESS?

Another fundamental ethical issue concerning prisons is the question of what kind of prison environment society should provide for prisoners. A number of voices are calling for tough, spartan-like prisons with no "frills" such as television, recreation facilities or athletic equipment. More traditional voices think that prison intrinsically involves a number of pains or deprivations and that we do not need to make it much tougher than it is. To these people, what looks like a frill may in fact be justified for one or more logical reasons.

Van den Haag (1975) is an example of a critic who argues for spartan prisons. He argues that prisoners should work many hours each day for the purpose of punishment and that such hard labor should be sufficient to tire them out. At night they would be so exhausted that they would just rest before bed. This type of prison would serve retributive, incapacitative and deterrent objectives. It would be tough punishment for crime, it would keep offenders off the streets and away from opportunities to commit crime, and it would serve to frighten potential offenders from committing crime because persons considering crime would not want to be sentenced to a hard-labor prison.

Bidinotto (1997) has criticized our nation's prisons for coddling prisoners. In an article originally published in *Reader's Digest*, he alleged that hard labor was out of fashion. In style, he said, were electronic exercise equipment, horseshoe pits, bocce, conjugal visits (even at such supposedly spartan prisons as Attica, New York) and opera appreciation classes.

More extreme critics argue for even tougher prisons. In addition to removing any frills or amenities from traditional prisons, these individuals contend that prison should be made as tough as possible. Possible changes would be very limited diets and the introduction of chain gangs. Chain gangs would add humiliation to prison labor. Prisoners would be chained to each other and forced to work outside prison walls so that the public could see them at work. In this scenario, scorn would return to the criminal justice system. (See the separate section below on chain gangs.)

More traditional voices note that prison already contains numerous painful features that are sufficient punishment for offenders. These inherent pains of prison are harsh enough to make prison punitive and also serve as a deterrent to potential offenders. Sykes (1958), for example, noted almost 50 years ago that prison involves a number of pains or deprivations. These are deprivation of freedom, autonomy, possessions, security and heterosexual contact. Deprivation of freedom or liberty is self-explanatory; inmates lose their freedom to come and go as they please. Deprivation of autonomy refers to the removal of choices; inmates are told what to do and when to do it by virtue of a schedule that governs every minute of the day. Unlike free citizens, inmates have no choices about when to get up in the morning, when to go to meals, what to eat, what to wear, when to watch television and when the lights go out. The prison dictates these decisions that all of us take for granted each day and treats the inmate like a child who is incapable of making autonomous decisions. Likewise with possessions, the administration allows only minimal possessions such as a picture or poster or two and no distinguishing clothing. In a society that exalts material possessions as signs of status, accomplishment and individuality, the prison restricts possessions to the minimum and thereby depersonalizes each inmate. Security is far from a given in prison. Inmate assaults are a real possibility, especially for the weak. Even the strong have to fear attacks from groups of inmates who can overpower any one individual (more on this below). Finally, deprivation of heterosexual contact is the norm in most prisons. Very few prisons allow conjugal visitation and a prisoner must be married to participate.

Guenther (1978) has noted some additional deprivations or pains. The subjective experience of time in prison can be very painful. For example, weekends are periods of "hard time" because the inmate does not have to go to a job that helps him pass the time during the week. Through the holiday season, inmates see holiday shows and advertisements that remind them that they are missing contact with loved ones at a special time of the year. Even letters from home can be painful because sometimes the letter writer expresses anger or hurt at the offender for the things the offender did to the writer. Children, for example, may express anger at their father for abandoning them and not being with them to do simple things like take them fishing. Visits can be occasions for other inmates to offer taunts. Other inmates may tease the inmate who receives a visit from his or her spouse, reminding the offender that the spouse is free and might be seeing other people behind the offender's back. Or a visit from a spouse may cause the inmate "to question how 'the government' can deny him sexual access to his spouse" (Guenther, 1978:602). At the very least, visitors have to be searched and they see the offender in prison clothing that reminds both the visitor and the offender that he or she is a lawbreaker who has been arrested and convicted.

Traditionalists argue that these inherent pains of prison are sufficient suffering. Additional torments such as removing exercise equipment or televisions and radios are unwarranted. Traditionalists also argue that amenities can serve to keep inmates occupied and thereby help prevent restlessness, attacks on other inmates, attacks on guards and, ultimately, prison riots.

Conrad (1982:313) frames the question aptly: "What do the undeserving deserve?" His answer is worthy of consideration. He argues that they deserve "safety, lawfulness, industriousness, and hope" (Conrad, 1982:328). Safety and lawfulness are self-explanatory; unfortunately, they are often lacking in our prisons. Inmates often fear that they will be victimized in some way while behind bars. By industriousness Conrad does not mean mere busywork but that "everyone puts in a full day of work at jobs that are worth doing and paid accordingly" (p. 328). Hope is the most important consideration: ". . . where everyone has some reason to hope for better things to come—or could have such a reason if he or she were willing to look for it—the prison will not only be safer, but it will also be a place in which its staff can take some pride" (Conrad, 1982:328).

Sometimes the debate over prison conditions can make it sound like prisoners are living in expensive luxury resorts in which every whim is satisfied, but "[i]f our prisons are such resorts, simply open the gates and see how many run out . . . and how many walk in" (Taylor, 1997:92).[2]

TREATMENT/REHABILITATION/PROGRAMMING

Related to the issue of the appropriate conditions for prisoners is the issue of whether treatment opportunities should be provided for prisoners. Although rehabilitation was once routinely provided, many voices question providing anything other than punishment to inmates.

There is no question that most prisoners are in need of various types of assistance. Many prisoners are high-school dropouts, do not have employable skills, had drug and/or alcohol problems prior to entering prison, and may suffer from psychological difficulties such as lack of self-esteem.

An argument for providing services to offenders is that such services may help reduce recidivism when the inmate is released. Employment, for example, has been shown to be a clear correlate of success on parole (Pritchard, 1979). Similarly, recent studies of intensive supervision have demonstrated that offenders who received treatment for various problems recidivated less (were less likely to reoffend) than offenders who did not receive appropriate treatment (Petersilia & Turner, 1993). Such empirical evidence for the efficacy of treatment (see also, Gendreau, 1996) suggests that the ethically correct course of action is to provide treatment opportunities.

In spite of such effectiveness, some still argue that treatment is not appropriate for prisoners. One argument is the principle of least eligibility, which maintains that prisoners do not deserve anything better than the least eligible in our society. Since many people cannot afford college or vocational training or psychological counseling, a strict adherent of this principle might argue that prisoners should not benefit from any such treatments. To do so would give them something better than that had by a significant minority of the free population.

One response to this is that the deprived status of the neediest in American society is not sufficient justification for depriving inmates. The answer is to address both problems. Law-abiding citizens deserve the opportunity to attend college or learn a vocational trade. Prisoners too should have such opportunities, which will hopefully help prevent any return to crime. Years ago the Vienna correctional facility in Illinois attempted to solve the problem by opening up a number of prison programs to any interested citizens from the community. That way the area residents did not feel that the inmates were benefiting from programs that were not available to them (Silberman, 1978).

Another argument against services for inmates is that the prison environment is highly likely to sabotage such efforts. Drawing on the prison research of Sykes (1958), the mental hospital research of Goffman (1961), and other research, some argue that so much suspicion, distrust and animosity arise between inmates and prison staff that it is impossible to offer meaningful treatment options in the prison environment. In Goffman's terms, inmates are so involved in seeking secondary adjustments that mitigate the intended punishments of prison that they would not benefit from treatment programs. In Sykes's terms, inmates are so busy trying to soften the pains of prison by such strategies as making home-brewed alcoholic beverages, achieving status by boisterousness or physical prowess, or prowling for sexual conquests that any treatment efforts would fall on deaf ears. The counter argument is that prison officials have often failed to implement rehabilitation programs as needed. Instead, wardens and guards put custody concerns over treatment concerns in terms of both dollars and emphasis. Thus, prison staff get what they want: custody rather than rehabilitation.

An important reminder in any debate over providing treatment is that most offenders will be released back into society. If society makes no effort to educate or train offenders for gainful employment after release, the offenders will not have a legal means of support and may well resort to crime. Releasing offenders without any improvement of their condition seems highly unlikely to improve their chances for success.

CHAIN GANGS

Chain gangs were reintroduced in Alabama in 1995, but the move was followed by court challenges. Governor Fob James justified their use as a way to save money and to make incarceration tougher. He argued that a prison guard can supervise only 20 unchained men on a road crew but the number doubles to 40 prisoners if the men are shackled. Concerning toughness, he argued that some men were declining parole because they thought incarceration was easier (Morris, 1997). An argument can also be made that chain gangs are constitutional because the Thirteenth Amendment to the United States Constitution prohibits involuntary servitude "except as punishment for crime."

A major argument against chain gangs is that they are discriminatory or, at best, give the appearance of discrimination. Observers have noted that 70 to 90 percent of the Alabama chain gang prisoners were black (Corsentino, 1997). For African-Americans, chain gangs are a reminder of the Reconstruction Era in the South when racism was still rampant. After the Civil War, the South needed to rebuild railroads and roads and prison labor was leased out to contractors to engage in such direly needed projects. Many of the prisoners were blacks, as the South used its criminal justice systems as a way to get around the legal abolition of slavery. As in slavery, the offenders were classified as "full hands" or "half hands," tacit recognition that slavery had simply taken another form (McKelvey, 1997). A consitutional question is whether the use of chain gangs violates the cruel and unusual punishment prohibition of the Eighth Amendment.

Another argument against reintroducing chain gangs is von Hirsch's (1990) principle of acceptable penal content. What he means is that sanctions are only acceptable if the offender can endure them and still maintain his or her human dignity. Von Hirsch, who argues that punishments such as bumper stickers on the cars of drunk drivers proclaiming their DUI (driving under the influence of alcohol) status are too demeaning, would oppose chain gangs because they are intrinsically humiliating and do not allow the offender the necessary minimum of human dignity.

Finally, it is important to consider what emotions might be generated in offenders by the use of measures like chain gangs, especially after release. Do we want offenders living next to us who have been humiliated and scorned? Or do we want offenders who feel that prison was a painful but appropriate punishment for the wrongs they committed?

SAFETY/SECURITY IN PRISON

As noted, Sykes (1958) listed deprivation of security as one of the pains that prisoners suffer. There is some controversy about how much lack of security prisoners should undergo.

A number of studies have detailed the victimization that many prisoners have had to face. Lockwood (1980), for example, found that approximately 25 percent of the male inmates he studied had been a target of sexual assault. Nacci and Kane (1983) did a similar study of federal prisoners and found that 9 percent of them had been targets of sexual aggression in any prison and that 2 percent had been targeted in a federal institution. Marquart (1986), conducting participant observation research, personally witnessed 50 guard beatings of inmates. Wachtler (1997), former Chief Judge of the New York Court of Appeals, reported being stabbed in a federal facility. Therefore, it appears that although federal facilities are supposed to be relatively safe and secure, even a prominent white-collar criminal has a considerable risk of being attacked in prison.

More generally, Bowker (1980) provides a thorough (but now-dated) catalogue of the various types of victimization that prisoners suffer. Irwin and Austin have argued that prison produces harmful effects on offenders: "The disturbing truth is that growing numbers of prisoners are leaving our prisons socially crippled and profoundly alienated" (1997:82). They are also concerned that the increasing use of maximum-security confinement compounds the harmful effects of prison so that contemporary prison systems are "spewing out such damaged human material" (Irwin & Austin, 1997:106). Indeed, a survey of prisoners revealed disciplinary practices, including beatings, that were characterized as capricious and brutal (Hamm et al., 1994).

Several studies, however, have painted a less negative picture. A study of coping in New York prisons concluded that "most prisoners serve fairly trouble-free terms" and that their overall experience in prison is "no more overwhelming to them than other constraining situations they have encountered in their lives" (Toch & Adams, 1989:254). A longitudinal study of the incarceration experience in Canada led Zamble and Porporino to compare a prison sentence to a "deep freeze" after which the offenders are unchanged: "As they had done on the outside, most of the inmates in this study followed a path of least resistance, and they focused on the fine line of present time passing" (1988:150). A 1990 review of prison studies failed "to show any sort of profound detrimental effects" (Bonta & Gendreau, 1994:57).

In summary, a number of studies have shown that victimization is problematic in at least some prisons or for some prisoners in many prisons. Other studies have shown that a number of prisons are relatively secure and safe and that a considerable number of offenders come out unscathed. The ethical mandate is to make all prisons safe and lawful. Even the undeserving deserve this minimal guarantee (Conrad, 1982).

ELDERLY PRISONERS

With longer sentences, mandatory sentences and "three strikes and you're out" laws, state prison systems and the federal prison system can expect an increase in the number of elderly offenders. This increase raises some ethical issues.

A basic question concerns the release of elderly prisoners once they are no longer a danger to others. In other words, given some of the changes in sentencing in the last 10 years, it is reasonable to expect that prison officials will see increasing numbers of prisoners in their sixties, seventies or eighties. As prisoners become elderly in prison, it is clear that many of them will be little or no danger to society. A prisoner who has Alzheimer's disease or arthritis or heart disease is hardly at risk of engaging in burglary, armed robbery or murder. At some point, age reduces the risk of further criminal behavior to zero or close to zero.

If there is little incapacitative or rehabilitative value in keeping such prisoners locked up, should we release them? Or does the goal of retribution dictate that they stay in prison for as long as their original sentence dictated? If a prisoner gets to the point at which he does not even understand where he or she is (for example, due to a disease like Alzheimer's), does it make any retributive sense to keep him or her confined? Doesn't punishment require that the prisoner understand what is being done to him or her?

Conversely, society may want to release elderly offenders to save money. As prisoners age, it is logical to expect that their health care expenses will rise. They generally will need increasing medical care. Should society keep these offenders in prison so that they can receive the medical attention they need or should society release them to save money? Parenthetically, a system of national health care could eliminate this dilemma by removing any incentive to release them.

WOMEN IN PRISON

Women make up a small but significant proportion of the United States prison population. At year-end 1996 there were 63,900 female prisoners in state and federal institutions, constituting almost 6 percent of the total prison population (Mumola & Beck, 1997).

Although prison conditions are not as violent for women as for men, there are some problems that are unique to women's prisons. Since women constitute a much smaller proportion of any state's prison population, there are usually fewer prisons for women and also fewer opportunities for education and training. Part of this is related to stereotyped conceptions of the appropriate role for women in society. Traditional notions of appropriate roles have played a part in providing programs to train women to become cosmetologists or cooks instead of auto mechanics or television repair workers. Traditional notions of appropriate female behavior have also led to prison disciplinary practices that can be more dictatorial than those found in men's prisons. Beliefs that women should be "prim and proper" have influenced many officials to enforce rules against arguing and talking back to guards more stringently in women's prisons than in men's prisons. Thus, while women's prisons may look more pleasant than men's prisons, the appearance of a softer regime may in fact belie an institution that oppresses by intruding into more dimensions of behavior than occurs in the typical male prison.

Perhaps the fundamental ethical question is that suggested by Durham (1994): Would it be right to treat women exactly like men when such a shift in orientation might very well take away some of the benefits—such as single rooms rather than cells—that have benefited many women prisoners? Equal treatment would mean some positive changes, such as increased opportunities for vocational training, but would the overall results be beneficial for women or would equal treatment actually mean generally worse conditions for women?

PRIVATIZATION

Another ethical issue is whether states should privatize prisons or continue to keep them public.

As noted in Chapter 16 on ethical issues in probation and parole, proponents of privatization argue several benefits for turning over prisons to private corporations. One alleged benefit is budgetary savings. Proponents claim that private enterprise can do things more efficiently and less expensively than the government. Government operation is equated with waste and inefficiency. Some of this is attributed to the civil service system that guarantees job tenure except in extreme circumstances when jobs are abolished. Civil service workers are not under the same pressures as workers in private industry who must constantly show a profit. Competition forces private industry to be effective, efficient and accountable (Logan, 1990).

Opponents of privatization argue that government agencies *can* be efficient and effective. Government offices can adopt strategies that enhance efficiency and effectiveness just as can privately run agencies.

A number of states have turned over some of their prisons to private corporations. Several evaluations of private prisons, jails and juvenile facilities have been conducted. In most of these studies a private prison and a public prison from the same state are compared in terms of costs and inmate and/or staff satisfaction. One reviewer of a number of such studies concluded that they "seem to show a somewhat lower cost and higher quality of services in private facilities" (Shichor, 1995:231). The reviewer went on to note, however, that one particular private prison has been the subject of several of the studies and that some of the researchers finding such positive results were "active supporters" of privatization rather than neutral observers (Shichor, 1995:231). Shichor thus agrees with the conclusion of the General Accounting Office study that private prisons have not yet been proven superior.

Perhaps the main argument against privatization is whether it is appropriate for the government to turn over functions as basic as correctional supervision of offenders to private businesses. Many question whether the symbolic task of punishing offenders can be handed over to workers who wear uniforms that say "Acme Corrections Company" rather than the "State Department of Corrections" (American Bar Association, 1986). The most dramatic example of this would be for "Brand X Corrections" to carry out capital punishment. Should the state surrender the symbolism of the state executing an offender? Less dramatically, is it right for the state to allow private companies to impose deprivation of liberty and serious disciplinary measures such as solitary confinement? Or does incarceration involve a basic right that ought not to be relinquished by the government? Going further, is it right to bring the profit motive into this area? One answer is that it is wrong to do so; "it can be found morally troubling that corporations will try to make a profit on the punishment of people (which is a deliberate cause of suffering by representatives of society)" (Shichor, 1995:258).

Another concern regarding privatization is whether the profit motive can debase corrections. For example, would private prisons be under pressure to keep clients incarcerated beyond an appropriate release time so as to keep prison populations and reimbursements high? Would these companies begin to lobby for lengthier sentences and fewer release opportunities? Would private prisons try to pay guards fair salaries or would profit pressures work to minimize salaries and benefits for officers? Would private agencies try to cut services for inmates (counseling, drug treatment) to a minimum?

In the nineteenth century, the profit motive did operate to cause significant problems in many state prison systems. In one juvenile system, for example, boys were leased out to private contractors for their labor. Hard working boys would be kept under supervision longer than necessary because the contractor did not want to lose their productivity (Pisciotta, 1982).

A response to such problems is spelling out a private agency's responsibilities to offenders in a carefully devised contract and then monitoring the implementation of the contract. If state inspectors enforce the contract conditions, then problems can be prevented or quickly resolved. If a private agency does not resolve any problems, they are in violation of the contract and the agency can be dropped. Opponents of privatization argue that there is a problem with this argument. If the state wants to end a contract, there may not be another service provider willing and able to step in and take over the contracted service. At the very least, it would take some time for another company to be ready to step in and provide the needed service.

Still another problem with privatization is that private agencies can be overly selective of the clients (offenders) they want to manage. Private agencies in corrections and in areas such as welfare (for example, training public assistance clients to become job ready) have been criticized for picking the most capable clients (Rosin, 1997). The criticism is that these individuals may have been able to succeed on probation or in getting off of public assistance with little or no help. Statistics showing them to be success stories are thereby misleading. The private agency selected the individuals most likely to succeed and ignored the individuals most in need of intervention. The state is left to deal with these more difficult cases.

Proponents of privatization argue that contracting of services can make spending on correctional services more visible. When the government operates its own prisons they "have been ignored by the public and given . . . 'hands-off' treatment by the courts" (Logan, 1990:256). Since some criticize contracting, there would be a number of eyes scrutinizing the privately run prisons.

In summary, proponents of prison privatization argue that private agencies can provide needed services more effectively and more efficiently than the government has done in the past. Opponents argue that government agencies can become more effective and efficient. Opponents also contend that there can be serious problems with privatization and question whether it is right to allow the state to give away the highly symbolic function of depriving citizens of their freedom and supervising that deprivation of liberty.

SUMMARY

This chapter has examined a number of ethical issues pertaining to prisons. Probably the most basic question is Conrad's: What do the undeserving deserve? One's choice of answer to this question permeates most of the other issues raised in this chapter. At this moment in our nation's history, it appears that many answer that prisoners deserve little or nothing. Because they treated their victims with no compassion, they deserve no compassion in return.

The three theories that form the framework for this book, however, suggest that the current answer to Conrad's question may not be the ethical answer. Kant's categorical imperative urges us to treat others as subjects. Utilitarianism urges us to consider the consequences of our actions, including the consequences of treating inmates very harshly for years and then simply releasing them back onto the streets. The peacemaking perspective reminds us that we are all connected, including offender, victim and public, and that caring is a basic ethical principle. It seems that all three ethical theories suggest that while punishment is appropriate, we cannot lose sight of the humanity of offenders even when they have appeared to lose sight of their own humanity and the humanity of others.

The challenge for the next century is to try to punish offenders in ways that are fitting and to remain mindful of the need to treat offenders with dignity. The Quakers and others tried to do this 200 years ago. It is not an easy task.

NOTES

1. For a more thorough analysis of the issue of prison composition, see Irwin & Austin (1997) and Braswell & Whitehead (1997). This section of the chapter relies heavily on the latter source.

2. Ironically one conservative critic of soft prisons, former Governor Fife Symington of Arizona, who removed many frills from his state's prisons, recently pleaded guilty to fraud. He may be forced to experience firsthand the tougher prison environment that he orchestrated.

REFERENCES

Alabama Code, 13A-3-23.

American Bar Association (1986). *Section of Criminal Justice, Report to the House of Delegates.* Chicago, IL: American Bar Association.

Applegate, B.K., Cullen, F.T., Turner, M.G. & Sundt, J.L. (1996). "Assessing Public Support for Three-Strikes-and-You're Out Laws: Global versus Specific Attitudes," *Crime and Delinquency*, 42: 517-534.

Beck, A.J. & Gillard, D.K. (1995). *Prisoners in 1994.* Washington, DC: U.S. Department of Justice.

Bidinotto, R.J. (1997). "Prisons Should Not Coddle Inmates." In Cozic, C.P. (Ed.) *America's Prisons: Opposing Viewpoints* (pp. 85-92). San Diego, CA: Greenhaven Press.

Bonta, J. & Gendreau, P. (1994). "Reexaminning the Cruel and Unusual Punishment of Prison Life." In M.C. Braswell, R.H. Montgomery & L.X. Lombardo (Eds.), *Prison Violence in America,* 2nd ed. (pp. 39-68). Cincinnati, OH: Anderson Publishing Co..

Bowker, L.H. (1980). *Prison Victimization.* New York: Elsevier.

Braswell, M. & Whitehead, J. (1997). "The Middle Way: The Debate about Prisons." Paper presented at the 1997 Annual Meeting of the Southern Criminal Justice Association in Richmond, VA.

Brownstein, H.H., Spunt, B.J., Crimmins, S.M., & Langley, S.C. (1995). "Women Who Kill in Drug Market Situations," *Justice Quarterly*, 12: 473-498.

Cohen, R.L. (1995). *Probation and Parole Violators in State Prison, 1991.* Washington, DC: U.S. Department of Justice.

Conrad, J.P. (1982). "What Do the Undeserving Deserve?" In R. Johnson & H. Toch (Eds.), *The Pains of Imprisonment* (pp. 313-330). Beverly Hills, CA: Sage Publication.

Corsentino, M. (1997). "Inmate Chain Gangs are an Improper Form of Punishment." In Cozic, C.P. (Ed.), *America's Prisons: Opposing Viewpoints* (pp. 120-127). San Diego, CA: Greenhaven Press.

DiIulio, J.J., Jr. (1994). "The Question of Black Crime," *The Public Interest*, 117: 3-32.

DiIulio, J.J., Jr. (1995). "White Lies about Black Crime," *The Public Interest*, 118: 30-44.

DiMascio, W.M. (1995). *Seeking Justice: Crime and Punishment in America*. New York: Edna McConnell Clark Foundation.

Durham, A.M. (1994). *Crisis and Reform: Current Issues in American Punishment*. Boston: Little, Brown & Co.

Gendreau, P. (1996). "The Principles of Effective Intervention with Offenders." In A.T. Harland (Ed.), *Choosing Correctional Options that Work: Defining the Demand and Evaluating the Supply* (pp. 117-130). Thousand Oaks, CA: Sage Publications.

Goffman, E. (1961). *Asylums: Essays on the Social Situation of Mental Patients and Other Inmates*. Garden City, NY: Anchor Books.

Guenther, A. (1978). "The Impact of Confinement." In N. Johnston & L.D. Savitz (Eds.), *Justice and Corrections* (pp. 596-603). New York: John Wiley & Sons.

Hamm, M.S., Coupez, T., Hoze, F.E. & Weinstein, C. (1994). "The Myth of Humane Imprisonment: A Critical Analysis of Severe Discipline in U.S. Maximum Security Prisons, 1945-1990." In M.C. Braswell, R.H. Montgomery & L.X. Lombardo (Eds.), *Prison Violence in America*, 2nd ed. (pp. 167-200). Cincinnati, OH: Anderson Publishing Co.

Inciardi, J.A., Horowitz, R. & Pottieger, A.E. (1993). *Street Kids, Street Drugs, Street Crime: An Examination of Drug Use and Serious Delinquency in Miami*. Belmont, CA: Wadsworth Publishing Co.

Irwin, J. & Austin, J. (1997). *It's About Time: America's Imprisonment Binge*, 2nd ed. Belmont, CA: Wadsworth Publishing Company.

Lockwood, D. (1980). *Prison Sexual Violence*. New York: Elsevier.

Logan, C.H. (1990). *Private Prisons: Cons and Pros*. New York: Oxford.

Maguire, K. & Pastore, A.L. (Eds.) (1996). *Sourcebook of Criminal Justice Statistics 1995*. Washington, DC: U.S. Department of Justice.

Marquart, J.W. (1986). "Doing Research in Prison: The Strengths and Weaknesses of Full Participation as a Guard," *Justice Quarterly*, 3: 15-32.

McKelvey, B. (1997). "American Prisons: A Study in American Social History Prior to 1915." In J.W. Marquart & J.R. Sorenson (Eds.), *Correctional Contexts: Contemporary and Classical Readings* (pp. 84-94). Los Angeles, CA: Roxbury Publishing Co.

Morris, R.L. (1997). "Inmate Chain Gangs are a Proper Form of Punishment." In C.P. Cozic (Ed.), *America's Prisons: Opposing Viewpoints* (pp. 111-119). San Diego, CA: Greenhaven Press.

Mumola, C.J. & Beck, A.J. (1997). "Prisoners in 1996." *Bureau of Justice Statistics Bulletin*. Washington, DC: U.S. Department of Justice.

Nacci, P.L. & Kane, T.R. (1983). "The Incidence of Sex and Sexual Aggression in Federal Prisons," *Federal Probation*, 7, 4: 31-36.

Petersilia, J. & Turner, S. (1993). "Intensive Probation and Parole." In M. Tonry (Ed.), *Crime and Justice: A Review of Research* (vol. 17). Chicago: University of Chicago Press.

Pisciotta, A.W. (1982). "Saving the Children: The Promise and Practice of *Parens Patriae*, 1838-98," *Crime and Delinquency*, 28: 410-425.

Pritchard, D.A. (1979). "Stable Predictors of Recidivism: A Summary," *Criminology*, 17: 15-21.

Rosin, H. (1997). "About Face: The Appearance of Welfare Success," *New Republic*, 217 (August, 4): 16-19.

Shichor, D. (1995). *Punishment for Profit: Private Prisons/Public Concerns*. Thousand Oaks, CA: Sage Publications.

Silberman, C.E (1978). *Criminal Violence, Criminal Justice*. New York: Random House.

Spelman, W. (1994). *Criminal Incapacitation*. New York: Plenum Press.

Sykes, G.M. (1958). *The Society of Captives: A Study of a Maximum Security Prison*. Princeton, NJ: Princeton University Press.

Taylor, J.M. (1997). "Prisons Do Not Coddle Inmates." In C.P. Cozic (Ed.), *America's Prisons: Opposing Viewpoints* (pp. 85-92). San Diego, CA: Greenhaven Press.

Toch, H. & Adams, K., with Grant, J.D. (1989). *Coping: Maladaptation in Prisons*. New Brunswick, NJ: Transaction Publishers.

Tonry, M. (1995). *Malign Neglect—Race, Crime, and Punishment in America*. New York: Oxford.

van den Haag, E. (1975). *Punishing Criminals: Concerning a Very Old and Painful Question*. New York: Basic Books.

von Hirsch, A. (1990). "The Ethics of Community-Based Sanctions," *Crime and Delinquency*, 36: 162-173.

Wachtler, S. (1997). *After the Madness: A Judge's Own Prison Memoir*. New York: Random House.

Walker, S., Spohn, C. & DeLone, M. (1996). *The Color of Justice: Race, Ethnicity, and Crime in America*. Belmont, CA: Wadsworth Publishing Company.

Wright, R.T. & Decker, S. (1994). *Burglars on the Job*. Boston, MA: Northeastern University Press.

Zamble, E. & Porporino, F.J. (1988). *Coping, Behavior, and Adaptation in Prison Inmates*. New York: Springer-Verlag.

Zimring, F.E. & Hawkins, G. (1995). *Incapacitation: Penal Confinement and the Restraint of Crime*. New York: Oxford University Press.

DISCUSSION QUESTIONS

1. What do you think the "undeserving deserve"? Describe an ethical prison. What it would look like? How would prisoners live? What would be their daily regimen? If you were a state commissioner of corrections and could design your own prison system, what it would be like? Could you sell your ideal system to the governor and to the public?

2. Is there any place for chain gangs or other harsh measures in an ethical prison? Why or why not?

3. Is there a point at which elderly offenders should be released even if they have five, 10 or more years to serve on their sentences? Discuss.

4. Should women prisoners be treated exactly like male prisoners? Would equal treatment be advantageous for female prisoners? Discuss.

5. Is it desirable for a state to contract out its prison operations to a private correctional company? What are the ethical considerations in doing so?

SECTION V

Ethical Issues in Crime Control Policy and Research

How should we approach problems related to crime control? We are spending increasing sums of money in areas of law enforcement and corrections and we have continued to pass new legislation with an eye toward developing more effective crime control policies. Still, crime continues to increase. In addition, we have to contend with public perceptions regarding crime and the justice system's response that are largely shaped by the media. Newspaper headlines, television programs and films each try to attract readers or viewers. How much is fact and how much is fiction? Whether founded entirely on fact or not, our citizens' fear of crime is certainly real to them.

An increasing awareness of the scope and nature of corporate crime challenges the abilities and resources of our justice system on additional fronts. Our traditional approach to controlling crime seems more comfortable when addressing familiar criminal behavior in such areas as burglary, robbery, and assault. The "bad guys" are typically more clearly defined. This is not always the case with much of corporate crime. Problems involving consumer safety, pollution and other related issues often involve business executives who are considered upstanding members of their communities, and with the rapid development of the computer, such crimes are increasingly difficult to track down. In some ways it seems that our traditional approach to administering justice is simply not adequate to resolve the more sophisticated problems of much of the corporate world. Still, the demands of culture can encourage and stimulate us to develop new ways of thinking about crime and, as a result, more innovative responses to crime-related problems.

There are also a variety of ethical concerns surrounding criminal justice research. The scientific life provides no barrier to unethical conduct. The problem of employing unethical means to an otherwise desirable end is ever present in the research setting, where scientists are sometimes tempted to sacrifice the well-being of their subjects for the sake of scientific knowledge. Subjects can easily come to be viewed as the means to an end when the products of scientific research are equated with the utilitarian's "greater good."

In the name of scientific research, subjects may experience invasions of privacy, unknowing participation in simulated research experiments, and physical and emotional stress. In experimental research designs, which systematically withhold an intervention from one group while exposing another, research subjects may be denied participation in programs offering medical, educational or psychological treatment.

Although the nature of the research task poses many ethical dilemmas, additional problems involve the political context of the research. No one wants to hear bad news about a popular new law enforcement or correctional program, least of all the people who administer the program. Researchers can find themselves in very difficult circumstances when results indicate that the program is not achieving its goals. Is the correct response to redo the results until a more palatable outcome is achieved, or to report findings honestly? How is this decision affected when the people administering the program are the same ones paying the researcher's salary?

Researchers should police themselves, using standards of professional ethics and censure to provide appropriate guidance. It must be recognized, however, that there are significant pressures against the objective exercise of such standards. Competition for research funds is considerable—few universities or research centers are interested in forfeiting research funds on ethical grounds, and few scholars are interested in creating any more obstacles for their research efforts than necessary. It is therefore very important to establish a climate of high ethical standards in the graduate schools that produce researchers and in the organizations ultimately responsible for conducting research.

CHAPTER 18

Crime, Criminals and Crime Control Policy Myths

Robert M. Bohm

INTRODUCTION

Despite recognition that the reality of crime is socially constructed, the task of debunking myths about crime, criminals and crime control policy has received only limited attention (Quinney, 1970; 1979; 1979b; Pearce, 1976; Milakovich & Weis, 1977; Reiman, 1979; Simon, 1981; Pepinsky & Jesilow, 1984; Walker, 1985). Myths continue to be perpetuated.[1] Moreover, some of them have become part of an ideology that informs, and is informed by, public interests in the area of social control in general and of crime and crime control in particular.[2] This has resulted in at least two undesirable consequences for the vast majority of Americans. First is a myopic focus on short-term interests of dubious value and a near total obliviousness to long-range interests which promise greater relief from criminal victimization. Obliviousness to future interests makes exploitation easier.[3] A second undesirable consequence for most Americans is the contradictions that occur when actions are based on myth-laden ideology. Though not inevitable, contradictions, when they arise, sometimes adversely affect both short- and long-term interests. For many people, control policies based on myth-laden ideology result in an exacerbation of harm and suffering.

> **KEY CONCEPTS:**
> crime control myths
> crime myths
> criminal myths
> undesirable consequences

The focus of this essay, however, is not crime control ideology per se, but rather the myths that inform that ideology. Specifically, the purpose is threefold: first, to identify some of the myths that inform the currently dominant crime

Reprinted with permission of the Academy of Criminal Justice Sciences. Robert M. Bohm, "Crime, Criminals and Crime Control Policy Myths" (1986). *Justice Quarterly* Volume 3, Number 2 (June): 193-214.

control ideology in the United States; second, to examine some of the sources of and reasons for the perpetuation of the myths; and third, to consider some of the contradictions and consequences of beliefs and policies based on myths.

CRIME, CRIMINAL AND CRIME CONTROL POLICY MYTHS

Due to space limitations, the following discussion considers only some of the myths that inform the prevailing "politically conservative," "law and order" ideology in the United States. Most of the myths examined are not new—testimony to both their enduring quality and their ability to be adapted to different, often opposing purposes.

Crime Myths

The foundation of the entire crime mythology edifice is the definition of crime. The problem is a lack of clarity as to what the concept of crime refers. Historically, crime has been used to label an extraordinarily large and a seemingly unrelated number of actions and inactions. A legal definition of crime, moreover, does not solve the problem. The law is rather arbitrary about what kinds of phenomena are regarded as crime and has generally expanded and contracted depending on the interests of the dominant groups in the social struggle. All definitions of crime, legal or otherwise, include actions or inactions that arguably should be excluded and exclude actions or inactions that arguably should be included. This is inevitable, given the political nature of crime. Consequently, a critical issue is whether there is a socially unacceptable and generally unknown bias in including or excluding certain actions or inactions as crime. Considerable evidence indicates that there is (Pepinsky & Jesilow, 1984; Simon & Eitzen, 1982; Reiman & Headlee, 1981:43; Reiman, 1979; Quinney, 1979:62; Lieberman, 1974; Mintz & Cohen, 1971:25-26; American Friends Service Committee, 1971). For example, consider the crime of murder. According to the 1982 *Crime in the United States*, there were 21,012 murders and nonnegligent manslaughters. These murders represent only a fraction of those killed intentionally or negligently. Conservative estimates indicate that each year at least 10,000 lives are lost to unnecessary surgeries, 20,000 to errors in prescribing drugs, 20,000 to doctors spreading diseases in hospitals, 100,000 to industrial disease, 14,000 to industrial accidents, 200,000 to environmentally caused cancer, and an unknown number from lethal industrial products (Reiman, 1979; Simon & Eitzen, 1982; Pepinsky & Jesilow, 1984). Yet, few of the latter actions or inactions are defined legally as murder or manslaughter. One reason is the myth that "white-collar crime" is nonviolent.

Another problem with criminal definitions that contributes to myths is the presumption that all laws are enforced and/or enforced fairly. Just as there is a socially unacceptable and generally unknown bias in the definition of crime, there is a similar bias in the enforcement of law. One reason so few white-collar crimes are brought to light, for example, is the inadequate enforcement mechanism. A myth that effectively obscures this inadequacy is that regulatory agencies can prevent white-collar crime. While there is little doubt that there would be more white-collar crime if regulatory agencies did not exist, it is not at all clear how much white-collar crime is prevented by their existence. In any event, the myth can be sustained only by ignoring the history of efforts at federal regulation of corporate crime. Humphries and Greenberg (1981:236) argue that "regulatory agencies were the Progressive Era's solution to the problem of controlling business in a manner that did not delegitimize capitalism by tarnishing capitalists with the stigma of criminality." Similarly, Pearce (1976:88) maintains that the state intentionally created agencies responsive to the interests of big business (also see Pepinsky & Jesilow, 1984:66-79). Furthermore, while the prosecution of corporate crime has increased dramatically in recent years, it may well be, as Pearce (1976:90) suggests, merely a symbolic effort to vindicate the myth that the state is neutral and to reinforce the myth that the law is applied uniformly to all persons. In the wake of lost legitimacy following Watergate and other scandals of the 1970s, an increase in the prosecution of elite criminality is not surprising. In any event, two problems lie at the heart of the myth of crime: the definitional problem and the enforcement problem.

Another myth is that crime in the United States is primarily violent. This myth is derived partly from the Uniform Crime Reports. These reports give the impression that the crime problem in the United States consists primarily of the eight "index offenses": murder and nonnegligent manslaughter, forcible rape, robbery, aggravated assault, burglary, larceny-theft, motor vehicle theft, and, beginning in 1979, arson. Three or possibly four of the eight "index crimes" are clearly "violent" (murder and nonnegligent manslaughter, forcible rape, aggravated assault and, possibly, robbery). Yet, according to recent Uniform Crime Reports, only about 10 percent of all the crime known to the police is violent. In addition, if the new arson category is excluded, no more than ten percent of all persons arrested are charged with *any* of the index crimes (Milakovich & Weis, 1977:339). It is hard to justify the crime problem, as conceptualized in the Uniform Crime Reports, as a problem of violence.

Another common myth is that crime is increasing. This myth is also sustained primarily by the data reported in the Uniform Crime Reports. However, if data in the Uniform Crime Reports are compared with the findings of the Census Bureau's National Crime Surveys from 1973 to 1980, one finds a major discrepancy. The Uniform Crime Reports show a substantial increase in the crime rate during the period, while the Census Bureau statistics indicate no increase in the proportion of victims reporting the same crimes. In some cases, the Census Bureau reports slight decreases (Paez & Dodge, 1982). Indeed, a careful examination of the historical record provides no basis for the belief that street crime, the type of crime most people fear, is rising: "People today are in no greater danger of being robbed or physically hurt than 150 years ago" (Pepinsky & Jesilow, 1984:22; also Ferdinand, 1977:353).

A final myth is that crime is an inevitable concomitant of complex, populous and industrialized societies. This myth has been advanced by Shelley in *Crime and Modernization: The Impact of Industrialization and Urbanization* (1981). Besides the serious problems with comparing crime statistics cross-culturally (cf. Sutherland & Cressey, 1974:25), there are at least four other problems with Shelley's proposition. First, it fails to account for the great variation in crime rates of different complex, populous and industrialized societies. For example, the crime rates of Japan and West Germany are much lower than those of the United States (Reiman, 1979:20; Martin & Conger, 1980; also see Clinard, 1978; Stack, 1984, especially Appendix 1). Second, the proposition fails to account for the great variation in crime rates within modern, complex, populous, and urbanized nations. For example, according to the 1984 Uniform Crime Report, the homicide rate in the United States varied from a low of one in New Hampshire to a high of 13.1 in Texas (per 100,000 persons). Similar variation is found for other crimes (cf. Lyerly & Skipper, 1981). Third, the proposition fails to account for the lack of correlation between a city's crime rate and its population and population density. According to the 1984 Uniform Crime Report, for example, the city with the highest homicide rate was Gary, Indiana. The three most populated cities in the United States—New York, Los Angeles, and Chicago—are not found among the top ten cities with the highest homicide rate (also see Reiman, 1979:21-23, especially Table 1). A fourth problem with the proposition is that the claim of inevitability in the social sciences is always tenuous and suspect.

Criminal Myths

Several myths inform popular conceptions of criminals. For example, one myth holds that some groups are more law abiding than others (Pepinsky & Jesilow, 1984:47). Evidence indicates however, that over 90 percent of all Americans have committed some crime for which they could be incarcerated (Silver, 1968; Wallerstein & Wyle, 1947). The observation does not deny that crime may be more concentrated in some groups, but only that it is unlikely to be absent in others. The myth seems credible because the crimes of some (e.g., physicians or corporate executives) are not easily detected, or there is not as much effort exerted detecting them. These two problems sustain another myth: that most crime is committed by poor, young males between the ages of 15 and 24 (Pepinsky & Jesilow, 1984; Reiman, 1979). As noted, if law enforcement were able or willing to detect all crimes, it would be more evenly distributed among rich and poor and all age groups, though it may remain more highly concentrated in some groups. With regard to age discrimination, an additional problem with the myth is that "the crime rate is growing much faster than either the absolute number of young people or their percentage of the population" (Reiman, 1979:24).

Crime Control Policy Myths

Myths about crime and criminals often form the basis of crime control policy. Historically, the use of myth in effecting crime legislation is perhaps the most transparent in the "educational campaign" mounted by the Federal Bureau of Narcotics to outlaw the consumption of marijuana (Grinspoon, 1977; Becker, 1973; Smith, 1970). Under the leadership of Commissioner H.J. Anslinger, the myth of the eleventh-century Persian Assassins was employed in the 1930s to substantiate a link between marijuana, violence, and crime. To obtain stiffer penalties in the 1950s, the attack on marijuana by Anslinger and the Federal Bureau of Narcotics shifted to the myth that marijuana use led to heroin use. Although there is speculation on the motives behind the campaign (cf. Helmer, 1975; Becker, 1973; Musto, 1973), suffice it to say that it was successful in achieving its ends. A result has been that somewhere between twelve and thirty-four million otherwise generally law-abiding citizens have been made criminals.

A number of myths inform public conceptions of law enforcement and law enforcement policy. One of the more pervasive myths is that the police are primarily crime-fighters. Nothing could be further from the truth. Only a small fraction of police time (perhaps less than 10%) is devoted to crime fighting. The vast majority of police time entails public service and traffic activities (Pepinsky, 1980:107; Manning, 1978; 1977:16; Bittner, 1975:42; 1967:700; Wilson, 1975:81; 1968:6; Garmire et al., 1972:25; Reiss, 1971:100).

Related to the myth of police as crime-fighters is one that holds that the police solve crimes. Evidence suggests otherwise (see sources cited in the paragraph above). According to recent editions of the Uniform Crime Report, the official overall clearance rate of the police in the United States is around 25 percent. The true rate, however, is probably closer to 13 percent (Walker, 1985:26).

A final myth of crime control policy to be considered is that eliminating injustices from the criminal justice system will reduce the level of serious crime. Eliminating injustices from the criminal justice system is certainly a worthwhile pursuit. However, it is unlikely to have an appreciable effect on serious crime. The causes of most crime are to be found in general social arrangements and not in the operation of the criminal justice system (Walker, 1985:206; Bohm, 1982).

The preceding list of myths is by no means exhaustive and is only intended as an indication of some of the myths that inform the now dominant "politically conservative," "law and order" ideology in the United States. Based largely on this ideology, crime prevention and enforcement resources have been expended recently on some of the following priorities: mandatory sentencing, habitual-criminal statutes, increased numbers of police officers, more effective police officers, changes in Miranda warnings, preventive detention, changes in plea bargaining, changes in the exclusionary rule, changes in the insanity defense, career criminal programs, prison industries and capital punishment. While each of these policies is intended to accomplish one or more bureaucratic goals (e.g., crime reduction, cost-effectiveness, or greater efficiency), none is likely to have a significant effect on the harm and suffering experienced by the vast majority of the American public. They do not adequately address the fundamental social structural elements of the crime problem (cf. Pepinsky & Jesilow, 1984; Walker, 1985; Bohm, 1982). The task now is to examine some of the sources of and reasons for the perpetuation of myths that do not contribute to pervasive harm and suffering.

SOURCES OF AND REASONS FOR THE MYTHS: CONTRADICTIONS AND CONSEQUENCES

Myths about crime, criminals and crime control policy are perpetuated because they serve a variety of interests. Among the interests served are those of the general public, the media, politicians, academic criminologists, criminal justice officials and social elites. One of the problems with previous discussions of crime-related mythology is the emphasis on the way elite interests are served (cf. Reiman, 1979; Quinney, 1979; 1979b). This emphasis is probably derived from the seminal observations of Marx and Engels, who wrote that "the ideas of the ruling class are in every epoch the ruling ideas . . ." (1970:64). They noted that in order for the ruling class to carry out its ideas, it is necessary for the ruling class "to represent its interest as the common interest of all the members of society, that is, expressed in ideal form: it has to give its ideas the form of universality and represent them as the only rational, universally valid ones" (Marx & Engels, 1970:65-6). This, of course, includes ideas about crime.

A problem with Marx's and Engels' observations is that they failed to distinguish between short- and long-term interests. While in the long-run elite interests are served by myths about crime, criminals and crime control policy, and the general public is duped into believing that their long-run interests are also served, it is unlikely that the myths could find such universal appeal if they did not also serve real short-term interests of the general public. It is maintained here that myths about crime, criminals and crime control policy are perpetuated because they actually do serve the general short-term interest, as well as long-term elite interests.

This section examines some of the ways that myths serve both general and elite interests. It also considers some of the contradictions and consequences of beliefs and policies based on myths. While there is obvious overlap in groups served by myths (e.g., members of the media, politicians, academic criminologists, criminal justice officials and elites are also part of the general public), the ways that each group contributes to and is served by myths are a little different. For this reason, each group is considered separately.

THE GENERAL PUBLIC

The general public contributes to their own myth-laden conception of crime in at least four ways. The first is by overgeneralizing from personal experience. If people have been crime victims, they may consider their own experience typical or representative of crime in general. A problem is that it is unlikely that there is such a thing as "typical" crime, and the crime most people know and experience is not representative of crime in general. A second way the public contributes to myths is by relying on inaccurate communication. Some people embellish crime experiences and thus distort their own conceptions or the conception of those to whom they communicate. A third way the public contributes to myths is by relying on atypical information. For those who are not aware that they have experienced crime, part of their conceptions of crime may come from atypical and unrepresentative experiences, embellished or otherwise, of family or friends, who may or may not have been victims themselves. Finally, the public contributes to myths through a lack of consciousness. There are many cases where the general public has no knowledge of victimization. For example, in cases of consumer fraud or medical negligence, people may never know that a crime has been perpetrated against them. In such cases, it would be difficult to conceptualize such actions as criminal.

The public perpetuates myths about crime, criminals and crime control policy because they serve at least three short-term interests: (1) they offer identities, (2) they aid comprehension by creating order, and (3) they help forge common bonds and create and reinforce a sense of community. Implicit in each of these interests, however, are important contradictions. Myths about "criminals" and "law-abiding citizens" offer identities. For many people, it is comforting to conceive of themselves as law-abiding citizens. Given the daily temptations to violate the law, those who do not, even in the face of great material deprivation, demonstrate a moral courage and a self-control that often forms the basis of their self-identities. Additionally, abiding by the law is considered by many an aspect of patriotism. This does not mean that law-violators necessarily consider themselves unpatriotic, but only that to be law-abiding and patriotic is an important part of many people's identities. This facet of patriotism is an emotion that politicians find it advantageous to exploit. For these reasons, many people find it in their interests to believe in and perpetuate the myth of the criminal and law-abiding citizen.

In reality, however, many self-conceived law-abiding citizens are engaging in self-delusion. No doubt there are a few paragons of virtue, but not many. Most people manifest common human frailties. For example, evidence suggests that over 90 percent of all Americans have committed some crime for which they could be incarcerated (Silver, 1968; Wallerstein & Wyle, 1947). This is not to imply that most Americans are murderers or robbers, for they are not. Criminality is a relative (and political) phenomenon. In his discussion of delinquency, Matza (1964) captures this relativity when he writes that juveniles drift between law-abiding and law-violating behavior. Whether a juvenile actually engages in a delinquent act depends on a host of factors, not the least of which is available opportunity. There are few delinquents or criminals whose entire life orientation is centered around delinquent or criminal activities. Consequently, it makes little sense to label an individual a "delinquent" or a "criminal" who occasionally gets into a fight, steals from a store, exceeds the speed limit, or cheats on income taxes. While these are "criminal" acts, the people who perpetrate them are not "criminals."

A contradiction is that the criminal role offers a different kind of identity to another segment of the population. For some, the criminal label is actively sought. The literature on juvenile delinquency is replete with examples of juveniles whose identity is based on their "rep" (reputation) for toughness, sexual prowess, institutional experience, etc. Many of those who assassinate or attempt to assassinate famous people are likely seeking a public identity that could not be achieved legitimately. This applies as well to many "notorious" criminals. A problem with labeling theory, in this regard, is an overemphasis on the negative consequences of the label or stigma—that individuals actively seek to avoid it. In many cases, as noted above, individuals actively seek the label as a goal. Myths do offer identities, criminal or otherwise, real or imagined; and people find it in their interest to believe in and perpetuate the myth of the criminal and law-abiding citizen.

Another way in which myths about crime and criminals contribute to identity is through the reinforcement and perpetuation of the myth of the individual. The concept of "individual," as used here, does not deny "individualism" but only refers in a limited sense to the idea of the "free-willed" being who acts on society without being acted on by society. Although the myth of the individual has informed philosophical and criminological thought at least since the Enlightenment, it became a part of popular consciousness and identity through existentialism and the human potential and other movements of the 1960s. It began influencing crime control policy again significantly by the mid-1970s.

However, as Foucault (1977:194) explains, "The individual is no doubt the fictitious atom of the 'ideological' representation of society. . . ." The idea of the individual, as used here and portrayed in existentialism, for example, is an illusion precisely because human beings are necessarily social. Not only are human beings social by virtue of the social nature of self-identity and of relations with others, but also because of the social component (e.g., language) in the ability of human beings to conceive of anything at all (Ollman, 1976; Mead, 1972).

The idea of the "free-willed individual" finds characteristic expression in the current politically conservative interpretation of the "criminal" and his or her behavior. In this view, the criminal is considered an isolated being whose social environment is generally inconsequential or, at least, legally irrelevant to his or her criminal actions. Kennedy (1976:39) maintains that the notion of the criminal as individual was the product of an historical transformation from "the ethic of shared responsibility for individual conduct (the cooperative ethic) to the ethic of individual responsibility." He adds that this transformation "was fundamental to the birth of crime and penal sanction" and "to political, economic, religious, and familistic transformation generally. . . ." Thus, states Kennedy (1976:38), "individualism as an attitude of self is basic to guilt, and as a premise of both civil and criminal law it is elemental to the whole legal practice of incrimination." A consequence is that the belief that the individual alone is responsible for his or her conduct diverts attention away from the structural elements in society that inevitably contribute to criminal behavior. (This last point will be discussed further in another context later.)

Another reason that myths find popular support is that they aid comprehension by creating order. Myths aid comprehension in two ways. They reduce contradictions and simplify complex phenomena.

As previously noted, myths about crime and criminals create a simple dichotomy that separates the "good guys" from the "bad guys." Quinney (1977:14) maintains that the myth of crime "provides the metaphor for our human nature; crime represents human nature in its 'less attractive form.'" Consequently, for many people, the "criminal" is conceived as abnormal, irrational, evil or untrustworthy, while the "law-abiding citizen" is normal, rational, good and trustworthy. While dichotomies such as these can be useful heuristic devices, they necessarily abstract and distort reality.

Myths also aid comprehension by reducing contradictions, which is especially important when it comes to public conceptions about crime and crime control. One of the major contradictions that confronts American society is that one of the wealthiest and technologically advanced countries in the world contains widespread poverty, unemployment and crime. Historically, a myth that has been perpetrated to resolve this contradiction is that crime is an individual problem, the result of personal defect—especially of poor, young males between the ages of 15 and 24. Conceived of in this way, it follows that there is no social or structural solution to the problem of crime.

Another contradiction that perplexes many Americans is that at a time when more effort was expended and more money spent on crime control, the worse the problem got. Myths help people cope with the knowledge that crime control efforts have not lived up to expectations. For example, during the heyday of LEAA, when billions of dollars were presumably spent on crime control, crime became, in the minds of many, epidemic. However, when LEAA was disbanded and the monies expended on crime control were greatly reduced, the crime problem, according to official statistics, decreased. No doubt other factors were operating, but the impression given to many people must have been that the more we do, the worse we fail, which for many is a very disconcerting observation. It is likely that the current punitive attitude of a large segment of the public and the call for a result to the punishment model in crime control can be attributed at least in part to the simple solution that the punishment model offers to a seemingly intractable problem. A result is that the United States currently holds the distinction of incarcerating more of its citizens than any other country in the world with the exception of the Soviet Union and South Africa, and it is among one of the last countries outside of Africa and Asia to impose the death penalty.

Finally, crime myths contribute to public fear which helps forge common bonds and creates and reinforces a sense of community. Fear of crime makes people feel that they share the same boat. Crime crosses social barriers. In reality, however, the chance of actual victimization from the crimes most people fear is very unevenly divided among social groupings. Nevertheless, that matters little, since it is the abstract fear that helps unite people. Fear of crime also creates and reinforces a sense of community. Recent enthusiasm over neighborhood watch programs and the recent increase in vigilantism are two examples of the way that fear of crime brings people together.

A contradiction is that fear of crime also inhibits community. Because of fear, people are afraid to leave their homes and are suspicious of strangers. It is fear of crime, moreover, that politicians play upon in their "law and order" campaigns. Weighted together, it is likely that factors that inhibit community are more influential than those that create community.

In sum, the public perpetuates myths about crime, criminals or crime control policy because they serve at least three short-term interests:

1) they offer identities;

2) they aid comprehension by creating order; and

3) they help forge common bonds and create and reinforce a sense of community.

THE MEDIA

Perhaps the most important source of common conceptions and myths of crime, criminals and crime control policy is the media. As Vold observed, "crime waves are now and probably always have been products of newspaper headlines" (1935:803; also see Fishman, 1978). One thing is certain: the media presents a distorted crime picture to the public. According to one study, the factors that influence crime news selection are the seriousness of the offense, whimsical or unusual elements, sentimental or dramatic aspects and the involvement of famous or high-status persons (Roshier, 1973:34-35; also see Graber, 1980; Sheley & Ashkins, 1981).

The entertainment media has a particularly distorting effect on public conceptions of crime, criminals and crime control policies. Crime-related television programs have been estimated to account for about one-third of all television entertainment shows (Dominick, 1978). Information that the public receives from these shows is anything but accurate. Studies have indicated that

1) the least committed crimes, such as murder and assault, appear more frequently than those crimes committed more often, such as burglary and larceny;

2) violent crimes are portrayed as caused by greed or attempts to avoid detection rather than by passion accompanying arguments as is more typical;

3) the necessary use of violence in police work is exaggerated;

4) the use of illegal police tactics is seemingly sanctioned;

5) police officers are unfettered by procedural law; and

6) the police nearly always capture the "bad guys," usually in violent confrontations (Dominick, 1973; Pandiani, 1978; Gitlin, 1979).

Perhaps the principal reason why the entertainment media perpetuates such myths is that they attract a large viewing audience which, in turn, sells advertising. Whether more accurate presentations would be less appealing, however, is an empirical question yet to be answered. In any event, whether intentional or not, crime myths perpetuated by the media often do serve elite interests by, among other things, portraying crime in a particular manner. (Other ways in which crime myths serve elite interests are examined in a later section.) The fact that most of the mass media in the United States are either owned by large corporations or are dependent on corporate advertising has been taken as evidence of a conspiracy among the elite to control public consciousness (Miliband, 1969; Halberstam, 1979; Dreier, 1982; Evans and Lundman, 1983). While such a view has a certain intuitive appeal and some empirical evidence to support it, the fact remains that the mass media, particularly of late, has been at the vanguard at exposing elite malfeasance. Whether the effort is sincere or merely an attempt to legitimate the media as an institution that serves the interests of the general public, as was the case with the federal regulation of corporate crime, is not clear. Intentions aside, there is no question that the mass media perpetuates a false conception of crime to the general public.

Another, though subtle, way the media affects common conceptions about crime, criminals and crime control policy is through public opinion polls. Erskine (1974) argues that the public's conception of crime may be the result of categories selected by pollsters. Erskine reports that 1965 was the first year (since 1935 when Gallup polled his first respondent) that crime appeared as a response to the question: "What do you think is the most important problem facing this country today?" The crime response, however, did not appear alone as a single category but was grouped in a category that included "immorality, crime and juvenile delinquency." Crime did not appear again as a response when the same question was asked until 1968 when it was grouped in a category of "crime and lawlessness, including riots, looting, and juvenile delinquency." The importance of the category in which crime is grouped in generating a response is underscored by Erskine who notes, "When categories such as unrest, polarization, student protest, moral decay, drugs, and youth problems began to be itemized separately, crime 'per se' began to rank relatively lower than it had previously" (1974:131). Furthermore, in response to the Harris Survey question—"In the past year, do you feel the crime rate in your neighborhood has been increasing, decreasing, or has it remained about the same as it was before?"—the conception of crime appears to be tied to a variety of events such as racial violence, assassination, war protest and campus unrest, as well as criminal activity (Erskine, 1974:131-2). In short, it is conceivable that people who were polled in both Gallup and Harris Surveys were responding either to non-criminal problems (e.g., unrest, polarization, student protest, moral decay, etc.) arbitrarily grouped together in a category that also included crime or to dramatic social events that artificially raised people's conceptions of the crime rate.

POLITICIANS

A third source of crime-related myths is politicians. As members of the public, politicians derive much of their knowledge in the same way as does the rest of the public. However, unlike much of the public, politicians also get knowledge about crime, criminals and crime control policy from academic criminologists and especially criminal justice officials. Since "law and order" rhetoric is often politically advantageous (for reasons already discussed), many politicians find it difficult not to disseminate popular myths.

ACADEMIC CRIMINOLOGISTS AND CRIMINAL JUSTICE OFFICIALS

A fourth source of crime-related myths is academic criminologists and criminal justice officials. Like politicians, they are members of the public and thus derive part of their conception of these subjects from their own experiences. However, if blame is to be leveled at any one group for perpetuating myths, then it should fall here, because academic criminologists and criminal justice officials should and often do know better. They are in the best position to dispel the myths. There are several reasons why they do not.

Many academic criminologists find it in both their short- and long-term interests to perpetuate myths. These interests, moreover, may be either cognitive or structural. Regarding the former, many academic criminologists, like other members of the general public, have internalized the myths as part of their social "reality." To challenge the myths would be, for many, to undermine long-established and fundamental conceptions of society. For many academic criminologists, what has been considered here as myth simply makes sense or attunes with preconceived ideas. To question the myths might create cognitive dissonance.

Other academic criminologists perpetuate myths because it is in their structural interests to do so. Platt (1975:106-7) suggests that this is because of academic repression and cooptation. My impression is that prestigious university appointments and promotions in general typically go to those academics whose work does not fundamentally challenge myths supportive of the status quo. It appears that prestigious journals rarely publish articles that radically deviate from an accepted, often myth-laden perspective (though this may reflect considerations other than ideology). Similarly, major research grants generally seem to be awarded to academics whose proposals do not fundamentally undermine privileged positions or deviate from preconceived, often myth-laden wisdom. Whether or not myths are perpetuated because of academic repression and cooptation, academic life is generally more pleasant for those who do not make waves.

Criminal justice officials perpetuate myths for at least four reasons. First, employment and advancement often depend on a responsiveness to the interests of political and economic elites. Administrators, in particular, are generally either elected to their positions or appointed to them by political electees. Since political election or appointment often depends on the support of political and economic elites, those who would dispel myths that serve interests of political and economic elites are not likely to find support forthcoming.

Second, in case of the police, the myth of increasing crime is used to justify larger budgets for more police officers and higher pay (Pepinsky & Jesilow, 1984:16-17 and 30). Third, as was the case with the general public, myths also provide order to the potentially chaotic role of the police officer. They allow police officers to believe that they can do the job (i.e., prevent or control crime). Finally, as was also the case with the general public, myths provide police officers with a basis of solidarity, common purpose and collective unity in the face of a hostile and potentially threatening environment.

SOCIAL ELITES

As part of the general public, social elites contribute to the perpetuation of myths in much the same way as do other members of the general public. It is doubtful, moreover, that political and economic elites conspire to perpetuate myths primarily because it is unnecessary for them to do so. Because myths serve at least the short-term interests of virtually all members of society, myths of crime, criminals and crime control policy probably would be perpetuated whether they served the interests of social elites or not. Nevertheless, social elites receive more significant and long-lasting advantages from the myths than any other social grouping. Social elites are also affected by the adverse consequences of the myths.

The principal way that myths about crime, criminals and crime control policy serve elite interests is by helping to secure and legitimate the social status quo with its gross disparities of wealth, privilege and opportunity. Two interrelated means by which myths help to accomplish this are by providing a scapegoat and by redirecting the defusing dissent.

In the first place, the "crime problem" in general has been used as a scapegoat for increasing political and economic distress (Quinney, 1977:6). Secondly, by focusing public attention on particular forms of crime (e.g., crimes of the poor), the belief that such crime is the basic cause of social problems obscures "the conditions of inequality, powerlessness, institutional violence, and so on, which lie at the bases of our tortured society" (Liazos, 1977:155).

In effect, almost every type of "reported crime" has served as a "scapegoat" for political and economic contradictions. Examples include: organized crime (Galliher & McCartney, 1977:376; Pearce, 1976; Simon, 1981), street crime (Center for Research on Criminal Justice, 1977:14), rape (Griffin, 1976:237), and juvenile delinquency (Platt, 1977:192; Foucault, 1977). Even the occasional prosecution of corporate crime has its advantages for social elites. It serves as a symbolic gesture that reinforces the belief that the law is applied uniformly to all persons (Pearce, 1976:90).

A major result of scapegoating is the polarization of the population into a "confident and supportive majority" and an "alienated and repressible minority" (Clements, 1974). By creating a readily identifiable criminal group through scapegoating, willing obedience and popular support of the "noncriminal" majority are made less problematic, thus reducing the need for compulsion. If polarization were not accomplished, or if people (e.g., the poor) were not divided through a fear of being criminally victimized, for example, then they might unite to the detriment of social elites to press for the realization of their common interests (Wright, 1973:21; Chambliss, 1976:7; Pearce, 1976:90; Quinney, 1979).

Another result of scapegoating and another way that myths serve the interest of social elites is by redirecting or defusing dissent. One means by which dissent is redirected is the perpetuation of the myth that crime is primarily the work of the poor. Belief in this myth diverts the attention to the poor from the social and economic exploitation they experience to the criminality of their own class (Chambliss, 1976:8). Furthermore, the myth "deflects the discontent and potential hostility of middle America away from the classes above them and toward the classes below them" (Reiman, 1979:5; also see Pepinsky and Jesilow, 1984:42). In both cases, myth has the effect of directing attention away from the sources of crime that have the most detrimental consequences for society.

A primary way that dissent is defused is by supervising or institutionalizing potential dissidents. As Gordon (1976:208) relates, "If the system did not effect this neutralization, if so many of the poor were not trapped in the debilitating system of crime and punishment, then they might otherwise gather the strength to oppose the system which reinforces their misery." Thus, the criminalization of the poor negates their potential "for developing an ideologically sophisticated understanding of their situation . . . and by incarcerating them it is made difficult for them to organize and realize their ideas" (Pearce, 1976:81).

Ultimately, the success or failure of redirecting or defusing dissent depends on the degree to which the public accepts myths of crime, criminals and crime control policy as accurate descriptions of reality. Fortunately for social elites, myths are likely to be critically accepted by the public for the following reasons (besides those already noted): First, the ethic of individual responsibility, a "legal fiction" which is both socially and psychologically insupportable, obscures the state's causal role in crime (Kennedy, 1976:48). Second, most individuals have been socialized, to varying extents, to behave in conformity with the law (Schumann, 1976:292). Third, most criminal behavior represents impulsive reactions to unspecific social conflicts which rarely victimize the opponent in the underlying conflict, thus obscuring the "real" sources of social conflict (Schumann, 1976:292). Ironically, for the exploited, "much, if not most, crime continues to victimize those who are already oppressed . . . and does little more than reproduce the existing order" (Quinney, 1977:103). Fourth, most individuals who commit crimes attempt to conceal their illegal behavior from others, and, thus, remain isolated instead of attempting to develop solidarity with others (Schumann, 1976:292). Finally, most individuals are insulated from any abridgment of justice so that interpretations of justice made by the state are credible. For example, "systematic elimination or incarceration of a certain 'criminal element' must always be the objective and professional pursuit of the role of law. . . ." (Clements, 1974:176).

CONCLUSION

As the preceding discussion shows, common conceptions of crime, criminals and crime control policy are to a rather large degree informed by myths. The myths are perpetuated not only because they serve elite interests, but also because they serve short-term interests of much of the general public.

Because myths serve elite interests by helping to secure and to legitimate the social status quo, and because social elites are less affected by the crimes most people fear, social elites have little incentive to dispel myths or to reduce crime. Ironically, social elites are the one group that could have a profound effect on changing the system that creates these problems (cf. Reiman, 1979).

The real irony is that the rest of the public helps perpetuate myths that inhibit the reduction of those actions or inactions that cause them harm and suffering. While myths do serve, in a perverted way, short-term interests of the general public, in the long-run, they inhibit comprehension of the fundamental changes necessary to bring about a reduction in harm and suffering. The poor, as a result, bear the bulk of the blame while continuing to be the most victimized; and the middle class, also victimized, must bear the bulk of the costs of policies that would not provide them the protection and the security they are seeking.

There are people who would like to perpetuate the myth that nothing can be done to significantly reduce crime in the United States. If the ameliorative reforms of the past are the sole indication, they may be right. However, there remains the possibility that a significant reduction can be achieved through, as yet tried, fundamental social change. Although the details of such a program are beyond the scope of this essay,[4] a first step is demystifying the myths that inform the ideology that inhibits fundamental social change. A promising means by which to achieve this goal is the development and the employment of a self-reflexive critical theory grounded in justifiable human interests (cf. Gouldner, 1976:292).

According to Ollman (1976), "reflexivity" may be distinguished by three characteristics. First is an awareness of oneself as an individual active in pursuing his own ends (Ollman, 1976:82). Evidence of this endowment includes:

1) the ability to choose whether or not to act in any given situation (this includes the ability to forego gratification of short-term interests for achievement of long-term interests); 2) a purposefulness or an ability to plan actions before engaging in them; and 3) a mental and physical flexibility in regard to one's tasks (Ollman, 1976:110-112). Second is an awareness that actions of others have aims similar to, and even connected to, one's own (Ollman, 1976:82). For this reason, human activity is always social: "Even when it is not done with or for other men, production is social because it is based on the assumptions and language of a particular society" (Ollman, 1976:112). The last characteristic is an awareness of a past, which is the record of one's successes and failures in attaining one's aims and of the possibilities which constitute one's failure (Ollman, 1976:82). In sum, "reflexivity" is the "conscious, willed, purposive, flexible, concentrated and social facets which enable man to pursue the unique demands of his species" (Ollman, 1976:112).

Critical theory involves the critique of contemporary society, especially "the system of information publicly available through the concretely organized mass media" (Gouldner, 1976:159). Critical theory makes problematic generally unquestioned traditional belief. In this sense, critical theory is similar to traditional sociology, except in two important respects: 1) in the emancipatory values it explicitly seeks and 2) in the reflexive relation it has toward its own value commitments (Gouldner, 1976:292).

A self-reflexive critical theory, then, does not transcend ideology because of the assumption that nearly all human actions, and ideologies that inform them, are necessarily grounded in partisan interests. Since ideology cannot be transcended, it can only be reconstituted around other interests. Consequently, self-reflexive critical theory grounds its ideology in justifiable human interests and makes these interests problematic or subject to examination in their own right. Ultimately, self-reflexive critical theory seeks to demonstrate connections between knowledge, belief and human interests. It is hoped that this essay has contributed to that effort.

NOTES

1. According to Nimmo and Combs (1980:6), "at best, myths are simplistic and distorted beliefs based upon emotion rather than rigorous analysis; at worst, myths are dangerous falsifications." Specifically, a "myth" is:

    > . . . a credible, dramatic, socially constructed re-presentation of perceived realities that people accept as permanent, fixed knowledge of reality while forgetting (if they were ever aware of it) its tentative, imaginative, created, and perhaps fictional qualities (Nimmo and Combs, 1980:16).

    For examples of myths of crime, criminals, and crime control policy, see especially Reiman, 1979; Pepinsky and Jesilow, 1984; Walker, 1985.

2. For Gouldner (1976:30), "ideology" is "a call to action—a 'command' grounded in social theory," ideology "presents a map of 'what is' in society; a 'report' of how it is working, how it is failing, and also how it could be changed" (Gouldner, 1976:30). "Interests," on the other hand, refer to "what it makes sense for people to want and do, given their overall situation" (Ollman, 1976:122). Although ideologies are partly legitimated by their claim to represent the "public interest," in practice, they nearly always represent private interests. This does not necessarily forebode undesirable social consequences however, because there is often hidden public value in vested private interests (Gouldner, 1976:282).

3. "Exploitation," in this context, refers to the activity of one group preventing another group from "getting what they may as yet have no idea of, and therefore do not desire, but would prefer to their present condition if only they knew about it" (Plamenatz, 1963:322).

4. For some interesting "new" ideas, see Pepinsky and Jesilow, 1984.

REFERENCES

American Friends Service Committee Working Party (1971). *Struggle for Justice.* New York: Hill and Wang.

Becker, H.S. (1973). *Outsiders: Studies in the Sociology of Deviance.* New York: Free Press.

Bittner, E. (1967). "The Police on Skid Row: A Study of Peace-Keeping." *American Sociological Review* 32:699-715.

_____ (1975). *The Functions of the Police in Modern Society.* New York: Jason Aronson.

Bohm, R.M. (1982). "Radical Criminology: An Explication." *Criminology* 19:565-589.

Center for Research on Criminal Justice (1977). *The Iron Fist and the Velvet Glove.* Berkeley: Center for Research on Criminal Justice.

Chambliss, W.J. (1976). "Functional and Conflict Theories of Crime: the Heritage of Emile Durkheim and Karl Marx." In W.J. Chambliss & M. Mankoff (eds.), *Whose Law What Order?* New York: Wiley.

Clements, J.M. (1974). "Repression: Beyond the Rhetoric." In C.E. Reasons (ed.), *The Criminologist: Crime and the Criminal.* Pacific Palisades, CA: Goodyear.

Clinard, M.B. (1978). *Cities with Little Crime: The Case of Switzerland.* Cambridge, England: Cambridge University Press.

Dominick, J.R. (1973). "Crime and Law Enforcement on Prime-time Television." *Public Opinion Quarterly* 37:241-250.

Dreier, P. (1982). "The Position of the Press in the U.S. Power Structure." *Social Problems* 29:298-310.

Erskine, H. (1974). "The Polls: Fear of Violence and Crime." *Public Opinion Quarterly,* (Spring) 131-145.

Evans, S.S. & R.J. Lundman (1983). "Newspaper Coverage of Corporate Price-Fixing: A Replication." *Criminology* 21:529-541.

Ferdinand, T.N. (1977). "The Criminal Patterns of Boston Since 1849." In J.F. Galliher & J.L. McCartney (eds.), *Criminology: Power, Crime and Criminal Law.* Homewood, IL: Dorsey.

Fishman, M. (1978). "Crime Waves as Ideology." *Social Problems* 25:531-543.

Foucault, M. (1977). *Discipline and Punish.* New York: Pantheon.

Galliher, J.F. & J.L. McCartney (1977). *Criminology: Power, Crime and Criminal Law.* Homewood, IL: Dorsey.

Garmire, F., J. Rubin & J.Q. Wilson (1972). *The Police and the Community.* Baltimore: Johns Hopkins University Press.

Gitlin, T. (1979). "Prime Time Ideology: The Hegemonic Process in Television Entertainment." *Social Problems* 26:251-266.

Gordon, D.M. (1976). "Class and the Economics of Crime." In W.J. Chambliss & M. Mankoff (eds.), *Whose Law What Order?* New York: Wiley.

Gouldner, A.W. (1976). *The Dialectic of Ideology and Technology: The Origins, Grammar, and Future of Ideology.* New York: Seabury.

Graber, D.A. (1980). *Crime News and the Public.* New York: Praeger.

Griffin, S. (1976). "Rape: the All-American Crime." In W.J. Chambliss and M. Mankoff (eds.), *Whose Law What Order?* New York: Wiley.

Grinspoon, L. (1977). *Marijuana Reconsidered,* Second Edition. Cambridge, MA: Harvard University Press.

Halberstam, D. (1979). *The Powers That Be.* New York: Knopf.

Helmer, J. (1975). *Drugs and Minority Oppression.* New York: Seabury.

Humphries, D. & D.F. Greenberg (1981). "The Dialectics of Crime Control." In D. Greenberg (ed.), *Crime and Capitalism.* Palo Alto, CA: Mayfield.

Kennedy, M.C. (1976). "Beyond Incrimination." In W.J. Chambliss & M. Mankoff (eds.), *Whose Law What Order?* New York: Wiley.

Liazos, A. (1977). "The Poverty of the Sociology of Deviance: Nuts, Sluts, and Perverts." In J.F. Galliher & J.L. McCartney (eds.), *Criminology: Power, Crime and Criminal Law.* Homewood, IL: Dorsey.

Lieberman, J.K. (1974). *How the Government Breaks the Law.* Baltimore: Penguin.

Lyerly, R.R. & J.K. Skipper, Jr. (1981). "Differential Rates of Rural-Urban Delinquency: A Social Control Approach." *Criminology* 19:385-399.

Manning, P. (1977). *Police Work.* Cambridge, MA: MIT Press.

——————— (1978). "Dramatic Aspects of Policing." In P. Wickman & P. Whitten (eds.), *Readings in Criminology.* Lexington, MA: D.C. Heath.

Martin, R.G. & R.D. Conger (1980). "A Comparison of Delinquency Trends: Japan and the United States." *Criminology* 18:53-61.

Marx, K. & F. Engels (1970). *The German Ideology.* New York: International Publishers.

Matza, D. (1964). *Delinquency and Drift.* New York: Wiley.

Mead, G.H. (1972). *On Social Psychology.* Chicago: The University of Chicago Press.

Milakovich, M.D. & K. Weis (1977). "Politics and Measures of Success in the War on Crime." In J.F. Galliher & J.M. McCartney (eds.), *Criminology: Power, Crime and Criminal Law.* Homewood, IL: Dorsey.

Miliband, R. (1969). *The State in Capitalist Society.* New York: Basic Books.

Mintz, M. & J.S. Cohen (1971). *American Inc.: Who Owns and Operates the United States?* New York: Dial.

Musto, D.F. (1973). *The American Disease: Origins of Narcotic Control.* New Haven: Yale University Press.

Nimmo, D. & J.E. Combs (1980). *Subliminal Politics: Myths and Mythmakers in America.* Englewood Cliffs, NJ: Prentice-Hall.

Ollman, B. (1976). *Alienation,* Second Edition. Cambridge: Cambridge University Press.

Paez, A.L. & R.W. Dodge (1982). "Criminal Victimization in the U.S." *Bureau of Justice Statistics Technical Report.* U.S. Department of Justice (July).

Pandiani, J.A. (1978). "Crime Time TV: If All We Know is What We Saw . . ." *Contemporary Crises* 2:237-258.

Pearce, F. (1976). *Crimes of the Powerful.* London: Pluto Press.

Pepinsky, H.E. (1980). *Crime Control Strategies: An Introduction to the Study of Crime.* New York: Oxford University Press.

Pepinsky, H.E. & P. Jesilow (1984). *Myths that Cause Crime.* Cabin John, MD: Seven Locks.

Plamenatz, J. (1963). *Man and Society,* Vol. 2 New York: McGraw Hill.

Platt, T. (1975). "Prospects for a Radical Criminology in the USA." In I. Taylor, P. Walton and J. Young (eds.), *Critical Criminology.* Boston: Routledge and Kegan Paul.

_____ (1977). *The Child Savers.* Chicago: The University of Chicago Press.

Quinney, R. (1970). *The Social Reality of Crime.* Boston: Little, Brown.

_____ (1977). *Class, State and Crime.* New York: David McKay.

_____ (1979). *Criminology,* Second Edition. Boston: Little, Brown.

_____ (1979b). "The Production of Criminology," *Criminology* 16:445-457.

Reiman, J.H. (1979). *The Rich Get Richer and the Poor Get Prison: Ideology, Class and Criminal Justice.* New York: Wiley.

_____ & S. Headlee (1981). "Marxism and Criminal Justice Policy." *Crime and Delinquency* 27:24-47.

Reiss, A. (1971). *The Police and the Public.* New Haven: Yale University Press.

Roshier, B. (1973). "The Selection of Crime News by the Press." In S. Cohen and J. Young (eds.), *The Manufacture of News.* Beverly Hills: Sage.

Schumann, K.F. (1976). "Theoretical Presuppositions for Criminology as a Critical Enterprise." *International Journal of Criminology and Penology* 4:285-294.

Sheley, J.F. & C.D. Ashkins (1981). "Crime, Crime News, and Crime Views." *Public Opinion Quarterly* 45:492-506.

Shelley, L.I. (1981). *Crime and Modernization: The Impact of Industrialization and Urbanization on Crime.* Carbondale, IL: Southern Illinois University Press.

Silver, I. (1968). *Introduction to The Challenge of Crime in a Free Society.* New York: Avon.

Simon, D.R. (1981). "The Political Economy of Crime." In S.G. McNall (eds.), *Political Economy: A Critique of American Society.* Glenview, IL: Scott, Foresman.

Simon, D.R. & D.S. Eitzen (1982). *Elite Deviance.* Boston: Allyn & Bacon.

Smith, R.C. (1970). "U.S. Marijuana Legislation and the Creation of a Social Problem." In D.E. Smith (ed.), *The New Social Drug: Cultural, Medical, and Legal Perspectives on Marijuana.* Englewood Cliffs, N.J.: Prentice-Hall.

Stack, S. (1984). "Income Inequality and Property Crime: A Cross-National Analysis of Relative Deprivation Theory." *Criminology* 22:229-257.

Sutherland, E.H. & D.R. Cressey (1974). *Criminology,* Ninth Edition. Philadelphia: J.B. Lippincott.

Vold, G.B. (1935). "The Amount and Nature of Crime." *American Journal of Sociology* 40:496-803.

Walker, S. (1985). *Sense and Nonsense About Crime: A Police Guide,* Monterey, CA: Brooks/Cole.

Wallerstein, J.S. & C.J. Wyle (1947). "Our Law-Abiding Lawbreakers." *Probation* 25:107-112.

Wilson, J.Q. (1968). *Varieties of Police Behavior.* Cambridge, MA: Harvard University Press.

———— (1975). *Thinking About Crime.* New York: Vintage.

Wright, E.O. (1973). *The Politics of Punishment.* New York: Harper Colophon.

DISCUSSION QUESTIONS

1. Bohm discusses a "self-reflexive critical theory grounded in justifiable human interests." What does he mean by this and how could it have a positive effect on myths and their consequences?

2. What role does the media play in perpetuating the current myths about crime and crime control policy? How do they exacerbate the problem and how could they be used to diminish the problem effectively?

3. Identify the myths as explained by Bohm. Discuss each one in detail and explain why you think they are relevant to the criminal justice system. Which one do you think is most relevant?

CHAPTER 19

Responsible Corporations
and Regulatory Agencies

Frank Pearce

Large corporations claim to be socially responsible but they rarely spell out what conditions would have to be fulfilled in order that they could consistently act in a responsible way. In this paper I outline the arguments that they present to justify their claim that they are normally responsible "political citizens" and then I challenge them. I argue that corporations cannot be left to regulate themselves because there is always a potential contradiction between the imperatives of profitability and a willingness to take account of social goals. Further, I show that if a corporation's executives were to act in a socially responsible way in a market economy in the absence of externally imposed and effective regulation then the economic viability of that corporation would often be put at risk; many of its competitors would gain an advantage by ignoring such responsibilities. Nevertheless, I believe that it is possible to show how they could act more responsibly but only if there are significant changes in their form of

KEY CONCEPTS:

actus reus

amoral calculator

company law

mens rea

political citizen

regulatory agency

socially responsible

organization, in how they relate to other organizations and groups of individuals and in their operating environment. When a version of this paper was presented in April 1989 at a symposium on "The Management of Safety in the Chemical Industry" at the Society of Chemical Industry it became clear that many who work within corporations are concerned to act responsibly, but equally that few had ready arguments to challenge the dominant assumptions of the corpo-

Reprinted with permission of *The Political Quarterly.* Frank Pearce, "Responsible Corporations and Regulatory Agencies" (1989). *The Political Quarterly* 61 (4): 415-430.

rate sector. What follows will hopefully help challenge these assumptions, provide practical suggestions and remain realistic about the costs of necessary reforms.

Large corporations claim that they are "political citizens," socially conscious, useful members of society; that they make a profit by safely and efficiently producing safe and useful products sold in highly competitive markets; that they can be trusted in self-regulating. Such corporations argue that they join together in trade associations in order to develop and pool useful knowledge, create common standards and to represent the industry's interests to the outside world. They often work with regulatory agencies which, provided that they are staffed by professionals who are realistic about the needs of industry, can play a useful social role. They can check and validate the research of individual corporations, provide corporations with relevant advice and keep them up to date with what is occurring in other countries. They sometimes have to help incompetent businesses to achieve reasonable standards by diagnosing unsafe or inefficient ways of working. These are usually small and relatively under-resourced firms which need advice rather than punishment. True, some small businesses are "amoral calculators"—they try to make money by any means at all. They may need to be sanctioned. But this does not disturb the general picture of business integrity since they are an atypical minority—small "fly by night operations" run by "cowboys."[1]

Corporations claim that they are willing to accept reasonable state intervention but they believe that unqualified, irrational political actors—trade unionists, ecologists, socialists and others with little practical sense—put pressure on the state to interfere with market forces and the internal workings of the professionally run corporation. Unreasonable laws can be passed, excessive damages awarded, unworkable regulations promulgated, and product certification unfairly denied. Such individuals and attitudess—a belief in a risk-free society, for example—can gain excessive influence within democratic assemblies, in the courts, in juries and can capture regulatory agencies.[2] Given this danger, and since most corporations are self-regulating responsible political citizens, a minimum of external regulation is the preferred option.

Let us provide some concrete examples of such corporate reasoning. Recently, when it publicly took the lead in phasing out the use of fluorocarbons, DuPont's vice president demanded assurances that the substitutes for CFCs [chlorofluorocarbons] being developed will be found acceptable to regulatory agencies in the long run.[3] A few months earlier, the Chairman and Chief Executive of Monsanto argued that the high cost of litigation in the U.S. inhibits product innovation. His own company:

> . . . abandoned a possible substitute product for asbestos just before commercialization, not because it was unsafe or ineffective, but because a whole generation of lawyers had been schooled in asbestos liability theories that could possibly be turned against the substitute.

> The punitive damages system makes it too easy for lawyers to persuade a jury—possessing little scientific knowledge but believing in the possibility of a risk free society—to enrich plaintiffs and contingent-fee lawyers with multimillion dollar windfalls.[4]

Approximately $2.5 billion was "received by 60,000 claimants in the Johns-Manville asbestos suit."[5]

In the early 1970s, the chemical industry had opposed a proposed Federal PVC standard because it would cost $65 billion and two million jobs. It "was simply beyond the compliance capacity of the industry."[6] In 1976 the overall administrative cost of regulation in the U.S. was $3.2 billion and the compliance cost $62.9 billion—a total of $66.1 billion. In 1975 Federal regulations had increased the average price of a car by $449.41, forcing the auto industry and consumers to spend an additional $3.025 billion on cars. Both industry and consumers could have spent this money more productively elsewhere.[7]

Here, I will briefly comment on these statements and arguments. If we examine CFCs (and their possible replacements) we find that there is a genuine dilemma about how much of a trade off there was and is between the possible risks of using CFCs compared to the usefulness of refrigeration. But this can hardly be said to apply to their use in most aerosols or any fast food packaging. These latter were the frivolous market for two-thirds of CFC production during the many years when Du Pont, and in Britain ICI, were denying its dangers. If we turn to the question of the litigation concerning asbestos there is something particularly offensive about industry leaders citing the problems produced by this litigation without condemning the behaviour of the North American asbestos producers. One reason for these high settlements is that Johns-Manville, and other major companies from the 1920s on, concealed from their workers and the public a mass of accumulating evidence of the dangers of asbestos.[8] They were amoral calculators and they should be condemned by corporations and corporate executives who claim to be political citizens.

I cited some of the figures that manufacturers' associations and others have produced on the costs of regulation. These also need to be examined carefully. First, the PVC [Polyvinyl Chloride] standard: despite industry's objections, a virtually identical standard to that originally proposed was adopted in the U.S. and this sector of industry continued to flourish, without job losses and at only five percent of the expected cost.[9] If we then turn to Weidenbaum and de Fina's figures and, for the sake of argument, accept them, we must note that, although health and safety and environmental regulations cost a great deal of money, they also cut down on the destruction of property and on the cost of deaths and injuries to individuals, their families and the community as a whole. A 1979 study, for example, found that air pollution control in the U.S.A. (due largely to the implementation of the Clean Air Act of 1970) benefited the health of individuals, stopped the soiling of property and diminished the costs of cleaning it, and limited damage to vegetation. In 1978 the estimate was that something like 13,900 lives were saved and if, as this study suggests, lives were valued at $1 million each, the overall saving was $19.7 billion (in 1978 dollars).[10] Regulations protect the health and wealth of individuals and communities and force polluters to internalize the cost of controlling their "externalities."

Similarly, although increased expenditure on making cars safer may have simply been an additional cost for car manufacturers, this was not true for the community as a whole. The additional $3.025 billion spent on the purchase of cars must be balanced against the estimated savings of $2.5 billion by exhaust fume control and a saving from reductions in accidents of over $5.5 billion, even if we restrict ourselves to insurance and litigation based estimates of the value of life and limb. From the point of view of the rest of the community, there was a net benefit from this regulation of about £5 billion [5 billion British pounds]. A related way in which state and court action can force companies to internalize the cost of controlling externalities and thereby increase both business and social efficiency is by increasing the cost of worker compensation. The annual cost of this rose to $26 billion in 1988, and is expected to reach $60 billion by 1998. This rise stimulated Chrysler to invest more time and money in accident prevention and on therapy for the injured, thereby in 1987 saving them (and the community) a net $48 million or so in health care costs.[11]

Further, while expenditure on pollution may simply be a cost for polluting industries it tends "to stimulate economic growth, not retard it. In the 1970s in the U.S. some 20,000 employees were put out of work because of plant closings, but over 600,000 were employed in various pollution-related activities."[12] A cost for a specific industry and companies may be a business opportunity for others. When he was the environment minister, Mr. William Waldegrave pointed out that the British pollution control industry was losing out:

> Inferior environmental regulations and a lack of government support is undermining the £2 billion plus industry. . . . He defended the long standing practice of requiring industries to develop the best practicable means of reducing their pollution . . . The British industry . . . was losing home markets because other countries had higher environmental standards or forced the pace of technological development by setting standards unachievable with existing technology.[13]

Such technology forcing was remarkably effective in the case of the production of PVC.[14] This is also true in many cases where industries have been forced to monitor and register emissions of dangerous chemicals. The director of the U.S. Office of Toxic Substances at the Environmental Protection Agency recently demonstrated that "savings from controlling waste and improving process efficiencies often more than outweigh the costs."[15]

Socially Responsible and Amorally Calculating Firms

We must now turn to the distinction that is drawn between the socially responsible large corporation, allegedly the vast majority, and the amoral calculators that are supposedly relatively marginal and small businesses. The evidence is sketchy but lends little support to such a distinction. For example, the recent major U.S. study of corporate illegalities found that even allowing for their large market share large corporations tended to commit as many, if not more, recorded offenses than medium and small companies.[16] If we turn to a more specific example, this time associated with self-regulation, we find that:

> In 1981, OSHA [Occupational Safety and Health Administration] decided that if a review of a company's log of occupational injuries showed that its injury rates were below average, the first would be exempt from a full "wall to wall" inspection. Many companies responded exactly as they should have been expected to—they falsified their records. An OSHA crackdown against such offenders in 1986 and 1987 resulted in charges against Union Carbide, Chrysler, Caterpillar Tractor, Ford, General Dynamics, Shell and other major corporations.[17]

One company exempted from inspection by OSHA because, according to its company logs, it had a better than average safety record was Film Recovery System Corporation.[18] In June 1985, this Corporation and three of its executives were successfully prosecuted for murdering an employee and sentenced to 25 years in prison and a $10,000 fine. They ignored health and safety regulations and complaints from workers about headaches, nausea and vomiting when working with vats of sodium cyanide. Warnings about chemicals were printed only in English; the workers were employed because they were non-English speakers.[19]

This prosecution was not unconnected with an earlier case. When, in the 1970s, Ford discovered that the Pinto design was dangerous, they nevertheless decided not to change it. According to their estimates the costs of modifying "what they knew to be an unsafe fuel tank were nearly three times the expected costs of suits arising from the deaths and injuries."[20] Similarly General Motors sold the notoriously unsafe Chevrolet Corvair after it had been warned of its dangers by its own engineers,[21] and then when, twenty years later, it was again warned that a gas tank in another car "was vulnerable to puncture during some high speed crashes" it did not move it "to a more protected location" although this would have cost less than $12.00 per car.[22] Some large corporations, then, act at times as ruthless and knowing "amoral calculators." What is probably more typical of all businesses, however, is that, only too often, safety measures and those concerning environmental protection are considered secondary to the goal of making as much money as possible. In other words they do not always mean it when they say "Production at a cost: safety at any cost," to quote one of Union Carbide's slogans.

Carson found in his 1970 study of the British Factory Inspectorate that every one of the 200 firms he visited—*whatever their size*—violated the health and safety laws at least twice, and the average number of violations per firm was 19. More recently, between 1986 and 1988, the HSE has prosecuted the following large companies—Austin Rover, BOC, BP, British Gas, BSC, GEC, ICI, Balfour Beatty, John Laing Construction, Sir Alfred McAlpine, Tarmac Regional Construction, Wimpey Construction. In 75% of maintenance accidents in the chemical industry the HSE found site management was "wholly or partly responsible for failing to take all reasonably practicable precautions to prevent an accident." Large corporations, in fact, often find ways to subcontract out particularly dirty and risky activities to small firms. There is little doubt that in the U.S. one reason why there is such a problem about the inadequate disposal of, and illegal dumping of toxic waste by small companies, is that large corporations successfully blocked proposals that the generators of hazardous wastes should have the legal duty of seeing that they were disposed of safely. Instead there developed a free market in hazardous waste disposal, characterized by inadequate regulation and cut-throat competition with extensive participation by firms controlled by organized crime.[23] Smaller firms may be more vulnerable to prosecution than large firms because it is easier for regulatory agencies to mount a successful prosecution against them. It is, of course, true that one of the areas which has recently shown the largest accident rates—the construction industry—is characterized by a large number of firms. In the summer of 1987 the Factory Inspectorate concentrated on construction sites. As a result of inspecting the work of about 4,500 contractors, 868 prohibition notices were issued to stop work immediately because of dangerous conditions—that is conditions were so bad that some work in approximately one in five building sites could not be allowed to continue.[24] There is an organizational issue at stake here—the site agent should be made responsible for safety on the site. Further, when the experiment in self-regulation in the construction industry was abandoned because of a fatality and rumours of an increased accident rate[,] it is important to note that the company involved was one of the major ones in the industry.

Large corporations have been responsible for many accidents which could have been avoided if state of the art technologies and safety procedures had been used. This is true of the bulk of the fatal accidents in the offshore oil industry[25] and the tragedies at Flixborough, Seveso, Mexico City, Bhopal, and Sandoz. A recent Dutch analysis of 251 serious accidents in the international chemical industry, massively dominated by transnational corporations, showed that they were primarily caused by poor plant design and inadequate standards of basic maintenance, which are clearly the responsibility of management.[26]

THE ROLE OF MANAGEMENT

This, then, reopens the question: why are companies accident and disaster prone? HSE Inspectorates are quite clear that bad management is the major cause of fatal accidents—for "two out of three deaths in general manufacturing"[27] [and] "three out of five farm deaths."[28] Braithwaite's analysis of 39 coal mine disasters worldwide indicated that inadequate organization, general inefficiency and a poor safety record are related. On the other hand, the coal companies in the U.S. that are safety leaders:

1. Give a lot of informal clout to top management backing to their safety inspectors.

2. Make sure that clearly defined accountability for safety performance is imposed on line managers.

3. Monitor safety performance carefully and let managers know when it is not up to standard.

4. Have mostly formal programs . . . for ensuring:

    (a) that safety training and supervision (by foremen in particular) is never neglected;

    (b) that safety problems are quickly communicated to those who can act on them;

    (c) that a plan of attack exists dealing with all identified hazards.[29]

Furthermore, these were profitable firms and they seem to be competent self-regulators which suggests that safe firms are efficient firms, and vice versa.

Many of these firms were subdivisions of such large corporations as U.S. Steel, Bethlehem Steel, Du Pont and Sohio. The complex division of labor within corporate giants means that they are usually self-conscious about their organization, that they tend to have specialist safety engineers, and that economies of scale reduce the costs of quite extensive safety measures to only a fraction of their operating budget. Such large corporations certainly have the capacity to act safely. However, the safety records of these corporations are by no means consistently good and some previously had a distinctly poor record, so the sheer size of such firms is at best a partial explanation. In fact, their safety performance only improved after strong pressure from OSHA in the context of increasingly strict mine safety laws. Research on the American coal-mining industry concluded

> that most of the variance in fatality rates could be explained by . . . the size of the federal government's budget allocation to coal mine health and safety regulation. . . . The research indicated that strong safety laws reduce coal mine fatalities and that, if laws are strong, coal mine fatalities decrease with increases in federal spending on mine health and safety.[30]

While safety is often associated with efficiency and profitability, this is not necessarily the case. Profits and safety can be at odds with each other. In the absence of effective external regulation, safe, efficient firms may become unprofitable. Their products may become overpriced relative to those of other firms which, with impunity, engage in business in a risky and unsafe way. This may lead to a general drop in standards. For example, many American passenger airlines have in recent years remained profitable in part through dangerously extending the life of aircraft by replacing only those parts which have obviously worn out. These problems are compounded by the fact that there is something of a bottleneck in the production of new aircraft due to a shortage of plant and skilled personnel; this in turn has led some aircraft manufacturers to overuse both.[31] What, under these circumstances, may be economically rational behaviour from the point of view of the corporation is not rational from the point of view of employees, consumers or the community.

Other situations where profits and safety may be at odds with each other include those when a company that has recently expanded plant capacity is then confronted by a declining market, or when its production processes are rendered obsolete and inefficient by new production processes or products. In Bhopal, Union Carbide India Ltd., having increased its capacity to produce carbamate pesticides, was then confronted with a declining market both because of severe problems with India's "green revolution" and because of the growing popularity of other kinds of pesticides, organophosphates and new synthetic pyrethroids. It reacted by employing fewer operatives (who were given inadequate training) and by cutting back on maintenance and other operating costs. These cutbacks played a major role in causing the 1984 accident which led to the deaths of more than 3,000 people. Union Carbide, which owned a controlling interest in its subsidiary, could have simply absorbed any losses—after all in the same year it wrote off $241 million worth of plant in other parts of the world—but instead allowed safety to be compromised.[32] Union Carbide settled out of court (for $470 million, of which $200 million was covered by insurance), never accepted responsibility for the accident and indeed attempted to shift the blame to the Indian authorities. It claimed that:

> the Indian government may have granted a license for the Bhopal plant without adequate checks on the plant; that the relevant controlling agencies responsible for the plant were grossly understaffed, lacked powers and had little impact on conditions in the field. More particularly, the Bhopal department of labor office had only two inspectors, neither of whom had any knowledge of chemical hazards. . . .[33]

It is not clear if the statement is an accurate description of the Indian regulatory agencies, although it is likely that regulation was less severe there than in the U.S. However, it seems extremely unlikely that Union Carbide really wanted effective regulation—it did not demand this before the accident—but it may have wished to export hazard[34] to a less regulated country. That the return on capital is potentially higher in less regulated countries can be inferred from the amount of money that the U.S. chemical industry spent in 1975 and 1976 on pollution control equipment (approximately 9% and 12% of capital expenditure) when it would have only expected to spend half this amount overseas.[35] What the Bhopal case suggests is that it is only if all companies producing within an economy are equally (and effectively) subject to the compulsion to engage in adequate expenditure on safety and pollution control measures that they will do so.

The distinction drawn between the essentially socially responsible corporation and the atypical amoral calculator seems untenable. This does not, however, mean that corporations, corporate executives and professionals such as chemical engineers always act as amoral calculators. What it does indicate is that there are certain empirical realities that need to be taken account of by those who wish to act in a socially responsible way: they must actively organize to bring pressure to bear on their superiors, shareholders, trade associations *and* the state to articulate and enforce realistic standards of conduct; they must acknowledge that, on occasion, their industry, their corporations, their colleagues, and even their professional associations, may not act responsibly. It is precisely because many corporations act, on occasion, as amoral calculators that adequate laws and their rigorous enforcement by regulatory agencies play an essential role in safety and in the protection of the environment.

What, then, could the claim that corporations are political citizens mean and what would industry have to do to demonstrate to people that this is what corporations really are? How can a legal framework be set up in such a way that it helps corporations, corporate executives and engineers to be responsible citizens while still engaging in productive business activity? Could "responsible" corporate executives persuade their shareholders that they should act ethically? We know that because of pressure for high immediate returns on investments, the threat from corporate raiders, etc. etc., many executives are finding any kind of long term planning and investment problematic, never mind those associated with health and safety and pollution control. How can engineers and other employees, committed to high standards of health and safety and pollution control, press the board of their companies to act responsibly? How can corporations and corporate executives who wish to act unethically (and often thereby steal a competitive advantage) be stopped from doing so[?] In other words, how can the ethical be empowered to be responsible without being disadvantaged *vis-à-vis* irresponsible competitors and colleagues? To answer these questions we must spell out in some detail what is meant by certain key terms and what their implications are.

SOME PROPOSITIONS FOR REFORM

1. Individuals or corporations can be citizens of the world community, one or more common markets, various nation states and many local communities. Any meaningful concept of political citizenship must include a commitment to the continued viability of the community, which means a commitment to bring (net) benefits to it now and to help secure its future.

2. The major transnational corporations are all based in democratic countries. As members of a democratic political community corporations have a right to participate in the political process and must therefore also recognize that others also have this right, even when this may involve a challenge to some corporate interests. Corporations are answerable to the democratic assemblies of their shareholders and (formally, at least) acknowledge the right of their employees to democratically choose whether or not to be represented through democratic trade unions. In such a democratic community there is a commitment to the equal treatment of others and the development of universal standards.

3. A responsible corporation would presumably accept that workers, consumers, members of local communities have a right to know whether or not they are being exposed to danger and what these dangers are. It must accept the responsibility of generating and making available this information.

4. A responsible corporation would accept that it bears responsibility for the dangerous side effects of its productive processes, its products and the waste that it generates. What economists call externalities must be recognized as corporate responsibilities and treated as internal costs. This will inevitably add to the expense of engaging in production. Industry must be honest about these costs. Moreover these costs will not be evenly spread across all industries and will affect some, such as the chemical industry, more than others. If companies wish to engage in chemical production or if countries want a viable chemical industry then they may have to subsidize chemical manufacture.

5. A responsible corporation would recognize that calculations of cost and benefit do not only involve its own costs and benefits but also costs and benefits to present and future members of communities.

6. Responsible corporations would produce safe commodities. If there are risks then the community would be apprised of them. Risks would only be countenanced if there seem to be corresponding benefits to the community. (It may be worth risking the production of CFCs for refrigeration but not for aerosols or fast food containers.)

7. Industry must accept that the community has a right to call all its members to account. This can be achieved, in part, through market mechanisms; in part, through litigation; in part, through regulatory agencies. Both individual citizens and regulatory agencies must have readily available to them detailed information about the nature

of corporate activities and products and about the decisions and decision-making processes of corporations. There must exist the capacity effectively to bring corporations and their executives to account for their actions. Industry must accept the need for effective external regulation.

8.   Corporations must organize production safety. Braithwaite's analysis of the "organizational characteristics" that "make for safe mining" apply equally well to all large-scale manufacturing, *viz*:

> clout for the safety department, clearly defined accountability for safety imposed on line managers, top management commitment to and monitoring of safety performance, programs for guaranteeing safety training/supervision, effective communication and, most important of all, effective plans to cope with hazards.[36]

While a safe firm is usually an efficient firm and vice versa, in some situations there will be financial advantages in engaging in less than safe production; but a responsible corporation would put safety first. Such a corporation would know that there may exist competing corporations who are not so scrupulous. The only way that a corporation can remain ethical and not be disadvantaged is for irresponsible corporations to be publicly sanctioned. This is both for reasons of justice and so that the responsible corporation knows that others are stopped from engaging in unfair practices. An executive vice-president of Dow put this well when he pointed out that, by resisting expenditure on air pollution control, some companies are able "to establish a margin of advantage over their competitors. Such conduct is hurting the rest of industry and should not be defended or tolerated."[37] It is thus quite understandable that in her study of pollution control Brittan found that firms whose discharges complied with water control standards "favored a hard line on enforcement."[38]

9.   It is important to recognize that effective regulation requires that irresponsible corporations and irresponsible senior executives can be called to account for what they do.[39] Currently, if a company is prosecuted for health and safety violations it is the corporate entity that is charged and not particular senior executives. Fines are often treated as little more than a tax and hence provide scant incentive to obey the law.

Company law, whilst increasingly specific about financial responsibilities (and with a possibility of criminal prosecution for negligence as in Section 89 of the 1986 Insolvency Act), is extremely vague about those concerned with managing safety, thus creating problems in determining individual and collective responsibility for disasters and accidents. But the present law can also easily be reformed to make directors and chief executives legally as well as morally responsible for accidents and disasters whilst still providing them with a reasonable defense if they are not in fact to blame. This will also make prosecution easier and hence a more rational option for the inspectorates.

Recently, in a judgment concerning the coroner's verdict on the Zeebrugge disaster, the court of Queen's Bench Division found that a corporation may be indicted for manslaughter, where the *mens rea* (intent) and *actus reus* (circumstances) of manslaughter can be established against those who are identified as the embodiment of the corporation itself.[40] However, they also argued that "manslaughter could not be found on the aggregation of the individual acts or omissions of those employed by a corporate body."[41] In other words, while the looseness of the organizational structure of a company can contribute to an accident, it also helps its executives to escape prosecution. In this case, however, the DPP [Director of Public Prosecution] has subsequently issued eight summonses for manslaughter: seven to employees (including two company directors) and one against P&O European Ferries (Dover) Ltd. (formerly Townsend Car Ferries). Although the outcome must be awaited, particularly as to what corporate manslaughter might entail, it is undeniable that "the notion of corporate manslaughter is now entering popular vocabulary"[42] and influencing legal reasoning.

What remains clear is that the law must be changed to force companies to tighten up their organizational structure and their management of health and safety. Provisions of the 1974 HASAWA [Health and Safety at Work Act] could be adapted to make it more difficult for them to avoid responsibility. Section 2(3) of the 1974 Act imposes a duty upon employers to produce a written statement of their general policy for the health and safety of their employees. This must include not only the overall policy but must also set out the organization and arrangements currently in force for carrying out that general policy.[43] This could provide the basis for a satisfactory safety policy but it does not specify how top corporate executives can be made responsible for safety nor how safety should be monitored and policed.

Section 79 of the 1974 Act[44] and Schedule 7 of the Companies Act 1985, which deals with directors' annual reports, [enable] the Secretary of State to prescribe cases whereby [directors'] reports will contain information about arrangements on health and safety. If such action was taken by the Secretary of State, senior executives would not be able to plead ignorance and thus escape responsibility. The obligation was made dependent upon the issuing of regulations. It is high time that these were laid. They could include a duty on companies that are responsible for the health and safety of large numbers of people (whether employees or the general public) to have:

- a named Director with overall responsibility for safety;

- reporting to a named Director, a qualified Safety Engineer who has a thorough understanding of the relevant hazards, applicable regulations, and emergency system and procedures;

- formal safety systems and means of enforcement;

- formal risk assessment as a way of minimizing risk.[45]

10. Corporations should be legally required to have an independent auditing unit within the corporation that reports to another named director and who has the responsibility of policing company activities including those involving health and safety. Lower level employees need protecting, too; there is always a danger that they will be scapegoated. Equally, senior executives can avoid prosecution by the device of offering lacklustre executives accelerated promotion as "vice-presidents responsible for going to jail."[46] To avoid both of these possibilities all such named directors should report directly to the chief executive and their reports should be the basis of the annual safety profile, i.e., published. The chief executive would then also be personally liable and it is likely that his concern with safety would then be well developed. As Dr. Cullen of the Health and Safety Commission recently stated, the possibility of "a jail sentence would help to concentrate the minds of employers who might not be carrying out their duties under health and safety laws."[47]

In this context it is also worth noting that the existence of strict regulations that are effectively enforced provides ammunition for engineers and others concerned with safety and pollution control when arguing with accountants and others at head office about such expenditure. Brittan, for example, quotes an executive working for a subsidiary of an American company—"Treatment plant is capital investment. We can't spend this money without prior authority from the States. If you use legislation as a reason, it usually receives favourable action."[48]

11. Effective regulation requires agencies that are independent and which have a clear mandate to protect people and the environment. The major problem is not that environmentalists capture agencies but rather that they become subordinate to the interests of those that they are meant to regulate.[49] An extreme example is that of the water authorities which, as Mr. Nicholas Ridley, the then Environment Secretary, pointed out "act as 'both gamekeepers and poachers' supplying water and setting the regulatory framework."[50] Whether this requires water privatization is another matter. A more

typical problem is that some regulatory agencies are associated with ministries dedicated to the active promotion of the economic development of the industries whose dangers they are meant to be mitigating with strict regulations.[51] One under-reported aspect of the recent Exxon oil spill in Alaska is that it would have been dealt with much more effectively if the industry consortium Alyeska Pipeline Service Company had not, in a penny-pinching move in 1981, disbanded a response team trained to deal with emergency clean-ups. The Alaskan Department of the Environment Conservation had not stopped it doing this. However, the latter organization was and is underfunded and the oil industry has been a major opponent of any increase in its funding. More generally, to save costs in a deregulatory era the number of local coast guards were recently cut back and the quality of their radar system downgraded.[52] It is time that "responsible" corporate executives recognized where the major problems in achieving adequate regulation actually lie.

12. Regulatory agencies require effective powers and adequate financing. This is the only valid implication of Union Carbide's comments about the Indian government and its role in the Bhopal disaster.

13. Effective regulation equalizes conditions. It should equalize the conditions to which all are subject. Thus, we can only applaud the responsibility and rationality of the Chemical Manufacturer's Association of the U.S.A., which, according to W. Stover, its Vice President, Government Relations,

> supports the adoption and enforcement of the hazardous materials regulations by State and Local governments. We believe it is essential for State and Local enforcement personnel to ensure industry compliance with the national regulatory scheme.[53]

But this should be true nationally and internationally. The same safety standards should apply throughout the world, thus equalizing the conditions under which corporations compete. This would generate new markets. It would force technological development. It would help sustain and enhance the quality of life.

In the context of the current development of large trading blocs there exists the possibility of producing adequate regulatory frameworks which will be binding on the major corporations if they wish to produce for and sell in their major markets. The safety conscious public is not without leverage. It is no coincidence that in its eagerness to gain access to the profitable French agricultural producer markets Union Carbide agreed to French trade union demands that in its pesticide plant at Beziers expenditure on safety would increase to 20% from the more usual 3.5%. Thus, if corporations are serious about their social responsibilities, they will accept the kinds of changes that have been advocated in this article. They would not be painless or cost free. But if corporations do not accept the need for change then we can only assume that their self-representation as socially responsible organizations and as "political citizens," committed to the long-term interests of the communities in which they operate, is little more than a public relations ploy. The suggestions in this article, like the recently enunciated "Valdez Principles,"[54] then, should be construed as both a set of practical measures and as a challenge.

NOTES

1. I have adapted these terms from the social science literature on the regulation of corporations. See, in particular, Kagan, R. and Scholz, J., "The Criminology of the Corporation and Regulatory Enforcement Strategies" in Hawkins, K. and Thomas, J. (eds.), *Enforcing Regulation*, Kluwer-Nijhoff Publishing, Boston, 1984; Hawkins, K., *Environment and Enforcement*, Clarendon Press, Oxford, 1984; Sutherland, E.H., *White Collar Crime: The Uncut Version*, Yale University Press, New Haven, 1983; Pearce, F. and Tombs, S., "Ideology, Hegemony and Empiricism—Compliance Theories of Regulation," *British Journal of Criminology*, Summer 1990.

2. Weaver, P., "Regulation, Social Policy and Class Conflict" in Jacobs, D.P. (ed.), *Regulating Business: The Search for an Optimum*, Institute for Contemporary Studies, San Francisco, 1978. See also Wilson, J.Q. (ed.), *The Politics of Regulation*, Basic Books, New York, 1980.

3. *The Globe and Mail*, 6 March 1989.

4. Mahoney, Richard J., "Punitive Damages: The Costs are Curbing Creativity," *The New York Times*, 11 December 1988.

5. *The Los Angeles Times*, 22 February 1989. See also *The New York Times*, 2 April 1989.

6. Rattner, Steve, "Did Industry Cry Wolf?," *The New York Times*, 28 December 1975.

7. Weidenbaum, M. and de Fina, R., *The Costs of Federal Regulation of Economic Activity*, AEI Reprint No. 88, American Enterprise Institute, Washington DC, 1978.

8. Brodeur, P., *Outrageous Misconduct: The Asbestos Industry on Trial*, Pantheon, New York, 1985.

9. Wilson, D.K., *The Politics of Safety and Health: Occupational Safety and Health in the United States and Britain*, Clarendon Press, Oxford, 1985, pp. 15-16.

10. Freeman, A.M., "The Benefits of Air and Water Pollution Control: A Review and Synthesis of Recent Estimates," *A Report Prepared for the Council on Environmental Quality*, 1979. See also Wilson, G.K., *The Politics of Safety and Health: Occupational Safety and Health in the United States and Britain*, Clarendon Press, Oxford, 1985.

11. *The New York Times*, 19 March 1989.

12. Marcus, A., "Environmental Protection Agency" in Wilson, J.Q. (ed.), *The Politics of Regulation, op. cit.*.

13. *The Guardian*, 2 May 1989.

14. Rattner, S., "Did Industry Cry Wolf?," *New York Times*, 28 December 1975; and Castleman, B.I., "The Double Standard in Industrial Hazards" in Ives, J. (ed.), *The Export of Hazard*, Routledge, London, 1986.

15. Elkins, C., "Corporate Citizenship—Toxic Chemicals, the Right Response," *New York Times*, 13 November 1989, p. 3.

16. Clinard, M.B. and Yeager, P.C., *Corporate Crime*, Free Press, New York, 1980.

17. Coleman, J., *The Criminal Elite: The Sociology of White Collar Crime*, St. Martin's Press, New York, 1989, p. 164.

18. *The New York Times*, March 1988.

19. Coleman, J., *The Criminal Elite, op. cit.*

20. Reasons, C., "Crime and the Abuse of Power: Offenses and Offenders Beyond the Reach of the Law" in Wickham, P. and Daley, T. (eds.), *White-Collar and Economic Crime: Multidisciplinary and Cross-National Perspectives*, Lexington Books, DC: Heath and Co., Lexington, [MA], 1982.

21. Coleman, J., *The Criminal Elite, op. cit.*, p. 218.

22. Mokhiber, R. and Falloon, E.V., "The 10 Worst Corporations of 1988," *Multinational Monitor*, December 1988.

23. Ironically, under Superfund legislation in "designated" sites, companies are strictly liable for the hazardous waste they have generated. See Szasz, A., "Corporations, Organized Crime, and the Disposal of Hazardous Waste: An Examination of the Making of a Criminogenic Regulatory Structure," *Criminology*, vol. 24, no. 1, 1986; and Block, A. and Scarpitti, F., *Poisoning for Profit: The Mafia and Toxic Waste in America*, William Morrow, New York, 1985.

24. *Occupational Safety and Health*, December 1987. Similarly, while enforcement notices are issued at an average of 0.03% a visit, a recent factory inspectorate proactive initiative on small textile firms issued such notices at a rate of 7%; prosecutions were taken out on 0.7% of visits as opposed to 0.005% normally; 191 of the 300 premises inspected were not even registered (*Health and Safety at Work*, April 1985).

25. Carson, W.G., *The Other Price of Britain's Oil*. Martin Robertson, Oxford, 1982.

26. Smith, M.H., *The Chemical Industry After Bhopal: An International Symposium Held in London*, IBC Technical Services, London, 1986, pp. 261-3.

27. Chief Factory Inspector's Report, 1982.

28. Chief Agricultural Inspector's Report, 1986.

29. Braithwaite, J. *To Punish or Persuade: Enforcement of Coal Mine Safety*, State University of New York Press, Albany New York, 1985, p. 65.

30. Braithwaite, J., *op. cit.*, pp. 77-81.

31. *The Guardian*, 27 and 31 January 1989.

32. Pearce, F. and Tombs, S., "Bhopal" in *Social Justice*, June 1989.

33. Muchlinski, P.T., "The Bhopal Case: Controlling Ultrahazardous Industrial Activities Undertaken by Foreign Investors," *The Modern Law Review* 50, 5, September 1987.

34. Ives, J. (ed.), *The Export of Hazard, op. cit.*

35. Castleman, B.I., "The Export of Hazardous Factories to Developing Nations," *International Journal of Health Services*, vol. 9, no. 4, 1979; and Wilson, G.K., *The Politics of Safety and Health: Occupational Safety and Health in the United States and Britain, op. cit.*

36. Braithwaite, J., *op. cit.*, p. 71.

37. Brown, M.H., *The Toxic Cloud*, Harper and Row, New York, 1987, p. 242.

38. Brittan, Y., *The Impact of Water Pollution Control on Industry: A Case Study of Fifty Dischargers*, Centre for Socio-Legal Studies, Oxford, 1984, p. 79.

39. These arguments are discussed at more length in Pearce, F. and Tombs, S., "Bhopal,", *op. cit.;* and in the *Employment Law Bulletin* Issue No. 18 (Summer 1988).

40. *The Times*, 10 October 1987 (Law Report).

41. *The Guardian*, 15 October 1987 (Law Report).

42. Wells, C., "What can we do if the guilty parties are corporations?," *The Guardian*, 26 August 1988, p. 31.

43. Fife, I. and Machin, E.A., *Redgrave's Health and Safety in Factories*, Second Edition, Butterworths, London, 1982, p. 416.

44. Fife, I. and Machin, E.A., *Redgrave's Health and Safety in Factories, op. cit.*, p. 540.

45. *Health and Safety at Work*, vol. 9, no. 11 (November 1987).

46. Braithwaite, J. and Fisse, B., "Self Regulation and the Control of Corporate Crime," in Shearing, C.D. and Stenning, P.C. (eds.), *Private Policing*, Sage Publications, Newbury Park, 1987.

47. Cited in *Health and Safety at Work*, March 1988:5.

48. Brittan, Y., *The Impact of Water Pollution Control on Industry: A Case Study of Fifty Dischargers, op. cit.*, p. 47.

49. Stigler, G.J., "The Theory of Economic Regulation," *Bell Journal of Economics and Managerial Science*, no. 2 (Spring 1971).

50. *The Guardian*, 25 September 1988.

51. Carson, W.G., *The Other Price of Britain's Oil, op. cit.*

52. *The New York Times*, 2 April 1989.

53. Stover, W., "A Field Day for Legislators: Bhopal and its Effect on the Enactment of New Laws in the United States," in Smith, M. (ed.) *The Chemical Industry after Bhopal: An International Symposium held in London 7/8th November 1985,* IBC Technical Services Ltd., London, 1986.

54. *The New York Times*, 10 September 1989.

DISCUSSION QUESTIONS

1. What are some examples of *corporate reasoning*? What does Pearce have to say about this kind of rationale?

2. Should corporations be held legally responsible for accidents? Should they be tried in civil or criminal courts? Do you think that a chief executive officer (CEO) from a corporation should serve prison time for an infraction perpetrated by his or her company? What if the CEO had no knowledge of the event?

3. What points does Pearce make about the safest coal companies in the United States? How is the role of management important?

4. Discuss Pearce's points of reform for corporations. Do you agree or disagree with them? Why?

CHAPTER 20

The Ford Pinto Case and Beyond: Assessing Blame

Francis T. Cullen, William J. Maakestad
& Gray Cavender

In 1968 the President's Commission on Law Enforcement and Administration of Justice concluded that "the public tends to be indifferent to business crime or even to sympathize with the offenders who have been caught" (1968:84). Now some might question the accuracy of the commission's assessment; indeed, it appears that the public has never been quite so sanguine about white-collar crime as governmental officials and academicians have led us to believe (see Braithwaite, 1982a:732-733). Nevertheless, it would be too much to assert that the commission's evaluation of the views of the American citizenry was fully without empirical referent. For if the commission underestimated the willingness of the public to punish criminals of any sort, it was perhaps more correct in sensing that citizens had yet to define white-collar and corporate criminality as anything approaching a social problem.

KEY CONCEPTS:

corporate misconduct

political ethics

white-collar crime

By contrast, few social commentators today would seek to sustain the notion that the public considers upperworld illegality as "morally neutral conduct" (Kadish, 1963). To be sure, there are now and undoubtedly will continue to be calls for citizens both to sharpen their awareness of the dangers posed by the lawlessness of the rich and to demand that the state take steps to shield them from this victimization. Nonetheless, public awareness of white-collar and corporate crime has reached the point where the concept has become part of the common vernacular. Further, survey data indicate that the public judges such criminality to be more serious than ever before, is quite prepared to sanction

Adapted from Frances T. Cullen, William J. Maakestad and Gray Cavender, *Corporate Crime Under Attack: The Ford Pinto Case and Beyond* (Cincinnati, OH: Anderson Publishing Co.), 1989.

white-collar offenders, and is far more cognizant of the costs of upperworld crime than had been previously imagined (Cullen, Clark, et al., 1982; Cullen et al., 1982; Cullen et al., 1983).

In light of the events of the past decade and a half, the finding that upperworld crime has emerged as an increasingly salient social issue is not surprising. Indeed, during this time we have witnessed what Katz (1980) has termed "the social movement against white collar crime" (Clinard & Yeager, 1978:258-262; 1980:12-15). Thus with Watergate and Abscam representing the more celebrated examples, prosecutions for political corruption have climbed markedly (Katz, 1980:161-164). Similarly, consumer groups have scrutinized corporate activities and asked what officials planned to do to put a halt to "crime in the suites" (Nader and Green, 1972). Meanwhile, investigative news reporters and news shows such as "60 Minutes" have told us much about improprieties ranging from kickbacks to the illegal dumping of chemical wastes that endanger lives (Brown, 1980). Mistrust has run so deep that physicians are now suspected of fraudulent Medicaid schemes, and hence states have moved to establish enforcement agencies to combat this possibility (Cullen & Heiner, 1979; Pontell et al., 1982). In 1977 the notion that white-collar crime is a serious problem received further reification when U.S. Attorney General Griffin Bell remarked that he would make such illegality his "number one priority."

It is clear, then, that consciousness about upperworld lawlessness rose, perhaps substantially, since the President's Commission on Law Enforcement and Administration of Justice [President's Commission] (1968) characterized public opinion about such matters as essentially disinterested. However, it is equally important to be sensitive to the particular content that this consciousness came to assume. On the one hand the social movement Katz speaks of alerted people to the enormous costs incurred by white-collar crime (Conklin, 1977; Schrager and Short, 1978) yet it did much more than this: It provided the additional message that the rich and powerful could exact these harms with impunity. Consequently, questions of justice and moral right were immediately suggested. The matter was thus not merely one of preventing victimization but of confronting why crime allows "the rich to get richer and the poor to get prison" (Reiman, 1979). As Katz (1980:178-179) has observed:

> The demand supporting the movement to date has been much more than a utilitarian concern for the efficient deterrence of antisocial conduct. . . . In order to understand the expansion of "white collar crime," we must understand the demand that unjust enrichment and unjustly acquired power be made criminal; not just that it be made unprofitable but that it be defined officially as abominable, that it be treated as qualitatively alien to the basic moral character of society.

In short, a core element of the movement against white-collar crime was to assert that the harms committed by the more and less advantaged be subject to the same moral mandates, particularly within our courts. Of course the very attempt to reshape moral boundaries is itself a manifestation of broader changes in the social context of any historical era (Erikson, 1966; Gusfield, 1967; Farrell & Swigert, 1982:27-51). While a complicated matter, two circumstances would appear to have done much to encourage and structure the nature of the attack on upperworld criminality that has emerged in recent times.

First, the unfolding of the civil rights movement focused attention on the intimate link between social and criminal justice. Pernicious patterns of racism and class discrimination were thus seen to be reproduced within the legal system. In turn it became incumbent upon political elites to explain why such inequities were allowed to prevail in our courts. Significantly, a second circumstance made answering this charge of perpetuating injustice an essential task for those in government: the "legitimacy crisis" facing the state (Friedrichs, 1979). Indeed such poignant happenings as Attica, Kent State, Vietnam, and Watergate, as well as the failure of the "Great Society" programs to fulfill promises of greater distributive justice, all combined to shake people's trust in the benevolence of the government (Rothman, 1978). In response, elected officials (like Jimmy Carter) felt compelled to campaign on their integrity and to claim that they would not show favor to criminals of any class. That is, political elites, under the press of the call for "equal justice," were placed in the position of having to publicly support the notion that the harms of the rich be brought within the reach of the criminal law. And as Piven and Cloward (1971, 1977) have demonstrated, when necessity moves political elites to define existing arrangements as unfair, the possibility of a social movement to refashion the social order is greatly enhanced. It would thus appear that, at least in part, elite definitions lent legitimacy and helped give life to the movement against white-collar crime.

Now, in this social climate, the behavior of corporations took on new meaning. The world of big business was seen to suffer, in Durkheim's (1951) terms, from "chronic anomie," a breakdown of any sense of ethical regulation. It was thus common to encounter articles which first asked, "How lawless are big companies?" and then answered that "a surprising number of them have been involved in blatant illegalities" (Ross, 1980). What is more, these infringements of existing legal and administrative standards not only involved enormous and ostensibly intentional harm, but also were seen to be greeted only rarely with the full force of the criminal law. Corporate actors were thus depicted as readily sacrificing human well-being for unjustly acquired profits with little worry over paying any real price; meanwhile those who had the misfortune of stealing lesser amounts through more customary means could anticipate no immunity from state sanction.

Notably, such imagery helped to precipitate not only public discussion and popular accounts about corporate malfeasance (e.g., Vandivier, 1972; Rodgers, 1974; Stern, 1976; Caudill, 1977; Dowie, 1979; Wright, 1979), but a proliferation of scholarship on the topic as well (e.g., Fisse, 1971, 1973, 1981; Geis, 1972; Geis & Edelhertz, 1973; Coleman, 1975; Elkins, 1976; Kriesberg, 1976; Duchnick & Imhoff, 1978; Yoder, 1979; Braithwaite, 1979, 1982b; Kramer, 1979; Braithwaite & Geis, 1982). Typically these academic writings followed a pattern of initially identifying the large costs of corporate illegality and lamenting the failure of existing enforcement strategies to diminish this pressing problem. The commentary would then turn to a consideration of whether such activity should be brought under the umbrella of the criminal law. In particular, two issues were debated: (1) Should corporations and their executives be held responsible for unlawful acts just as street criminals are? (2) Will efforts to use criminal sanctions really result in a reduction of corporate illegality?

These latter concerns as well as those discussed previously furnish a context for understanding both the very occurrence and importance of Ford Motor Company's prosecution for reckless homicide by the State of Indiana. It appears that the Ford Pinto case was very much a child of the times; succinctly stated, it is doubtful that Ford would have been brought to trial during a previous era. Yet, as the case is best seen as a manifestation of the broad movement against white-collar crime—and, in particular, against corporate crime—it is also unique in the legal precedent it set, the publicity it received, and in the opportunity it provides to examine how more theoretical insights on corporate responsibility and control are shaped by the realities of the courtroom.

With these issues in mind the current endeavor attempts to present a case study of Ford's prosecution.[1] To be more exact, four matters are discussed below: Why was an indictment brought against Ford in Indiana? Why did the courts permit a corporation itself to be tried for a criminal offense? What transpired at the trial? And what will be the meaning of the case in the time ahead?

ASSESSING BLAME

On August 10, 1978, Judy and Lyn Ulrich and their cousin visiting from Illinois, Donna Ulrich, set out to play volleyball at a church some twenty miles away. While on U.S. Highway 33 in northern Indiana, the yellow 1973 Pinto they were driving was struck in the rear by a van. Within seconds their car was engulfed in flames. Two of the teenagers, trapped inside the vehicle, died quickly; the driver, Judy was thrown clear of the blazing Pinto with third-degree burns on more than 95 percent of her body. Though conscious following the accident, she died at a hospital eight hours later (Strobel, 1980).

As might be anticipated, the accident stunned those who witnessed the aftermath of the crash and soon sent shock waves throughout the local community of Elkhart. Yet, like many other fatal collisions, this might have been defined exclusively as a tragedy. Or, if wrongdoing was involved, law enforcement officials might have prosecuted the driver of the van. Indeed, as a 21-year-old who had just recently reacquired a suspended license and who was driving a van which was labeled "Peace Train" and contained half-empty beer bottles as well as the remains of marijuana cigarettes scattered on the floor, he would have made a likely candidate to take the rap.

However, both the particulars of the accident and the tenor of the times led the blame to be placed elsewhere. In particular the observations of State Trooper Neil Graves were crucial in determining that this was not a "normal crime"

(Sudnow, 1965). After arriving at the scene of the crash, Graves discovered that gasoline had somehow soaked the front floorboard of the car. He found as well that the van had sustained only minor damage, and its driver, Richard Duggar, was only mildly injured. By contrast, the Ulrichs' Pinto was viciously crushed in the rear and, of course, badly charred. This oddity was made even more poignant when eyewitnesses reported that the van was not speeding and that it looked initially like the accident was going to be nothing more than a fender-bender (Strobel, 1980).

These inconsistencies might have been set aside had it not been that Trooper Graves recalled reading an exposé about the Pinto some months before. This piece, written by Mark Dowie (1977) and entitled "Pinto Madness," alleged that the placement of the gas tank on the Pinto constituted a lethal hazard. Specifically, Dowie noted that the location of the tank adjacent to the rear bumper made it highly susceptible to puncture by the fender's bolts during a rear-end collision. In turn, this meant that the Pinto would experience considerable fuel leakage and hence fires when hit even at low speeds.

Yet this is not all that Dowie claimed. Far more controversial was his assertion that Ford was fully aware of this problem in the initial stages of production but chose not to fix the Pinto's defect because it was not cost efficient. To bolster this conclusion, he presented secret Ford memoranda which revealed that the financial loss of a recall exceeded the loss incurred as the result of injuries and fatalities "associated with crash-induced fuel leakage and fires." In the name of profit, Dowie believed, "for seven years the Ford Motor Company sold cars in which it knew hundreds of people would needlessly burn to death."[2]

Sensitized to the potential dangers of the Pinto, Graves was thus aware that the blame for the accident might rest with Ford. This sentiment was reinforced when he began to receive calls from news reporters around the country inquiring about the crash and the possibility that the fuel tank defect may have been responsible for the deaths of the three teenagers. Meanwhile, Michael A. Cosentino, Elkhart County's State's Attorney, was apprised of the accident. When he had an opportunity to review photographs of the crash, he too was troubled by the discrepancy between the minimal damage to the van and the wreckage of the Ulrich girls' Pinto. And then there was the emotional, human side to the accident: the pictures of the charred remains of the victims and the reality that three teenagers had suffered a terrible death (Strobel, 1980; Cosentino interview).

As a 41-year-old conservative Republican county prosecutor, Cosentino was an unlikely candidate to try to bring Ford Motor Company within the reach of the criminal law. Like many people at this time, he had heard about the problems associated with the Pinto and about the recall of the car that Ford had begun earlier in the summer. However, he had not read Dowie's article, and he was not inclined to attack corporations because of an ideological persuasion that they constituted a menace to society. Indeed, even now, Cosentino is convinced that the civil law should be used to deal with "99 percent" of all cases involving alleged corporate misbehavior (Cosentino interview).

Yet in light of the facts surrounding the accident and of conversations with Neil Graves (who by this time had called and talked with Mark Dowie), Cosentino could not easily put the matter aside. He was aware as well that Indiana's revised criminal code, which had become effective on October 1, 1977, less than a year before the accident, contained a provision for the offense of "reckless homicide." Section 35-42-1-5 of the Indiana Code thus read: "A person who recklessly kills another human being commits reckless homicide." Taken together, these considerations led Cosentino to wonder whether the Ford Motor Company could or should be criminally prosecuted. Because of the novelty of the case, the power of Ford, and the difficulty of piercing the corporate veil, Cosentino did not seriously consider prosecuting individual Ford executives (Cosentino interview).

Cosentino, however, set out to explore whether Ford could in fact be prosecuted under Indiana law. Since Section 35-41-1-2 of the penal code included "corporation" under its definition of "person," his staff reported that a prosecution was legally permissible. This conclusion was corroborated by William Conour of the Indiana Prosecuting Attorney's Office, who had been involved in drafting the reckless homicide statute (Strobel, 1980).

But even though the potential for prosecution seemed to exist, the question remained whether Ford really should be charged with a criminal offense. Research conducted by Cosentino and his staff suggested that it should be. Particularly influential were the conversations with and documents supplied by those involved in civil judgments against Ford. The prosecutor was in contact, for example, with automobile experts who had testified against Ford in civil hearings and with Mark Robinson, who was the lawyer in the Alan Grimshaw case.[3] As the evidence from these varied sources who had been close to the Pinto scene accumulated, it became clear that Ford knew that its Pinto was defective and chose to risk human life by not moving quickly to fix it. Thoughts of criminal culpability did not seem out of place in this context.

It is important to note here that, without the mounting attention concerning Ford's handling of the Pinto, it would have been unlikely that Cosentino would have come to blame Ford for the deaths of the three teenagers. Had the accident occurred several years before, he might have been forced, perhaps reluctantly, to put aside the peculiarities of the crash and move on to other cases. Yet now the social climate worked against this option and, alternatively, made a criminal prosecution seem plausible, if not obligatory. By August of 1978 the attack against Ford and its Pinto had emerged as a "symbolic crusade" (Gusfield, 1967), a movement aimed at showing that Ford, like other powerful corporations, felt comfortable in operating outside accepted moral boundaries in its irresponsible pursuit of profit. Ford's handling of the Pinto thus came to symbolize what was wrong with corporate America.

In general terms Dowie's (1977) "Pinto Madness" article, its release trumpeted at a press conference sponsored by Ralph Nader, signaled the beginning of the "crusade" against Ford. With concern over corporate crime running high,

Dowie's article earned national exposure. In February of 1978 the movement intensified still further with the announcement of the exorbitant financial damages awarded in the Grimshaw civil case. At the same time the National Highway Traffic Safety Administration (NHTSA), a federal regulatory body, had undertaken tests on the Pinto. In May of 1978, NHTSA notified Ford that there had been "an initial determination of the existence of a safety-related defect" (quoted in Strobel, 1980:23). Denying any wrongdoing but faced with pressure on all sides, Ford subsequently issued a recall of all Pintos manufactured from 1971-1976 and all 1975-1976 Bobcats, a total of 1.5 million cars (Strobel, 1980). As might be expected, this series of events sparked a marked escalation in the focus placed by the media on Pinto issues (Swigert and Farrell, 1980-1981). Indeed, it was clear that reporters had come to view the Ford Pinto matter as a fascinating and eminently newsworthy upperworld scandal.

Thus it is significant that Mike Cosentino confronted the Ulrichs' tragic accident in the midst of a general crusade against Ford, for in several ways this necessarily shaped what the case could and did come to mean to him. First, unlike the traffic fatalities he had processed in the past, the numerous calls that his office and Neil Graves received from reporters across the nation alerted him, if only vaguely at the start, to the fact that any Pinto crash was potentially of national concern. Second, the movement against Ford, while certainly informal and unorganized, nevertheless created invaluable informational networks. This meant that in a matter of days Cosentino acquired revealing documents and expert feedback from parties who harbored strong sentiments against Ford. Under normal circumstances, such material would have either been unavailable or taken months to uncover, a task beyond the resources of a county prosecutor. Third, the ideological framework of the Pinto crusade provided the conservative state's attorney with a vocabulary about the case that encouraged a response by the criminal law. As Swigert and Farrell (1980-1981) have demonstrated, accounts of the Pinto appearing at this time increasingly characterized Ford as willfully and without repentance inflicting harm on innocent citizens. In a sense, then, Ford was being designated as a sociopath which knew no social responsibility.

In short Cosentino quickly learned that the death of the Ulrich girls was not a local or isolated occurrence and that Ford, like the worst of criminals, endangered its victims not inadvertently but intentionally. He was aware as well that evidence existed that made a prosecution feasible. Taken together, these considerations personally convinced Cosentino that Ford had acted recklessly and should be prosecuted. Again he did not wish to initiate a campaign calling for the use of criminal sanctions to deal with all corporate wrongdoing. However, it was manifest to him that Ford had been largely unaffected by traditional forms of control; after all, Ford's conduct surrounding the Pinto had already triggered nearly every legal response possible other than criminal prosecution: civil cases involving compensatory damages, civil cases involving both compensatory and punitive damages, and federal administrative agency actions. In absence of effective regulation and where corporate behavior is so outrageous as to affront moral sensibilities, Cosentino could see the application of the criminal law as appropriate. And from what he knew of the Pinto case, it seemed that this was just such an instance, where justice demanded that a corporation be held criminally responsible for its behavior (Cosentino interview; Maakestad, forthcoming). However, the very novelty of this idea caused Cosentino to exercise caution. While he believed that Ford should be indicted and that he possessed the authority to do so, he was not certain that the community would support such a prosecution. Consequently, he convened a grand jury to consider an indictment under the reckless homicide statute. From the beginning of the hearing, Cosentino consciously made every effort not to sway the grand jury one way or the other (Cosentino interview). Nevertheless, after entertaining testimony from both Ford officials and safety experts who had previously served as witnesses in civil cases against Ford, the grand jury unanimously returned indictments against Ford Motor Company for three counts of reckless homicide. In essence, the six-member panel agreed with Cosentino that there was sufficient evidence to believe that Ford had acted with moral irresponsibility. Swigert and Farrell (1980-1981:180) captured this point when they wrote:

> The indictment against Ford may be viewed as an attempt on the part of the state to assert moral integrity in the face of enemy deviation. In its decision to contest civil suits, the corporation refused to recognize that moral boundaries had been transgressed. This opened the way to a definition of the manufacturer as a force against whom the power of the law must be directed.[4]

GETTING TO TRIAL

Word of Ford's indictment immediately received front-page attention in newspapers across the nation. It now appeared that Ford Motor Company, at that moment the fourth largest corporation in the world (Clinard & Yeager, 1980:3), would go to trial for reckless homicide. While a guilty verdict would bring only a $30,000 fine ($10,000 on each count), company officials viewed the prospect of a trial with considerable consternation. With Pinto sales already down 40 percent, due to the recent recall, a lengthy, highly publicized criminal case could only serve to erode still further consumer confidence in the car and, more generally, in the corporation. Equally troubling was that a prosecution could encourage state's attorneys elsewhere to bring criminal charges against the company and alert other Pinto victims (or surviving families) to the fact that Ford should be held civilly liable for burn injuries occurring in rear-end collisions (Strobel, 1980). Moreover, executives realized that a criminal conviction would be powerful evidence of Ford's culpability in any subsequent civil suits. With the potential costs of a prosecution running high, Ford thus quickly mobilized to see that the case would never come before a jury.

The task of preventing a trial was given to the prestigious Chicago law firm of Mayer, Brown, and Platt. With a ten-member team assigned to the case, the result of the firm's efforts was a 55-page motion which argued that the criminal indictment should be dismissed on both conceptual and constitutional grounds. In fashioning a response to this attack, Cosentino and his small staff realized that they could well benefit from additional assistance. However, all such help would have to come from volunteers. Cosentino had asked Elkhart County for a special fund of $20,000 to try the case, and he had promised not to request any additional moneys. This figure would have to be stretched far in the fight against Ford; in fact, Cosentino would eventually spend money of his own to defray expenses (Strobel, 1980). Yet, given the prevailing social context, finding law professors to join the prosecution's team did not prove overly difficult. After all, corporate liability and the criminal law was a "hot topic," and the Pinto case obviously possessed both important national and legal ramifications. Again, whether a local prosecutor could have so readily acquired such expert assistance in a previous decade or on a different case is questionable. Bruce Berner, one of the two law professors who worked full time on the case,[5] wrote that "originally, of course, I got involved because of the novel legal questions presented by the indictment." However, it should also be realized that, after agreeing to become part of the prosecution's staff, the appeal of legal novelties was not all that sustained the commitment of volunteers to the case. There was also and always the reality of the horrible deaths of the Ulrich girls. In Berner's words (letter to author, February 21, 1982):

> It was only after I became involved that I saw the photographs [of the girls following the crash] and met the families of the girls. It is nevertheless hard for me to separate the motivating force of the legal issues from that of the personal aspect of the tragedy. . . . Part of what we were saying is that a corporation like all other persons must be forced at all times to look at the very personal tragedies it causes. It seems to me that Ford's whole effort in keeping the pictures of the girls out of evidence, including the pictures of them while they were alive, was in part a way to disconnect themselves from what they had wrought to some very nice people. All I can say about the "Car Wars" photos was that they made me ill and that I cannot, to this day, get them out of my head.[6]

While numerous arguments were voiced in the debate over whether Ford could be brought to trial, the continued vitality of the indictment hinged on two central issues (Maakestad, 1980, 1981). To begin with, Ford's legal brief contended that conceptually the reckless homicide statute could not be applied to corporate entities. For one thing the statute defines the offense as "a person who recklessly kills another human being." Ford claimed in turn that the meaning of "another" was "one of the same kind." Consequently, since the victim is referred to as "another human being," it followed that the perpetrator of the crime must also be human (Clark, 1979). For another thing, the brief asserted that the use of the word "person" in other places in the criminal code clearly is not meant to apply to corporations. Conceptual consistency thus would preclude corporations from being charged with violently oriented offenses like reckless homicide. Quoting Ford's memorandum:

> There are numerous examples in the Criminal Code where the legis-lature has used the word "person" to refer exclusively to human beings. See, e.g., the section prohibiting rape. . . . ("A person who knowingly or intentionally has sexual intercourse with a member of the opposite sex . . .") Thus, although corporations may generally be covered by the definition of "persons," there are clearly crimes—essentially crimes of violence against other human beings—where it is irrational to read the statutes as applying to corporations.

In response to this line of reasoning, the prosecution initially turned to the penal code itself. First, it observed that the code distinguishes between a "per-son" ("a human being, corporation, partnership, unincorporated association, or governmental entity") and a "human being" ("an individual who is born and alive"). Because the statute defines reckless homicide as a "person who reck-lessly kills another human being," rather than as a "human being who reckless-ly kills another human being," it is evident that the legislative intent here is to encompass corporate behavior. Second, the prosecution noted that the Indiana criminal code explicitly reads that a corporation "may be prosecuted for any offense . . . if it is proved that the offense was committed by its agent within the scope of his authority." Finally, the state's brief dismissed the idea that "corpo-rations" cannot physically commit violent crimes like rape and homicide by emphasizing the realities of the corporation as a legal fiction:

> The major premise that "person" cannot include corporation in the rape statute is simply incorrect. This argument patently exploits the corporate fiction. It attempts to show corporate inability to commit rape. . . . Of course, a corporation cannot itself engage in sexual inter-course; a corporation cannot itself do anything. As it is a fictional per-son, it can act only through its natural-person agents. A corporation has no genitals, to be sure, but neither does it have a trigger finger, a hand to forge a check, an arm to extend a bribe nor a mind to form an intent or to "consciously disregard" the safety of others. Nevertheless, a corporation is liable for all crimes of its agents acting within their authority. The unlikelihood of corporate rape liability is because sex-ual intercourse by its agents will almost always be outside the scope of their authority—not because the crime is definitionally ridiculous.

Apart from conceptual considerations Ford maintained that there were two constitutional barriers to its being brought to trial. First, there was the matter that the National Traffic and Motor Vehicle Safety Act had already created a federal apparatus to supervise the automobile industry. Consequently, Ford argued, Con-gress intended that this system would preempt any state, including Indiana, from regulating the same field. In rebuttal, the prosecution argued that the federal mea-sure was not invoked to deprive states of their police power, and they observed that Ford was unable to cite "a single case where a traditional, general criminal statute was found to have been preempted by a federal regulatory scheme."

Yet there was a second, more serious constitutional matter raised by Ford's lawyers: the ex post facto provision of both the Indiana and U.S. Constitutions. As may be recalled, the revised Indiana code which contained the new reckless homicide crime category became law only on October 1, 1977. Moreover, it was not until July 1, 1978—41 days prior to the Ulrichs' crash—that the reckless homicide offense was amended to include acts of omission as well as commission. Significantly, it is the amended version of the statute which was employed to indict Ford. In light of these two dates, Ford reminded the court that it was being charged with recklessly designing and manufacturing a car that was a 1973 model. It was thus being prosecuted for an act that had transpired several years before enactment of the very law under which it was being charged. Even if its acts were reckless, such ex post facto application of the law constitutionally barred prosecution.

The prosecution assaulted Ford's logic on two fronts. First, issue was taken with Ford's interpretation of when its offense occurred. Contrary to Ford's assertions, the prosecution argued that it is the date the offense is completed, not the date of the first element of the crime, that determines whether ex post facto provisions have been violated. Thus, since the accident postdated the reckless homicide law, the company was potentially subject to criminal sanction. Second, the prosecution maintained that the defendant's omissions in regard to its obligation to either repair the Ulrichs' 1973 Pinto or warn them of the car's hazards were important elements of the offense. That is, Ford was being charged with reckless homicide not only for an act of commission (building a dangerous vehicle), but for an act of omission (ignoring its duty to protect owners from the Pinto's known dangers). The prosecution then went on to propose that once either proscribed acts or omissions are shown to have taken place after a criminal statute is enacted, all of the defendant's prior acts and omissions can properly and constitutionally be considered by the court.

On February 2, 1979, Judge Donald W. Jones succinctly rendered his decision: "There are substantial factors in this case for which there are no precedents. The indictment is sufficient. I therefore deny the motion to dismiss" (quoted in Strobel, 1980:55). In large part Judge Jones embraced the prosecution's reasoning, agreeing that Indiana law does permit a corporation to be charged for reckless homicide and that federal regulatory statutes did not in this instance preempt the state's rights to seek retributive and deterrent goals unique to the criminal sanction. However, he was only partially persuaded by the prosecution's thoughts on the ex post facto aspects of the case, and thus he attempted to clarify exactly what Ford could and could not be tried under.

In essence Jones's ruling declared that since the vehicle was marketed in 1973, Ford could not be charged for recklessly designing and manufacturing the Pinto. Instead, its actions with regard to the actual production of the Pinto were relevant only to the extent that they constituted antecedents for Ford's alleged recklessness in repairing the vehicle. Alternatively, Ford could be charged with

failure to fulfill its obligation to repair, because such recklessness could potentially have occurred in the 41 days between the enactment of the omission
amendment to the reckless homicide statute on July 1 and the Ulrich girls' deaths
on August 10.

The problems surrounding the ex post facto issue clearly complicated the
prosecution's case. At least in theory it would no longer be sufficient to convince
the jury that Ford had recklessly assembled the Pinto. To be sure, this much
would have to be proven in order to show that Ford knew its product was unsafe
and thus had a duty to warn its customers, including the Ulrichs, of this fact.
However, Ford could now only be convicted if it could also be revealed that the
company had recklessly ignored its duty to inform the Ulrichs of the Pinto's
dangers in the period following July 1.

In sum, with the help of law professors and other volunteers, Cosentino had
succeeded in getting Ford to trial. However, the legal constraints on his case, the
realities of the courtroom, and the resources at his opponent's disposal would
make getting a conviction another matter.

TRYING FORD

Ford's failure to quash the indictment taught the company that their foes
were perhaps more formidable than initially imagined. It was now manifest that
nothing could be spared in order to avert the shame of a criminal stigmatization.
In particular, Ford's lawyers would be given a blank check; they would be free
to craft the best defense money could buy.

For Ford two orders of business were immediately at hand. First, there was
the crucial matter of whom to select to head the defense team. The choice proved
to be a wise, if expensive, one; James J. Neal, a former special prosecutor during Watergate.[7] The second pressing concern was to move Cosentino off his
home turf by securing a change of venue. Based on evidence gathered from a
survey of Elkhart residents about the case (commissioned by Ford) and the testimony of $1000-a-day consultant Hans Zeisel (co-author with Harry Kalven of
The American Jury), Ford argued that it could not receive a fair trial in Elkhart.[8]
Judge Jones agreed, and the case was moved to Winamac, a town of 2450 locat-
ed in Pulaski County some 55 miles southwest. Sixty-year-old Judge Harold
Staffeldt would preside over the trial (Strobel, 1980).

The move to Winamac and the additional living expenses this entailed further strained the prosecution's budget; Cosentino himself would shoulder much
of this new burden. However, as would become evident throughout the trial,
there appeared to be no limit to the resources that Ford was able and willing to
devote to its defense. The cost of the survey employed to justify the change of
venue itself approximated the entire Cosentino budget. Other facts are equally
revealing. For instance, after the place of the trial became known Ford quickly
made an attractive offer to and succeeded in retaining a local Winamac lawyer

who was a close friend of Judge Staffeldt and who had practiced with the judge for 22 years. Similarly, the bill for housing the Ford defense team, which at times reached 40, ran to $27,000 a month. Later they would undertake additional crash tests on Pintos at a cost of around $80,000. Importantly, they were also able to purchase daily transcripts of the trial at $9 a page, with the total expenditure for the trial transcripts being $50,000 (Strobel, 1980). Since the complexity and length of the trial meant that a private firm supplied the court stenographers and thus that the transcripts were not available free to the prosecution, budgetary constraints precluded Cosentino from having access to this material. In his opinion the inability to review previous testimony (e.g., to prepare for cross-examination) was one of the largest disadvantages plaguing the prosecution (Cosentino interview). In the end it is estimated that Ford may have spent anywhere from $1.5 million to $2 million on its defense.

In launching its case, the prosecution wanted to impress upon the members of the jury that they were not merely dealing with statistical casualties; like other homicide cases, they were being asked to assess whether Ford should be held responsible for the horrible burn deaths of three vibrant teenagers. James Neal, however, fully realized that it would be important to neutralize this emotional factor. In a skillful maneuver he thus submitted a document which first admitted that the Ulrich girls had died as a result of burns and then declared that there was no need for the jury to see the grotesque pictures of or hear testimony about the girls' charred bodies. The prosecution countered that Neal was endeavoring to "sanitize" the girls' deaths and that it is common practice to present evidence on cause of death in a homicide trial. Somewhat amazingly, Judge Staffeldt agreed with Neal and prevented the jury from seeing or hearing about what the reality of the crash entailed. Stymied on this front, the emotional advantage of the prosecution was largely confined to the remarks of the victims' mother, Mrs. Mattie Ulrich, who told the court that she would have gotten rid of the Pinto had she known of its dangers. She then remarked that she had in fact received notice of the Pinto recall; however, it came to her house in February of 1979, several months after the crash in which her two daughters and niece had perished (Strobel, 1980).

Despite this setback the prosecution remained optimistic. After all, the foundation of its case was not erected upon the angle of playing on the jurors' sympathies. Instead, Cosentino felt that the Pinto had a defective fuel tank placement. This material included internal Ford memos and documents commenting on the Pinto's safety as well as the results of crash tests on 1971 and 1972 models, conducted by Ford and the government, showing that the vehicle exploded in flames at low impact speeds. These tests would be crucial, Cosentino reasoned, because they revealed that in planning the production of the 1973 Pinto, Ford had concrete evidence of the car's defects yet chose not to rectify them. Moreover, Cosentino did not have crash tests at low speeds for the 1973 model, and his tight budget precluded his conducting them at this stage.

Recognizing the damaging nature of this evidence, Neal moved quickly to challenge the admission of any testimony or tests that were not directly related to the 1973 Pinto, the model year of the Ulrichs' car. In a series of rulings over the course of the trial, Judge Staffeldt concurred with Neal and barred nearly all materials that predated 1973. Needless to say, this had the result of seriously undermining the state's case. In the end, only a small percentage, perhaps as low as 5 percent, of the documents the prosecution had compiled were admitted as evidence (Anderson, 1981:370, n.20).

The judge's reluctance to permit the jury to consider the totality of the prosecution's case points up the difficulty of transporting what has traditionally been a product liability case from civil into criminal court. To a large extent it appears that the rural judge was never fully comfortable in knowing how this was to be done. Indeed, his grabbing onto 1973 as his evidentiary standard reveals that he either did not fully comprehend the logic of the prosecution's case or did not embrace the legal theory on which it was based. It seems that he wished to treat the 1973 Pinto as he would any other weapon in a homicide case: Since it was this weapon that caused the crime, evidence on other weapons was irrelevant. Of course, at the heart of the prosecution's case was the understanding that Ford's recklessness with regard to the 1973 Pinto was intimately contingent on what the corporation had done in its product development of the car line in the previous years. Whether rightly or wrongly, Judge Staffeldt failed to appreciate this distinction between the recklessness of corporate decisionmaking and that involved in more traditional forms of criminality.

Now with much of its case set aside, the prosecution presented two major lines of argument to the jury. First, it called in auto safety experts, including a former Ford executive who testified that the fuel tank on the Pinto was placed in a potentially lethal position. Second, Cosentino relied upon eyewitnesses to prove that Duggar's van was traveling at 50 miles per hour or less and that the Ulrichs' Pinto was still moving when hit from behind. Taken together, these facts indicated that the speed differential at the moment of impact was around 30. In turn, establishing this low differential was crucial to the prosecution's case because it explained both why so little damage was done to the van and why the girls died from their burns but not from injuries sustained in the crash, as would be expected in a high-velocity collision. Most importantly, however, it showed that the Pinto the girls were driving exploded despite being hit at a relatively low speed. The implication was thus clear: Because of Ford's reckless construction of the Pinto, three girls died in an accident that should have been little more than a fender-bender.

Having done much to diminish the force of the prosecution's case, James Neal began Ford's defense by vigorously rejecting the claim that the Pinto was an unsafe vehicle. For instance, Neal brought his own automotive experts before the jury to testify that the 1973 Pinto met prevailing federal automotive standards and was just as safe as comparable subcompacts manufactured at that time. He also produced Ford executives who testified that they had such faith in the car that they had purchased Pintos for members of their own families. Neal then challenged the prosecution's version of the speed differential between the van and the Ulrichs' Pinto. Crucial in this regard were the dramatic accounts of two surprise witnesses; both claimed that prior to her death in the hospital Judy Ulrich had said that her car was stopped on the highway. If so, the speed at impact would have been 50 miles per hour, a collision that no small car could have withstood. This reasoning was given added credence when Ford presented newly conducted crash tests which showed that at 50 miles per hour a van would sustain only minimal damage despite the large crushing effect it exerted on the rear of the Pinto. Neal thus concluded from this that the small front-end wreckage of Duggar's van was not evidence of a low-impact accident but was normal, even at speeds exceeding 50 (Strobel, 1980).

The defense also took pains to remind the jurors that Ford itself had voluntarily agreed to recall the Pinto two months before the Ulrich accident and thus during all 41 days following the enactment of the omission amendment to the reckless homicide statute. Ford employees testified that during this period the company had pressured them to contact Pinto owners about the recall as quickly as possible. To accomplish this task, workers were given overtime pay, and airplanes were used to hurry recall kits across the nation. With 1.5 million customers it was not surprising, though of course terribly regrettable, that the Ulrichs' notification did not arrive until February 1979. Indeed, Ford had done everything feasible to warn Pinto owners; it certainly had not been reckless in this duty (Strobel, 1980).

After four days of exhausting deliberations, the jurors returned their verdict: not guilty. The initial vote was 8-4 to acquit. Twenty-five ballots later, the final holdout changed his mind and joined the majority. Some on the jury felt that the hazards of the Pinto were basically inherent in all small cars and that owners took certain risks when they chose a vehicle that was less costly and consequently less sturdy. A number of other jurors, however, were convinced that Ford had marketed a defective automobile, but that the prosecution simply had not proven that the corporation was reckless in its recall efforts during the 41 days in which it was criminally liable (Strobel, 1980). Regardless, the ten-week Ford Pinto trial was now over. As might be anticipated, there was much jubilation and relief at Ford headquarters in Dearborn, Michigan (*Time*, 1980). Meanwhile, Cosentino and his staff were left to contemplate the bitterness of an unsuccessful crusade and to wonder what might have occurred had a different judge presided over the case and the prosecution not been burdened by a tight budget and ex post facto considerations.

CONCLUSION: THE FORD PINTO CASE

The Ford Pinto trial was regularly hailed in the media as "one of the most significant criminal court trials in American corporate history" (*Newsweek*, 1980). This notoriety clearly signifies the uniqueness of the case. While Ford's prosecution was not totally devoid of legal precedents (Maakestad, 1981), it was certainly the most poignant example of a corporation being brought within the reach of the criminal law for allegedly visiting violence upon innocent citizens (Anderson, 1981). In this light it thus provided a rare and concrete glimpse of the power that corporations can bring to bear in order to avoid conviction. Similarly, it revealed that prosecution of corporations for offenses of a product liability type will necessarily involve legal theories with which participants in the criminal justice system are only vaguely familiar and perhaps find inappropriate for their arena. Indeed, from an ideological standpoint, the potential for irony here is pronounced: We can expect conservative jurists now to be inclined to look favorably on the rights of the defendant (the corporation) and their more liberal brethren to furnish a more generous interpretation of the prerogatives enjoyed by the state. Finally, the very fact of prosecution is notable not merely for its role in bolstering formal legal precedent but in breaking psychological barriers. The legal community is now sensitized to the possibility that companies that recklessly endanger the physical well-being of the public may, even by a local state's attorney, be held criminally responsible for their conduct.

Yet the special character of the Pinto case should not mask the realization that Ford's prosecution was very much a social product. As argued earlier, the more general crusade against the Pinto, itself a manifestation of a broader movement attacking corporate crime that sought to question the appropriate moral boundaries of corporate behavior, was integral in creating the opportunity for Cosentino to prosecute Ford. In turn this perspective suggests that the ultimate, long-range meaning of the Pinto trial may depend less on the legal precedent that has been set and more on the nature of the social context that comes to prevail. That is, will the time ahead sustain the movement against corporate crime and thus encourage attempts to build upon the Pinto prosecution, or will concern with upperworld illegality diminish any interest in criminally sanctioning corporations commensurately decline?

The answer to the question is by no means certain. To be sure, the Reagan Administration moved to reinterpret the moral character of corporate America and to officially clarify what "real" crime is (Reiman, 1979). Thus Reagan's loosening of regulatory controls on business was accompanied by a renewed concern over violent street crimes and the trafficking of drugs; meanwhile, white-collar and corporate criminality were placed on the back burner (Gordon, 1980; Cullen & Wozniak, 1982). Notably, like many of his other social policies, Reagan's crime control agenda was informed by his implicit view of human nature: the productive respond to incentives (opportunities for profit), while the unproductive respond to punishments, thus the need for harsh sanctions for the crimes of the poor (Piven and Cloward, 1982:39).

However, these policies and the sentiments that underlie them may very well have the unanticipated consequence of fueling the public's concern over upperworld lawlessness. The ostensible failure of Reagan's domestic programs to effect promised benefits for working people made his administration susceptible to charges of injustice, an image that Democrats across the nation constantly tried to make more salient. In this climate, sensitivity to collusion between government and big business, as in the EPA incident involving the dumping of chemical wastes, should run high (*Time,* 1983). Corporate conduct should thus remain a matter of continuing public concern, and in turn it will be difficult for the state to retain legitimacy if it chooses to ignore flagrant affronts to existing moral boundaries. If this analysis is correct, we should see additional, if only intermittent, criminal prosecutions within the immediate future of corporations who persist in recklessly endangering the public's well-being.

NOTES

1. The account of the Pinto case presented here was drawn from four sources: (1) several telephone interviews by the authors with prosecutor Michael Cosentino; these were conducted in late February 1983; (2) the personal observations of one of the authors, William J. Maakestad, who served as Special Deputy Prosecuting Attorney during the case; (3) the detailed information compiled by newsman Lee Strobel (1980) in his fascinating chronicle of the case; and (4) news reports and scholarly commentary written about the trial. Please note that data taken from the talks with Cosentino is cited in the text as "Cosentino interview."

2. The estimated cost of fixing the fuel tank defect has generally been placed at $11, though the price has at times been set as low as $6. Also it should be noted that the memo printed by Dowie in which Ford calculated the costs of fixing the Pinto versus the financial loss due to death and injury pertained to problems in the fuel tank during rollover tests conducted by Ford and not during rear-end crash tests. Nevertheless, the mode of thinking suggested by the memo vividly reinforces Dowie's point that, with regard to the Pinto, profit was more important to Ford than consumer safety.

3. In this latter instance, Grimshaw, who had undergone over 50 operations to correct burn injuries suffered during a Pinto crash-turned-inferno, was awarded $2.8 million in compensatory damages and $125 million in punitive damages (reduced to a total of $6.6 million two weeks after the trial).

4. Interestingly, Swigert and Farrell reached this conclusion without talking with Cosentino. Thus, while their observations were drawn from a broad understanding of the social meaning of the case, their comments captured much of what was going on inside prosecutor Consentino's mind.

5. Berner was on the law faculty at Valparaiso. The second professor working full time on the case was Terry Kiely of DePaul University. A few other lawyers, including author William Maakestad, also volunteered substantial amounts of time at points in the case. Finally, Berner and Kiely recruited up to 15 law students to conduct research and otherwise assist the prosecution.

6. During the course of the trial, tired members of the prosecution's team, especially the law students helping with research, would look at the post-crash photographs of the girls in order to remember what the case was really about and hence bolster their resolve to continue working.

7. As Strobel (1980:60) noted, Neal's salary in other cases is reputed to have been as much as $800,000.

8. The survey showed that 56% of the residents sampled felt that Ford was either guilty or probably guilty (Strobel, 1980:66). Interestingly, Cosentino believed that about half his community initially supported the idea of prosecuting Ford, while the other half thought he was "crazy." However, by the time of the trial, it was his perception that the vast majority of his constituents were in his camp (Cosentino interview).

REFERENCES

Anderson, D. (1981). "Corporate Homicide: The Stark Realities of Artificial Beings and Legal Fictions." *Pepperdine Law Review* 8: 367-417.

Braithwaite, J. (1979). "Transnational Corporations and Corruption: Towards Some International Solutions," *International Journal of Sociology of Law* 7: 125-142.

Braithwaite, J. (1980). "Inegalitarian Consequences of Egalitarian Reforms to Control Corporate Crime," *Temple Law Quarterly* 53: 1127-1146.

Braithwaite, J. (1982a). "Challenging Just Deserts: Punishing White Collar Criminals," *Journal of Criminal Law and Criminology* 73 (Summer): 723-763.

Braithwaite, J. (1982b). "Enforced Self-Regulation: A New Strategy for Corporate Crime Control," *Michigan Law Review* 80 (June): 1466-1507.

Braithwaite, J. & G. Geis (1982). "On Theory and Action for Corporate Crime Control," *Crime and Delinquency* 28 (April): 292-314.

Brown, M. (1980). *Laying Waste: The Poisoning of America by Toxic Chemicals.* New York: Pantheon.

Caudill, H. (1977). "Manslaughter in a Coal Mine." *Nation* 224 (April 23): 492-497.

Clark, G. (1979). "Corporate Homicide: A New Assault on Corporate Decision-Making." *Notre Dame Lawyer* 54 (June): 911-924.

Clinard, M. & P. Yeager (1978). "Corporate Crime: Issues in Research." *Criminology* 16 (August): 255-272.

Clinard, M. & P. Yeager (1980). *Corporate Crime.* New York: Free Press.

Clinard, M., P. Yeager, J. Brissette, D. Petrashek & E. Harries (1979). *Illegal Corporate Behavior.* Washington DC: Government Printing Office.

Coleman, B. (1975). "Is Corporate Criminal Liability Really Necessary?" *Southwestern Law Journal* 29: 908-927.

Conklin, J. (1977). *Illegal but Not Criminal: Business Crime in America.* Englewood Cliffs, NJ: Prentice-Hall.

Cullen, F. & K. Heiner (1979). "Provider Medicaid Fraud: A Note on White-Coat Crime." Presented at the annual meeting of the American Society of Criminology.

Cullen, F. & J. Wozniak (1982). "Fighting the Appeal of Repression." *Crime and Social Justice* IX (Winter): 23-33.

Cullen, F., B. Link & C. Polanzi (1982). "The Seriousness of Crime Revisited; Have Attitudes Toward White Collar Crime Changed?" *Criminology* 20 (May): 82-102.

Cullen, F., R. Mathers, G. Clark & J. Cullen (1983). "Public Support for Punishing White Collar Crime: Blaming the Victim Revisited." *Journal of Criminal Justice* 11, 6: 481-493.

Cullen, F., G. Clark, B. Link, R. Mathers, J. Lee & M. Sheahan (1982). "Dissecting White Collar Crime: Offense-Type and Punitiveness." Presented at the annual meeting of the Academy of Criminal Justice Sciences.

Dowie, M. (1977). "Pinto Madness," *Mother Jones* (September-October): 18-32.

Dowie, M. (1979). "The Corporate Crime of the Century." *Mother Jones* (November): 23-38, 49.

Duchnick, J. & M. Imhoff (1978). "A New Outlook on the White Collar Criminal as it Relates to Deterring White Collar Crime," *Criminal Justice Journal* 2 (Winter): 57-76.

Durkheim, E. (1951). *Suicide.* New York: Free Press.

Elkins, J. (1976). "Corporations and the Criminal Law: An Uneasy Alliance," *Kentucky Law Journal* 65: 73-129.

Erikson, K. (1966). *Wayward Puritans.* New York: John Wiley.

Farrell, R. & V. Swigert (1982). *Deviance and Social Control.* Glenview, IL: Scott, Foresman.

Fisse, B. (1971). "The Use of Publicity as a Criminal Sanction Against Business Corporations," *Melbourne University Law Review* 8 (June): 107-150.

Fisse, B. (1973). "Responsibility, Prevention, and Corporate Crime," *New Zealand University Law Review* 5 (April): 250-279.

Fisse, B. (1981). "Community Service as a Sanction Against Corporations," *Wisconsin Law Review* (September): 970-1017.

Friedrichs, D. (1979). "The Law and the Legitimacy Crisis: A Critical Issue for Criminal Justice," pp. 290-311 in R. Iacovetta & D. Chang (eds.). *Critical Issues in Criminal Justice.* Durham, NC: Carolina Academic Press.

Geis, G. (1972). "Criminal Penalties for Corporate Criminals," *Criminal Law Bulletin* 8 (June): 377-392.

Geis, G. & H. Edelhertz (1973). "Criminal Law and Consumer Fraud: A Sociological View," *American Criminal Law Review* 11 (Summer): 989-1010.

Gordon, D. (1980). *Doing Violence to the Crime Problem: A Response to the Attorney General's Task Force.* Hackensack, NJ: NCCD.

Gusfield, J. (1967). "Moral Passage: The Symbolic Process in Public Designations of Deviance," *Social Problems* 15 (Fall): 175-188.

Kadish, S. (1963). "Some Observations on the Use of Criminal Sanctions in Enforcing Economic Regulations." *University of Chicago Law Review* 30 (Spring): 423-449.

Katz, J. (1980). "The Social Movement Against White Collar Crime," pp. 161-184 in E. Bittner & S. Messinger (eds.), *Criminology Review Yearbook,* Volume 2. Beverly Hills: Sage.

Kramer, R. (1979). "The Ford Pinto Homicide Prosecution: Criminological Questions and Issues Concerning the Control of Corporate Crime." Presented at the annual meeting of the American Society of Criminology.

Kriesberg, S. (1976). "Decisionmaking Models and the Control of Corporate Crime," *Yale Law Journal* 85 (July): 1091-1129.

Maakestad, W. (1980). "The Pinto Case: Conceptual and Constitutional Problems in the Criminal Indictment of an American Corporation." Presented at the annual meeting of the American Business Law Association.

Maakestad, W. (1981). "A Historical Survey of Corporate Homicide in the United States: Could it be Prosecuted in Illinois?" *Illinois Bar Journal* 69 (August): 2-7.

Nader, R. & M. Green (1972). "Crime in the Suites: Coddling the Corporations," *New Republic* 166 (April 20): 18.

Newsweek (1980). "Ford's Pinto: Not Guilty." Volume 95 (March 24): 74.

Piven, F. & R. Cloward (1971). *Regulating the Poor: The Functions of Public Welfare.* New York: Pantheon.

Piven, F. & R. Cloward (1977). *Poor People's Movements: Why They Succeed, How They Fail.* New York: Pantheon.

Piven, F. & R. Cloward (1982). *The New Class War: Reagan's Attack of the Welfare State and Its Consequences.* New York: Pantheon.

Pontell, H., P. Jesilow & G. Geis (1982). "Policing Physicians: Practitioner Fraud and Abuse in a Government Medicaid Program," *Social Problems* 30 (October): 117-125.

President's Commission on Law Enforcement and Administration of Justice (1968). *Challenge of Crime in a Free Society.* New York: Avon.

Reiman, J. (1979). *The Rich Get Richer and the Poor Get Prison.* New York: John Wiley.

Rodgers, W. (1974). "IBM on Trial," *Harper's Magazine* 248 (May): 79-84.

Ross, I. (1980). "How Lawless are Big Companies?" *Fortune* 102 (December 1): 56-64.

Rothman, D. (1978). "The State as Parent: Social Policy in the Progressive Era," pp. 67-96 in W. Gaylin et al., *Doing Good: The Limits of Benevolence.* New York: Pantheon.

Schrager, L. & J. Short (1978). "Toward a Sociology of Organizational Crime," *Social Problems* 25 (April): 407-419.

Stern, G. (1976). *The Buffalo Creek Disaster.* New York: Vintage.

Strobel, L. (1980). *Reckless Homicide? Ford's Pinto Trial.* South Bend, IN: And Books.

Sudnow, D. (1965). "Normal Crimes: Sociological Features of the Penal Code in a Public Defender's Office," *Social Problems* 12 (Winter): 255-276.

Swigert, V. & R. Farrell (1980-1981). "Corporate Homicide: Definitional Processes in the Creation of Deviance," *Law & Society Review* 15, 1: 171-182.

Time (1980). "Three Cheers in Dearborn." (March 24): 24.

Time (1983). "Superfund, Supermess." (February 21): 14-16.

Vandivier, K. (1972). "The Aircraft Brake Scandal," *Harper's Magazine* 244 (April): 45-52.

Wright, J. (1979). *On a Clear Day You Can See General Motors: John A. DeLorean's Look Inside the Automotive Giant.* New York: Avon.

Yoder, S. (1979). "Criminal Sanctions for Corporate Illegality," *Journal of Criminal Law and Criminology* 69 (Spring): 40-58.

DISCUSSION QUESTIONS

1. What role did the 21-year-old driver of the "peace train" van play in the events as evidenced in the Ford case? Should he have been implicated? Why or why not? Explain.

2. List some additional "corporate crimes" that are committed today that you feel should be dealt with on the criminal level?

3. Should corporations be held equally responsible for unlawful acts as compared to street criminals? If so, would the same penalties and sanctions work on white-collar criminals?

4. What features are shared by organized and white-collar criminals? How does the ideology of criminal justice policy work to obscure these similarities?

CHAPTER 21

Ethics in Public Service:
Higher Standards and
Double Standards

Edwin Delattre

Some time ago, a colleague who is a chief of police telephoned me during the twenty-first hour of a hostage negotiation. The day before, a former student from a nearby university who had inflicted brain damage on himself by using illegal narcotics had, unfortunately, been released from a psychiatric hospital. He had borrowed or stolen a car and, he told police, had gone in search of "the perfect beauty parlor." He meant a beauty parlor that would be difficult for police to storm, and he found it—in an old bank building. There, at gunpoint, he took hostage seven women and a child.

KEY CONCEPTS:

double standard

good character

higher standard

integrity

legalized corruption

Police negotiators and command and patrol personnel, including snipers, were brought to the scene. Once communication was established, the difficulty of satisfying the hostage-taker became clear: he demanded the materials to build a time machine.

The police met his specific demands for tools and materials. By the twenty-first hour, they had negotiated the child and six women to freedom, out of harm's way. On several occasions, snipers could have shot the perpetrator of the crime, but the chief refused to authorize that action because he and his top advisors believed that the hostages were not in immediate, life-threatening peril, and they held out to save all the lives.

But by the time the chief called, negotiations were stalled, the hostage-taker was growing weary and therefore impatient, and the immediate danger to the remaining hostage was rising. Less than three hours later, the gunman announced

Edwin J. Delattre, "Ethics in Public Service: Higher Standards and Double Standards," (as appeared in *Criminal Justice Ethics*, Volume 8, Number 2 [Summer/Fall 1989] pp. 2, 79-83). Reprinted by permission of the Institute for Criminal Justice Ethics, 899 Tenth Avenue, New York, NY 10019-1029.

that he had a bomb in a suitcase and intended to kill the hostage and himself. His threat had to be taken at face value. The chief authorized the snipers, the young man was shot to death, and the last hostage was returned to safety.

Some people will wonder whether the suitcase actually contained a bomb, but when the chief and I spoke again after the crisis, we did not discuss that. The gun itself was real enough. Some may argue that the chief should not have waited so long, others that he should have waited longer. But he is a man of experience and seasoned judgment, and I am glad that such a person had the authority and responsibility to decide.

My central point is that he *did* decide: with regard for high ideals, including respect for all the lives involved, and for hard realities, including the fact that he might need deadly force to save the last hostage. The chief did not shirk the ordeal of judgment that accompanies his office. He did not behave with a cynical disregard for the life of the perpetrator or a naive expectation that every human conflict can be resolved peacefully. He was and is a realistic idealist who takes the conduct of life seriously—the kind of person who is fit to bear the trust of others in public and private.

In September 1796, in his Farewell Address to the People of the United States, George Washington said, "The period for a new election of a citizen to administer the executive government being not far distant . . . your thoughts must be employed in designating the person who is to be clothed with that important trust."[1]

Washington's idea of public office as a public trust was not new, of course. The idea had been treated explicitly and in depth fifty years earlier by the Scottish philosopher Francis Hutcheson, who wrote, "Our children are dear to us, so are our wives, our kinsmen, our friends and acquaintance(s). But our country contains within it all these objects of endearment, and preserves them to us."[2]

Hutcheson believed that constituted governments could treat our loved ones more securely, justly, and humanely than others. They could close *both* of the doors to the temple of tyranny—totalitarian government *and* government so weak and ineffectual that it cannot prevent citizens from preying on each other. Hutcheson therefore argued that "the constituting of civil power is the most important transaction in human affairs."[3]

For this reason, we have a right to insist that the *obligations* of public servants are "very high and sacred." Indeed, the "obligation on rules to a faithful administration" is a higher duty than "that on the subjects to obedience." The rights of rulers are "less divine than those of the people" because the former are designed "for the preservation of the latter."[4] Hutcheson took the sacredness of the duties of public service to imply that "for crimes against the publik rights of a people, or the gross abuses of power, or attempts against the plan of polity to increase their own power or influence there should be no impunity."[5] Though Hutcheson described precisely the form that modern undercover sting operations would take and even recommended immunity and other deals to "turn" informants in investigations of private crimes, he held that violations of the public trust are unpardonable.

Despite this history—which has its antecedents in antiquity—Walter Lippmann could still write in 1930:

> The American ideal of government as a public trust to be carried on by disinterested men represents not the actuality but a long step ahead in the evolution of man. . . . It is a very difficult ideal to attain, and I know of no man in America even in our time who has felt able to be completely loyal to it. . . . The campaign . . . on behalf of the idea of trust is no mere repairing of something perfect that has broken down, but the implanting of a new habit of acting in the ancient consciousness of man.[6]

Some of the public servants I work with in the three branches of government do not understand the idea of public trust; some understand but are unmoved by it. Often, they do not see that worthiness to bear the public trust is a matter of personal character, as James Madison wrote when his brother decided to run for country office: "If he wishes to establish himself in the good will of the Country, the only durable as well as honorable plan will be to establish a character that merits it."[7] In this, Madison echoed Socrates, Xenophon, and Cicero, among others.

Some public servants, unlike the chief I described earlier, claim in private that there is no difference between a higher standard for public servants than for the general citizenry and a double standard within government that is by definition unfair. They do not appreciate that a higher standard is not a double standard. It is instead a reflection of the fact that when a person voluntarily accepts a position of public trust, he takes on new obligations. If he does not want to live up to them, he is free to decline the job. Not only is this a fair demand; granting authority without expecting public servants to live up to it would be unfair to everyone they are expected to serve.

Some law enforcement personnel, for example, object that the standards they are expected to meet in their use of authority and discretion seem unfair. A few have complained to me that although others are innocent until proven guilty, police seem to be presumed guilty by the citizens and the media whenever accused.

Though prejudice and presumption of guilt are unfair, there is nothing unfair in presumption of limits and an expectation that the burden of proof will be met by all public officials who have authority and use it. This presumption amounts to insistence that might does not make right, that officials will bear the public trust faithfully, and that they will accept the onus of showing that they are doing so. Accordingly, I tell public servants in my classes that if they have no stomach for such ordeals, they should choose another line of work.

Still, the problem of the double standard—the ability of agencies or individuals in government to treat themselves with favoritism and special privilege as compared to other branches of government (and often the public as well)—has been recognized for a long time, and it is perhaps as pressing now as ever before. Madison was sufficiently concerned that he devoted *Federalist #57* to arguments that apply to the problem. He asked there how republican government is to protect itself against a legislature that "favors the elevation of a few on the ruins of the many."[8] His question had been initially raised by opponents to ratification of the Constitution who argued that the House of Representatives would consist of men who, because of their class, would have little sympathy with the general public and would aim at "an ambitious sacrifice of the many to the aggrandizement of the few."[9]

Madison's answer was that "the aim of every political constitution is, or ought to be, first to obtain for rulers men who possess most wisdom to discern, and most virtue to pursue, the common good of the society; and in the next place, to take the most effectual precautions for keeping them virtuous while they continue to hold their public trust."[10] The instruments to this achievement he believed to be frequent elections, based on the principle that the legislature "can make no law which will not have its full operation on themselves and their friends, as well as on the great mass of society."[11] That principle, he wrote, "creates bonds between [the rulers and the people], that communion of interests and sympathy of sentiments . . . without which every government degenerates into tyranny."[12] How is the principle kept vital? By the "vigilant and manly spirit which actuates the people of America—a spirit which nourishes freedom, and in return is nourished by it," declared Madison. He added, "If this spirit ever be so far debased as to tolerate a law not obligatory on the legislature, as well as on the people, the people will be prepared to tolerate anything but liberty."[13]

In our times, the principle has been repeatedly violated, and in the past year, it has become commonplace for public servants and aspirants to office in Washington to vaunt ethical as well as legal double standards inside government that contradict the spirit Madison so cherished and trusted.

In practice, the situation that most imperils the public good is the one in which a public official can betray the public without fear of adverse consequences. Police and corrupt judges and defense attorneys sometimes achieve this by secrecy and conspiracies of silence. Legislators have, by the stroke of a pen, legalized their own untrammeled pursuit of self-interest at the public expense—an even better shield than conspiracy. In such cases, above all, weak and bad character in individuals leads to unrestrained behavior.

Specifically, in early 1987, the Congress and staff aides shared a 3 percent salary increase, but a much larger increase was proposed for members of Congress. In March 1987, Congress could have limited these large increases; instead, it "strategically 'missed' the deadline for voting to reject."[14] Since a vote was required to reject the large raises but not to receive them, members of Congress were able to profit by deliberate inaction. At a time of concern for government deficits, "missing" the deadline was a convenient way of being able to say, "I never voted for the raise."

But the resultant salary raises left a new gap between the salaries of Congressmen and the salaries of key aides. To fill the gap, just before Christmas 1987 in a "catchall continuing resolution . . . to fund operations of agencies whose budgets hadn't been approved by Congress at recess time," the Congress inserted four paragraphs "written in congressional legalese, a useful language when one wants to get a job done without anybody knowing what's being done"[15] that enabled some aides to receive raises of up to $10,000 in 1988. Other government employees do not benefit from this standard of compensation; in 1988, their increases were two percent.

I will not rehearse Congress's attempt to repeat these actions in 1988-89, or all the problems of Political Action Committees, or the difficulty of getting a hearing on the Hill without making financial contributions, but to those problems should be added the common practice among interest groups of paying speech honoraria in order to get a hearing. Perhaps such practices explain why so many people in Washington claim that lobbying is "an industry that loves working in the shadows."[16]

In 1961, "there were 365 registered lobbyists in Washington; by 1987, that number had risen to 23,011."[17] It is in this context that on March 8, 1988, William F. Weld, then head of the Justice Department's Criminal Division, said at the National Press Club that Congress enjoys the benefits of a double standard. He explained that members of the executive branch are prohibited from "handling matters in which they have a financial interest, from accepting money in addition to their government salaries for their duties, or from lobbying their former agencies on certain issues."[18] But such actions are "perfectly all right if committed by a member of Congress." Weld referred to legal payments of $2,000 by a coal company to each member of a congressional committee on mining legislation simply for touring its facilities.[19] And, in July 1988, *Newsweek*, in an ironic tone, reported other payments of the same kind:

> The most breathtaking of Congress's pioneering ethical practices, though, remains the *non*-speech honorarium. Last year, seven members of the House Armed Services Committee were paid $2,000 each by the Oshkosh Truck Corporation simply to attend a breakfast meeting. Later that very day, the committee ordered the Army to buy five hundred more 10-ton Oshkosh trucks than the Army wanted.[20]

Congress has awarded itself many other special privileges, establishing double standards in its own favor, that amount to legalized public corruption. As sociologist Amitai Etzioni observes, for example, members of Congress "vote on the allocation"[21] of "counterpart funds," enabling themselves to "buy thousands of dollars worth of trinkets" at no expense to themselves on junkets to underdeveloped countries. "These funds are generated when the U.S. Government sells underdeveloped countries some of its products" and accepts in payment "funds in the local currency, with the understanding that they must be spent in the particular country."[22]

When political campaign contributions are made, "the only step that is prohibited, and which hardly ever needs to be negotiated, even when the lobbyist and the member of Congress meet alone behind closed doors, is explicitly, openly and directly tying a contribution to a specific vote."[23] If only the letter of this law enjoys respect, then payoffs are entirely possible, even likely; all that is necessary is a little subtlety and common sense. Members of Congress themselves have acknowledged this: Representative Mike Synar of Oklahoma has testified in Congress that "it would be naive in the extreme to ignore the '*quid pro quo*' implicit in PAC contributions. The money is given . . . to influence the legislative process." Former Representative Bob Eckhardt of Texas has testified that "the process has all of the advantages of bribery and none of its risks."[24]

Legalized corruption and double standards are a problem in some states, as well as in the federal government. California, where no legislator has been found guilty of an ethics violation since the ethics committee was established over sixteen years ago, stands out. In Maryland, efforts of 1988 to reform campaign laws were abandoned, as they have been in years past, despite common knowledge of a history of political scandal and corruption. Committee Chairman Anne Perkins of Baltimore told *The Washington Post* that "General Assembly leaders and others were afraid of [legislators] appearing in the paper as some sleaze-balls' if campaign practices were debated on the House floor."[25] Perhaps these government officials have not learned that sometimes when people *appear* to be sleazeballs, it is because they *are* sleazeballs. Appearance and reality are not *always* different.

What is palpably worse than any of these specific actions is the debasement of the spirit of uniform standards of wisdom and virtue in government itself. In the past year, it has become fashionable in Washington to insist that *there should be* a double standard within government that calls for greater probity, self-control, and good judgment from some public servants than from others. The advocacy of a double standard is entirely different from the advocacy of a higher standard for all public servants, and I do not know of a time when the double standard has been so badly and thoughtlessly endorsed by government officials.

For example, on March 31, 1988, Senator Patrick Leahy of Vermont, in an interview on the MacNeil/Lehrer News Hour, insisted that the attorney general, then under investigation, had a duty to step aside. I agreed with this position because I knew from my work that the Justice Department was in fact without an agenda and that the attorney general was so preoccupied with self-defense that the Department threatened to be indefinitely adrift. But Leahy argued that it would be all right for a cabinet officer at HUD or Labor to continue in office under the circumstances—yet not all right for the attorney general. The attorney general had to live by a higher standard, he declared. When asked whether *he* would step aside if accused of similar offenses of which he believed himself innocent, Leahy replied, "If I were attorney general, of course I would have to step aside." Clearly, he meant that *as a senator*, he would not need to do so.

Later I called the senator's press secretary to offer the senator a chance to take a more defensible position before I included a description of the interview in my forthcoming book on ethics in policing. We spoke several times, and finally the press secretary said in a voice of complaint, "Well, Ed, you have to remember that the senator is not *accustomed* to being listened to this closely."

The same advocacy of a double standard arose in the confirmation hearings for John Tower as the nominee for Secretary of Defense. Many senators—and even Tower himself—held that the Secretary of Defense must be more temperate and trustworthy than other public servants because he is in the nuclear chain of command.

Now, I insist that the standards of temperance and trustworthiness for a secretary of defense must be very high. And I offer no comment here whatsoever about whether Tower should have been nominated or confirmed. My point is that the duties of a secretary of defense to the public and the public interest are no greater than those of congressmen and judges who enact laws and decide cases that profoundly affect for better or worse the lives of citizens every day. A congressman whose intemperance with alcohol diverts him from careful study of questions of enforceability of laws or from comprehensive planning of legislative programs regarding, say, narcotics is as great a threat to the public weal, to the safety of police, school teachers, and the general public, and to the prudent investment of personnel and money, as any other public servant could be. To do his job responsibly, he must be diligent and alert to every element of the supply and demand sides, including source control, interdiction, enforcement, education, prevention, treatment, the addiction of newborn children, the explosion of AIDS among intravenous users, the availability of prison space, and the proliferation of sophisticated firearms. A judge who drinks too much and listens to cases less attentively because he is hung over is a disgrace to the rights of due process every American is entitled to enjoy; he affects lives as immediately and dramatically as any secretary of defense has ever affected them. A cop who intemperately spends himself into debt is as vulnerable to corruption as an intelligence analyst or legislative staff member, and all three may be too distracted by worry to face crises with full attention. And if a *prospective* government official in the executive branch seems to be compromised by consulting contracts with industrial corporations *when he is not in office*, surely it is true that a congressman is at least as tainted by honoraria accepted from private interests when he is in office.

It is not difficult to extend the examples. Last year, nearly thirty building inspectors in New York were indicted for extortion. Did they need less excellence of character than a cabinet officer? In practice, a building inspector on the streets affects individual lives fully as much as a secretary of defense—and the misbehavior of a building inspector does not become tolerable simply because he cannot push a nuclear button. In fact, in the routine affairs of daily life, a building inspector who can be blackmailed over a drug habit or philandering is potentially more dangerous because he can act with greater independence than anyone in the nuclear chain of command can [—] and he is much less visible.

I infer that justice—and the facts of life in public service—imply that double standards are both wrong and foolish. But it should be clear that my opposition to double standards within government does not answer the question of how high uniform standards should be or how in different institutions they should be sustained. After all, falsifying a police report must be disciplined in different ways from manipulating data to the point of lying in congressional floor debate. The former depends on responsible command, the latter on conscientious rebuttal and exposure—even though neither method is all that reliable.

Furthermore, my position does not answer the question of how much of a person's private life is the public's business. And it does not address problems of changing standards over time.

Neither will much of the current talk about ethics in government. The sour, holier-than-thou moralizing and finger-pointing, the self-flagellation of the media, the preoccupation with supposed dilemmas that are not really dilemmas at all, the idea that individual wisdom and character can be replaced by ethics committees and legislation, are scarcely to be celebrated. In the end, they are as likely to give ethics a bad name as to accomplish anything better.

Part of what is needed is a public sense of what Madison meant by wisdom and good character: balanced perception and integrity. Integrity means wholeness in public and private life consisting of habits of justice, temperance, courage, compassion, honesty, fortitude, and disdain for self-pity.

One element of wisdom is a willingness to work hard enough to answer ethical questions responsibly. There can be no quick fixes. If we want to know, say, whether Gary Hart's sex life is public business, our questions cannot focus simply on sex. Rather, we need to ask whether it is relevant to a person's worthiness for office that he willfully abandons the expectations of his campaign volunteers and financial contributors to his transitory desires. Of his wisdom, we may ask whether a person who would both aspire to public office and place his public credibility in the hands of a private citizen who can by a single word destroy it— or blackmail him after the assumes office—is wise enough to serve us. Exactly the same question about wisdom or prudence can be asked about Ollie North, who, whether alone or in complicity, placed the credibility of the country in the hands of Iranians as surely as Gary Hart placed his own in the hands of Donna Rice. Of Jim Wright, we can ask whether a man who would stake a great deal on a distinction without a difference in fact, such as honoraria and, nominally, "royalties," or who would compound the problem by receiving royalties for two thousand more copies of his book than were ever printed,[26] has character enough to deserve the public trust.

Not all such matters can be governed by law and regulation. But where existing regulations are ignored or skirted with impunity, that vice will always forestall later enforcement of them. The whine, "Why now, why me?" gains power when standards have received only lip service before. It always ignores the plain truth that no one of decent character ever treats the nonenforcement of regulations against questionable behavior as an excuse to act questionably. No one of any moral substance takes refuge in the excuse that "others do it," any more than any thoughtful parent is swayed by a child's insistence that "the other kids' parents let them do it." And anyone of the slightest moral sensibility knows that preferring things we consider doing not be known by family, colleagues, constituents, or the press gives us a reason to suspect that such actions are shameful.

Wisdom and character in public servants, disdain for favoritism in one's own case, simple courage in ethics committees, informed voter participation, conscientious floor debate that reveals incompetence and manipulation of the truth, appointment of executive branch officials, including police and judges, on criteria of merit as established by careful background investigations, and so on, are needed. Much of this the Founders already knew. Personal respect for the spirit of law and regulation—itself an achievement of character—is irreplaceable.

But beware, we are told, of making the standards *too* high, or no one will participate in government. Really? No one? No one who is qualified? Where is the evidence that we would suffer a shortage of aspirants? And where is the evidence that if many who now hold or seek public office no longer did, we would be worse off? Surely, knowing—and acting—better than Jim Wright has does not take extraordinary personal standards. A person does not have to be all that decent to refuse to attack the careers and reputations of bank regulators in order to salvage S and L owners who raise funds for his own political party—as Wright did without remorse.[27]

Raise the salaries, we are encouraged, and then you can expect better. I doubt it. If the salaries are unbearably low, why do incumbents run over and again? Surely, not just to get the honoraria. Raise the salaries if the jobs merit higher pay but not in expectation of buying integrity. Nobody sells that. People who have it give it for free.

Realistic expectations based on due regard for the facts of human nature are surely imperative. But only because we must know ourselves to govern ourselves. Certainly not because we are so cynical as to believe that no one can both live up to such expectations *and* be interested in public life, and certainly not because we are afraid that if we seek wisdom and virtue in public servants, we will come up empty. Too many decent people in government and in the private sector belie by their lives such cynicism and such fear.

NOTES

1. George Washington, "Farewell Address," in 6 *A Collection of Orations from Homer to McKinley* 2511, 2513 (M. Hazeltine ed. 1902).

2. F. Hutcheson, *A Short Introduction to Moral Philosophy, in Three Books; Containing the Elements of Ethicks and the Law of Nature* 347 (Glasgow: Printed and Sold by Robert Foulis, Printer to the University of Glasgow, 1747).

3. F. Hutcheson, *A System of Moral Philosophy in Three Books* 285 (Glasgow: R. and A. Foulis, Printers to the University of Glasgow, 1755; reprint 1968).

4. Id.

5. Id. at 335.

6. Lippmann, "A Theory About Corruption," in *Political Corruption: Readings in Comparative Analysis* 296, 297 (A. Heidenheimer ed. 1970).

7. "James Madison to Ambrose Madison," October 11, 1787, in 10 *The Papers of James Madison* 192 (R. Rutland, et al. eds. 1977).

8. Alexander Hamilton, James Madison & John Jay, *The Federalist Papers,* #57 at 351 (C. Rossiter ed. 1961).

9. Id. at 350.

10. Id.

11. Id. at 352.

12. Id. at 352, 353.

13. Id. at 353.

14. Causey, "A Double Standard," *The Washington Post,* Feb. 25, 1988, at D2.

15. Id.

16. McAllister, "Lobbying: Bigger Money, Bigger Stakes," *The Washington Post,* Jan. 4, 1988, at A8.

17. Alice-Leone Moats, "Power Game Has Changed in D.C.," *The Philadelphia Inquirer,* May 3, 1988, at 27A.

18. Marcus, "Justice Official Assails Congress' Double Standard in Ethics," *The Washington Post,* Mar. 9, 1988, at A4.

19. Id.

20. Kaus, Noah & Clift, "Congress Faces an Ethics Gap," *Newsweek,* July 4, 1988, at 17.

21. A. Etzioni, *Capital Corruption* 18 (1984).

22. Id.

23. Id. at 58.

24. Id. at 59.

25. Schmidt, "Bill Limiting Funds to Campaigns Sinks," *The Washington Post,* Mar. 18, 1988, at G1, G10.

26. Babcock, "Behind Charges: 279 Pages of Detail," *The Washington Post,* Apr. 18, 1988, at G1, G10.

27. "Jim Wright and the S and Ls," *The Washington Post,* April 21, 1989, at A26.

DISCUSSION QUESTIONS

1. In your opinion, did the chief of police in this chapter act in what the author would explain as a higher standard or a double standard? Explain. What would you have done in the same circumstances? Justify your answers.

2. Is it fair to expect a higher standard of ethics from a public servant in contrast to a private citizen? Would you think a representative of Congress would have a greater impact on society or a private sector businessperson such as the chief executive officer (CEO) of an international chemical company? In your opinion, are ethics violations more serious in the public sector or private sector? Explain this in terms of the corrupt Congress representative and the white-collar criminal.

3. What are Delattre's strongest and weakest arguments regarding ethics in public service? Explain the "good" and "bad" points of each argument.

CHAPTER 22

Ethics and Criminal Justice Research

Belinda R. McCarthy

No area of life or work is free of ethical dilemmas, and the field of research is no exception. In recent years a number of scandals surrounding the profession-al behavior of academic researchers have made newspaper headlines and stirred government inquiries. In 1989, an individual charged with the responsibility of reviewing an article prior to publication was charged with plagiarism—steal-ing the prepublication results of the research reviewed and publishing them as the basis for his own work (*Chronicle of Higher Education,* 1989c). Another researcher, an award-winning scientist, was charged with falsifying laboratory records to indicate that tests never performed had been completed and publishing the results. The investigation of this event, including a review by the National Institute of Health and the eventual reprimanding of the Principal Investigator by his University, caused as much of an uproar as the allegations (*Chronicle of Higher Education,*

> **KEY CONCEPTS:**
>
> coercing
> participation
>
> confidentiality
>
> privacy
>
> randomization
>
> self-determination
>
> willingness to
> participate

1989a). Because the research was federally funded, legislative inquiries were con-sidered as a means of monitoring the investigation process.

In a very different vein, questions have been raised about the conduct of the two University of Utah professors who went to the media with their discovery of cold fusion prior to the publication of their results. Subsequent efforts to repli-cate their findings have been unproductive (*Chronicle of Higher Education,* 1989b). A different problem was confronted by the Stanford University student of Anthropology who while doing field work in China reportedly witnessed the performance of many third-trimester abortions forced on pregnant women in an effort to control population growth. The student made the decision to go to the international press with his observations and was subsequently asked to leave the country (*New York Times,* 1983).

One might think that scientific endeavors, with their objective and unbiased approach to the world, would create fewer dilemmas than other occupational activities. Although most researchers are not faced with the same kind of corrupting influences confronting street-level criminal justice officials, the pressures of "grantsmanship" and publication provide significant motivations. The dilemmas of working with human subjects in a political environment are equally challenging. Moreover, the goal of scientific purity, of unbiased objectivity, may be corrupting as well, as researchers are tempted to put scientific objectives before their concern for the welfare of others.

In this chapter we will examine the nature of ethical dilemmas confronting the criminal justice researcher. To a large degree these problems are comparable to those difficulties faced by other social scientists. Additional problems arise as a result of the particular focus of research on deviance and law-breaking.

PROBLEMS INVOLVING WORK WITH HUMAN SUBJECTS

Stuart Cook (1976) lists the following ethical considerations surrounding research with human subjects:

1. Involving people in research without their knowledge or consent

2. Coercing people to participate

3. Withholding from the participant the true nature of the research

4. Deceiving the research participant

5. Leading the research participants to commit acts which diminish their self-respect

6. Violating the right to self-determination: research on behavior control and character change

7. Exposing the research participant to physical or mental stress

8. Invading the privacy of the research participant

9. Withholding benefits from participants in control groups

10. Failing to treat research participants fairly and to show them consideration and respect. (p. 202)

INVOLVING PEOPLE IN RESEARCH WITHOUT THEIR KNOWLEDGE OR CONSENT

Often the best way to study human behavior is to observe people in a natural setting without their knowledge. Self-reported descriptions of behavior may be unreliable, because people forget or are uncertain about their actions. Although most people might tell you that they would attempt to return a lost wallet, a hidden camera focused on a wallet lying on the sidewalk might reveal very different behaviors. People who know they are being watched often act differently, especially when unethical, deviant or criminal behaviors are involved. For these reasons, studies of deviance often involve direct observation, which in scientific terminology involves listening as well as visual observation.

At times the observer participates to some degree in the activities being studied. Whyte's (1955) study of street-corner society involved just this form of participant observation. Humphreys's (1970) examination of homosexual behavior in public rest rooms, Short and Strodtbeck's (1965) study of delinquency in Chicago and Cohen's (1980) observations of female prostitutes in New York all involved the observation of persons who never consented to become research subjects.

Studies of persons on the other side of the criminal justice process have also been undertaken without the consent of those participating in the research. Meltzer (1953), for example, studied juror deliberations through the use of hidden microphones. The importance of discretion in the criminal justice process and the hidden nature of most decisionmaking support the greater use of such techniques in efforts to understand how police, prosecutors and correctional personnel carry out their duties.

The ethical dilemma, however, is a complicated one: Is the value of the research such that persons should be turned into study "subjects" without their permission? The conditions of the research are extremely important to this deliberation. If the behaviors being studied would have occurred without the researcher's intervention, the lack of consent seems less troubling. Such studies involve little personal cost to unknowing subjects. Unintrusive research that involves only behaviors that occur in public view is also less questionable, because the invasion of personal privacy is not at issue.

But what about experiments that create situations to which subjects must react, such as those involving a "lost" wallet? Or a study of witness response to crime that involves an actor or actress screaming and running from an apparent assailant down a crowded street? Observation might be the only method of determining how citizens would really respond, but the personal cost of being studied might be considerable.

Not only may such research be troubling for the persons involved, but when sensitive activities that are normally considered private or confidential are the subject of study, additional problems may arise. Cook (1976) reports that Meltzer encountered such difficulties in his study of jury deliberations:

> Members of Congress reacted to the jury recording as a threat to fundamental institutions. When the news of the study came out, a congressional investigation resulted. Following the investigation legislation was passed establishing a fine of a thousand dollars and imprisonment for a year for whoever might attempt to record the proceedings of any jury in the United States while the jury is deliberating or voting. (p. 205)

Although the response might be less severe, one can anticipate similar objections to the taping of discussions involving police, attorneys, judges, correctional officials and probation and parole authorities.

COERCING PEOPLE TO PARTICIPATE

You have probably received a questionnaire in the mail at some time that offered you some small incentive for completing the form—a free pencil, a few quarters. This practice is a common one, reflecting the assumption that people who are compensated for their efforts may be more likely to participate in a research endeavor than those who receive nothing. Similarly, college students are often provided a grade incentive for participation in their instructor's research. But when does compensation become coercion? When is the researcher justified to compel participation? The issues here involve the freedom *not* to participate, and the nature and quantity of the incentives that can be ethically provided without creating an undue influence.

The person receiving the questionnaire in the mail is free to keep the compensation and toss away the form. Students may be similarly free not to participate in their instructor's research, but the instructor's power over the grading process may make students feel quite ill at ease doing so.

It might seem that the easiest way out of this dilemma is to simply rely on volunteers for research subjects. But volunteers are different from others simply by virtue of their willingness to participate. At a minimum they are more highly motivated than nonvolunteers. It is important to obtain a more representative sample of participants, a group that mirrors the actual characteristics of those persons to whom study results will be applied.

This problem becomes especially critical when research subjects are vulnerable to coercion. Although students might be considered a captive population, jail and prison inmates are clearly the most vulnerable of research subjects.

The history of inmate involvement in research is not a very proud one. Prisoners have been used as "guinea pigs" by pharmaceutical companies that set up laboratories at correctional institutions. For minimal compensation, or the possibility that participation might assist in gaining parole, inmates have participated in a variety of medical research projects.

> In the United States, the first use of correctional subjects for medical experiments took place at the Mississippi state prison in 1914, when researchers attempted to discover the relationship between diet and pellagra. The Governor of Mississippi promised pardons to persons volunteering for the experiment. The situation may be contrasted to a more recent experiment in New York in which eight prisoners were inoculated with a venereal infection in order to test possible cures. For their voluntary participation the subjects, in their own words, "got syphilis and a carton of cigarettes." (Geis, 1980:226)

Today, prisoners are forbidden to engage in such research efforts, but inmates are frequently required to participate in efforts to evaluate the impact of correctional treatment, work or education programs. The reason for requiring participation is the same as that stated above. Volunteers are sufficiently different from others that relying on their participation would probably produce more positive outcomes than the intervention alone would warrant. Freedom of choice is highly valued in this society, but how much freedom of choice should prisoners have? Before denying a subject the opportunity to refuse participation, it should be clear that the overall value of the research outweighs the harm of coercion. In this consideration, the nature of the participation must be carefully evaluated—coercion to participate in weekly group therapy is quite different from coercion to participate in eight weeks of paramilitary training. One must also assess whether coercion is the only or best means available to obtain research results. Confronting this dilemma requires a balancing of such matters with a concern for individual rights.

WITHHOLDING FROM THE PARTICIPANT THE TRUE NATURE OF THE RESEARCH

Informed consent requires that subjects know fully the nature of the research, its possible effects and the uses to be made of the data collected. However, even in the most benign circumstances, written notification may deter further action. Full and complete notification has the added potential of prejudicing responses. Often more accurate assessments are achieved when the subject believes that one aspect of his or her behavior is the focus, when research interest is really on something else.

Researchers are understandably reluctant to provide too much information in this regard, especially in the early stages of a project, when the need to develop rapport and a willingness to cooperate are especially important. Ethically speaking, informed consent should precede involvement in the study, so that individuals are given a meaningful opportunity to decline further participation.

Balancing research interests and respect for human dignity requires that subjects be informed about all aspects of the research that might reasonably influence their willingness to participate. Any risks that the subjects may expect to face should be fully discussed. Geis (1980) recommends that researchers remember the example of Walter Reed, who participated as a subject in his own experiments on yellow fever because he could ask no one to undergo anything that he himself was not willing to suffer (p. 227).

DECEIVING THE RESEARCH PARTICIPANT

Perhaps the most flagrant example of deception in criminological research is provided by Humphreys's (1970) study, *Tearoom Trade.* Humphreys assumed the role of lookout in public rest rooms so that strangers unaware of his research objective could engage uninterrupted in homosexual activity. He copied down the automobile license tags of the subjects and obtained their addresses. Later he went to their homes, explaining that he was conducting a health survey. He asked the respondents many personal questions that became part of his research on public homosexual conduct.

The rationale for such deception emphasizes the importance of the research and the difficulties of obtaining accurate information through other means. All deceptive acts are not equal. There are differences between active lying and a conscious failure to provide all available information. Deception may be considered an affront to individual autonomy and self-respect, or an occasionally legitimate means to be used in service of a higher value (Cook, 1976).

One alternative to deception is to provide only general information about the research project prior to the experiment and offer full disclosure after the research has been completed. Another technique relies on subjects to role-play their behavior after the nature of the research project has been explained. There is mixed evidence, however, on the effectiveness of this technique (Cook, 1976).

In regard to deception, the researcher must evaluate the nature of the research and weigh its value against the impact of the deception on the integrity of participants. The degree to which privacy is invaded and the sensitivity of the behaviors involved are important considerations.

LEADING THE RESEARCH PARTICIPANTS TO COMMIT ACTS WHICH DIMINISH THEIR SELF-RESPECT

Research subjects have been experimentally induced into states of extreme passivity and extreme aggression. Efforts to provoke subjects to lie, cheat and steal have proven very effective. Cook (1976) describes a study in which students were recruited to participate in a theft of records from a business firm. The inducements described included an opportunity to perform a patriotic service for a department of federal government. A substantial number of students were significantly encouraged to take part in the theft, although ultimately the burglary was not carried out.

Research by Haney, Banks and Zimbardo (1973) involved the simulation of prison conditions, with 21 subjects assuming the roles of prisoners and guards. After a very short time, the guards began behaving in an aggressive and physically threatening manner. Their use of power became self-aggrandizing and self-perpetuating. The prisoners quickly experienced a loss of personal identity, exhibiting flattened affect and dependency; eventually they were emotionally emasculated by the encounters.

Because of the extreme nature of the subjects' responses, the project was terminated after only six days. The debriefing sessions that followed the research yielded the following comments:

Guards:

> "They (the prisoners) seemed to lose touch with the reality of the experiment—they took me so seriously."

> ". . . I didn't interfere with any of the guards' actions. Usually if what they were doing bothered me, I would walk out and take another duty."

> ". . . looking back, I am impressed by how little I felt for them . . ."

> "They (the prisoners) didn't see it as an experiment. It was real, and they were fighting to keep their identity. But we were always there to show them just who was boss."

> "I was tired of seeing the prisoners in their rags and smelling the strong odors of their bodies that filled the cells. I watched them tear at each other, on orders given by us."

> ". . . Acting authoritatively can be fun. Power can be a great pleasure."

> ". . . During the inspection, I went to cell 2 to mess up a bed which the prisoner had made and he grabbed me, screaming that he had just made it, and he wasn't going to let me mess it up. He grabbed my throat, and although he was laughing, I was pretty scared. I lashed out with my stick and hit him in the chin (although not very hard), and when I freed myself I became angry."

Prisoners:

> ". . . The way we were made to degrade ourselves really brought us down, and that's why we all sat docile towards the end of the experiment."

> ". . . I realize now (after it's over) that no matter how together I thought I was inside my head, my prison behavior was often less under my control than I realized. No matter how open, friendly and helpful I was with other prisoners I was still operating as an isolated, self-centered person, being rational rather than compassionate."

> ". . . I began to feel I was losing my identity, that the person I call _____, the person who volunteered to get me into this prison (because it was a prison to me, it *still* is a prison to me, I don't regard it as an experiment or a simulation . . .) was distant from me, was remote until finally I wasn't *that* person; I was 416. I was really my number, and 416 was really going to have to decide what to do."

> "I learned that people can easily forget that others are human."

In Milgram's (1974) research, participants showed "blind obedience" to a white-coated "researcher" who ordered them to provide what appeared to be electric shocks of increasing severity to subjects who failed to respond correctly to a series of questions. Although they were emotionally upset, the subjects continued to follow their instructions as the "shocked" subjects screamed in agony.

Follow-up research revealed that Milgram's subjects experienced only minor and temporary disturbances (Ring, Wallston & Corey, 1970). One might argue that the subjects even benefited from the project as a result of their greater self-awareness, but the fact that the educational experience occurred without their initial understanding or consent raises ethical concerns.

To what degree should subjects be asked to unknowingly engage in activities that may damage their self-esteem? Again, the researcher is required to engage in a balancing act, reconciling research objectives and the availability of alternative methods with a concern for the integrity of subjects. At a minimum, such research efforts should provide means to address any possible harm to subjects, including debriefings at the conclusion of the research and follow-up counseling as needed.

VIOLATING THE RIGHT TO SELF-DETERMINATION: RESEARCH ON BEHAVIOR CONTROL AND CHARACTER CHANGE

The film *A Clockwork Orange* provides an excellent illustration of the dilemmas of behavior-modifying research. In the film, a thoroughly violent and irredeemable individual named Alex is subjected to therapy that requires him to observe violent acts on film at the same time that the chemicals he has ingested make him physically ill. After a while, the acts that he has observed make him sick as well, and he is changed from a violent individual to one who avoids violence at all cost, including that required for his own self-defense. At the end of the film, the "powers that be" decide to reverse his treatment for political reasons.

Although there is little possibility of behavior modification being used to exact such effect in the near future, the question remains: To what extent should experimental efforts be made to alter human behavior against the will of the participant? Remembering the vulnerability of the inmate to coercion (in the film, Alex only participated in the violence control project because he thought it would help him gain early release), it becomes clear that the greatest desire to use behavior control strategies will be evident in areas involving those persons most vulnerable to coercion—criminals and persons with problems of substance abuse. Although research on crime prevention and control generally has only the most laudable aims, it should be remembered that it is often well-intentioned actions that pose the greatest threat to individual freedoms.

EXPOSING THE RESEARCH PARTICIPANT TO PHYSICAL OR MENTAL STRESS

How would you evaluate the ethics of the following research project: an evaluation of a treatment program, in which persons convicted of drunk driving are required to watch and listen to hours of films depicting gory automobile accidents, followed by horrifying emergency room visits and interviews with grieving relatives? Would it matter whether the actions of the drunk drivers had contributed to similar accidents? If your answer is yes, you are probably considering whether the viewers deserve the "punishment" of what they are forced to observe on film.

This not-so-hypothetical scenario raises a difficult issue. Is it acceptable for a research project to engage in activities that punish and perhaps harm the subject? To test various outcomes, subjects in different settings have been exposed to events provoking feelings of horror, shock, threatened sexual identity, personal failure, fear and emotional shock (Cook, 1976). The subjects in Haney, Banks and Zimbardo's research and Milgram's research were clearly stressed by their research experiences. To what extent is it acceptable to engage in these practices for the objective of scientific inquiry?

In most situations, it is impossible to observe human reactions such as those described above in their natural settings, so researchers feel justified in creating experiments that produce these reactions. The extent of possible harm raises ethical dilemmas, however, because theoretically there is no limit to what might be contrived to create a "researchable" reaction. The balancing of research objectives with a respect for human subjects is a delicate undertaking, requiring researchers to dispassionately scrutinize their objectives and the value of their proposed studies.

INVADING THE PRIVACY OF THE RESEARCH PARTICIPANT

The issues of privacy and confidentiality are related concerns. Ethical questions are raised by research that invades an individual's privacy without his or her consent. When information on subjects has been obtained for reasons other than research (e.g., the development of a criminal history file, probation or prison records), there are questions about the extent to which data should be released to researchers. Some records are more sensitive than others in this regard, depending on how easily the offender's identity can be obtained, and the quantity and nature of the information recorded. Even when consent has been given and the information has been gathered expressly for research purposes, maintaining the confidentiality of responses may be a difficult matter when the responses contain information of a sensitive and/or illegal nature.

CONFIDENTIALITY

The issue of confidentiality is especially important in the study of crime and deviance. Subjects will generally not agree to provide information in this area unless their responses are to remain confidential. This may be a more difficult task than it appears. Generally it is important to be able to identify a subject, so that his or her responses can be linked to other sources of data on the individual. Institutionalized delinquents might be asked in confidence about their involvement in drug use and other forms of misconduct during confinement. An important part of the research would involve gathering background information from the offender's institutional files to determine what types of offenders are most likely to be involved in institutional misconduct. To do this, the individual's confidential responses need to be identifiable, so complete anonymity is unfeasible.

As long as only dispassionate researchers have access to this information, there may be no problem. Difficulties arise when third parties, especially criminal justice authorities, become interested in the research responses. Then the issue becomes one of protecting the data (and the offender) from officials who have the power to invoke the criminal justice process.

One response to this dilemma is to store identifying information in a remote place; some researchers have even recommended sending sensitive information out of the country. Because the relationship between the researcher and his or her informants is not privileged, researchers can be called upon to provide information to the courts.

> Lewis Yablonsky, a criminologist/practitioner, while testifying in defense of Gridley White, one of Yablonsky's main informants in his hippie study, was asked by the judge nine times if he had witnessed Gridley smoking marijuana. Yablonsky refused to answer because of the rights guaranteed him in the Fifth Amendment of the U.S. Constitution. Although he was not legally sanctioned, he said the incident was humiliating and suggested that researchers should have guarantees of immunity. (Wolfgang, 1982:396)

It is also important that researchers prepare their presentation of research findings in a manner that ensures that the particular responses of an individual cannot be discerned. Presentation of only aggregate findings was especially important for Marvin Wolfgang (1982) when he reinterviewed persons included in his earlier study of delinquency in a birth cohort. His follow-up consisted of hour-long interviews with about 600 youths. The subjects were asked many personal questions, including those about involvement in delinquency and crime. Four of his respondents admitted committing criminal homicide, and 75 admitted to forcible rape. Many other serious crimes were also described, for which none of the participants had been arrested.

At the time of the research, all of the respondents were orally assured that the results of the research would remain confidential, but Wolfgang raises a number of ethical questions surrounding this practice. Should written consent forms have been provided to the subjects, detailing the nature of the research? Wolfgang concludes that such forms would have raised more questions than they answered. Could a court order impound the records? Could persons attempting to protect the data be prosecuted for their actions? Could the data be success-fully concealed?

The general willingness to protect subjects who admit to serious crimes also requires close ethical scrutiny. Wolfgang (1982) takes the traditional scientific stance on this issue, proposing that such information belongs to science. Because the information would have not been discovered without the research effort, its protection neither helps nor hinders police. The ethical judgment here requires a weighing of interests—the importance of scientific research balanced against society's interest in capturing a particular individual.

It should be noted that if researchers began to routinely inform on their sub-jects, all future research relying on self-reports would be jeopardized. Thus, the issue at hand is not simply that of the value of a particular study, but the value of all research utilizing subject disclosures. Researchers are generally advised not to undertake such research unless they feel comfortable about protecting their sources. This requires that all research involving the use of confidential information provide for controlled access to sensitive data and protect the infor-mation from unauthorized searches, inadvertent access and the compulsory legal process (Cook, 1976).

WITHHOLDING BENEFITS TO PARTICIPANTS IN CONTROL GROUPS

The necessity of excluding some potential beneficiaries from initial program participation arises whenever a classical experimental design is to be used to eval-uate the program. This research design requires the random assignment of subjects to experimental and control groups. Subjects in the control group are excluded from the program and/or receive "standard" rather than "experimental" treatment.

In a program evaluation, it is important that some subjects receive the ben-efits of the program while others do not, to ensure that the outcomes observed are the direct result of the experimental intervention and not something else (subject enthusiasm or background characteristics, for example). It is imperative that those who receive the intervention (the experimental group) and those who do not (the control group) be as identical in the aggregate as possible, so that a clear assessment of program impact, untainted by variation in the nature of sub-jects, can be obtained.

The best way to ensure that experimental and control subjects are identical is randomization. Randomization is to be distinguished from arbitrariness, in that randomization requires that every subject have an equal opportunity to be assigned to either the experimental or control group; arbitrariness involves no such equality of opportunity.

In many ways, randomization may be more fair than standard practice based on good intentions. Geis (1980) reports:

> For most of us, it would be unthinkable that a sample of armed robbers be divided into two groups on the basis of random assignment—one group to spend 10 years in prison, the second to receive a sentence of 2 years on probation. Nonetheless, at a federal judicial conference, after examining an elaborate presentence report concerning a bank robber, 17 judges said they would have imprisoned the man, while 10 indicated they favored probation. Those voting for imprisonment set sentences ranging from 6 months to 15 years. (p. 221)

Randomization is also acceptable under law, because its use is reasonably related to a governmental objective, i.e., testing the effectiveness of a program intervention (Erez, 1986).

Although randomization is inherently fair, it often appears less so to the subjects involved. Surveys of prisoners have indicated that need, merit and "first come, first served" are more acceptable criteria than a method that the offenders equated with gambler's luck (Erez, 1986). Consider Morris's (1966) description of "the burglar's nightmare":

> If eighty burglars alike in all relevant particulars were assigned randomly to experimental and control groups, forty each, with the experimentals to be released six months or a year earlier than they ordinarily would be and the control released at their regularly appointed time, how would the burglar assigned to the control group respond? It is unfair, unjust, unethical, he could say, for me to be put into the control group. If people like me, he might complain, are being released early, I too deserve the same treatment. (cited in Erez, 1986:394)

Program staff are also frequently unhappy with randomization, because it fails to utilize their clinical skills in the selection of appropriate candidates for intervention. Extending this line of thought, consider the likely response of judges requested to sentence burglary offenders randomly to prison or probation. While this might be the best method of determining the effectiveness of these sanctions, the judicial response (and perhaps community response as well) would probably be less than enthusiastic. This is because it is assumed, often without any evidence, that standard practice is achieving some reasonable objective, such as individualizing justice or preventing crime.

Randomization does produce winners and losers. Of critical importance in weighing the consequences of randomization are the differences in treatment experienced by the experimental and control groups. Six factors are relevant here:

1. Significance of the interest affected. Early release is of much greater consequence than a change of institutional diet.

2. Extent of difference. Six months' early release is of greater significance than one week's early release.

3. Comparison of the disparity with standard treatment. If both experimental and control group treatment is an improvement over standard treatment, then the discrepancy between the experimental and control group is of less concern.

4. Whether disparity reflects differences in qualifications of subjects. If the disparity is reasonably related to some characteristic of the subjects, the denial of benefits to the control group is less significant.

5. Whether the experimental treatment is harmful or beneficial to subjects compared with the treatment they would otherwise receive. A program that assigns members of the experimental group to six weeks of "boot camp" may be more demanding of inmates than the standard treatment of six months' incarceration.

6. Whether participation is mandatory or voluntary. Voluntary participation mitigates the concern of denial of benefit, while coercion exacerbates the dilemma. (Federal Judicial Center, 1981:31-40)

Similar to the management of other ethical dilemmas, an effort is required to balance values of human decency and justice with the need for accurate information on intervention effectiveness. Problems arise not in the extreme cases of disparity but in more routine circumstances. Consider the following example:

> . . . how do we judge a situation in which a foundation grant permits attorneys to be supplied for all cases being heard by a juvenile court where attorneys have previously appeared only in rare instances? A fundamental study hypothesis may be that the presence of an attorney tends to result in a more favorable disposition for the client. This idea may be tested by comparing dispositions prior to the beginning of the experiment with those ensuing subsequently, though it would be more satisfactory to supply attorneys to a sample of the cases and withhold them from the remainder, in order to calculate in a more experimentally uncontaminated manner the differences between the outcomes in the two situations.
>
> The matter takes on additional complexity if the researchers desire to determine what particular attorney role is the most efficacious in the juvenile court. They may suspect that an attorney who acts as a friend of the court, knowingly taking its viewpoint as parens patriae and attempting to interpret the court's interest to his client, will produce more desirable results than one who doggedly challenges the courtroom procedure and the judge's interpretation of fact, picks at the probation report, raises constant objections, and fights for his client as he would in a criminal court. But what results are "more desirable"? (Geis, 1980:222-223)

It could be contended that little is really known about how attorney roles influence dispositions, and that without the project no one would have any kind of representation. Over the long term, all juveniles stand to benefit. On the other hand, it could be argued that it is wrong to deprive anyone of the best judgment of his or her attorney by requiring a particular legal approach. What if there are only enough funds to supply one-half of the juveniles with attorneys anyway? Is randomization more or less fair than trying to decide which cases "need" representation the most?

Randomization imposes a special ethical burden because it purposefully counters efforts to determine the best course of action with the element of chance. The practice is justifiable because the pursuit of knowledge is a desirable objective—as long as the overall benefits outweigh the risks. The balancing of risks and benefits is complicated by the fact that judgments must often be made in a context of ambiguity, attempting to predict the benefits of an intervention that is being tested precisely because its impact is unknown.

The Federal Judicial Center (1981) recommends that program evaluations should only be considered when certain threshold conditions are met:

> First, the status quo warrants substantial improvements or is of doubtful effectiveness. Second, there must be significant uncertainty about the value or effectiveness of the innovation. Third, information needed to clarify the uncertainty must be feasibly obtainable by the program experimentation but not readily obtainable by other means. And fourth, the information sought must pertain directly to the decision whether or not to adopt the proposed innovation on a general, non-experimental basis. (p. 7)

Several conditions lessen the ethical burdens of evaluative research. Random assignment is especially acceptable when resources are scarce and demand for the benefit is high. Denying benefits to the control group is quite acceptable when members of the control group can participate at a later date. Finally, discrepancies between the treatment of experimental and control groups are decreased when the groups are geographically separated (Federal Judicial Center, 1981).

FAILING TO TREAT RESEARCH PARTICIPANTS FAIRLY AND TO SHOW THEM CONSIDERATION AND RESPECT

The basic tenets of professionalism require that researchers treat subjects with courtesy and fulfill the variety of commitments they make to subjects. In an effort to obtain cooperation, subjects are often promised a follow-up report on the findings of the research; such reports may be forgotten once the study has been completed. Subjects are often led to believe that they will achieve some personal benefit from the research. This may be one of the more difficult obligations to fulfill.

Researchers need to treat their human subjects with constant recognition of their integrity and their contribution to the research endeavor. This is especially important when subjects are powerless and vulnerable. Although such treatment may be a time-consuming chore, it is the only ethical way to practice scientific research.

BALANCING SCIENTIFIC AND ETHICAL CONCERNS

This discussion has emphasized the importance of balancing a concern for subjects against the potential benefits of the research. Cook (1976) identifies the following potential benefits of a research project:

1. Advances in scientific theory that contribute to a general understanding of human behavior.

2. Advances in knowledge of practical value to society.

3. Gains for the research participant, such as increased understanding, satisfaction in making a contribution to science or to the solution of social problems, needed money or special privileges, knowledge of social science or of research methods, and so on. (p. 235)

The potential costs to subjects are considerable, however, and it is often difficult for the researcher to be objective in assessing the issues. For this reason, many professional associations have established guidelines and procedures for ethical research conduct. Generally the professional is honor-bound to follow these guidelines, as little active monitoring occurs.

To ensure that their faculty follow acceptable procedures (and to protect themselves from liability), universities have established Institutional Review Boards to scrutinize each research project that involves the use of human subjects. These review boards serve a valuable function in that they review the specifications of each research project prior to implementation. These boards are also generally incapable of providing direct monitoring of projects, so again, the responsibility for ethical conduct falls on the researcher.

ETHICAL/POLITICAL CONSIDERATIONS

Applied social research, that is, research that examines the effectiveness of social policies and programs, carries with it additional ethical responsibilities. Such research influences the course of human events in a direct fashion—often work, education, future opportunities and deeply held values and beliefs are affected by the outcomes. Researchers must be prepared to deal with a variety of pressures and demands as they undertake the practice and dissemination of research.

It is generally acknowledged that organizations asked to measure their own effectiveness often produce biased results. Crime statistics provide a notorious example of data that tend to be used to show either an effective police department (falling crime figures) or a need for more resources (rising crime figures). Criminal justice researchers are often asked to study matters that are equally sensitive. A correctional treatment program found to be ineffective may lose its funding. A study that reveals extensive use of plea bargaining may cost a prosecutor his or her election.

Often the truth is complicated. A survey that reveals that drug use is declining in the general population may prove troublesome for those trying to lobby for the establishment of more drug treatment facilities. The survey results may lead the public to believe that there is no problem at the same time that the need for treatment facilities for the indigent is substantial.

Such research has been known to produce unintended consequences. The publication of selected results of a study on the effectiveness of correctional treatment programs (Martinson, 1974) was used by many persons to justify limiting funds for education and treatment programs in correctional institutions. The research revealed that there was little evidence that correctional treatment programs were effective means of reducing recidivism (a finding that has been widely challenged). Rather than stimulating the development of more theoretically sound programs and rigorous evaluations of these efforts, the apparent product of the research was a decrease in the humaneness of conditions of confinement.

Sometimes research results conflict with cherished beliefs. Studies of preventive police patrol (Kelling, Page, Dieckman and Browne, 1974) and detective investigations (Chaiken, Greenwood and Petersilia, 1977) both revealed that these practices, long assumed to be essential elements of effective law enforcement, were of little value. Researchers can expect findings such as these to meet with considerable resistance.

Researchers may be asked to utilize their skills and their aura of objectivity to provide an organization or agency with what it wants. When the group that pays the bills has a direct interest in the nature of the outcome, the pressures can be considerable. Marvin Wolfgang (1982) reports:

> I was once invited to do research by an organization whose views are almost completely antithetical to mine on the issue of gun control. Complete freedom and a considerable amount of money to explore the relationship between gun control legislation and robbery were promised. I would not perform the research under those auspices. But the real clincher in the decision was that if the research produced conclusions opposite from that the organization wanted, the agency would not publish the results nor allow me to publish them. Perhaps their behavior, within their ideological framework, was not unethical. But within my framework, as a scientist who values freedom of publication as well as of scientific inquiry, I would have engaged in an unethical act of prostituting my integrity had I accepted those conditions. (p. 395)

In-house researchers, who are employed by the organization for which the research is being conducted, face special problems in this regard, because they lack the freedom to pick and choose their research topic. These problems must balance their concern for rigorous scientific inquiry with their need for continued employment.

Generally the issues confronted are subtle and complex. Although researchers may be directly told to conceal or falsify results, more often they are subtly encouraged to design their research with an eye toward the desired results. The greatest barrier to such pressures is the development of a truly independent professional research unit within the organization. Such independence protects the researcher from political pressures, while at the same time promotes the credibility of the research being conducted. Without this protection, the individual is left to his or her own devices and standards of ethical conduct.

THE PURITY OF SCIENTIFIC RESEARCH

The ideal of scientific inquiry is the pure, objective examination of the empirical world, untainted by personal prejudice. But research is carried out by human beings, not automatons, who have a variety of motivations for undertaking the research that they do. Topics may be selected because of curiosity or perceived need to address a specific social problem, but the availability of grants in a particular field may also encourage researchers to direct their attention to these areas. This is critical if one is working for a research organization dependent upon "soft" money. The need for university faculty to publish and establish a name for themselves in a particular area may encourage them to seek "hot" topics for their research, or to identify an extremely narrow research focus in which they can become identified as an expert.

There is some evidence that the nature of one's research findings influences the likelihood of publication (*Chronicle of Higher Education,* 1989d). A curious author submitted almost identical articles to a number of journals. The manuscripts differed only in one respect—the nature of the conclusions. One version of the article showed that the experiment had no effect; the other described a positive result. His experiment produced some interesting findings—the article with positive outcomes was more likely to be accepted for publication than the other manuscript.

If research that concludes that "the experiment didn't work" or that "differences between Groups A and B were insignificant" are indeed less likely to see the light of day, then pressures to revise one's research focus or rewrite one's hypotheses to match the results produced can be anticipated.

None of the practices described above involve scandalous violations of ethical conduct. Their presentation should function, however, to remind us that actions justified in the name of scientific inquiry may be motivated by factors far less "pure" than the objective they serve.

PUBLIC POLICY PRONOUNCEMENTS AND TEACHING CRIMINAL JUSTICE

When is a researcher speaking from the facts and when is he or she promoting personal ideology? If there were any fully conclusive and definitive studies in the social sciences, this question would not arise. However, research findings are always tentative, and statements describing them invariably require conditional language. On the other hand, researchers have values and beliefs like everyone else, and few of us want to employ the same conditional language required to discuss research when we state our views on matters of public policy and morality. Researchers thus have a special obligation to carefully evaluate their remarks and clearly distinguish between opinion and apparent empirical fact. This is not always an easy task, but it is the only way to safeguard the objectivity that is critically important to scientific inquiry.

CONCLUSION

Conducting scientific research in criminal justice and criminology in an ethical fashion is a difficult task. It requires a constant weighing and balancing of objectives and motivations. It would be nice to conclude that the best research is that which is undertaken in an ethical fashion, but such a statement would skirt the dilemma. This is the exact nature of the problem—those actions required to meet the demands of scientific rigor sometimes run counter to ethical behavior.

Evaluating rather than avoiding ethical dilemmas does provide a learning experience, though, the benefits of which can be expected to spill over into all aspects of human endeavor. Thinking and doing in an ethical fashion requires practice, and conducting research provides considerable opportunity for the development of experience.

REFERENCES

Chaiken, Jan, Peter Greenwood & Joan Petersilia (1977). "The Criminal Investigation Process: A Summary Report," *Policy Analysis* 3: 187-217.

Chronicle of Higher Education (1989a), January 25:A44.

Chronicle of Higher Education (1989b), June 14:A44.

Chronicle of Higher Education (1989c), July 19:A4.

Chronicle of Higher Education (1989d), August 2:A5.

Cohen, Bernard (1980). *Deviant Street Networks: Prostitution in New York City.* Cambridge, MA: Lexington Books.

Cook, Stuart W. (1976). "Ethical Issues in the Conduct of Research in Social Relations." In *Research Methods in Social Relations,* 3rd ed., Claire Sellitz, Lawrence Rightsman & Stuart Cook, (eds.) New York: Holt, Rinehart and Winston.

Erez, Edna (1986). "Randomized Experiments in Correctional Context: Legal, Ethical and Practical Concerns," *Journal of Criminal Justice* 14: 389-400.

Federal Judicial Center (1981). Experimentation in the Law. Report of the Federal Judicial Center Advisory Committee on Experimentation in the Law. Washington, DC: Federal Judicial Center.

Geis, Gilbert (1980). "Ethical and Legal Issues in Experiments with Offender Populations." In *Criminal Justice Research: Approaches, Problems & Policy,* Susette Talarico (ed.), Cincinnati: Anderson.

Haney, Craig, Curtis Banks & Phillip Zimbardo (1973). "Interpersonal Dynamics in a Simulated Prison," *International Journal of Criminology and Penology* 1: 69-97.

Humphreys, Laud (1970). *Tearoom Trade.* Chicago: Aldine.

Kelling, George L., Tony Page, Duance Dieckman & Charles E. Browne (1974). *The Kansas City Preventive Patrol Experiment.* Washington, DC: The Police Foundation.

Martinson, Robert (1974). "What Works?—Questions and Answers About Prison Reform," *Public Interest* 35: 25-54.

Meltzer, B.A. (1953). "A Projected Study of the Jury as a Working Institution," *The Annals of the American Academy of Political and Social Sciences* 287: 97-102.

Milgram, Stanley (1974). *Obedience to Authority: An Experimental View.* New York: Harper and Row.

Morris, Norval (1966). "Impediments to Penal Reform," *Chicago Law Review* 33: 646-653.

New York Times (1983). February 26: 7.

Ring, K., K. Wallston & M. Corey (1970). "Mode of Debriefing as a Factor Affecting Subjective Reaction to a Milgram Type Obedience Experience: An Ethical Inquiry," *Representative Research in Social Psychology* 1: 67-88.

Short, James F., Jr. & Fred Strodtbeck (1965). *Group Processes and Gang Delinquency.* Chicago: University of Chicago Press.

Whyte, William F. (1955). *Streetcorner Society.* Chicago: University of Chicago Press.

Wolfgang, Marvin (1982). "Ethics and Research." In *Ethics, Public Policy and Criminal Justice,* Frederick Elliston & Norman Bowie (eds.), Cambridge, MA: Oelgeschlager, Gunn and Hain.

DISCUSSION QUESTIONS

1. Are there any circumstances in which it is acceptable for a research project to engage in activities that punish and perhaps harm the subject? Where should the researcher draw the line? Can you think of any situation in which the ends justify the means? Support your answer.

2. What are some of the benefits to be gained by doing a research project? Do the benefits outweigh the costs to the subjects and participants? Explain. What are some of the pressures that may be placed on researchers that could compromise the integrity of their research results?

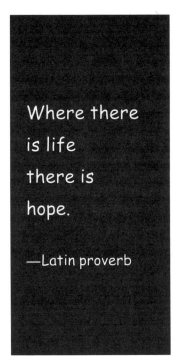

Where there
is life
there is
hope.

—Latin proverb

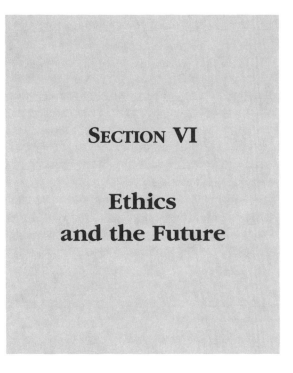

Section VI

Ethics
and the Future

When thinking about the future of our institutions of justice and other processes that are related to them, a number of questions come to mind. What philosophical model or models will guide us personally and professionally? How will we attempt to balance the rights of the individual with the needs of the larger community? How will these same models help to define and redefine the roles of the courts, policing, and corrections? The heart and mind of our system of justice from which our policies and programs spring forth is composed of our personal and professional philosophical models. Will our collective heart and mind of justice use its long arms of the law to simply keep the peace or will it begin to try to encourage and contribute to the peace? And how will all the interrelated aspects of this process be evaluated? How will we define success in the future?

It seems evident that as we come to the last section of this book, there are many more questions than answers. Perhaps that is as it should be. As we look to our future, we may find the beginnings of the answers we seek through the asking of clear, accurate, meaningful questions about our personal sense of justice and how it is expressed through our formal justice process.

CHAPTER 23

Criminal Justice:
An Ethic for the Future

Michael C. Braswell

Now that we have come to the end of this volume, we would like to finish by once again considering its beginning. The first three chapters were concerned with developing a philosophical framework through which we could consider the ethical implications of a variety of criminal justice issues from personal, social and criminal justice perspectives. Now that we have attempted to examine contemporary issues within this framework, we are challenged to look toward the future of criminal justice, a future that is found hidden in its present. How are we to find the eyes to see such a future—a vision that can empower us to contribute to its promise? Will our contributions as individuals and institutions be expressed in the context of a community of hope or a community of fear and cynicism? Will we protect and serve the status quo (focus on the criminal), or will we move ahead, riding the crest of a long shot—that the larger sense of justice is what will be accentuated and that the possibility of social peace can increasingly become a reality? Are we only to be engaged in colorful, crisis-minded rhetoric, or can we translate contemporary justice dilemmas into opportunities for encouraging more substantial policies and practical applications toward restitution and reconciliation?

KEY CONCEPTS:

mindfulness

order-keeping

peacemaking

If we choose to commit to seeking justice and peace in a community of hope, we will need to begin acting on an enlarged vision that includes an ethic for the future. Of course, to some, this sort of thinking may seem to be too romantic a notion when considered against the hard realities of today's justice problems. Still, it would appear that an attitude of hope that empowers us on a personal as well as systemic level, and is anchored in something more than another blue-ribbon task force or budget increase, is worth pursuing. Whether in reference to offenders, victims, citizens or criminal justice professionals, it seems to be in our best interests to recognize and encourage an attitude of person empowerment, that perhaps we need to restore the balance of our interaction with our environment, that problems and solutions come from the inside-out as well as from the outside-in. Thich Nhat Hanh writes,

The problem is to see reality as it is. A pessimistic attitude can never create the calm. But, in fact, when we are angry, *we ourselves* are anger. When we are happy, we ourselves are happiness. When we have certain thoughts, *we are those thoughts*. . . . In a family, if there is one person who practices mindfulness, the entire family will be mindful. . . . And in one class, if one student lives in mindfulness, the entire class is influenced." (pp. 40, 52, 64)

THE NEED FOR MINDFULNESS

If we are to develop an ethic for the future of criminal justice, we need to become more mindful and conscious of ethical truths concerning justice that are found in the present. For example, the utilitarian's priority for community good and the individual integrity of the deontologist become conscious of one another in the context of connectedness and, more importantly, reconciled in an ongoing response of active care. At some point in our lives, we are inclined to become aware that no matter how strong our personal needs and interests are, no one is an island. We need to be with other people in community in order to survive and grow.

Whether we live in suburbia, the inner city or rural America, we begin to realize that we are connected: parents to children, teachers to students, guards to prisoners and offenders to victims. We like the ideas of "one for all and all for one" and "one nation under God with liberty and justice for all," and we are also connected to our environment. Drought, acid rain, forest fires and oil spills all raise our consciousness of our interdependence with our physical environment as well.

The dynamic interaction between the community and the individual along a continuum of connectedness and care can be demonstrated in a specifically criminal justice context. We may still find it necessary to remove an offender from society. We may decide to place this person in prison "for the good of the community," yet, even in prison, we need to realize that offenders are entitled to certain rights of basic care and safety. In other words, we need to see that they are treated humanely on ethical and moral grounds, even if in some cases we may feel they are not deserving because of the crimes they have committed or that our correctional treatment efforts have little effect on their behavior.

Although the offender may be inside prison and we may be outside in the community, we are still connected in a number of ways. We are bound together from the past by the fear and suffering of the victim and the vicarious feelings and perceptions of our citizens. There is also the fear and suffering of the offender and the offender's family, who may also be victims. We are brought together in the present through the quality of life of the prison staff, who are also members of the community and are tied to the offenders they supervise and with whom they interact. The promise of the future connects us in the knowledge that, especially with current overcrowding problems, most offenders will eventually return to our communities. We might even consider the notion that how we as a community allow prisoners to be treated in prison and in correctional programs may say much about how we see ourselves and expect to be treated. Becoming more mindful can allow us, as individuals and communities, to take greater care in seeing and responding more meaningfully to the connections that bind us together in relationships.

ORDER-KEEPING AND PEACEMAKING

Hans Mattick (in Conrad, 1981) once said, "If I could sum up my entire education experience and reflection in a single sentence, it would be: 'Things are not what they seem'" (p. 14). Yet, often in our haste to find and keep order, we try to do just the opposite of what Mattick suggests: we try to eliminate the ambiguity and paradox from human behavior—we try to make things "be as they seem." If we limit our search for justice to crime and criminals, we are likely to miss the larger truth of Mattick's point. Our search for justice can instead become subverted to a search for order. It is even possible that the ambiguity that is an inevitable part of democracy's birthright can, over time, be replaced by the certainty and predictability of a totalitarian society.

Too much emphasis on order-keeping encourages us to review problems or failures in the justice process as technological difficulties that can be corrected through sound engineering rather than fundamental problems of design. We imagine that if we can just do things more efficiently, crime and justice problems can eventually be solved, or at least reduced to an insignificant level. Unfortunately, an order-keeping focus may inhibit us from expanding our area of concern to include the impact of the interaction within the larger social arena, which addresses more specific crime and justice issues. It is worth remembering that if we have not asked the right questions, which include a variety of diverse perspectives, our solutions—no matter how efficiently implemented—are no solutions at all; rather, they simply add another layer to the confusion and difficulty that already exists, and end up creating additional problems and suffering.

The importance of viewing criminal justice and related issues from a variety of perspectives is well illustrated by a Sufi writer: "What is fate?," Nasrudin was asked by a scholar. "An endless succession of intertwined events influencing each other," Nasrudin replied. "That is hardly a satisfactory answer. I believe in cause and effect." "Very well," said the Mulla, "look at that." He pointed to a procession passing in the street. "That man is being taken to be hanged. Is that because someone gave him a silver piece to buy the knife with which he committed murder, or because someone saw him do it, or because nobody stopped him?" (Meredith, 1984, p. 48).

While keeping the order is important, keeping the peace is more than that. Peacekeeping represents a larger vision with potentially profound implications for the individual and the community. Peacekeeping can in fact emerge into a practice of peacemaking. Such a practice requires that we encourage a greater sense of mindfulness that allows us to remain conscious that human behavior is not an either/or proposition but a continuum that includes and connects offenders, victims and nonoffenders. Order-keeping focuses on the "guilty few" while the mindfulness of peacekeeping and peacemaking remind us that "few may be guilty, but all are responsible" (Quinney, 1980).

Isaiah (32:17) states, "Justice will bring about peace, right will produce calm and security." Is that what is happening in our crime and justice conscious culture? Are our citizens experiencing a greater sense of peace, calm and security? How can we in a meaningful and balanced way maintain that order yet keep and even contribute to the peacefulness, calm and security in our communities? Such existential questions seem challenging at best and overwhelming at worst. It is easy enough to think and talk about peacemaking, but quite another thing to put it into mindful action. Hubert Van Zeller (in Castle, 1988) adds yet another twist when he writes, "Thinking about interior peace destroys interior peace. The patient who constantly feels his pulse is not getting better" (p. 180). Van Zeller would lead us to believe that if we are able to contribute to the peacefulness, calmness and security of our community, we must learn to be more peaceful, calm and secure within ourselves. Can we offer calm if we are angry, security if we are fearful, or hope if we are cynical? It seems that if we are to contribute to a more just society, we must not simply think, talk or write about peacekeeping and peacemaking but personally struggle to increasingly *be* peace. Quinney (1987) writes, "Rather than attempting to create a good society first, and then trying to make ourselves better human beings, we have to work on the two simultaneously. . . . Without peace within us and in our actions, there can be no peace in our results" (p. 19, 23). Critics of peacemaking as a viable way to improve our justice process would point to its impracticality. Such an approach seems to have little in common with popular notions such as "getting tough on crime." Unfortunately, while such popular notions may get people elected to political office and make many of us feel better emotionally, their practical applications have done little to reduce crime or increase the calm and security of citizens. Although perhaps requiring an alternative mind set, peacemaking may not be as impractical as many critics would suggest. Dass and Gorman (1985) offer an account by a police officer who struggled to see himself primarily as a peacekeeper and peacemaker:

> Now there are two theories about crime and how to deal with it. Anti-crime guys say, "You have to think like a criminal." And some police learn that so well they get a kind of criminal mentality themselves.

> How I'm working with it is really pretty different. I see that man is essentially pure and innocent and of one good nature. That's who he is by birthright. And that's what I'm affirming in the course of a day on the job. In fact, that is my job. The "cop" part of it . . . well, they call us "cops," to me, my job is *I'm a peace officer.*

> So I work not only to prevent the crime but to eliminate its causes— its causes in fear and greed, not just the social causes everyone talks about.

Even when it gets to conflict. I had arrested a very angry black man who singled me out for real animosity. When I had to take him to a paddy wagon, he spit in my face—that was something—and he went after me with a chair. We handcuffed him and put him in the truck. Well, on the way I just had to get past this picture of things, and again I affirmed to myself, "This guy and I are brothers. . . . When I got to the station, I was moved spontaneously to say, "Look, if I've done anything to offend you, I apologize." The paddy wagon driver looked at me as if I was totally nuts.

The next day I had to take him from where he'd been housed overnight to criminal court. When I picked him up, I thought, "Well, if you trust this vision, you're not going to have to handcuff him." And I didn't. We got to a spot in the middle of the corridor which was the place where he'd have jumped me if he had that intention, and he stopped suddenly. So did I. Then he said, "You know, I thought about what you said yesterday, and I want to apologize." I just feel deep appreciation.

Turned out on his rap sheet he'd done a lot of time in Michigan and had trouble with guards in jail. I symbolized something. And I saw that turn around, saw a kind of healing, I believe.

So what really happens if you're going to explore whether or not this vision of nature really has power? Maybe people will say you're taking chances. But you're taking chances without any vision; your vision is your protection. Maybe they'll say you're sentimentalizing people. But it's not about people. It's about principle and truth. It's about how the universe is. Maybe they'll think it's idealistic; things could never be this way. Well, for me, things are this way already; it's just up to us to know that more clearly.

I see that my work is to hold to an image of who we all truly are and to be guided by that. And I have been guided by that, to greater strength and security . . . within myself and on the street.

SOME SUGGESTIONS FOR CRIMINAL JUSTICE

If we are to look to the future of criminal justice with some measure of hope rather than a growing sense of cynicism, we must seek out fresh possibilities rather than defend traditional certainties. We need not be naive to remain open to creative alternatives concerning justice philosophy, policy and programming. As Geis (1984) suggests, we need to "stand apart from the parade" to see old problems with a new perspective. Nettler (1982) exhorts us to spend more time and energy in asking the right questions *before* seeking answers. We need reflection before action. Lozoff puts our dilemma in perspective when he writes, "We all want to know the way, but very few of us are willing to study the maps" (1989:3).

It seems more important than ever for us to look past our individual and agency interests into the larger community of which we are a part. The corporate body of this larger community includes both the best and the worst that we have to offer. The sinner and saint, offender and victim all share the consequences of our formal and informal responses to matters of crime and justice. The choice between prevention, intervention or no response at all holds meaning for each part of our community as well as the whole. We have to keep trying to look at the problems of crime and justice with fresh eyes, through the eyes of overworked bureaucrats, prison guards, caseworkers, and through the eyes of the victims and offenders as well. We need to look beyond the next career opportunity and try to see through the eyes of our children, and even their children, for we are responsible to them as well.

The following suggestions are offered as observations to consider, as food for thought.

Law and Justice

Can legal statutes or the justice system make up for our lack of community, for our feelings and experiences of fragmentation? Can morality or a responsible and caring community be legislated? The answer to both questions is, of course, no. However, the way we define laws and the way our justice system enforces them can enhance or diminish our opportunities for more peaceful and orderly communities. While conflict and ambiguity are an inevitable part of how social ills are connected to problems of crime and justice, intervention (in the form of prevention efforts) must occur before as well as after crimes are committed. Adequate health care and opportunities for meaningful work are as (or more) important than simply improving the efficiency of the criminal justice process. As we consider how laws must be changed and our justice system needs to be improved, an expanded vision can allow us to create a space in which we can more honestly address differences between how we view the justice process ideally and how it often functions in reality. Myths—such as (a) white-collar crime is nonviolent, (b) the rich and poor are equal before the law, (c) the punishment can fit the crime, and (d) law makes people behave—can be examined and responded to in a more enlightened context of community.

There are also issues of law and justice that must be struggled with on a personal basis both in terms of our being criminal justice professionals and as members of families and social communities. For example, it seems that many persons have come to believe that a legal act and a moral act are essentially the same. Politicians or corporate executives charged with crimes typically declare to the press and the public that they have done nothing illegal and indeed, they may often be correct. But does that make it right? Can legal behavior be immoral and illegal behavior moral? Were Martin Luther King, Jr. and Mahatma Gandhi criminals or heroes? In a society in which success is measured primarily in terms of money and prestige, are we encouraged to do whatever is necessary within (and sometimes outside) the law to be successful (Braswell &

LaFollette, 1988)? We are appalled when public figures are convicted of large-scale fraud, yet we may consider cheating on our income taxes or college exams acceptable. It seems as if we are saying, "It's all right to do something wrong as long as we don't get caught at it." Of course, in life or in criminal court, when we do get caught our plea is for mercy. From minor greed to major fraud, when we are the victim we are inclined to want retribution, yet when we are the offender we want mercy. This contrasting desire seems true in personal relationships as well as in a professional or criminal justice context. Can we truly have it both ways: mercy when we are the offender and retribution or revenge when we are the victim? Or do we need to accept responsibility and make a stand for one way or the other?

Policing

With more minorities and women entering police work, the opportunity exists for a greater openness in defining and redefining police roles and function. In addition, as issues surrounding the family such as domestic violence and child abuse are translated into law and criminal justice policies, a clearer focus concerning the need for police officers to possess meaningful communication and interpersonal skills should become more apparent. It seems ironic that police officers are expected to intervene with families who are in crisis, while few, if any, helping services are available to many of them when they experience family crisis situations. Shift work and a closed professional system are just several of the factors that can contribute to difficulties regarding family life. To make matters worse, in some instances a stigma perceived as weakness is identified with those officers who do seek professional help for family-related problems (Miller & Braswell, 1997).

Police agencies are also responsible for detaining offenders in jails until courts dispense with them. Current problems associated with prison overcrowding have also spilled over into jails, turning many of them into little more than institutions for extended incarceration. Most jails are operated by law enforcement agencies more inclined toward enforcement and order maintenance strategies than correctional intervention with offenders. And the offenders who end up in jail are typically from the underclass and represent the least in the community since they often cannot afford bail. Suggestions for more creative options such as pretrial release, diversion programs and speedier trials have long been a possibility, but they are often not utilized. Such an attitude of neglect has additional implications for one of the criminal justice system's most missed opportunities: its potential impact on first-time offenders who have their initial contact with the system at the jail. It seems ironic that the point in the justice process at which the first-time offender is usually the most open to intervention is also the place where the least resources are allocated.

Are police officers tough, unyielding crime fighters, or are they much more than that? Many police officers consider social services calls as "garbage calls," not worthy of their time and effort, yet the majority of their typical work day is spent dealing with human service situations. Paradoxically, the more mindful they are of the ethic of care, as translated through effective communication and interpersonal skills, the less likely they are to have to get tough with the people with whom they come in contact. Still, the image persists: Dirty Harry, crime fighter or peacemaker? it is interesting to note that an informal survey given each semester to introductory criminal justice students consistently reveals that the overwhelming majority of them would prefer, all things being equal (i.e., job responsibilities, pay, etc.), to be identified as a police officer or deputy sheriff rather than as a public safety officer. How can we enlarge our vision of police work to include a primary emphasis on peacemaking as well as law enforcement? It is not just a matter of knowing how to shoot well but also knowing when to shoot—as well as being open to possible nonviolent alternatives. Given the litigious nature of today's world, such an orientation has pragmatic as well as peacemaking advantages. It is unfortunate that the nature and tradition of contemporary police work would make the previous example of the police officer who saw himself as primarily a peace officer seem so unusual (Dass & Gorman, 1985). With so much research focused on police corruption and deviance, we might find it worthwhile to follow A.H. Maslow's (1954) example and turn our attention to what motivates well-adjusted, creative and psychologically healthy police officers. Given the discretion and immediacy of response necessary for police officers in the community setting, there is perhaps no other criminal justice professional who is as connected to the community and who has as great an opportunity to contribute to the community's sense of care and well-being. There are a number of positive developments in policing, particularly in the area of community policing (Trojanowicz et al., 1998).

Corrections

Corrections directly addresses the "least of the community"—the two-time losers, the nuisance factor, the disenfranchised and the violent. Along the continuum of connectedness, offenders appear to be the least useful to the community. They have demonstrated their disdain or inability to do their duty as citizens, to adequately contribute to the common good, or to provide meaningful care. As a result, the larger community often retributively feels that such persons themselves are deserving of the least care. Ironically, while we want them to pay for crimes and be corrected, we are not particularly supportive of their feeling good about themselves. The paradox "be good, but don't feel good about it" can often put our correctional process at odds with itself. Is our priority to provide corrections or punishment? Is our emphasis to repair the connection and restore both offender and victim to our community, or to disconnect and distance one or the other or both from community? Are we to be more interested in restitution and reconciliation whenever possible, or in retribution? Thomas Merton writes, "You cannot save the world with merely a system. You cannot have peace without charity" (in Quinney, 1988, p. 71).

While the effectiveness of correctional treatment is a worthy and important topic for debate between the pro- and anti-rehabilitation factions in criminal justice (Cullen & Gilbert, 1982; Whitehead & Lab, 1989), is it the only (or even the most important) basis for funding and providing correctional treatment services for offenders? Are the moral and ethical grounds for treating offenders at least as important, if not more so, than the utilitarian demands for effectiveness? Perhaps we need to develop and articulate a treatment ethic that is restorative in nature and that more honestly addresses the community's (including its least members) sense of duty to itself. Such a turn of focus also allows us to pay closer attention to the art of correctional treatment rather than strictly to its scientific aspect— to the creation as well as the operation of correctional process. The restorative justice and peacemaking movements, through such nonprofit organizations as The Prison Fellowship (Van Ness & Strong, 1997) and Human Kindness Foundation (Lozoff & Braswell, 1989), offer a correctional alternative that encourages offenders to take responsibility for their actions and be restored to a sense of community in which personal and spiritual transformation can take place.

It is interesting that when we think of correctional treatment interventions we are inclined to think of them more as treatment systems or clinical approaches to be evaluated and less as existential processes to be experienced. While this tendency may also be true of our psychotherapeutic colleagues, there are more among them that are sensitive to and grounded in a vital sense of the existential that makes the philosophy and science of theory come alive in the art and process of relationship (Rogers, 1980; Satir, 1973). It is worth noting the substantial and continually evolving research of Robert Carkhuff and his associates (1969; 1987), which indicates that the further graduate students progress in clinical help professions, the more proficient they become in diagnostic, assessment and evaluation skills, but the less effective they seem to become in demonstrating meaningful and effective communication skills.

To put the "art of treatment" perspective into a more specifically correctional context, we can turn to the groundbreaking work of John Augustus and Alexander Maconochie. We can become so enamored of their innovative approaches that we can easily forget, or at least take for granted, the inner aspect of who they were that made their approaches come alive in experience. David Dressler (1959) writes of John Augustus's interaction with offenders in a police court: "It is probable that some of them know him, for as he walks to the box two or three turn their blood-shot eyes toward him with eager glances. . . . In a moment he is with them, gently reproving the hardened ones, and cheering . . . those in whom are visible signs of penitence" (p. 25). Dressler continues in commenting on Maconochie's restorative impact on an incorrigible and disturbed inmate: "He was out of touch with reality most of the time, unaware of what was going on about him, but when Maconochie, his wife, or their children, visited him, he returned to reality, recognized his callers. He showed affection for them to the day he died" (p. 67). It is true that evaluating treatment effectiveness is important, as is educating and training competent clinical professionals in diagnostic, assessment and evaluation skills. However, the art of helping requires more than cognitive or affective sensitivity; it requires a synthesis of both these dimensions and more—emerging from within and lived out in experience with others. "A staff person who's calm and strong and happy is worth his or her weight in gold. People who are living examples of truthfulness, good humor, patience, and courage are going to change more lives—even if they're employed as janitors—than the counselors who can't get their own lives in order" (Lozoff & Braswell, 1989, p. 52).

Perhaps we can begin to rethink our attitude regarding corrections. Do we really want it to work or not? Is corrections to be little more than an opportunity for an incomplete community to express its feelings of retribution, or can it be more than that? Can we realize the possibility that corrections, even with its need for punishment, can also include restitution, rehabilitation and restoration as a means for the community to experience reconciliation? After speaking to a local Kiwanis group about juvenile crime and corrections in their community, one speaker was asked by one of the group members what they could do to help. His response: "Create recreation opportunities for the least of your community and for yourselves—join the local PTA."

JUSTICE AS A WAY RATHER THAN A DESTINATION

It is in our best interests to begin to see justice as an evolutionary way of service rather than as an efficiently engineered technological destination. We need an ethic for our future that will empower us to act on an enlarged vision of what justice is about—a vision that will include the community of which we are all a part, the best of us and the worst of us (and the best in each of us and the worst in each of us). We need a prophetic vision to energize the empowerment of such an ethic. The passion of prophetic vision resounds in the words of Amos (5:24) and is repeated by Martin Luther King, Jr. in a striking address: "Let justice roll down like waters. And righteousness like a mighty stream." Quinney (1980) adds, "For the prophets, justice is like a mighty stream, not merely a category or mechanical process. In contrast, the moralists discuss, suggest, counsel; the prophets proclaim, demand, insist" (p. 25).

Justice as a way of service requires more than just the passionate zeal of the visionary, it also requires the mindfulness of quiet compassion. Creative and humane policies and plans are one thing, but making them work is something else. It is the compassionate professionals in public schools, courts, law enforcement, corrections and other human service agencies that make the ethic of care come alive in the community. Such persons are mindful of the suffering that crime and social injustice creates for victims and offenders. Their mindfulness is born of their own suffering as well. Dietrich Bonhoeffer, himself incarcerated and finally executed in a Nazi prison camp, writes (in Castle, 1988), "We must learn to respond to people less in the light of what they do or omit to do, and more in the light of what they suffer." Seeing a Ted Bundy or Charles Manson through the eyes of compassion keeps us from closing ourselves off from the terrible suffering they have given and received. Their acts are not excused, nor is our irresponsibility in choosing not to commit our collective resources and energies toward preventing the creation of future Bundys or Mansons. Compassionate professionals realize it is not how much they do, but rather how mindfully they do whatever they do. To put it another way, as Mother Teresa suggests, "It is not how much you do, but how much you do with love." From a compassionate way of service comes a sense of peace and well-being.

Success, happiness, even justice are all preludes at best, and second-rate substitutes at worst, to what we really seek—peace. Only peace has the potential to remain calm and resolute even in the midst of suffering that connects each of us to the other in community. Peace comes from the inside out. It cannot be implemented organizationally from the top down. People at peace with themselves create peaceful organizations that can then become instruments for peacemaking in the larger community. To reiterate Dass and Gorman's (1985) cogent observation: "If we ourselves cannot know peace, be peaceful, how will our acts disarm hatred and violence?" (p. 165). And to borrow once again from Isaiah (2:17): "How else will our justice system bring about peace, produce calm and security for our people?"

REFERENCES

Amos 5:24.

Braswell, Michael C. (1989). "Correctional Treatment and the Human Spirit: A Focus on Relationship," *Federal Probation* (June): 49-60.

_____ & Hugh LaFollette (1988). "Seeking Justice: The Advantages and Disadvantages of Being Educated," *American Journal of Criminal Justice* (Spring): 135-147.

Carkhuff, Robert (1987). *The Art of Helping III*. Amherst, MA: Human Resource Development Press.

_____ (1969). *Helping Human Relations, Vol. II*. New York: Holt, Rinehart, and Winston.

Castle, Tony (1988). *The New Book of Christian Quotations*. New York: Crossroad.

Conrad, John (1981). *Justice and Consequences*. Lexington, MA: Lexington Books.

Cullen, Francis & Karen Gilbert (1982). *Reaffirming Rehabilitation*. Cincinnati, OH: Anderson.

Dass, Ram & Paul Gorman (1985). *How Can I Help?* New York: Alfred A. Knopf.

Dressler, David (1959). *Practice and Theory of Probation and Parole*. New York: Columbia University Press.

Geis, Gilbert (1984). "Foreword" In Harold Pepinsky & Paul Jesilow, *Myths that Cause Crime*. Cabin John, MD: Seven Locks Press.

Gendreau, Paul & Robert Ron (1987). "Revivification of Rehabilitation: Evidence from the 1980's." *Justice Quarterly* 4: 349-409.

Hanh, Thich Nhat (1987). *Being Peace*. Berkeley, CA: Parallax Press.

Isaiah 32:17.

Lozoff, Bo (1989). "Editorial," *Human Kindness Foundation Newsletter*, 3.

Lozoff, Bo (1987). *We're All Doing Time*. Chapel Hill, NC: Human Kindness Foundation.

Lozoff, Bo & Michael Braswell (1989). *Inner Corrections: Finding Peace and Peace Making*. Cincinnati, OH: Anderson.

Maslow, Abraham (1954). *Motivation and Personality*. New York: Harper.

Meredith, Nikki (1984). "The Murder Epidemic," *Science* (December): 48.

Miller, Larry & Michael Braswell (1997). *Human Relations and Police Work,* 4th ed. Prospect Heights, IL: Waveland Press.

Nettler, Gwynn (1982). *Explaining Criminals*. Cincinnati, OH: Anderson.

Pepinsky, Harold & Paul Jesilow (1984). *Myths That Cause Crime*. Cabin John, MD: Seven Locks Press.

Quinney, Richard (1988). "Crime, Suffering, and Service: Toward a Criminology of Peacemaking," *The Quest* (Winter): 71.

Quinney, Richard (1987). "The Way of Peace: On Crime, Suffering, and Service," unpublished paper, (November): 19, 23.

Quinney, Richard (1980). *Providence: The Reconstruction of Social and Moral Order*. New York: Longman.

Rogers, Carl (1980). *A Way of Being*. Palo Alto, CA: Houghton-Mifflin.

Satir, Virginia (1973). *Peoplemaking*. Palo Alto, CA: Science and Behavior Books.

Trojanowicz, Robert, Victor E. Kappeler, Larry K. Gaines & Bonnie Bucqueroux (1998). *Community Policing: A Contemporary Perspective*, 2nd ed. Cincinnati, OH: Anderson.

Van Ness, Daniel & Karen Heetderks Strong (1997). *Restoring Justice*. Cincinnati, OH: Anderson.

Whitehead, John & Steve Lab (1989). A Response to "Does Correctional Treatment Work?" unpublished paper.

Discussion Questions

1. Can legal behavior be immoral and illegal behavior moral? Give your opinion on this statement and defend your answer with examples.

2. Braswell thinks an ethic for the future can improve the criminal justice system. Do you agree or disagree with his viewpoint? Why or why not?

3. Why is mindfulness important to one's personal and professional life? Can you think of any personal example?

Index

407

About the Authors

Michael C. Braswell

Michael C. Braswell, Professor in the Department of Criminal Justice and Criminology at East Tennessee State University. Braswell received his Ph.D. in Counseling Psychology from the University of Southern Mississippi. In addition to his academic position, Braswell has also served as a correctional psychologist, a marital/family therapist and a consultant to a variety of law enforcement and corrections organizations. Braswell's writing and research has focused on ethics, correctional treatment and peacemaking. His books include: *American Criminal Justice: An Introduction* (by Bartollas and Braswell), *Correctional Counseling and Rehabilitation* (by Van Voorhis, Braswell and Lester), *Inner Corrections: Finding Peace and Peacemaking* (by Lozoff and Braswell) and *Human Relations in Corrections* (by Braswell, Miller and Fletcher).

Belinda R. McCarthy

Belinda R. McCarthy, Professor of Criminal Justice and Dean of the College of Health and Public Affairs at the University of Central Florida. McCarthy received her Ph.D. from the School of Criminal Justice at the State University of New York at Albany. Her research and writing have focused on such topics as prison furloughs, older offenders and AIDS education for juvenile offenders. McCarthy is the editor or author of several books, author or co-author of numerous scholarly articles and book chapters, and a frequent presenter at various professional conferences. Her books include: *Intermediate Punishments: Intensive Supervision, Home Confinement and Electronic Surveillance; Older Offenders: Perspectives in Criminology and Criminal Justice;* and *Easy Time: Female Inmates on Temporary Release.*

Bernard J. McCarthy

Bernard J. McCarthy is Professor and Chair of the Department of Criminal Justice and Legal Studies at the University of Central Florida. McCarthy received his Ph.D. from the School of Criminology, Florida State University. His teaching areas include ethics, community corrections, criminal justice policy analysis and terrorism. He is the co-author of *Community Based Corrections* (by McCarthy and McCarthy). His present research includes an assessment of the impact of jail programs on offender behavior and an evaluation of Drug Courts in Central Florida.